Adaptive Church

Collaboration and Community in a Changing World

Dustin D. Benac

BAYLOR UNIVERSITY PRESS

© 2022 by Baylor University Press
Waco, Texas 76798

All Rights Reserved. No part of this publication may be reproduced, stored in a retrieval system, or transmitted, in any form or by any means, electronic, mechanical, photocopying, recording, or otherwise, without the prior permission in writing of Baylor University Press.

Cover and book design by Kasey McBeath
Cover art courtesy of Unsplash/Max Williams

The Library of Congress has cataloged this book under ISBN 978-1-4813-1708-5.

Library of Congress Control Number: 2022938313

To Casey
With gratitude and hope.

Contents

Acknowledgments ix
List of Tables xv
List of Figures xvii
List of Photographs xix

    Introduction 1
        Collaboration, Community, and Change in the Pacific Northwest

I Organizational Environments

    1 "The Church Has Always Been Nimble" 17
        Church Engagement on the Edge of Christendom

    2 "Hope and Care in the Neighborhood" 39
        Refounding the Church in Local Community

II The Nexus of Collaborative Work

    3 The Structure of Adaptive Change 67
        Organizing Challenges and Values for Communities of Faith

    4 Anchors and Webs 103
        Hubs as Fields, Networks, and Ecologies

III A Practical Theology for an Adaptive Church

    5 Reimagining Church 131
        Pastoral and Ecclesial Imagination for Adaptive Change

    6 Adaptive Church 153
        Patterned Practice for a Way of Life

IV A Theological Paradigm for a Changing World

   7 "We're Better Together"   183
       Wisdom, Presence, and Leadership for Adaptive Change

   8 **A Moment of Renovating Virtue**   217
       Adaptive Possibility beyond Certainty

Appendix A: Naming: Networks, Data, Methods, and Names	233
Appendix B: Interviewee Phase and Date	239
Appendix C: Phase I Interview Guide	243
Appendix D: Phase II Interview Guide	247
Appendix E: Phase III Interview Guide	251
Appendix F: Two-Day Focus Group Gathering	253
Appendix G: Informed Consent Form	255
Notes	257
Bibliography	299
Index of Subjects	317
Index of Names	323
Index of Scripture	327

Acknowledgments

This book is the result of extravagant generosity that extends for more than a decade. While many lament how the craft of writing requires a solitary endeavor, this work stitched me into a broader structure of belonging. I am indebted to those who believed in this project, even before it was a fully formed concept and question, and to the many others who listened, hosted, or asked questions along the way. Your support for this volume, which bears witness to the words and wisdom of an adaptive church, gives me hope.

First, to the many participants in this study who shared insight, stories, and care, thank you for trusting me with your words and work. To the small group of individuals who participated in the first phase of my research, thank you for having a vision for this project and saying yes to an interview. Your support gave a fledgling concept the momentum it needed to move forward. To the founders, organizers, and participants from the Office of Church Engagement (OCE) and Parish Collective (PC), thank you for your generous presence and hospitable spirit. You model a hopeful posture that has helped me see how much better we are together. I offer these words back to you as a token of appreciation for your hopeful and transformative work. To those who hosted me or provided hospitality during many trips to the Pacific Northwest—Ethan and Caroline Smith, Ben Ross, Curtis and Alicia Powell—thank you for your friendship and generosity.

Craig Dykstra nurtured an early version of this project, my dissertation. This work bears Craig's imprint through his support and conversation as a doctoral advisor. Many of the ideas presented here are simply reflections on Craig's insights and his vision for what is possible through a more connected ecclesial ecology. Beyond his work as a guide, Craig introduced me to a broader community of scholars and practitioners who exemplify the kind of practical wisdom I describe here. Thank you Craig for creating the intellectual and institutional space for this work to take form. A fantastic doctoral committee also supported this work: Mark Chaves, Fred Edie, L. Gregory Jones, and Patricia Killen. Mark introduced me to organizational studies and guided a young theologian into the world of social scientific inquiry. Fred enriched my reflections through study and conversation over many years about the formation of individuals and communities. Greg provided gracious support and conversation that opened my imagination to a field of inquiry that I had long searched for but didn't have the language to identify. Patricia's expertise on religion in the Pacific Northwest and astute scholarly sensibilities clarified and enriched this entire project. With characteristic grace, Kavin Rowe guided my work on Luke-Acts and the broader theological interpretation of Scripture as a member of my preliminary exam committee. Thank you all for your investment in this project and vision for its eventual impact.

I benefited from a wonderful intellectual community at Duke University and in Durham, N.C. Our Friday dinner group during our first three years in Durham created an ideal environment for curiosity to grow through conversation over good meals. Corey and Juli Kalbaugh, John and Minda Zambenini, Tim and Caitlin McCleod, Justin and Allie Hughes, Alice Brower, Ryan and Kendra Juskus, and so many others are practiced in the art of friendship.

Upon entering a doctoral program, I found both generous conversation partners across disciplines and good friends: Aminah Bradford, Emily Dubie, Mike Grigoni, Sarah Jobe, Ryan Juskus, Alberto La Rosa, Adam Perez, Philip Porter, Katrina Schaafsma, Nate Tilley, and Greg Williams. To these and so many others, who worked on the "line" in the library basement or gathered for lunch, thank you for creating a space marked by humility, curiosity, and care. The formation of Duke's Theology, Religion, and Qualitative Methods Network provided space to refine questions of methodology and interdisciplinary inquiry alongside others who were at a similar stage. I am particularly grateful for Luke Bretherton's role as the faculty advisor for this group, and to Ed Balleisen's leadership of Duke Interdisciplinary Studies, who funded this project. This working group also provided an opportunity to work with and learn from Todd Whitmore during a key phase of my writing, for which I am grateful.

This project would not have come to fruition without my colleagues in Duke Divinity School's Convocation of Christian Leaders. To my ACCL cohort—Jennifer Ayres, Nannette Banks, Kat Banakis, Amanda Drury, Jill Duffield, Scott Hoffman, Bernadette Hickman-Maynard, Emily Hull McGee, Hardy Kim, Andy Kort, Mihee Kim-Kort, Aaron Kuecker, Kermit Moss, Christian

Peele, Patrick Reyes, Fernando Rodriguez, Rob Saler, Sarah Schreiber, Mindy McGarrah Sharp, Erin Weber-Johnson, Trey Wince, Kevin Kim Wright—you embody this work. The Convocation became a gestation space for this project. Many ideas advanced in these pages were first conceived, tested, or refined in conversation with colleagues from ACCL. I also want to express my profound appreciation and gratitude to Craig Dykstra, Dave Odom, Gretchen Ziegenhals, Victoria White, Donielle Cyprian, and Mary Floyd Page for the leadership, intentionality, and hospitality that characterized this group.

I could not have completed this research without support from several organizations and individuals. The M. J. Murdock Charitable Trust provided a grant for the first phase of this research and helped convene leaders for the final phase of my research.[1] Without their timely support it is difficult to imagine how this project could have gotten off the ground or concluded as it did. Their early investment in and vision for my research reflects their broader commitment to enrich the vitality of religious and social life in the Pacific Northwest. To Steve Moore and Kimberly Thornbury, thank you for inviting me into your catalytic work.

Fellowships and research grants from university partners also supported my research and training. The John Hope Franklin Humanities Institute provided funding to serve as a fellow in the PhD Lab in Digital Knowledge. The PhD Lab provided space to explore network visualization techniques. A 2017 grant from Duke Interdisciplinary Studies enabled me to pursue advanced training in qualitative methods through the Inter-university Consortium for Political and Social Research Summer Program at the University of North Carolina's Odum Institute. A writing retreat at the Collegeville Institute provided an environment to translate my early research in the Pacific Northwest into a coherent argument and line of inquiry. A 2018 grant from the Information Initiative at Duke provided funding to translate insights and methods from my research to an undergraduate setting. A 2019 Research Fellowship from Saint Louis University's Lived Religion in a Digital Age project provided funding to attend the OCE and PC annual conferences. An appointment as a visiting research fellow at the University of Victoria's Centre for Studies in Religion and Society provided an environment to present and discuss my work as I finalized this project.

Several other individuals and organizations provided support, feedback, and resources at critical stages in this project. Leadership Education at Duke Divinity School provided an innovation grant in 2017 that allowed me to explore how teams support the conditions for adaptive work. A dissertation support fellowship from the Center for the Study of Philanthropy and Volunteerism at Duke's Sanford School of Public Policy provided release time during the final year of my research and writing. A postdoctoral fellowship from the Louisville Institute created space to revise and update my research in the wake of the social and ecclesial crisis of 2020–2021. To Edwin Aponte and the Louisville Institute Team, thank you for your generous investment in this project and the communities I hope this work will serve. Finally, unsolicited gifts from three individuals (who asked to remain anonymous) provided funding to continue this research at critical junctures. In each case, I remain grateful for the commitment to generosity these individuals and organizations express for the scholarship and ecclesial vision this project pursues.

Just as I was preparing to submit an early version of this project to my dissertation committee, the world turned upside down. In mid-March 2020, after spending nearly five years studying how communities of faith adapt to uncertainty, I watched communities of faith around the world adapt and innovate like never before. I also found myself in a liminal space, marked by uncertainty and creative possibility. My work with Kate Bowler, Katherine Smith, Jessica Richie, and Harriet Putnam at the Everything Happens Project during the belly of a pandemic was a shot of hope, inviting me to consider what is possible on the other side of uncertainty. Thank you Kate and Katherine for the gift of time and good conversation that allowed me to translate this project into a book. I also had the privilege during this pandemic time to coedit *Crisis and Care: Meditations on Faith and Philanthropy* with Erin Weber-Johnson. To Erin and our remarkable contributors, thank you for offering these words into a world searching for meaning; they gave me language to sustain a hopeful imagination in the wake of crisis.

My dean at Baylor University's George W. Truett Theological Seminary, Todd Still, as well as my colleagues and students have encouraged me to move this work toward publication. My students in Leadership for Ministry and Leading in the Kingdom classes read and provided feedback on chapters 4 and 7. Paul Putz kindly read and provided expert comments on an early version of the introduction. Savannah Green prepared the index. To these colleagues and the broader Baylor community, thank you for modeling how a commitment to local faith communities *and* research can nourish a more adaptive church.

I am forever grateful for the many editorial experts who shaped this project overall and each paragraph. To John Zambenini, who read and reviewed an early version, I am the beneficiary of your masterful work with words. To Cade Jarrell, my editor at Baylor University Press, thank you for your vision for this project and tending to the editorial process with an abundance of care. To the two anonymous peer reviewers and my copyeditor, thank you for your contributions, which added clarity and depth to my overall argument. And to the broader team at Baylor University Press, I am grateful for your commitment to local communities of faith and scholarly communities; this work is better because of you. Any errors that remain are mine alone.

Versions of this work appeared at conferences and in select publications. An early version of the opening vignette first appeared in *The Presbyterian Outlook*, and portions of chapter 6 first appeared in *The Bonhoeffer Legacy*. They appear here with the editors' permission, and with my gratitude to Jill Duffield and Terry Lovat for invitations to translate my research for a broader audience.

Family created the container for this work to take form. My parents, Dan and Dianne, nurtured many of the contextual and intellectual sensibilities that now find their form in this work. My brothers and their spouses, Drew, David, Dylan, Hannah, Kaity, and Savannah, provided encouragement and endured endless conversations about these topics. My in-laws, Bill and Cindy, and the broader Blohm/Roberts family—Justin, Kim, Jenni, Roger, Jacque, and Steve—cheered on this work to completion. Finally, to Casey, thank you for taking a chance on this idea and the more connected common life we're creating. You remind me each day how much better we are together. To our children, Cade and Ellie, who often woke to Dad writing in the morning, thank you for your notes in my books and gentle invitations to "come read with us."

I am overwhelmed by the embarrassment of connection and care that surrounds this project. To those named here, those who have gone unnamed, and all those who read this work, thank you for adding your wisdom and witness to support a more adaptive church.

List of Tables

1-1	Research Process	11
3-1	Summary of Values Identified across OCE and PC	72
3-2	OCE Total Challenges vs. Individuals Who Identify Challenges	76
3-3	PC Total Challenges vs. Individuals Who Identify Challenges	78
3-4	Summary of Challenges Identified across OCE and PC	80
7-1	Summary Table for Six Modes of Leadership	198

List of Figures

2-1	Parish Collective Flywheel. Parish Collective.	49
2-2	Map of Parish Collective Portal in Pacific Northwest. Parish Collective online platform.	50
2-3	Topographic Map of Pacific Northwest. University of Washington, "Climate in the Pacific Northwest," accessed February 18, 2020, https://cig.uw.edu/learn/.	54
4-1	OCE Partners Network Visualization (National). Generated by author with Tableau.	113
4-2	OCE Partners Network Visualization (Regional). Generated by author with Tableau.	114
4-3	OCE Partners Network Visualization (City). Generated by author with Tableau.	115
4-4	PC Online Portal (Pacific Northwest). Parish Collective online platform.	116
4-5	OCE and PC Relational Network. Created by author.	118
7-1	Six Modes of Being With. Created by author.	188
7-2	Leadership Teams. Created by author.	202
7-3	Centers and Ranges. Created by author.	204
7-4	Polarities. Created by author.	207
7-5	Axes of Leadership. Created by author.	211
A-1	Reflexive Ecclesiology Network. Created by author.	234

List of Photographs

1	The OCE's annual Ministry Summit in 2019. Used with permission of the OCE.	61
2	The PC's annual Inhabit Conference, with Tim Soerens and Christiana Rice in conversation. Used with permission of the PC.	61
3	The PC's board chair, Jonathan Brooks, speaking at a gathering in 2019. Used with permission of the PC.	62
4	The OCE's Jerry Sittser (far left) engaged in conversation with presenters for an online event in 2020. Used with permission of the OCE.	63
5	The OCE's team gathered in collaboration. Used with permission of the OCE.	63
6	Parish leaders gathered for an outdoor meal in 2016. Used with permission of the PC.	64

Introduction

*Collaboration, Community, and Change
in the Pacific Northwest*

Our systems that we have relied on to undergird ministry for so long no longer support or sustain the ministry necessary for the new age.

Rev. Erin Martin

[The Pacific Northwest is] a laboratory to learn where the rest of the country is going.[1]

Matthew Kaemingk

Treading carefully on a cracked and rolling sidewalk in Portland, Oregon, I pass toothless pumpkins that grin in the early morning light. Once a level and safe passage, the sidewalk now lies rippled and rifted from the pressure of unseen roots that have grown up from below. In the silence that comes to the city only on the day after Halloween, I breathe in the stillness of this neighborhood. Just moments earlier, I heard Bon Jovi's "Livin' on a Prayer" on my commute to this out-of-the-way part of the city. Listening to the chorus, "Woah, we're halfway there, Woah, livin' on a prayer," I thought to myself, "How true that is for many Christian communities in the Pacific Northwest."

I pause at a gray brick house on the corner before walking up its seven steps, passing more pumpkins and a sign extending welcome to all. Part pilgrim and part researcher, I offer an anxious knock, and enter to a fire on the hearth and an equally warm welcome.

I have come for morning prayer, but I have also come to listen and learn from the witness of this particular community. Those gathered include a young couple with their newborn baby, a visiting Catholic nun, a mainline denominational leader, a scholar with a Ph.D. from an East Coast university, and several others who have been part of this community for thirty years. As I will later come to learn, the community's life reflects the rippled and rifted sidewalks just outside its door. Over time, as the neighborhood changed and grew, they were stretched to discern how to adapt to its shifting composition. And yet, even through times of apparent fracture and disagreement in the community, they still carry those in their midst—like me—toward greater communion with God.

After singing, a time of prayer, and passing the peace, I accompany two members to a nearby coffee shop. Sipping our drinks, they share about the challenges facing pastors and Christian communities in their context. Erin Martin, who lives in the community and served as Portland's United Methodist district superintendent at the time, writes: "Our systems that we have relied on to undergird ministry for so long no longer support or sustain the ministry necessary for the new age.... We need systemic overhaul.... How to do it? I have no idea."[2] Recognizing that "new age" refers to patterns of individual and collective life—not some form of New Age spirituality—her language draws me in. Indeed, the "systems" that support and sustain Christian communities, congregations, and educational institutions within and beyond the Pacific Northwest require renewal.

In her book *Traveling Mercies*, Anne Lamott describes the frailty that was her life and faith in a way that reflects the experience of many who inhabit the "system" of Christian communities and educational institutions. "The cracks webbed all the way through me," she writes, "I believed that I would die soon, from a fall or an overdose. I knew there was an afterlife but felt that the odds of me living long enough to get into heaven were almost nil."[3] Drunk in life and captivated by the fear of death, Lamott expresses the collective experience of many who serve or support these communities of faith on the edge of certainty.

The fragility of communities of faith, organizations, and "systems" is more often felt before it is spoken aloud. There is a hope for a better future, but faith communities and those who lead them are worn and weary. Like the rippled and rifted sidewalk I traveled in the predawn light, the landscape on which many Christian communities and institutions were built has shifted. In other cases, unseen, subterranean forces are working their way up from beneath. As expressed by an individual interviewed for this work, these challenges present in seven different forms: relational engagement; leadership development; boundary-zone work; post-Christendom; financial stability; loneliness and isolation; and connection to place. Although this catalogue reflects aspects of broader national and cultural trends that confront communities, my description contextualizes these challenges in relation to the lived experience and histories that ground faith in particular communities. In both cases, these visible and invisible challenges reflect a shifting landscape of organized religious life,[4] shooting cracks through the social terrain that surrounds the life of faith.[5] A system-wide realignment is occurring.[6]

New forms of organizational life are emerging in this pockmarked landscape. As a result, these phenomena can simultaneously induce *both* optimism about the latent possibilities and a listlessness that may lapse into despair. Even in a region researchers have dubbed the "None Zone,"[7] new possibilities for Christian education, organization, and leadership are emerging out of the institutional and imaginative "cracks" such as I witnessed in that early morning encounter in Portland.[8] Christian organizations and those who lead them are imagining and pursing adaptive responses to the challenges they face.

The rippled and rifted state of Christian communities and educational institutions invites and requires new frameworks to direct Christian education and leadership in this "new age." Research on congregations, religious higher education, and related organizations over the last decade paints a fairly consistent picture: engagement in existing institutions is declining and religious organizations are marked by pronounced fragility.[9] Although there are ample examples of vitality and resilience,[10] these cases should not conceal the decisive shift that is taking place in communities of faith and those who serve them. As one leader in the Pacific Northwest observed, there is a need for a "bridge to a post-Christendom era." Amid the crumbling of Christendom, the ecclesial ecology that comprises the life of faith needs a "new institutionality"; new templates *are* required.[11]

THE PACIFIC NORTHWEST AS THE AMERICAN RELIGIOUS FUTURE

This book tells the story of two communities in the Pacific Northwest who are adapting to the challenges they face through collaborative approaches to Christian education, organization, and leadership. The Pacific Northwest, as Mark Silk has observed, is "the American religious future."[12] Comprised of Washington, Oregon, and Idaho and located in the northwestern corner of the United States, the region has a history of religious entrepreneurship and a marginal social position for religious organizations. To be a religious organization in the region requires an entrepreneurial spirit. As one leader shared, "[Innovation] is in the water we drink."[13] And it is precisely at this point that the stories of these two communities can address the needs of other faith communities and leaders.[14] Uncertainty. Collaborative partnership. Caring for the needs of local communities. As faith communities inhabit a shifting landscape, nimbleness is required.

Adaptive Church explores what it takes for communities of faith to respond to uncertainty and shifting organizational environments. Based on fifty-one interviews, focus groups, attendance at key events, and more than five years of research on religious life in the Pacific Northwest, I tell the story of these adaptive ecclesial communities and their emerging organizational forms. I employ a novel method to identify two sites where communities are responding to adaptive challenges through collaborative approaches to religious organization, education, and leadership: The Parish Collective (Seattle, Wash.) and The Office of Church Engagement (Spokane, Wash.). Rather than focusing on a single organizational form (e.g., congregations, theological schools, nonprofits, philanthropy, church plants), I identify contexts where leaders are partnering across these organizational sectors. Drawn from research that spans the pandemic, these two collaborative hubs provide a template for the connection and collaboration that can guide a post-COVID church. By "hub" I refer to a densely networked organizational form that anchors religious life within a particular community and facilitates webs of connection across a broader ecclesial ecology through partnership, education, and leadership development.[15] This concept is not strictly synonymous with "Christian nonprofit, parachurch ministry,"[16] even though these two communities serve and work alongside several congregations. Much as Thad Austin has observed: "As the church enters a post-pandemic world, collaboration is required."[17]

These two communities in the Pacific Northwest provide a fitting context to consider the challenges and opportunities that invite new forms of adaptation, partnership, and creativity.[18] Individuals who enter the Pacific Northwest typically "experience a loosening of connection to social institutions."[19] Patricia Killen explains:

> Each person who enters the region must choose whether, if, and how to reconnect. That choice is part of a larger question of community in the Pacific Northwest, a question about how an individual can be fully free, in nature, and part of society. People seek community, often through churches, and yet feel ambivalent about the constraints that community entails. This ambivalence leads some out of churches and drives others toward intense commitment and ownership.[20]

The dynamic Killen identifies represents a historic and ongoing challenge within the region. For example, in 1914 the Great Divide "seemed too steep for church letters" and "the air of the Northwest seemed too rare for prayer."[21] More recently, a columnist in *The Seattle Times* noted how the region's "mulish independent streak" can translate to a distrust of authority and supporting social structures.[22] A study of church plants in Seattle similarly noted the challenges transplants encounter finding "meaningful community."[23] Here, in a region that prizes idealism, autonomy, and self-expression, the social landscape is marked by a countervailing desire for connection in the wake of institutions. As a result, organizational adaptations in religious organization and leadership emerge from a context where individuals are ambivalent about inherited templates for tradition-bound religious organizations and desire connection that occurs in—but also *beyond*—the traditional boundaries of organized religious life.

The Pacific Northwest displays the dual challenge and possibility of creating alternative structures to organize a common life. For the broader study of religious and cultural change, the distinguishing features of the Pacific Northwest make it a "regional laboratory of demography indicating where North America north of the Mexico border is headed when it comes to religion."[24] Killen aptly summarizes the consequence of the Pacific Northwest for this broader study when she describes Cascadia—a subset of the region—as the "canary in the mine" and "an experiment about the consciousness and conscience of humanity." Noting how the region readily surfaces more questions than answers for those who serve in religious organizations, she queries, "[C]an the possibilities of sustainable community become sufficiently compelling that the institutionally averse will feel so powerfully claimed by living beings other than themselves that they are capable of sacrifice?" Indeed, as Killen observes, the tensions, possibilities, and challenges that are inherent to the Pacific Northwest provide an opportunity to consider ways of life that may emerge on the other side of Christendom.[25] Here—where shifting geographical, social, and cultural landscapes meet shifting conventions for religious organization and practice—there is the possibility of discerning the practices and practical wisdom required for this "new age."[26]

The Pacific Northwest also expresses the possibility of resilient Christian witness amid the crumbling of Christendom. Writing from Vancouver, British Columbia, Jason Byassee notes how "Christendom has long come and gone in the Pacific Northwest and British Columbia, if it was ever there to begin with."[27] And yet, the story of Christian communities in the region displays resilience, hopefulness, and creativity. As Sunia Gibbs, a pastor, artist, and community organizer in Portland, observes, the need for experimentation released her to attend to the local context, where she "found new conversations, concerns, and perspectives."[28] Gibbs' story displays the arc of the creative, contextual, and connective resilience that is emerging in the region. Driven by the needs for innovation and wisdom born of local communities, the Pacific Northwest provides a "nurse log" for adaptive possibilities.[29] Church plants are taking root in Seattle, exploring a range of postures to pursue mission and ministry.[30] Local churches, nonprofits, and Christian colleges are partnering to extend hospitality to immigrant communities. Historic congregations are being restored and local mission reinvigorated amid closures of many peer congregations.[31] Deeply rooted missional experiments in hospitality, neighborliness, and faithful presence are starting across the region.[32]

If the Pacific Northwest displays the promise of the American religious future, it first illustrates how the story of Christian witness and ministry requires a more complex narrative than statistics of decline can tell. While national data displays unrelenting trends in disaffiliation, institutional distrust, and declining participation in local congregations, local ministry and practice display creativity, care, and vitality. The stories of these two adaptive communities, the Parish Collective (PC) and the Office of Church Engagement (OCE), demands a more complex narrative of the American religious future. Second, it directs attention to local communities as the site to discern the form(s) of organization, education, and leadership that can sustain a future church. Amid a moment of dramatic reshuffling of American religious life—a "hinge time," as one participant observed—the adaptability and resilience of Christian witness in the Pacific Northwest invites careful attention and care. As other communities and leaders attempt to craft their faithful work and witness, the work and stories of these two communities can provide a spark of imagination.

Finally, the story of these two communities in the Pacific Northwest displays the promise and complexity of caring for an adaptive church. While each stewards their work in response to the contextual demands of the people they serve, they also pursue strikingly similar adaptive responses. As other communities face mounting challenges and calls for innovation, the stories of these communities provide a template for the organizational forms and practical wisdom that can guide communities and those who lead them amid the challenges they face.

PRACTICAL THEOLOGY AND CHRISTIAN PRACTICAL WISDOM

Practical Theology

Historical, social scientific, and organizational explanations can illumine the adaptive processes and social structures that organize both the Office of Church Engagement and the Parish Collective. But the development of alternative structures principally requires a *theological* form of inquiry. More specifically, it requires a practical theological inquiry that considers the conditions, practical wisdom, and imagination that enable adaptation within these two collaborative hubs. Accordingly, practical theology provides the primary disciplinary basis for this research and, in turn, supports the form of interdisciplinary engagement that it pursues.

Practical theology explores the challenges that confront individuals and communities in relation to the activities of their everyday life of faith. As Bonnie Miller-McLemore notes, practical theology involves "an exploration of activities of faith in their encounter with the challenges of everyday embodiment."[33] Practical theology may attend to and enrich a way of life, a discipline, a method, and a curriculum. As a way of life, practical theology is organized by the dually individual and ecclesial forms of practice (e.g., suffering, singing, forgiving) that shape and emerge from the life of faith.[34] As a discipline, practical theology emerges from communities of faith. It seeks to enrich the formation of people of faith, communities' leadership, and the forms of critical reflection and practices—which includes scholarship—that these communities pursue.[35] As a method, practical theology represents an interdisciplinary and integrative approach that seeks to "bridge the academic study of theology and the practice of faith."[36] Finally, as a curriculum, practical theology contributes to the training of religious leadership as well as the formation of a wider community of faith. When considered together, these four valences of "practical theology" describe an approach and form of knowledge that cannot be separated from communities of faith and the traditioned reflection that constitutes the Church's historic and ongoing common life. Miller-McLemore summarizes:

> In all four parts, practical theology is a general way of doing theology concerned with the embodiment of religious belief in the day-to-day lives of individuals and communities. It engages personal, ecclesial, and social experience to discern the meaning of divine presence and to enable faithful human response.... Ultimately, practical theology is normatively and eschatologically oriented. It not only describes how people live as people of faith in communities and society. It also considers how they might do so more fully.[37]

As such, practical theology emerges from the challenges that confront communities of faith, requires contextual and interdisciplinary approaches to research and scholarship, is organized by attention to practice, and seeks to nurture the conditions where individuals and communities may live faithfully in relation to God and others.

The need for "systemic overhaul" named in the opening scene requires an interdisciplinary approach. Practical theology and organizational theory, as intrinsically interdisciplinary fields, provide suitable guides for the form of inquiry that can respond to the call for new templates to organize, educate, and lead. Practical theology provides theories and interpretive tools to consider faith formation and leadership development through local communities and across generations. Organizational theory offers theories and empirical research about how individuals in communities respond to change, individually as well as collectively. Connected by a shared disciplinary interest in the structures and processes that contribute to change, practical theology and organizational theory provide complementary insights.

While the need for change is shared across communities of faith, the practices that guide it are contextually determined. For this reason, I have purposefully focused on two specific hubs, detailing their history, networks, and surrounding communities. With context as an anchor for inquiry, I tell the story of how these two communities of practice are nimble and adaptive, expressing a porous way of life that resists strict disciplinary definition. As these two communities work to build alternative structures, they do so in light of the reality and possibilities of God. Accordingly, practical theology and organizational theory provide a disciplinary pair to describe each adaptive response,[38] accenting the structural features of their collective work, and how alternative structures aim to rekindle ecclesial imagination. Much like two hinges on a door, this interdisciplinary pairing provides a disciplinary scaffolding on which to hang this inquiry and the rhetorical fulcrum on which the argument turns.

The renewal that is envisioned in the early-morning Portland encounter also requires a systems-level analysis that attends to the broader environment where faith is formed and leadership takes shape: the broader ecclesial ecology instead of a single congregation, leader, or organization. By "ecclesial ecology," I mean the constellation of identifiable forms of organized, ecclesial life, such as congregations, theological schools, Christian colleges and universities, philanthropic centers, and nonprofits, as well as experiments and expressions of creative deviance that take place in the boundary spaces between existing and emerging orders.[39] The challenges that confront communities of faith, however, are not restricted to a single place or position; they cross sectors and create systems-level disruption. Research that aims to attend to and support "systemic overhaul" requires an adequate form of analysis that locates particular expressions of Christian life and leadership in relation to the broader ecclesial ecology.[40]

The practical theologian also begins from the situation of the contemporary church and the practices that organize its common life. The challenges posed by this situation invite various sources of knowledge in order to understand and describe the practices and structures that order individuals' and communities' engagement in and with the world. When enlivened and illumined by attention to theology, Scripture, and other forms of theory, practical theological reflection enriches and refracts contemporary practice. As John Swinton and Harriet Mowat conclude: "The primary task of Practical Theology is not simply to see differently, but to enable that revised vision to create changes in the way that Christians and Christian communities perform the faith. Practical Theology is certainly a reflective discipline, but above all else it is a *theology of action*."[41] Further, the use of qualitative methods in practical theology, to borrow language from Bent Flyvbjerg, reflects a form of "phronetic social science."[42] Qualitative methods direct the practical theologian's attention to the forms of practice, conditions, and structures of community that cultivate forms of Christian practical wisdom. Practical theological inquiry of this kind attempts to understand and describe the conditions that enable and release the transformation of individuals and communities.

CHRISTIAN PRACTICAL WISDOM

If practical theology and organizational studies are the hinges on which this argument turns, Christian practical wisdom is the pin that holds the story together. Representing more than disciplinary insight or technical expertise, this wisdom contributes to the vitality of an ecclesial ecology that can adapt to a shifting environment. Attending to wisdom is the work of practical theology,[43] but it is also the work of everyday people of faith. As Miller-McLemore observes: "In its focus on concrete instances of religious life, its objective is both to understand and influence religious wisdom or faith in action in congregations and public life more generally."[44] The systems-level change that is required invites a form of wisdom that renews the collective imagination of an adaptive church.

In a collaborative work with Dorothy Bass, Kathleen Cahalan, James Nieman, and Christian Scharen, *Christian Practical Wisdom: What It Is, Why It Matters*, Miller-McLemore and colleagues provide an account of the source of knowledge that habituates a faith-filled form of knowing. If, as Cahalan notes, "wisdom is born of practice and . . . those who desire it must practice their way to it,"[45] *Christian Practical Wisdom* offers an account of the "practice" required for Christian knowledge. Christian practical wisdom is

> morally attuned, rooted in a tradition that affirms the good, and driven toward aims that seek the good. It is . . . open and adaptive to new situations. It is nimble and at times even self-critical. Most of all, this knowledge is practical, grounded in ordinary experience, and learned over time in the company of others and for the sake of others.[46]

Practical theology's particular methodological and epistemic commitments position it to attend to and describe the form(s) of Christian practical wisdom that are emerging in response to the challenges communities are facing in the Pacific Northwest.[47] Miller-McLemore clarifies this point: "Through its close attention to practice and lived experience in the last several decades, practical theology stands among the most recent and most sustained efforts to recover, honor, articulate, refine, and advance forms of practical knowledge."[48] Hence, the challenges that confront communities in the Pacific Northwest invite an inquiry attentive to Christian practical wisdom that guides communities' adaptive responses.

The wisdom that guides an adaptive church also requires an adequate individual and collective imagination. This wisdom contributes to the vitality of an ecclesial ecology nurtured by an imagination that sees the connection between individuals and a broader community of practice, and between a community of practice and God's entanglement in history. As Miller-McLemore and her colleagues note, Christian practical wisdom is "learned over time in the company of others and for the sake of others."[49] This collective learning cultivates an ecclesial imagination in which individuals-in-communities are able to see the possibilities in the adaptive challenges they face. When embedded in an ecclesial ecology where faith is form and leadership is fostered, a vibrant ecclesial imagination enables communities of faith to pursue nimble and adaptive responses to the challenges that trouble the Church.

Nevertheless, communities of faith face an "imagination deficit disorder."[50] As noted in the opening scene from the Portland coffee shop, there is a tacit understanding that "we need systemic overhaul"; however, much like the denominational leader, we often conclude: "How to do it? I have no idea." If communities of faith—within and beyond the Pacific Northwest—are to adapt to these challenges, our communities require a renewal of a ecclesial imagination. To this end, the formation and expression of an ecclesial imagination that guides an adaptive church is the organizing theological concern for this book. As a broader ecclesial ecology adapts to a shifting organizational environment, how may the formation of an ecclesial imagination shape a common life? An adequate response to this question requires contextual, interdisciplinary engagement that attends to social structures and wisdom that grounds responses, but it also invites a theological account of what is possible in light of the reality and promises of God. As people gather, connect, and collaborate in new ways, the structure that sustains an adaptive church invites others to do the same by creating space for God's ongoing creative and recreative work. Hence, in telling the story of the conditions, practices, and conceptual frameworks that nurture an ecclesial imagination of this kind, I aim to encourage and invigorate other expressions. When this form of local practice is considered in relation to the broader Christian witness, *Adaptive Church* theologically redescribes the practice and possibility of change in order to renew ecclesial imagination.

OVERVIEW

The story of an adaptive church emerges as an account of hubs where leaders from various types of Christian organizations gather to address common challenges. As argued in the chapters that follow, these two hubs represent a novel organizational form that attempts to reimagine church. When located in a broader network of Christian thought and practice, their work and wisdom

Table 1-1 Research Process

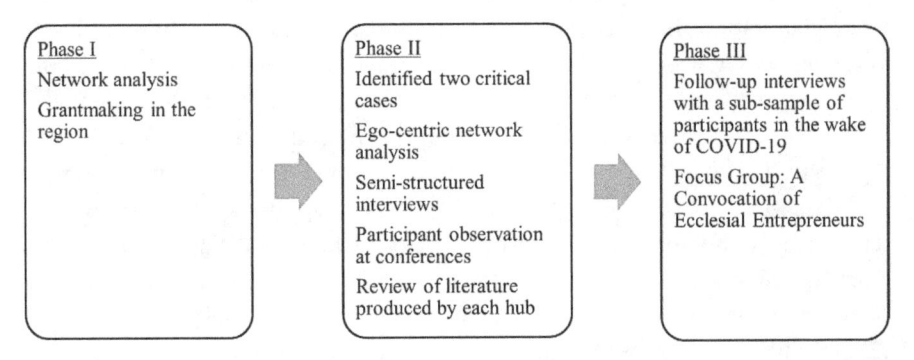

Phase I	Phase II	Phase III
Network analysis Grantmaking in the region	Identified two critical cases Ego-centric network analysis Semi-structured interviews Participant observation at conferences Review of literature produced by each hub	Follow-up interviews with a sub-sample of participants in the wake of COVID-19 Focus Group: A Convocation of Ecclesial Entrepreneurs

enriches the ecclesial ecology that supports and sustains faith formation and leadership development.

Through sustained attention to and participation within this particular organizational field, I examine the challenges and values that organize these hubs, the organizational structures that emerge from and sustain adaptive work at these sites, and the practices of organizational leadership that are embedded in these adaptive responses. I completed my research over three phases. The first phase included a network analysis that combined interviews with diverse stakeholders in the region and a review of grantmaking patterns. Based on this work, I identified two critical cases where individuals across different types of organizations are engaged in collaborative responses to the challenges they face: I designated these cases, the OCE and the PC, as "hubs."[51] At the time, I didn't have a clear definition for this category; I simply identified these organizations as novel ecclesial activity that prioritized collaboration. The second phase included an egocentric network analysis based on semi-structured interviews with thirty-eight individuals across these hubs, attendance at conferences, and a review of literature produced by founders and participants. In the third phase, I completed follow-up interviews with a sub-sample of participants in the wake of the interlocking crises of 2020 and convened a gathering of key organizers from each hub for a focus group. Based on early findings of my research, I called this gathering A Convocation of Ecclesial Entrepreneurs (ACEE).[52] Appendix B lists interviewees and corresponding interview dates. With participants' permission, I attribute comments to specific individuals in the course of telling the story of these hubs. I also distinguish four different forms of connection to their collaborative work: founders, key organizers, participants, and partners. While the richly collaborative nature of each hub resists rigid distinctions between these roles, these categories clarify the different ways individuals collaborate to start and sustain expressions of adaptive church. Appendices C, D, E, F, and G include interview guides and informed consent materials for the three phases of research.

These three phases provided a means to identify a common form of adaptive collaboration that organizes these two hubs. Although each hub cultivates and supports networks of Christian leaders, neither hub is connected to the other, despite being less than 250 miles apart—or about a seventy-minute flight. Rather, these adaptive responses emerge from the confluence of distinct theological traditions with unique organizational arrangements and in relation to the particularity of their geographical contexts. In response to the "striking similarities and fundamental differences"[53] between these two adaptive responses, Christian practical wisdom and ecclesial imagination provide the through line of this inquiry. Emerging from the adaptive ethos that characterizes organized religious life in the Pacific Northwest, these two hubs are pursuing and cultivating a form of Christian practical wisdom that characterizes what I describe as an Adaptive Church. As these and other communities respond to the adaptive challenges confronting Christian communities, precisely this kind of Christian practical wisdom is required to enrich the ecclesial ecology that surrounds a life of faith. Further, as these hubs cultivate an ecclesial imagination through presence and partnership, they display the kind of dually organizational and ecclesial adaptation that is required in this new age. As expressed by individuals across each hub, they represent kindred attempts to reimagine church.

WHAT TO EXPECT IN THIS BOOK

Part I introduces each hub and locates their work in relation to the Pacific Northwest's entrepreneurial ethos. If, as Mark Silk observes, the Pacific Northwest is a "regional laboratory of demography indicating where North America north of the Mexico border is headed when it comes to religion,"[54] the region provides a context to consider the forms of organization and leadership that can sustain communities of faith amid uncertainty. Accordingly, I frame their similar adaptive responses as independent expressions that reflect each hub's particular organizational environment. Chapter 1 introduces the Office of Church Engagement, noting how this particular ecclesial adaptation emerged in proximity to the mainline tradition and in a fixed set of organizational arrangements. A "fixed set" describes an organizational setting in which primary partners and relationships are adequately defined in order to pursue a common objective. Individuals in a fixed set of organizational arrangements may continue to negotiate the priority of particular functions that direct their collective activity, but the parameters of their partnership have sufficient definition to sustain collaborative projects. Chapter 2 introduces the Parish Collective, noting how it emerged alongside a neighborhood-centered Emerging-Missional tradition and in an ambiguous set of organizational arrangements. An "ambiguous set" describes an organizational setting where identifiable partners exist, but the relationships among these partners are not clearly defined. Despite distinctive differences between these hubs, they share the Pacific Northwest's entrepreneurial ethos and a history of engagement with local communities of faith. Part I concludes by noting the striking similarities and fundamental differences between these two cases.

Part II offers an in-depth analysis of the challenges and organizational structure(s) that give rise to their collaborative work. As considered in chapter 3, "The Structure of Adaptive Change," seven primary challenges confront these hubs: relational engagement; leadership development; boundary-zone work; post-Christendom; financial stability; loneliness and isolation; and connection to place. As Ronald Heifetz's theory of adaptive change suggests, these challenges are adaptive challenges. They represent "conflicts in the values people hold" that are expressed in "[a] gap between the values people stand for and the reality they face."[55] Organizers across both hubs have responded to these challenges through collaborative approaches to religious organization, education, and leadership. Accordingly, chapter 4, "Anchors and Webs," offers the first in-depth analysis of a novel form of organizing religious life, which I identify as a "hub." Neither a megachurch nor a denomination, a hub is a densely networked organizational form that anchors religious life within a particular community and facilitates webs of connection across a broader ecclesial ecology.

Part III is a practical theological account of adaptive work that draws on field-driven concepts in conversation with Craig Dykstra, Dietrich Bonhoeffer, and Luke-Acts. In response to each hub's stated aim to reimagine church, chapter 5, "Reimagining Church," identifies the diverse "places" (e.g., congregations, higher education institutions, and theological educational institutions) that support adaptive change. Second, this chapter considers how a broader ecclesial ecology serves as a "prism," refracting leaders' and communities' engagement with the challenges they face. Chapter 6, "Adaptive Church," outlines how collaboration across an ecclesial ecology enables the adaptive work each hub pursues. In conversation with Bonhoeffer's work and Luke-Acts, this chapter also theologically redescribes the organizational and ecclesial transformation each hub pursues.

Finally, Part IV offers a conceptual framework to understand and cultivate the Christian practical wisdom that sustains an adaptive church. Chapter 7, "'We're Better Together,'" describes six complementary modes of leadership that support community and organizational change: the Caretaker, the Catalyst, the Champion, the Connector-Convener, the Surveyor, and the Guide. Chapter 8 concludes by outlining the adaptive possibilities of this work for these hubs, for a broader ecclesial ecology, and for the changing landscape of religious life beyond the Pacific Northwest.

Like the different facets on a cut gem, these eight chapters figuratively cast the "light" of this inquiry in different directions even as they are each positioned in relation to the others. Moreover, the extended case study across these two hubs proceeds on the basis that the defining characteristics and relationships between the facets of each hub have a degree of correspondence. Taking them together illumines the Christian practical wisdom and ecclesial imagination at play within each case. Ultimately, imitating the practical wisdom evinced by these hubs, *Adaptive Church* offers a theological paradigm for collaboration and community in a changing world.

I
Organizational Environments

1

"The Church Has Always Been Nimble"

Church Engagement on the Edge of Christendom

Standing beneath ponderosa pines, college students, each in a red shirt, accompany a group of elementary-aged kids. The children's parents, many of whom are pastors, mill around as they hand off their kids for a morning of activities during the Office of Church Engagement's Ministry Summit. There is a restless bustle as a crowd migrates to the Chapel, but nobody is concerned about being late. Here, in Spokane, at the gateway to the Inland Northwest on the western edge of the Rockies individuals embodying the church in new ways have gathered, but they neither seem worried nor rushed.[1]

Amid the chatter and bustle, I recall lines from Mary Oliver: "When I am among the trees, / . . . I would almost say that they save me, daily."[2] Indeed, the mingling of ecclesial and ecological life in the Pacific Northwest resembles Oliver's poetic imagination: community, ecology, and an eschatological horizon meet in this moment. As Charles Goodrich, Kathleen Moore, and Frederick Swanson note, "Landscapes tell stories, if we know how to listen."[3] If these trees and landscapes could talk, they would tell stories of the people, spaces, and conversations that have changed beneath them. They would tell of Seeley Mudd Chapel, a red, sandstone building, that serves both as the Chapel at Whitworth University and houses the Office of Church Engagement (OCE). Originally dedicated in 1978,[4] an annex was added in 2018 to house the OCE and Whitworth's Theology faculty.[5] With a glass-paneled interior, clean lines, and a modern feel, this adjacent space is a symbol for the ongoing evolution of Christian thought and practice in the region: existing institutional structures and buildings are adapted to meet the changing needs of people of faith.

Simultaneously, the place conveys stories of both familiar and new people passing through these spaces. The OCE's cofounders, Terry McGonigal and Jerry Sittser, each served at Whitworth for more than twenty years before starting the OCE. Mindy Smith served as a campus pastor for ten years before joining the OCE. Alumni and friends—like myself—periodically return to this space.[6] And new faces gather around the OCE's connective and collaborative work. In these passing moments beneath ponderosa pines, the stories of this place, each of our stories, and the evolving story of organizational and ecclesial adaptation in the Pacific Northwest converge.

OFFICE OF CHURCH ENGAGEMENT: MISSION

The Office of Church Engagement at Whitworth resources and supports adaptive forms of Christianity as congregations and related Christian organizations across the Pacific Northwest respond to the challenges they face. The mission of the OCE expresses these commitments in the following manner:

> The Office of Church Engagement (OCE) partners with churches and other Christian ministries as they discern how to be the church and do ministry in the western region of the United States and around the world. Church engagement functions as a resource for vision-casting, planning and developing new forms of ministry capable of effectively engaging our rapidly changing culture.[7]

When asked about the OCE's mission, its two primary organizers, McGonigal and Sittser, emphasize different aspects of the OCE's work and mission. According to McGonigal—who served as the Dean of Spiritual Life at Whitworth for twenty years before becoming the director of the OCE in 2014—the OCE "partners with churches to equip disciples and engage culture with the good news in Jesus." As he explains, discipleship is "interrelated" with "engag[ing] the culture," which, in turn, requires a "biblical-theological-communal foundation." Even though the OCE's work reflects a form of practical wisdom that is both attentive to the needs of particular communities and emerges from listening and relationships, these four elements reflect McGonigal's sense for the mission: partnership, discipleship, cultural engagement, and the good news of Jesus.

Sittser, who serves as a professor of theology and as a senior fellow in the OCE, accents the OCE's commitment to forming partnerships amid the challenges that face communities of faith. For example, Sittser notes their commitment to working "in partnerships with" congregations by "building bridges in relationship between Whitworth and local and regional churches." Sitter's narration, and, specifically, his use of "with," "in," and "between," evinces the distinctly connectional and relational qualities that characterize the OCE's partnerships.

Further, he geographically specifies the distinction between local and regional partners. Although the OCE's mission statement identifies their commitment to churches and ministries both in the western region of the United States and around the world, the primary focus of their current partnerships remains locally and regionally determined. In 2019, 57 percent of their ministry partners were from Washington, Oregon, Idaho, or Wyoming. Indeed, if their organization and work represent a particular form of Christian practical wisdom, their local and regional embeddedness provide boundaries by which to consider the particular form of organization, leadership, and education their context requires.

Sittser notes the challenges that confront congregations and ministries throughout the region. When asked about the experiences that inform the way he thinks about his work, Sittser begins by talking about forms of relationship and connection that have been lost, and the need to recover them. "There's an older model [of Christian higher education], an older ecology of relationship that's been lost in historical memory, where it was the college of the community, and pastors were on the board of trustees, and students attended local churches, and there were all kinds of connections. And I think, not all—I don't want to exaggerate—but much of that has been lost." He then transitions to offer a dually historical and theological diagnosis of the challenges that confront communities, which occasions the OCE's work: "I think in our increasingly post-Christendom setting, we would all be wise if we reestablished some of those connections. Otherwise, we're all going to have to go at it alone."

As Sittser notes, the social-ecclesial environment that surrounds people of faith and religious organizations in the region is changing. Accordingly, the OCE pursues and promotes partnerships as alternative avenues for communities of faith to respond to the challenges they face. Mindy Smith, who joined in the OCE in July 2018 after ten years as a campus pastor, reflects that amid the challenges that face congregations, the OCE "equip[s] the church" as it "move[s] into this new season." Kathryn McInturff, who directs communications and the OCE's Fellows (e.g., internship) program at the time of our conversation, describes the OCE's mission and vision in relational terms, noting what has been broken and the hope for repair: "I think the best analogy or vision, I guess, I've given about what the OCE's purpose is, is that the OCE is here to rebuild a relationship that's been broken historically between the academy, the university, higher education, and the church."

Their complementary diagnoses raise many questions (e.g., Who is the we/our in Sittser's diagnosis? What are the specific markers of "post-Christendom"? and What factors have contributed to the gulf between ecclesial educational institutions and communities of faith?). Still, they collectively express the presenting challenge that occasions the OCE's work: the network of connections that once surrounded congregations and Christian educational institutions has frayed. Meanwhile, broader cultural transitions invite new forms of organization and partnership in their current institutional landscape. Although these questions cannot be explored in detail at this point, chapter 3 will detail the challenges that organize this collaborative work.

Finally, the OCE is formally connected to a university and, as such, its work contributes to the broader educational mission of Whitworth University. The ecclesial vision that organizes the OCE's work, however, extends beyond both the OCE and Whitworth by creating conditions in which congregations and Christian organizations can discover and explore partnerships independent of either organizational entity. As McGonigal notes:

> What we're saying is we want you to invest in this network of relationships so that the relationship isn't just Whitworth to X, Y, Z church, but in the end, we want the network to be all these churches participating together in a common vision of ministry. [The grant that sustained the OCE's early work] will go away some day. Our hope is that by the time this grant is gone, these churches have really said, "We're partners together in this."

Through this collaborative and convening work, the OCE aims to support and sustain the conditions where congregations, church-related educational institutions, emerging forms of Christianity, and nonprofit partners can gather together in response to the challenges they face. As partners and related organizations adapt to a shifting institutional landscape, the OCE's connecting and convening work invites partners to enrich the ecclesial ecology that supports religious life in the region. Specifically, they invite faith communities to join an expanded range of organizations and community partners. If, at some point, the OCE or its specific programs no longer exist, the founders understand its work as a catalyst for adaptation that supports congregations and Christian ministry in the Pacific Northwest. "The church has always been nimble," McGonigal reflects, "When it's at its best, the church is nimble to identify those changes and then respond in ways that are appropriately gospel in the best sense of that term."

ADAPTATION AND A HISTORY OF PARTNERSHIPS

The OCE launched in 2014, but it emerged from more than three decades of relationships within and beyond the region. As Rob Fairbanks, who is a local church planter and pastor, observes: "My connection with the OCE is almost exclusively relational. . . . I'd consider Jerry [Sittser] in the circle of some of my best friends. . . . Terry [McGonigal], we've known each other for close to thirty years. We've known each other a long time." In one form or another, Fairbanks' sentiment echoes throughout the narratives of the OCE's founding: existing relational contacts formed through ministry and scholarship created the context for a collaborative, adaptive response to emerge.

The OCE also emerged in proximity to an established organization, Whitworth University, and its related partner organizations. Two points of relational contact catalyzed the collaborations that birthed the OCE. First, the OCE reflects a history of collaboration between McGonigal and Sittser. McGonigal arrived at Whitworth in 1994 to serve as the Dean of Spiritual Life. His work in this role involved supporting students, serving on the president's cabinet, and forming partnerships and relationships with congregations and other church entities. At age sixty-two, he transitioned to serve as the director of the OCE. This opportunity provided a chance to continue much of the work he had been doing while also having the chance to start and support a new initiative that reflected Whitworth's mission. As McGonigal reflects, "At that point, I was twenty years in—I was sixty-two—I thought, 'Well, this is kind of fun. I get to do a new venture at this stage of my life. How many people get that chance?'" As described by others who have served alongside McGonigal, the transition to this role also reflected a continuation of his history of service to individuals and communities throughout the region. Indeed, the OCE's work reflects his animating "passion"—to borrow language from one colleague—in a way that aligns with the trajectory of his vocational ministry.

Sittser, who joined Whitworth in 1989, has built bridges between the church and the academy across his thirty-year tenure. His research and writing provide a platform to engage ecclesial and academic audiences. Meanwhile, a dense network of relationships marks his service in the OCE, crafting relational contours to an ecclesial vision for how a Christian institution, such as Whitworth, serves and supports the local church. For example, when asked about the formative developments in the history of the OCE, he identifies the relationships with pastors in the region, an institutional commitment to reward scholarship *and* service to the local church, the trajectory of his own scholarship and writing, and the friendships within and beyond the institution that enliven his work. He then adds: "I would say [another important thing] is that two old guys decided to do something new in their sixties. Terry and I are best friends who decided to do something creative rather than sputter." In language used by a member of one long-standing partner congregation in their network: "These guys are joined at the hip and at the heart." The creativity, Sittser notes, is glossed as entrepreneurialism by Beck Taylor, Whitworth's president from 2010 to 2021, who introduces Sittser and Taylor as "serial entrepreneurs." Fittingly, Sittser describes himself as a "catalyst for the think tank part" of the OCE. As such, his work and service involve reaching back to consider and describe the history of Christian practice and reaching forward to articulate and support the forms of faithfulness that will buttress the next generation of Christians.[8]

Second, a long-standing personal and institutional relationship with Lilly Endowment Inc. catalyzed the OCE's formation. At an individual level, a friendship between John Wimmer, who served as a program director at Lilly Endowment from 2002 to 2020,[9] and Sittser provided an avenue to consider the intersection between Lilly's funding priorities and the network of relationships that had emerged around McGonigal and Sittser's multi-decade service throughout the region. McGonigal recounts how this relationship served as a catalyst for the OCE's early work:

> The way we got into this was John and Jerry just catching up because they were both doctoral students in Chicago decades ago, and somehow the conversation drifted towards Jerry describing some of the connections that we had at the churches here in the Pacific Northwest—primarily through our summer conference, which we used to call WIM, Whitworth Institute of Ministry.
>
> John said to Jerry, "Well, we're looking for a West Coast partner"—because they invest in these regional sites for church support and renewal—"We don't have anybody on the West Coast and, frankly, we've never seen a university that's as interested in the church as you are, particularly in the West Coast." Beck and Jerry and I spent about nine months crafting this grant, and going back and forth in conversations with John, and finally, we kind of nailed an idea, and it was clear that they wanted to launch something here, so we got the first million dollar grant.

This initial grant supported the formation of the Ekklesia Project, which sought to "enlarge and develop Whitworth's ability to function as a catalyst, center and resource for conversation, vision-casting, planning and programing" for "churches and other Christian organizations in the region."[10] This grant did not formally establish the OCE; it did, however, catalyze efforts to consider the institutional infrastructure required to support their emerging service to the church and community. Early grants from the M. J. Murdock Charitable Trust and the Pacific Northwest Presbytery similarly expanded the OCE's capacity to serve the church and students in this manner.

Lest this narrative obscure the history of partnership between Whitworth and Lilly, the two institutions have a longer funding relationship. For example, Whitworth received a $2 million grant in 2002 through Lilly's grantmaking initiative to support vocational discernment among college students[11] and a $500,000 sustainability grant for this program in 2005.[12] The Lilly-funded project "Discerning Vocation: Community, Context and Commitments" was described by Whitworth's then president, Bill Robinson, as a chance to enhance Whitworth's long-standing commitment to "preparing people for the kind of lay and professional church leadership that responds to the deepest needs of our culture."[13] It would do so by "encouraging all students to explore the theological implication of their life commitments and vocational choices."[14] Although envisioned as a five-year grant, McGonigal directed an effort to stretch the funding to twelve years. As McGonigal notes, the conclusion of this extended grant period corresponded with the start of the OCE: "Literally, the day that that grant closed was December 31, 2013, and we opened up the Office of Church Engagement the very next day." Whitworth has since received a total of $4,049,572 in grants from Lilly since 2013.[15] Thus, the combination of a long-standing personal relationship between Sittser and Wimmer and a history of institutional partnership created the context to explore and catalyze the collaborative work that led to the formation of the OCE. Much like the "thick" relationships the OCE aims to foster, this history of partnership creates an environment to imagine and then pursue their work.

In addition to this external partnership, senior institutional leadership championed the OCE's work. Beck Taylor, who began serving as Whitworth's president in 2010, also nurtured the entrepreneurial activity that led to the OCE's formation. While McGonigal and Sittser were the principal founders and conveners, the two collaborated with Taylor to conceptualize the vision for the OCE. And Taylor has remained its champion. Reflecting on his role in relation to the OCE, Taylor shares: "I have spent my career in church-related higher education and have served other institutions that saw as part of their missions that connection to the church. And so, I think I bring a natural champion's perspective for that kind of work. I see it as integral to the work of the institution." As a scholar of entrepreneurial organizations, Taylor understands both the need for collaborative approaches to entrepreneurship and the need for institutional conditions that release the creativity adaptation requires.[16] Moreover, Taylor regards the work of the OCE as directly related to Whitworth's mission, even as it also redounds to the university. He expresses his excitement about the OCE, sharing:

> Dustin, as an aside, this has been one of the most exciting things that has happened at Whitworth in the last seven years is this renewed emphasis on our [church connections]. Whitworth was founded for the church and by the church; so if the church doesn't continue to be one of our primary constituencies, then we're failing in our mission.

When combined, a dense network of different kinds of relationships within a host institution created an environment in which this dually organizational and ecclesial adaptation could unfold.[17]

PROGRAMMATIC STRUCTURE

The OCE pursues its mission through a programmatic structure, comprised of five elements. It seeks to strengthen connections between leaders in the region and support congregations and those who serve them. Its endeavor includes: a partnership network, an annual gathering, leadership development initiatives, contextual "Calling Communities," and print and online resources. In the language of one organizer, these elements, which emerge from relational contact and listening to the needs of particular communities, reinforce one another and serve to "thicken" relationships across the network. Short descriptions of each aspect of the OCE's programmatic structure provide an introduction to the work and organization of this particular hub.

The Ministry Partner Network is the focal programmatic element that connects congregations and those who serve them. Churches may join the Ministry Partner Network for $500 a year. As of 2018, the OCE's Ministry Partner Network included thirty-nine congregations, ranging in worship attendance between eighty and five thousand individuals. Organizers estimate the average size of congregations that join the Network is between 250 and 600 in worship attendance.[18] By joining the Ministry Partner Network, congregations may access an expanded range of resources, partnerships, and direct support. For example, partner congregations can request an undergraduate student fellow during a summer; they can access a catalogue of print and online training resources called The Academy of Christian Discipleship; they receive a scholarship to attend the OCE's annual summer conference;[19] and they have access to the OCE-sponsored Calling Communities that take place year-round.

OCE organizers and staff also purposefully pursue relationships with the lay and ordained leadership of partner congregations. Ministry Partners, in turn, express how much they value a reciprocal relationship. Courtney Arntzen, who serves as an associate pastor at First Presbyterian Church in Missoula, Montana when we first spoke, shares: "[The Ministry Partnership] gives us great access to staff. . . . They just have had a really fluid relationship with us, and have shown up whenever they've been asked to, for whatever we've asked them to." Abby Leman, who serves as the primary connection between Spokane First Church and the OCE, similarly expresses the impact of the relational connection with the OCE staff. When asked about the nature of their partnership with the OCE, she shares: "Frankly, I felt valued. . . . They verbally spoke just respect towards me as a female leader in a small church. I'm not ordained or anything. I could just tell I was seen by them, seen and heard. And when you get pursued like that, as an individual or as a group, or as a family, or as an organization, you tend to gravitate towards those type of people."

As expressed repeatedly throughout the OCE's network, partnering is an organizing practice across this hub. A few brief examples of how founders explain the importance of partnerships illustrate the organizational and individual forms of connection that distinguish the Ministry Partnership Network. Noting the priority of partnership, McGonigal shares:

> [Everything] is done in partnerships. The key here is partnering, and the approach isn't "we want to deal with individuals in churches," [but] "we want to partner with churches," and we only want to partner on those things the church wants us to partner on. . . . We are in complete response mode. . . . That to me has been the genius of the whole thing, because churches feel like we're their partners not their competitors.

McGonigal later describes how deep listening to the needs of local congregations—what he describes as their "listening mode"—provides the basis for the partnerships they pursue and the specific programmatic offerings they provide to Partner congregations. Sittser provides a complementary perspective when he notes the need for both interpersonal and institutional connections in order to create and sustain the "thick relationships" that they envision with congregations who join the Ministry Partnership Network. As Sittser explains,

> [U]nderneath [the services we provide] is a desire for a real relationship, what we call thick relationships, between Whitworth, the people at Whitworth, and actual local churches and the people at the church. So, we're looking for two kinds of relationships. One is more interpersonal—my friendship with the board of a session and a pastor and a youth worker—and then institutional relationship. And for us to be successful . . . it has to be both. If it's merely interpersonal, it's too fragile; it's too dependent on me as a person, and when I retire, the thing will fall apart. Or when the pastor leaves, the thing will fall apart. If it's merely institutional, then it becomes nothing but a form, a piece of paper you sign, and that kind of thing.

As Sittser explains, the Ministry Partnership Network creates forums to pursue and deepen relationships between the OCE and congregations throughout the region. It requires two interlocking elements: that partner congregations find value in this partnership and that the OCE staff is able to maintain relational contact in order to ensure that the partnership is not exclusively institutional in nature.[20] As described by another central organizer, Mindy Smith, these partnerships provide ecclesial connection: "[W]e just keep saying, 'We love the church, and we want to serve the church.'" As Smith and others narrate it, this church-centric approach to partnership reflects Sittser and McGonigal's common vocation—i.e., resourcing the local church—and the OCE's mission to partner with congregations in the Pacific Northwest as a resource to ministry leaders throughout the region.

Nevertheless, there are obstacles to the development and growth of the Ministry Partnership Network, and more on the horizon. First, the OCE has to overcome the obstacle posed by the membership fee for some congregations. The OCE cites some reluctance on the part of congregations to join at $500. For congregations in the rural areas of the Inland Northwest, $500 can be a considerable commitment. Those who have been members of the Ministry Partnership Network have written the membership fee in as a line item on their annual budget. The OCE must also overcome the obstacle of distrust of educational institutions.[21] Acknowledging a history of division between the local church and educational institutions, the OCE approaches their work with local congregations by "building bridges in relationship" with local and regional congregations and "rebuilding trust" in educational institutions within congregations. At the same time, the Ministry Partnership Network faces the challenge of transitioning the trust-laden relationships that organize their work to the next generation of leadership. The OCE's work and partnership emerges from almost sixty years of combined teaching and service within the region by its two founders. Even as this has created a dense network of existing relationships, it also presents a formidable challenge for the strength and durability of the relational connections integral to the forms of partnership in this emerging network. While Sittser and McGonigal's extensive networks catalyzed the OCE's early work, a structure is now required to sustain it. Sittser and McGonigal, Whitworth's president, and the OCE staff each acknowledge the approaching challenge. As of this writing, they are beginning to explore when and how to introduce new leadership and transfer the relational capital; it remains to be seen whether the Ministry Partnership Network and related programs will weather a leadership transition given the importance of interpersonal connections to the formation and durability of the OCE's network.

The OCE also hosts an annual conference, The Whitworth Ministry Summit, to convene members of the Church Ministry Partnership network and provide an avenue for other members and congregations from the region to gather. Whitworth has hosted the Whitworth Institute of Ministry (WIM) for over forty years, which predates either organizer's arrival at Whitworth. In 2019, which marks the forty-fourth anniversary of the founding of WIM, this program was "rebranded" as the Whitworth Ministry Summit—or, simply, Summit. Smith, who directs the planning and organization of the event, describes Summit as "a three-day conference in which we're streamlining our [Calling] Communities to come and get resourced in the specifics of what that community's trying to do." The Calling Communities, described in more detail below, are contextual learning communities built around eight different focus areas.[22] Members of the Ministry Partnership Network are the primary audience for Summit; however, membership is not required to attend. Any pastor or ministry leader is welcome to join. As a result, Summit provides both a platform to bring various groups and partners together and a potential on-ramp for other people who are interested in the OCE's work and resources.

The OCE's Summit both reflects their animating mission and demonstrates the particular challenges that they have identified as important to discuss and engage in this collective setting. For example, advertisements for the 2018 WIM invite participants "to come and see how they may be called by God to kingdom work in a post-Christendom setting—a situation in which Christianity and the church no longer hold a position of cultural privilege and power."[23] When ministry partners were asked about the challenges they faced, they repeatedly used the language of "post-Christendom" to describe their ministry contexts. As one participant queried: "In a world that is less Christian, which is a world that seems to be on the way, how does the church work?" Adapting to a shifting cultural-ecclesial environment is a central concern of connecting and educational work.

For example, a promotional video for a 2019 gathering depicts the centrality of this concept.[24] After an irenic view of a rushing river overlaid with the text of Isaiah 40:31,[25] the video flashes through scenes of conflict and protest: protesters and police clashing, a gathering of (mostly white) individuals outside what looks like a governmental building, a march or rally in an urban setting with a "Black Lives Matter" sign in the center of the frame, and a scene of a protester being arrested by NYPD officers. A female narrator interprets these scenes: "We look around and see chaos dividing our world, our church, our communities, and our daily lives." Then the images pivot to urban settings, without protest and conflict, as the narrator continues, "Where do we find hope? How do we rise above the chaos and reconcile with our neighbor and live out our faith?" A male narrator, speaking over urban scenes and clips of conference speakers, then describes the OCE's response: "Together, through Jesus, we're building hope for the future of the church. We're living out our calling and caring for our communities. We're making connections that strengthen the work of the gospel. And we're learning what it means, what it truly means, to be made in the image of God." The narrator and text then conclude with an invitation: "Join us for this hope." As suggested by the textual presentation of this message, which reads "**Join us** in this **HOPE**," the invitation accents a collective response oriented toward hope.

Leadership development programs are the third programmatic element of the OCE's work. This includes the OCE Academy of Christian Discipleship and the Student Fellowship Program. The Academy of Christian Discipleship provides online training modules and print materials congregations can use to support lay education within their communities. The initiative emerged from conversations between the OCE's early partners across the region about the kinds of resources that could support the changing needs of congregations. As McGonigal recalls, they heard partners say, "We want lay-level theological and practical training." The purpose of the Academy of Christian Discipleship is "to train people in godliness, to form disciples into lifelong apprentices to Jesus, and to strengthen the life of the local church."[26] The OCE currently has eight courses taught by Whitworth faculty or ministry partners available through the Academy of Christian Discipleship. They include: The Gospel of Mark, The Gospel of Luke, The Gospel of John, The Third Way, Deepening the Root System, Introduction to the Bible, On Mission, and Christian Leadership. Ministry Partners may access the training modules and online materials for $100 per track and $25 for the tracks on the four Gospels. Ministry Partners may also access the Library of the Academy of Christian Discipleship. Organizers estimate that five hundred people have participated in the Academy of Christian Discipleship.[27]

Mostly, Ministry Partners express how the Academy has enriched their congregational life. A member of First Presbyterian Missoula expresses how the Academy has strengthened the church's training of lay leaders: "I think that what we've seen is that the people that have been engaged in the Academy are willing to take the next step and be engaged in leadership. . . . I think, also, that there's been longevity added to those positions." Another minister of a local Presbyterian congregation expresses his enthusiasm, saying, "I'll use whatever they put out." Nevertheless, other partners are either more measured in their assessment of the Academy or identify other aspects of the OCE's work as of greater value (e.g., access to an expanded network of partners). The ambivalence expressed by some partners and ministry leaders suggests the ongoing challenge of creating a sustainable educational platform for the OCE's curricular offerings. Although Ministry Partners have access to the online training modules and print resources for a small fee, this still appears to represent a barrier to entry. As the organizers observe, when similar training resources are available for free online, it is difficult to compete. Moreover, mainline—and especially Presbyterian—congregations are willing to adopt the Academy of Christian Discipleship, but the Academy's course offerings have generated less interest beyond the mainline tradition.

Meanwhile, the OCE's Fellows Program provides leadership development for Whitworth undergraduate students and recent graduates. The Fellows Program was catalyzed by a grant from the M. J. Murdock Charitable Trust and is directed by Kathryn McInturff. The program emerged in response to members of the Ministry Partner Network requesting to have students serve in ministry with them during the summer months.[28] Whitworth undergraduate students can apply for a ten-week summer placement anytime between the summer after their freshman year and the summer after graduating. Students receive a $3,000 stipend during their placement, which includes placements in congregations, nonprofits, and parachurch ministries; students themselves are expected to raise $750 before the fellowship period.[29] Host sites place students in a home stay, provide mentoring for fellows, and allow students to do substantive ministry. Fellows have served in placements within the Pacific Northwest, beyond the region (e.g., California and Alaska), and internationally (e.g., Scotland and Estonia). The OCE staff estimates that they have sent out 215 fellows in four years.

The Fellows Program supports the leadership development of students and thickens relationships with partner ministries within and beyond the region. For McInturff, the Fellows Program rebuilds trust between students and local congregations. She shares:

> I see a lot of what my role is, specifically with students going to churches and then churches being a part of the Fellowship Program, as very trust building between the two and trying to say, "Yes you had reasons not to trust before." . . . I mean there's a laundry list of things I feel like I'm talking to students about all the time—that the church is either out of touch or that the church wants nothing to do with it, or that the church is actually antagonistic about having those conversations. So, for students, as they're preparing to go work in churches, I think it's an opportunity for them to, in most cases, be really proven wrong.

The Fellows Program also provides an additional relational point of contact between the OCE and Ministry Partners, which the OCE pursues through regular relational engagement before, during, and after the fellowship period. Students who completed the Fellows Program speak about how the program enabled them to transition into ministry and professional settings, as well as about how their relationships with OCE staff have contributed to their vocational development. Andrew Goodwin serves as a Digital Communications Assistant for World Relief Spokane after his OCE fellowship there. Goodwin describes how the program provided a "bridge" to his current work. As he shares, "[H]aving the fellowship gave me an opportunity to pop into the work. . . . To just jump in with two feet, figure out if this is where I'm being called for this season. And it also provided a community of people who are doing the same thing and trying to follow God in the same way." According to another fellow, who currently serves in a community engagement role for a local nonprofit, the internship gave her experience contacting local congregations, which she describes as the "X factor" that helped her land her current position.[30]

The Calling Communities provide a fourth programmatic element of the OCE's work and ministry.[31] This emerging dimension of the OCE's work, which they formalized in 2018 through a nearly $1.5 million grant from Lilly Endowment Inc., gathers groups from churches around contextually specific concerns that enrich the broader ministry of a congregation. Sittser explains: "Our goal there is to get, not an individual, but groups from churches that are called into a particular area.... We don't want just one person, we want three or four, and then as they start to grow in their obedience to Christ.... We hope that they become salt, leaven, and light in the larger congregation; and part of our goal is to equip them so that they know how to do that in congregations."[32] This work, much like the OCE's other programmatic initiatives, emerges in response to the particular needs and questions that animate partner congregations. "We gathered about 110 ministry leaders for the Pacific Northwest for a listening day last summer, summer of 2017," recalls McGonigal. They framed their work as an attempt to think about and explore the ways of life that organize communities who follow Jesus "without any sense of power and privilege."[33] Six foci emerged: youth ministry, refugees and immigrants, creation care, reconciliation, called to the city, and church planting.

A ministry practitioner leads each Calling Community, combining theological and practical insight to enrich their shared work. Each Calling Community's specific focus varies, but the OCE provides administrative support and funding to launch these collaborative initiatives. For example, Rob Fairbanks, who has worked locally in Spokane as a church planter and internationally as the president of the church-planting organization Christian Associates, convenes the Church Planting Learning Community. His work in this role continues his collaboration with the OCE staff, but it is also informed by his ongoing collaboration with a team of pastors in the region who envisioned the Pacific Northwest Church Planting Movement. Fairbanks hopes that the "marriage" between an educational institution like Whitworth and local church planters can help individuals and communities reimagine the church and the forms of ministry and training required to support and sustain it. As this case demonstrates, the work of these Calling Communities reinforces existing collaborative networks within the region.[34] As a result, the OCE serves as a connective hub, convening and catalyzing these contextual Calling Communities, as congregations and church-related organizations across the region adapt to the shifting landscape of religious life.

Finally, the OCE also serves as a hub for teaching and thought leadership within the region. Although this aspect of their work takes a less formal expression, it is present across all aspects of their work. Participants across the OCE's network speak to the impact of the teaching, books, and similar print materials produced by the OCE, but the value they identify is regularly indexed to their relationship with one of the founders. For example, Mike McKay, who now serves as a lay leader at First Presbyterian, Missoula, notes the importance of Sittser's work *A Grace Disguised* at an early point in his faith journey.[35] Several years later, after sending his children to Whitworth, McKay began to build a relationship with McGonigal and Sittser. Over time, the combination of these factors with a broader alumni network in Missoula created the conditions for First Presbyterian to become an early ministry partner for the OCE's work within the region.

The OCE also develops language schemas that describe and direct ministry within the Pacific Northwest. The use of the term "post-Christendom" within and across this network provides a prime example. Although this research did not begin with the intent to surface and understand this concept, post-Christendom emerged as a pronounced theme throughout the OCE's work. Of the nineteen individuals interviewed in connection to the OCE, five used the language of "post-Christendom" or "Christendom,"[36] and others discussed the challenges associated with broader cultural transitions. For interviewees, "post-Christendom" describes the marginal position of Christianity, but it is hermeneutically distinct from "post-Christian." As Sittser explains: "We're not 'post-Christian' in this country; we're saturated with Christianity. . . . What I mean is that Christianity has lost its favorite place, especially in more elite circumstances: entertainment, education, so on and so forth, and it's presenting churches in America with some challenges they probably had not had to face before." Through OCE programs and founders' teaching, this language schema has worked its way into the parlance of participants within the network. For example, after Andrew Goodwin used the language of "post-Christendom" at several points in our conversation, I inquired about the source of this language. Here's an excerpt of our conversation:

Benac You've also used the language of post-Christendom once or twice.

Goodwin Yeah.

Benac Do you have a sense for where you picked up that language? Or how it worked its way into the way you think about the world?

Goodwin That's a good question. I don't know if I would have used the word post-Christendom before going to Whitworth. . . . I think I picked that up at Whitworth. That was also part of the program in Third Way. In a world that is less Christian, which is a world that seems to be on the way, how does the church work? Because the church shouldn't need to segment itself off into its own thing.[37]

A commitment to faith formation connects the various programmatic features of the OCE's work. Drawing upon a history of engagement in the region and the contextual contours of each partner, they work to form people of faith as well as more durable partnerships. When combined with the other four aspects of their work, the OCE serves as a hub where people from across the region come to consider the forms of Christian thought and practice that can enrich congregations, Christian organizations, and those who inhabit them.

GEOGRAPHIC AND URBAN CONTEXT

Ecclesial adaptation requires place. Geography and locality combine to shape adaptive expressions, carving the imaginative contours of the OCE's and PC's collective work. More specifically, the geographic and urban region that surrounds each hub contributes to its particular form of organizational and ecclesial adaptation. Even as the Pacific Northwest has been characterized as an "open religious environment,"[38] one that invites innovation and religious entrepreneurship,[39] the distinct, place-based characteristics of Spokane and Seattle inform the adaptation that each hub pursues. Much like the movement of water across land, the work of imagination takes place in and is shaped by space. As water moves down river, riverbanks and topography directs its movement; over time, this water also reshapes the land. In a similar way, urban settings, surrounding geography, and adaptive forms of religious life are shaped and reshaped by the practical wisdom that emerges from these hubs. Conjoined in a symbiotic relationship, the particulars of this place and the practical wisdom these hubs foster are remaking the fabric of belonging in the Pacific Northwest.

For the OCE, three features of its urban and geographic setting contribute to the form of adaptation that it pursues. First, located in Spokane, the OCE emerges from an urban setting that is geographically and culturally positioned at the gateway to the Inland Northwest. Spokane is home to 217,000 residents as of 2017;[40] its municipal neighbor, Spokane Valley, is a city of nearly 100,000.[41] Together, they comprise the largest metro area between Seattle and Minneapolis. The two cities are 87.1 percent white,[42] which was frequently noted by interviewees, but also has a growing immigrant population and history of black activism.[43] Railroads, gold mining in nearby Idaho, and the Spokane River once made Spokane "the hub of the Inland Northwest" in the early part of the twentieth century.[44] However, the decline of these industries and changing patterns of transportation set off a period of decline. Spokane's downtown district has undergone periods of urban renewal,[45] but the city has not experienced the economic and population boom that has characterized other cities in the Pacific Northwest.[46] In addition to Whitworth, Spokane is home to three other universities: Gonzaga University,

Eastern Washington University, and Great Northern University.[47] At a regional level, the Inland Northwest has a significantly lower population density than the coastal areas of the region.

Geographically, Spokane sits on the eastern edge of the Columbia Plateau in eastern Washington. This semi-arid, high-desert landscape creates a climate that departs from the common stereotype of the Pacific Northwest as rainy with mild temperatures. The Spokane River flows from northwestern Idaho through downtown Spokane on its way to the Columbia River. This massive watershed, which produces the second largest river in the lower forty-eight (behind the Mississippi River), flows from the Rocky Mountains of southwestern Canada to the Pacific Ocean. To the east of Spokane, the foothills of the Rocky Mountains roll down from Montana through the Idaho panhandle. Between the Cascades to the west and the Rockies to the east, agriculture is a prominent industry across the Columbia Plateau. While the work of the OCE extends beyond the Cascades to the west and across the Rockies to the east, its emergence and ongoing work reflects the distinctive characteristics of Spokane and the broader geographic features of the Inland Northwest. The relational gravity is rooted in Spokane, inviting local leaders into meaningful partnership and ministry, and yet the region's boundary-crossing ethos drives their work across barriers that can inhibit the transformation they envision: denominational distinctions, disconnection between congregations and educational institutions, political polarization, and geographic borders.

The region's economic and political characteristics also mark the OCE's work. Economically, the median income for Spokane is $44,768,[48] which is comparable to the other two urban centers within the Inland Northwest, Boise, Idaho and Missoula, Montana.[49] One organizer observed: "The scale of economics on the other side of the Cascades, on the I-5 corridor, and what we experience here is just, they're light years apart." Politically, Spokane is at the confluence of liberal and conservative views. While western Washington has historically been a left-leaning region, as one moves along I-90 to the east, the electoral map gradually becomes more red.[50] Interviewees within the OCE's network repeatedly attested to the divided political climate in the region. Courtney Arntzen observes: "In a culture that is so polarized, it's hard to even teach people how to listen to one another, or to listen to somebody who has had a different experience."

This particular urban setting contributes to the organization, programmatic offerings, and ongoing development of the OCE's collaborative and adaptive work. As McGonigal observes, the particular combination of features creates a scenario in which Spokane sometimes feels like the "Nazareth of the Pacific Northwest" that leads some to question, like Nathanael in John 1:46: "Can anything good come out of Spokane?" Organizationally, the office has a history of being "frugal" with the grants they receives and extending their reach through its partnerships. This resourcefulness has enabled them to sustain programs well beyond the initial grant periods, partnering with ministries, congregations, and students throughout the region. Similarly, their attention to the needs of Spokane contributes to the programs they offer, as expressed in the organization of their Calling Communities. In each case, the OCE's relationship with community leaders in the region and their attention to their particular place influences the specific initiatives they pursue. Their shared work reflects a vision for the church that "is going to require churches to move away from programs and be much more neighborhood focused and neighborhood based," according to McGonigal. Churches and church-related organizations will need to attend to local wisdom and become the "church in context."

Nevertheless, the development of the OCE's specific understanding of its work and service within the region also reflects its struggle to define and pursue its mission from an urban setting that is positioned so far inland within the Pacific Northwest. The historic concentration of resources and people on the western side of the state can disproportionately direct time, attention, and resources in a similar direction for the OCE. Indeed, reflecting the westward movement of the Spokane River into the Columbia and out to the Pacific, turning westward is also figuratively downhill for a collaborative center such as the OCE, whose work requires partnership and resources. Mike McKay at First Presbyterian in Missoula reflects on the potential impact of this approach to communities further east:

> Spokane and Whitworth are largely, not one-hundred percent, but largely guilty of waking up and looking west towards the Seattle area to see how they stand up in society. It's a natural inclination to say that they're Washingtonians and it's a Washington State, University of Washington rivalry sort of mindset that the East pits itself against the West and tries to stand up to that. And I've somewhat accused and challenged [Whitworth and the OCE's senior leaders], that when they wake up and look to the West, they turn their back to the East. And I said, "There's a big area out here that is clamoring for help and you're not seeing it because you're not looking this direction."[51]

For the OCE and PC, this insight surfaces a fundamental tension for place-based ecclesial expressions: the centers of economic activity that are required to catalyze innovation are not always proximate. Even as both hubs accentuate the priority of local connections, including the latent resources a community already has, financial sustainability requires partnering across locales. For the OCE, as a collaborative organization that depends upon partnerships for its long-term sustainability, their work requires nurturing partnerships to support communities in a less densely populated and less affluent region.

As a result, much like Spokane, the OCE is as a gateway to congregations and Christian ministries in the Inland Northwest, but it must serve this role in a different manner than the city once did. Instead of serving as the primary thoroughfare for goods and commerce, the OCE can serve as a point of confluence where individuals and communities gather at crossroads between distinct ways of life in the region. In this institutional space and across this particular city, individuals and communities meet and gather at the gate to the Inland Northwest. Here, in this liminal urban and geographic space, the wealthy and the less affluent, the politically liberal and the conservative, individuals from majority-white communities and those that have a predominately minority population, refugees and those who provide refuge, practitioners of established forms of Christianity and those with vision for new expressions, all are welcome to gather in response to the challenges they face.

THE MAINLINE TRADITION

Finally, the OCE's work reflects a history of engagement within the mainline tradition, even as its work and partnerships look beyond it. As described by organizers, the OCE reflects its "rootedness" in the mainline tradition and in a historically Presbyterian educational institution. "We cherish and celebrate the relationships that we've had and continue to have with larger ecclesiastical bodies," shares President Taylor, "We have a long history, as you know, of connection and support from and to the Presbyterian Church USA and its mainline antecedents."[52] For the OCE, more specifically, the history of partnerships between Whitworth, Presbyterian congregations, and other mainline churches has translated to a large percentage of the members in their Ministry Partnership Network coming from the mainline tradition. As Sittser notes, the denominational connections have also translated to a higher percentage of the regional partners coming from the Presbyterian tradition. He observes: "At the regional level, the connection is more Presbyterian. What we've found is that, at a regional level, more than at the local level, there's a kind of sweet spot." Congregations tend to be large enough to have some resources—somewhere between 250 and 600 in worship attendance—and there tends to be some history of relationship with Whitworth or the OCE founders. At the local level, they are able to pursue relationships and sustain partnerships with smaller congregations—such as First Church in Spokane[53]—where the OCE is able to maintain a higher level of relational contact, as well as larger congregations. In both regional and local contexts, the OCE works to strengthen and "thicken" relationships with partners, enriching and expanding the collaborative partnerships congregations and ministry leaders desire.

Although the OCE pursues its work in close proximity to the mainline tradition, organizers simultaneously acknowledge the potential limitations of mainline thought and practice. Informed by her work with students and youth, Smith articulates the approaching challenges for mainline congregations: "I think because of my work with college students, I have a sensitive ear to what young people are looking for. If they are even looking anymore for a church home, I think that is unique," she shares, "I think the traditional mainline church is not a place as much that young people are interested in. They're looking for more creative, authentic outlets in which they can worship in a variety of different ways." Without denigrating their mainline heritage and partnerships, the OCE's founders and staff express a hope to find pockets of vitality within and beyond the mainline tradition. McInturff notes how a majority of the placements in congregations tend to be Presbyterian, but these congregations are "doing other aspects of ministry that are less characteristic of mainline churches." Although the distinguishing markers of these less characteristic mainline churches are not specified, the OCE's work and organization reflects an attempt to identify communities who pursue *both* vital Christian practice and innovative, contextual ministry. As these reflections imply, these features—whether rightly or wrongly—are not always associated with mainline congregations. For example, speaking of Whitworth as an institution, Sittser shares, "So we're very peculiar as an institution in that we're very mainline and we're very Christian at the same time."

The OCE's work and network also extends beyond congregations from the mainline tradition and established Christian ministries. At a local level, nearly 30 percent ($n = 12$) of the members of 2018 Ministry Partnership Network do not include a mainline identification in their church or ministry name. In addition to this network, a host of more fluid relationships across the ecclesial landscape of Spokane and the surrounding area reach beyond the mainline. For example, the development of the OCE's work and organizing mission has emerged in close conversations with pastors from a large Foursquare Church in Spokane, LifeCenter, and local church plants, such as Immanuel in the West Central neighborhood. While LifeCenter has a regular worship attendance of around five thousand, Immanuel has a regular worship attendance of two hundred. In both cases, the OCE has connections with these congregations because of existing relationships between their pastors and OCE founders. Further, the thickening of this relationship through the OCE's church planting Calling Community occurs alongside the formation of the Pacific Northwest Church Planting Movement. The church planting Calling Community seeks to deepen the OCE's engagement with expressions of Christianity that are less reflective of mainline thought and practice. As they engage with a wide range of communities and leaders from mainline and nondenominational churches—and the range of ecclesial expressions that fall between these two extremes—the OCE notes how these communities face similar challenges within the region. As McGonigal notes: "They know the current models aren't working. I'm talking about nondenoms, denominational, Presbyterian, even the big, big churches, both Presbyterian and nondenom. They're swimming really hard just to stay even. Everybody recognizes that there are challenges, that we don't control these factors." McGonigal then concludes with a question: "How do we imagine being church in the future?"

The adaptive challenges that confront faith communities require systems-level change. Even as the OCE works to care for and connect local faith communities and those who serve them, they also aim to enrich a broader ecclesial ecology. Hence, the ecumenical and boundary-crossing "we" that activates McGonigal's question reflects the region's peculiar religious environment and the OCE's collaborative mode of engagement. When pursued in a contextually attentive manner, the Pacific Northwest's distinct religious environment creates the context for this kind of local, collaborative, and boundary-crossing work.[54] On the one hand, when a small number of faith communities occupy a marginal social position, they must collaborate in order to get anything done. On the other hand, the perceived scarcity of resources—including both funding and followers—can introduce and heighten boundary-maintaining practices that emphasize the distinction of one community over and against another. And precisely in this moment, as they imagine new ways of gathering, pastors, practitioners, and theological educators, McGonigal's ecumenical, denominationally porous, and boundary-crossing "we" invites those who gather around the OCE to explore new ways of organizing a common life. Without flattening or eliminating particularity and history, this question expresses the OCE's commitment to the church and its hope for the future.

2

"Hope and Care in the Neighborhood"
Refounding the Church in Local Community

A steady stream of twenty- and thirtysomethings unbundle after they walk through the door of a neighborhood coffee shop, rubbing their hands together as they talk. Although it is early February, a heavy snowfall has closed schools across Seattle, and the allure of hot coffee and conversation draws a steady crowd. With walls covered with Latinx-inspired art, t-shirts, and handmade goods from local artisans, it is also a multi-event space with a bay door that opens in the rear. Digital denizens bring their laptops in for a warm place to work for the morning. A couple with a two-year-old, who rests in a blanketed cocoon, sip on drinks and nibble a croissant, as the dad snaps pictures of his little girl. There is a play area in the corner with mats and toys for children. Watching over all of these happenings, like the Spirit hovering over creation, a painting on the wall reads: "Resistencia *Re•sis•ten•ci•a (rā,sēsten'syā)*: 'A local community standing up against adversity with **relentless hope** and care for everyone in the neighborhood." With "relentless hope" as its interpretive key, this dually communal and commercial definition reflects a broader ecclesial vision for the transformation of its neighborhood.

Located in the South Park neighborhood of Seattle, Resistencia Coffee is co-owned by Tim and Coté Soerens. I have come to Resistencia and South Park to meet with Tim and also with Paul Sparks; the two serve as cofounding directors for the Parish Collective. Catalyzed within the last decade among restless creatives in Seattle, Tacoma, and Portland, the Parish Collective has grown into an international network of neighborhood-based (i.e., parish) expressions, but it does not occupy a specific geographic locale. Indeed, much like this "scruffy, geographically isolated enclave" that attracts "creative entrepreneurs,"[1] as the *New York Times* describes South Park, the Parish Collective is host and home to ecclesial entrepreneurs pursuing an ecclesial life that reflects a dense, neighborhood-based network of relationships.

PARISH COLLECTIVE: MISSION

The Parish Collective's mission is to "grow roots and weave links" among followers of Jesus who seek to grow "expression[s] of love and care in the[ir] neighborhood."[2] For the founders, three animating commitments guide their collaborative work. First, the neighborhood, or the parish, is the principal contextual center for a transformative ecclesial life. As explained in their collaborative work with Dwight Friesen, *The New Parish: How Neighborhood Churches Are Transforming Mission, Discipleship and Community*, the parish "refers to all the relationships (including the land) where the local church lives out its faith together."[3] This reoriented ecclesial life, as a "life together in a definable place," provides a "geography large enough to live life together (live, work, play, etc.) and small enough to be known as a character within it."[4] As Soerens explains: "Part of what we found [and] that we're still finding is that . . . when you have the neighborhood or the parish as the primary context of engagement, then—for better or worse, and it's always both—neighborhood pushes back." Expressing more than a social enterprise or a commitment to the common good, this description reflects a vision to see and encounter God through a place-based ecclesial life. As Sparks notes: "The work is guided by a theological understanding of the neighborhood as the place where followers of Jesus may pursue a form of being together that seeks God's shalom. This is the telos." As a result, the parish becomes the contextual center out of which connections, mission, and partnerships emerge from the "particulars of ordinary life."[5] Focus on the neighborhood directs and disciplines the ecclesial parish-based expressions as Jesus followers are linked within and across neighborhoods.

The PC's mission is based on an animating commitment that parish-based expressions are already happening, but the individuals pursuing this work are isolated and do not know one another. As Sparks and Soerens reflect on the genesis of their work, isolation is both a catalyst and ongoing challenge. About eleven years ago, as they were experimenting with neighborhood-based church expressions, they began meeting other parish expressions across the region. As they listened, they discerned a gap between individuals' desires and their experiences, sometimes from individuals who lived just a few streets away. People wanted to reimagine church in the neighborhood, but they felt isolated. As Sparks and Soerens reflect on their early experience, they met individuals doing neighborhood work who felt like a sideshow to more mainstream ecclesial expressions. They heard common refrains as they listened: "[W]e feel like it's really profound and beautiful, gritty and resilient and we feel alone. We don't know if what we're doing really matters that much. Our denominations, or our networks, or whatever church planting network oftentimes give us permission to do what we are doing—to be kind of thinking publicly about a neighborhood, or parish—but it's also kind of seen as on the side." As people frequently observed: "We just feel alone." As expressed here, the fluid "we" reflects the collective and personal needs that catalyzed their work. In these encounters and conversations, others' isolation and loneliness resonated with Sparks' and Soerens' own experience. Their sense of emerging new possibilities led them to consider new forms to organize and support this kind of parish-based work.[6]

The PC's founders started connecting parish-based leaders because of a sense that local, ecclesial work is already happening.[7] They frequently express this commitment in terms of abundance. "[W]e see the abundance we have—individually, as neighbors and in this place of ours," write Sparks, Soerens, and Friesen.[8] Anna Golladay, who served as a pastor and community organizer before beginning to support Parish Collective events, corroborates this sentiment:

> When [*The New Parish*] came out six years ago, I was leading a congregation, and we were fully lay-led at this point. The church was a hundred years old, was down to about twenty members, and a group of us laity came in to initially revitalize the congregation, but we ended up replanting it. . . . [W]e were doing a lot of deeply rooted work in the neighborhood where this church existed, and it also happened to be the neighborhood where I lived. . . . As we were doing this work, I heard that this book was coming out, and I was intrigued by it, and I got a copy, and I realized that the work we were doing was very much in line with the work the book was asking folks to do.[9]

As a result, in the face of the challenges that confront individuals and communities, the PC seeks to organize and connect individuals and communities around the assumption, as Sparks and Soerens observe, "that we will find the resources for our complex problem, among us."

With the neighborhood as the "ecclesial center,"[10] new possibilities emerge for a "way of life." Nevertheless, the vitality of neighborhoods and parish expressions requires relational connections in order to reimagine the structure of a common life. Accordingly, the PC creates an arena for the resources and relational connections required to start, support, and sustain neighborhood-based parish expressions. As Sparks describes it, they understand the PC as a both "a network and a platform." He explains: "The network represents the relational connectivity, the platform represents the 'grease' that you apply to those links to make good connections happen." Like a cyclist's upstroke and downstroke of pedals on a bike, these interrelated features build momentum for the PC's work.

As a result, the PC does not solely connect isolated ministry leaders who are experimenting with new forms of Christian organization and community. Nor do they solely revitalize ecclesial expression by enriching the ordinary life within one's neighborhood. Rather, these two dimensions of their work—connecting parish-based expressions and enriching the ordinary life of the neighborhood—direct and reinforce the other. To borrow language from Peter Block—whom the organizers identify as a friend and key conversation partner—each feature represents an attempt to "discover and create the means ... that bring a new possibility into being."[11] As pursued over a decade, the PC's collaborative, connective, and ecclesial work creates the conditions where new possibilities emerge through encounters in the neighborhood and between parish-based experiments.

As one practitioner observes, the encounters with neighbors in the neighborhood invite transformation. "[I]t's my neighbors that are saving me, because it's just like the harvest;[12] it feeds us," he notes. "I think there's a mutual transformation that's happening," he continues, "When I'm engaging with them, I'm engaging with God." The "mutual transformation" envisioned here represents an understanding of salvation that is found in the neighborhood through encounters with one's neighbors. As another participant notes, "I do not go to the neighborhood to seek converts; I go into the neighborhood for my own conversion."

Finally, the combination of these three animating commitments represents what the founders and practitioners alike describe as a "movement." Soerens and Christiana Rice, who is both an early partner and now a key organizer, express this when they write: "Beyond our church growth charts and measurement sticks there is a movement bursting up from the ground, a counter-narrative to the anxious grip of the past. A movement is growing to reclaim the ancient idea of the parish for the 21st century."[13] Similarly, when Sparks and Soerens reflect on the history of the PC, they note: "[W]e felt like maybe there's a movement because people who feel like they are alone, actually aren't. And so, the nucleus of a lot of our work began [with the idea that] if we can identify and connect those people, it feels like there's a movement already. It feels like it just needs to be uncovered; it needs to be connected."[14] Although there is variation among founders and participants about whether they are starting a movement or joining an existing one,[15] this shared language invokes a sense in which the Spirit is on the move through a parish-based renewal.[16] The remainder of this chapter provides an introduction to the history and work of the PC in order to frame a broader consideration of the Christian practical wisdom that organizes the PC's and the OCE's work.

ADAPTATION AND COLLABORATIVE PARTNERSHIP

The PC's ecclesial adaptation emerges from a dense network of relationships and catalytic events. The PC, as an identifiable entity, is approximately ten years old,[17] and trust-filled relationships, formed over decades of service in the region, preceded its formation. Trust and friendship are the characteristic relational properties of the regional network that has formed around the PC. Nevertheless, a loose organizational structure also marks the organization of this highly relational and adaptive work. As one participant, who has journeyed with founders for thirteen years, observes: "[T]here's still no organizational flow charts, no organizational structure; it is so loose—in some ways it drives me nuts—but I've been most changed because it's this organic, beautiful weaving of love and care." While the relational network enables the PC's work to remain nimble and responsive, its rapid growth now requires more attention to the structure of the collective work it seeks to support and encourage.

For example, the PC has a history of a "grassroots," "organic," and "collaborative" approach that responds to the needs of local communities and seeks to identify and support new forms of missional practice and presence within local neighborhoods. Sparks and Soerens serve as the PC's cofounding directors, but the broader history of this organization reflects a porous core of early collaborators. Dwight Friesen and Ben Katt, specifically, contributed to the formation and animating vision that launched the PC. Through this collaborative effort, decades of service, organizing, and friendship within the region eventually coalesced as a collaborative vision to support and connect neighborhood-based ecclesial expressions.

The early development of the PC travels along relational lines rather than a strict strategic progression. For example, Sparks has spent his life in the Pacific Northwest, but Soerens, Friesen, and Katt are all transplants. In some capacity or another, each served as a pastor or church planter, experimenting with neighborhood-based church expressions and deconstructing pastor-centric models of leadership and church growth. Sparks was working in Tacoma, Soerens planted a church after graduating from The Seattle School of Theology & Psychology, Katt planted Awake Church in Seattle, and Friesen served as a pastor in Seattle before joining the faculty at The Seattle School of Theology & Psychology. Nevertheless, they also experienced a degree of disenchantment with prevailing models of congregational life and pastoral leadership. Each expresses this in different ways: as the limits of the "attractional model" for church growth; a "Christendom shift . . .

away from congregation as church and recovering Christians in the neighborhood as church"; an unshakeable sense of loneliness on the "fringes" of established forms of ecclesial life; and "a shrinking connection with what it meant to be the church together in the everyday realities of life."[18] Through a series of "chance meet up[s]," as Sparks describes it, these four began to intersect with one another and with other "experiments" in the region.[19] As neighborhood-centered relational encounters continued, synergy began to build, kindling a growing sense of an alternative vision for ecclesial life. Katt recounts it this way:

> I remember I was out and I was near Tim Soerens' neighborhood. . . . I remember very clearly one day tracking down Tim in his neighborhood because I had had this idea to get our churches together, because we are both trying to be church in the neighborhood. . . . I remember talking with Tim and he was like, "You've got to meet my friend Paul Sparks." I don't think I had met Paul then, and Paul had similarly been talking about "live local," or something like that, and I had this idea of "parish projects."[20]

As Katt recalls, this encounter took place in the neighborhood where Soerens lived, and catalyzed collaborative response. Further, anticipating the collective nature of the PC's work, Soerens linked Katt to Sparks, expanding their shared connection and enriching the possibility for collective work among them. This relational connection occurred in the context of a particular neighborhood and in response to the experience of isolation, perceived insignificance, and marginalization. More than anything, however, friendships provided the context to imagine and explore alternative forms of ecclesial organization, leadership, and education. As an incubator for adaptive possibilities, friendships provide a relational point of resistance to the separation of ideation from place. Over time, these friendships and partnerships would foster a common adaptive vision to center context—and neighborhood more particularly—in order to promote and connect neighborhood-based experiments.[21]

Simultaneously, a growing practice of listening redirected individual and collective reflection on the common challenges early PC organizers experienced, namely perceived limitations of existing models for ministry and leadership. Sparks characterizes this turn as "a profound awakening to the need for listening" that emerged both alongside his friendships and out of his experience trying to deconstruct a predominantly Gen X church in Tacoma. Their practice then expanded to listening to other neighborhood expressions within the region. Soerens reflects on the impact of their listening journey: "[I]t was when we started meeting more and more people in Portland, Oregon, and hearing more and more of the same things that it felt like, 'I wonder if there is a deepening vocational call to nurture what we're hearing?'" With Sparks nodding along, Soerens continues:

Soerens [W]e would literally wake up at six or seven in the morning, drive down for a whole day of meetings—this was before the Parish Collective existed as an entity—just to meet with people.... [A]nd it felt like every meeting was like that narrative about not knowing anybody else. And we would say, "We're literally going to meet this person, [do] you know them? No? They're four neighborhoods away, or they're literally going to come here after this meeting."

Sparks Or they're across the street!

Soerens I mean it's crazy!

Through the practices of listening and gathering in neighborhoods and across the region, they sensed the possibility of God's movement at the margins, moving to connect isolated expressions and enliven ecclesial witness. "It spoke to us, that, that maybe, maybe in fact this is something God was up to," Sparks reflects, "One of the craziest things we experienced was that nearly every neighborhood that we went to we would encounter experiments." And, in contrast to the prevailing pastor-centric model, they also point to possible signs of God's movement when individuals began to gather independently of Sparks' and Soerens' charisma. As Soerens recalls, "We were convening people in Seattle and we couldn't be there for some reason, but the event continued without us. That is when we realized the Spirit may be at work here."

A series of catalytic events provided further avenues to organize and connect individuals and communities. Early organizers and practitioners gathered around a vision for parish-based expressions to link followers of Jesus who were inhabiting their parish. First, Katt, Sparks, and Soerens received a series of Health and Renewal grants from the Christian Reformed Church (Katt's sponsoring denomination) through funding from the Lilly Endowment Inc. The initial grant provided resources to gather their three congregations for an evening of music, speakers, and learning about neighborhood-based ecclesial expressions. It was called "The Parish Project." When they received a second Health and Renewal grant, they started an annual conference, Inhabit, which "opened up" the initial conversation between their three congregations to others interested in experimenting with parish-centric models for ecclesial life.

Hosted at The Seattle School for Theology & Psychology, Inhabit also initiated collaboration between what was becoming the PC and the school.[22] Located in a three-story red brick building in downtown Seattle, a block away from the Puget Sound and less than a mile from Pike Place Market, The Seattle School of

Theology & Psychology describes itself as "liv[ing] at the intersection of theology, psychology, and culture, training artists, pastors, therapists, counselors, and change-makers to join God—Father, Son, and Spirit—in the restoration of their communities." Founded in 1997, with a "quasi-evangelical or at least progressive evangelical" vision—as one interviewee described the institution's history—it employs an "integrative and interdisciplinary" approach.[23]

With Friesen now on faculty at The Seattle School of Theology & Psychology and Soerens as an alumnus—and former student of Friesen—this institutional partnership provided legitimacy to a growing conversation about the importance of place and the relationship between the church and neighborhood, and the neighborhood as parish. It also provided an avenue for further catalytic funding to resource this growing conversation. For example, in 2013 The Seattle School of Theology & Psychology received an $82,000 grant from the M. J. Murdock Charitable Trust.[24] The grant was designed to support early efforts to translate the learnings and conversations emerging through the PC's collaborative work into a format that could support the training of leaders in theological education. Directly, the funding helped launch the Leadership in the New Parish certificate through The Seattle School. Indirectly, it provided opportunities for co-teaching and conversation among Soerens, Sparks, and Friesen through the Leadership in the New Parish certificate, which eventually led to the publication of *The New Parish* in 2014.[25]

This series of catalytic events, when combined, created the conditions for the PC to form and grow. Although it is impossible to trace a linear development, this particular combination of resources, relationships, and platforms provided avenues to continue to identify and connect new parish-based experiments. In language that we will explore in chapters 5 and 6, they provided avenues to reimagine the form of collective, ecclesial life that could release adaptive possibilities in and for local and ecclesial communities.

Within this porous organizational environment, a small group of neighborhood-rooted pastors—and Soerens and Sparks in particular—began to organize and participate in more events. At a local level, they continued to develop platforms to share stories of neighborhood work and to connect practitioners. This included Parish Story Nights, in which to share stories of neighborhood work, and where people engaged in parish work across Portland, Tacoma, and Seattle could convene and connect. Beyond the region, organizers began to work with local parish leaders in Cincinnati, San Diego, and Ottawa, Ontario, to connect with similar experimentation occurring elsewhere. The events were organized around the concerns of a given regional context and centered the work of local organizers in their neighborhoods. While participants and founders suggest that the PC has not sought to "scale" its work, this expanded regional activity represents an attempt to replicate the conditions that catalyzed a movement of neighborhood work in the Pacific Northwest.

New partnerships also began to form alongside this expanded relational and programmatic platform. For example, the PC's work began to invite conversations with denominational bodies within the region (e.g., the United Methodist Church), parachurch and nonprofit organizations (e.g., The Navigators), and organizations that had a similar vision to resource and support emerging forms of Christianity (e.g., Thresholds, Fresh Expressions). The form of partnership across these organizations varies, but they collectively represent a growing relational network around the PC's work. Some partnerships involve more of a financial contract—in which the PC founders provide resources or training—while others involve a higher degree of relational reciprocity. The relationship between The Navigators and the PC provides one example. According to Kirk Lauckner, who works for The Navigators in Seattle and serves on the PC's board, the work of The Navigators and the mission of the PC complement one another. "[For The Navigators] there's a real emphasis on life-on-life. . . . [T]here's this cross-over in a way because the Parish Collective wants to help in any way that they can to make that connecting happen," he shares, "I see both of those ministries really dovetailing well. That's why I think that this partnership that we currently have will continue on."

Rather than pursuing a series of strategic initiatives and partnerships, PC founders navigate this phase of expansion in a responsive mode. According to Christiana Rice, who has recently moved into a leadership role in the PC, the PC's work proceeds from a responsive posture. "Everything we do is a response," she observes, "I often use the metaphors of wildflowers. . . . It's like, 'oh whoa,' it's happening there, too, it's growing there, too. And so we kinda go where the wind continues to blow." At the same time, the PC represents a purposefully decentralized, collaborative form of leadership. Reflecting the ethos of a startup, the PC uses a lean and nimble approach that responds to the needs of individuals and communities. As the PC grew, they were selective about the strategic partnerships that sustained their work.

The PC—as a formal organization—does not occupy a single facility; organizers and key partners are spread across the region and the country. The organization says it has run on approximately 80 to 90 percent earned income; there was not a single person working in a full-time capacity until 2019. As one central organizer described the history of this work, they have prioritized integrity and personal relationships, but "it's like working out of a garage."[26] Those who have been involved in this work are also keen to remove the sheen that others attribute to it. As Sparks, Soerens, and Friesen write: "It would be nice to tie up all three of our stories with a nice little bow and tell you how amazing each one of our stories turned out. Although many wonderful things have happened, the truth is that the narrative of our churches and neighborhoods has been a rough ride, with ups and downs and trials and joys just like before. But here's the thing: we're still in the story."[27]

Although the PC emerged in proximity to existing organizations, it also catalyzed new partnerships. A single organization never became its primary sponsor, although various organizations played timely roles in the formation and development of its organizing mission and neighborhood-based engagement. Indeed, it is difficult to imagine how the PC could have gotten off the ground without a partnership with The Seattle School of Theology & Psychology, early funding from Lilly Endowment Inc. and the Murdock Charitable Trust, plus denominational contracts to sustain the PC's work. At the same time, however, the PC emerged from a liminal space as founders and other early organizers navigated the dynamics of working within, with, and between various existing organizations and practitioners pursuing their life together in neighborhoods. As Soerens shares, their work requires "dancing well with institutions" and discerning the appropriate form of local response.

The partnerships that catalyzed and emerged from the PC also reflect a distinguishing of the adaptive change they pursue. As one practitioner reflected on his six years of engagement with the PC, he identified a dialectic between organized activity and local expressions as a tension for the PC's organized work. As he queried, "How do you build an organization that," and concluded after a long pause, "is not an organization?" That is to say, how do you organize a network that seeks to connect and support local parish expressions, but do so in a manner that always allows the needs and concerns of the neighborhood to talk back?

PROGRAMMATIC STRUCTURE

The PC's programmatic structure organizes their collaborative effort to connect and resourced local, parish-based engagement. The PC's organizational "flywheel" has three components: organizing, training, and events. When taken together, these components "work together in mutually reinforcing ways to grow connection and belonging across a particular city-region."[28] The PC's description and graphical presentation demonstrates how they understand and present these programmatic relations. A brief explanation of each element demonstrates how the PC's mission and history of adaptation informs their specific programs.

Parish Collective Flywheel

The Flywheel describes the way our Organizing, Events, and Training work together in mutually reinforcing ways to grow connection and belonging across a particular city-region.

Fig. 2-1 Parish Collective Flywheel

The first component of the PC's flywheel approach, organizing, reflects its commitment to support and connect local, neighborhood-based parish expressions. The primary aim is to "foster relational connectivity" through online and on-the-ground organizing.[29] Reflecting the connective and collaborative approach that marked the early phases of the PC, organizing creates a "tertiary network" that does not replace existing forms of religious networks (e.g., denominations), but enriches and strengthens them. Sparks describes the importance of this relational connectivity: "[P]art of our early journey as friends was the recognition that, while the local neighborhood form was critical, the only way you could sustain or grow, or discover from your blind spots about your current reality in the neighborhood was through networks. You need to be connecting with other parties who are experiencing it from their particulars and who, who could see from the outside what was going on in your place." With this intention in view, individuals can digitally link with other parish-based expressions and discover other practitioners within and beyond their region through a free, online portal.[30] As of May 2019, 2,587 members have joined the PC's platform and identified themselves as involved or interested in some kind of parish-related work.[31] Members of the online platform can also see where other practitioners are located by accessing a map function on the website. Figure 2-2 below shows the concentration of members within the Pacific Northwest. Thus, reflecting the spirit of the face-to-face listening conversations and convenings that marked their early work, this digital platform shows people they are not alone, providing avenues for individuals and communities to link their place-based expressions across neighborhoods and regions.

The PC also supports on-the-ground organizing by identifying and resourcing local organizers they identify as "area connectors," who link parish expressions

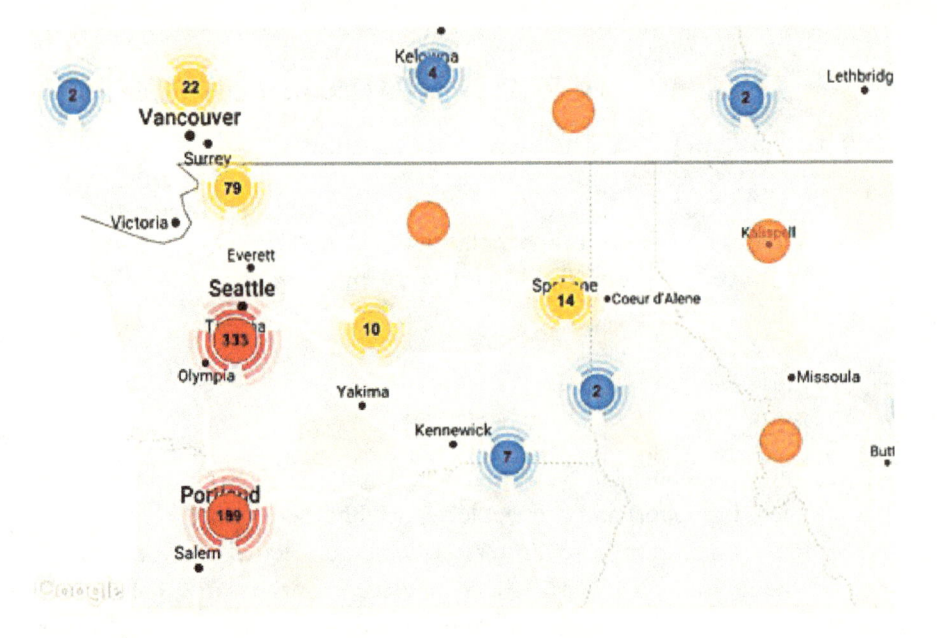

Fig. 2-2 Map of Parish Collective Portal in Pacific Northwest

within their areas. Area connectors typically have a history of engagement within their local context as well as a connection to the PC. They are contextually embedded, relational resources who connect individuals, communities, and projects. In doing so, they seek to support the flourishing of their context. The PC's paradigm for area-level organizing draws heavily on John McKnight's approach to asset-based community development.[32] For example, when asked what else he needs to continue his work, area connector Rich Jones replied: "Need? I don't know about need. Again, we have everything we need. [We only] need more awareness of the abundance that's already there, the gifts that are already there.... I don't know if I need anything other than to stay curious and listen."

Training is the second component to the PC's flywheel programmatic structure. Their training "helps individuals and congregations live into a new way of being the church together in the everyday life of the neighborhood."[33] The Leadership in the New Parish certificate, co-taught by Sparks, Soerens, and Friesen, provided an initial platform to develop pedagogy and methodology to support, train, and resource new parish leaders throughout the Pacific Northwest. The program combines contextual experience in neighborhoods, narrative work around personal trauma, sharing and listening to what has been learned from participants' deep roots in the neighborhood, and identifying and cultivating "rooting" and "linking" practices. To date, sixty-seven people have completed the Leadership in the New Parish certificate over five cohorts. However, the program was discontinued by The Seattle School of Theology & Psychology in 2019, pointing to the ongoing ambiguity of the organizational arrangements that surround the PC's work.

The PC has recently translated its contextual approach to training into a Learning Communities model in order to provide regional forums for training and contextual reflection. Launched regionally in 2019 through a partnership with the Pacific Northwest Conference of the United Methodist Church, this pilot program seeks to "spark [the] collective imagination."[34] It entails regional intensive training programs, "guided practice," and curated fieldwork through parish immersions.[35] In partnership with parachurch organizations and denominations, they have also employed a similar approach to train and resource local ministry leaders.

The third element of the PC's flywheel, events, curates gatherings that provide opportunities for parish leaders to connect and "celebrate the stories, ideas, and practices" that are "re-founding the church in the neighborhood."[36] Modeled after the template of Inhabit, these regional gatherings combine worship, stories from local neighborhoods,[37] plenary conversations, breakout training sessions, neighborhood tours, and ample time on the margins for mingling and conversation between friends and fellow practitioners. With events in San Diego, Cincinnati, Birmingham, United Kingdom, and Hamilton, Ontario, this convening work aims to enliven the "imagination" that directs the engagement within neighborhoods and across cities.[38] It also counteracts the all-too-common loneliness many organizers and practitioners identify as a central challenge for their work.

For example, Rice works to curate events in ways that attend to how individuals "come together around an experience that is going to shape our imagination about who God is and what God's up to." Both a practitioner—she lives within a network of neighborhood church communities that she helped found ten years ago—and a curator of environments, she combines a relational, place-based sensitivity with attention to the collective experience that occurs when people gather. Regarding her work curating events in relation the PC's broader work, Rice notes that "Christ is our unifier" before adding that she works to curate an environment that is "nourishing to the soul," includes "attention to place," "deep learning," and "inspiration from stories." Because the PC's events typically include a myriad of practitioners, stories, musicians, plenary speakers, and training sessions,[39] Rice's approach is highly relational, but it also attends to the particular details that invite people to consider "what is God doing to transform lives, and how does that impact the culture of a neighborhood?" She intends gatherings to be a pattern for people to "think about how to be together in the room in the way they want to be together in the neighborhood." As Rice reflects on a recent gathering, she suggests the environment can only be described as "God-breathed." The result, according to Rice, is a reorientation of the individual and collective imagination that situates the work of God and the work of a community of faith within a particular place. She observes: "We're not telling church stories anymore; we're not telling self-glorifying stories anymore; we truly are telling the stories of God's renewal and restoration of a place in view of everyday stories of real people."[40]

For participants, the PC's events provide an avenue to explore a broader vision for the neighborhood, to learn from the everyday stories of other communities, and to connect with practitioners who engaged in similar place-based experiments. For example, Lauren Goldbloom serves as an area connector in Spokane and is planting a neighborhood-based church in the Cliff/Cannon neighborhood near South Hill in Spokane. She first encountered the PC as an attendee of Inhabit. She recalls:

> I randomly went to my first Inhabit three years ago.... We had just moved into our neighborhood, so I was exploring a lot of questions about mission, and about vocation and calling. So, it just felt like a good time to go. When I went, they were advertising their leadership program [Leadership in the New Parish]. I went to an info lunch about that, and I was like, "I'm in; let's do this."

When asked how her engagement with the PC and Inhabit have impacted her work in the neighborhood, she first notes the value of the relationships, which she describes as "richly personal and relational," before reflecting: "The Inhabit Conference itself has been extremely formative; it allows me to see myself as doing the work.... There's also this new imagination for what [being a pastor] means; that I am a parish pastor. So, whether or not I have an institution giving me such a title, that's who I am to my neighbors as I walk my streets; I'm caring for them, I'm feeding the flock." For Goldbloom, as for many others who are drawn to parish-based work, the "new imagination" reflects a new way of seeing one's particular place and the attendant pastoral vocation that enables one to be with a people.

Thus, through these three interlocking and mutually reinforcing dimensions, the PC's "flywheel effect" seeks to enliven neighborhood work by connecting various experiments within a city and across a region. As Soerens observes, "By naming the parish as the unit of change, we reclaim the parish as the literal ground where our practiced faith becomes a powerful and even subversive organizing platform. The parish gives shape and definition to our imagination as we dream about real people and places and their very real stories."[41] For founders and participants across the PC, the formation and transformation of imagination takes place at the parish level through a practiced faith. Ultimately, their work aims to cultivate a new imagination for the kind of leadership that is required to be in a neighborhood in this way, contributing to the transformation of neighborhoods and cities.

GEOGRAPHIC AND URBAN CONTEXT

The parish-based vision that organizes the PC emerges both from the distinctive ethos of the coastal region of the Pacific Northwest and the particular neighborhoods that comprise it. Although the PC's network has extended well beyond the region over the last ten years, the majority of parish expressions are still found in and around Portland, Seattle, and Vancouver,[42] together known as "Cascadia." Cascadia refers to a distinct cultural and geographical context that emerges through the encounter between urban and geographic landscapes on the western edge of the Pacific Northwest.[43] As Douglas Todd explains in his introduction to *Cascadia: The Elusive Utopia*, Cascadia represents a "cohesive bioregion" that also has an "interconnected urban culture."[44] Positioned between the Cascade Mountains and the Pacific Ocean, Cascadia is no more than 100 miles wide in some portions. Portland, Seattle, and Vancouver are its three largest cities. As Patricia Killen observes, here "social and geographic landscapes are intertwined" in a way that invites a "rethinking of identity and community."[45]

Lest this description of Cascadia's social landscape mischaracterize the PC's work, an entrepreneurial spirit also creates the possibility for experiments in new forms of community to emerge. Seattle is lauded as the nation's "fastest growing tech hub,"[46] with visions for an expanded corridor that extends from Seattle to Vancouver, B.C.[47] Beyond technology, the Puget Sound is celebrated as a "hotbed for innovation" that provides a distinct cultural climate for inventive, collaborative, and world-changing ideas.[48]

For religious communities, the region's open religious environment creates a context that fosters a tradition of religious entrepreneurship that finds fertile cultural soil (and souls) in the region. For example, James Wellman's comparative study of evangelical and liberal congregations within the region leads him to conclude: "[E]ntrepreneurial evangelicals have carved out a foothold in the region."[49] Similarly, even though the region has been designated as the "none zone" that is "home to the least institutionally religious people in North America,"[50] Christopher James identified 105 new churches in Seattle that were "started, rebirthed, and/or relocated" between January 1, 2001 and June 1, 2014.[51] Of the 105 churches, approximately 25 percent reflect what he identifies as the Neighborhood Incarnation model,[52] which draws heavily on the PC's work.

Further, as the organizing vision of the PC suggests, individuals within the region desire connection and belonging; one need only listen to the needs of a given place and reimagine how to gather. As Sparks observes, "The neighborhood

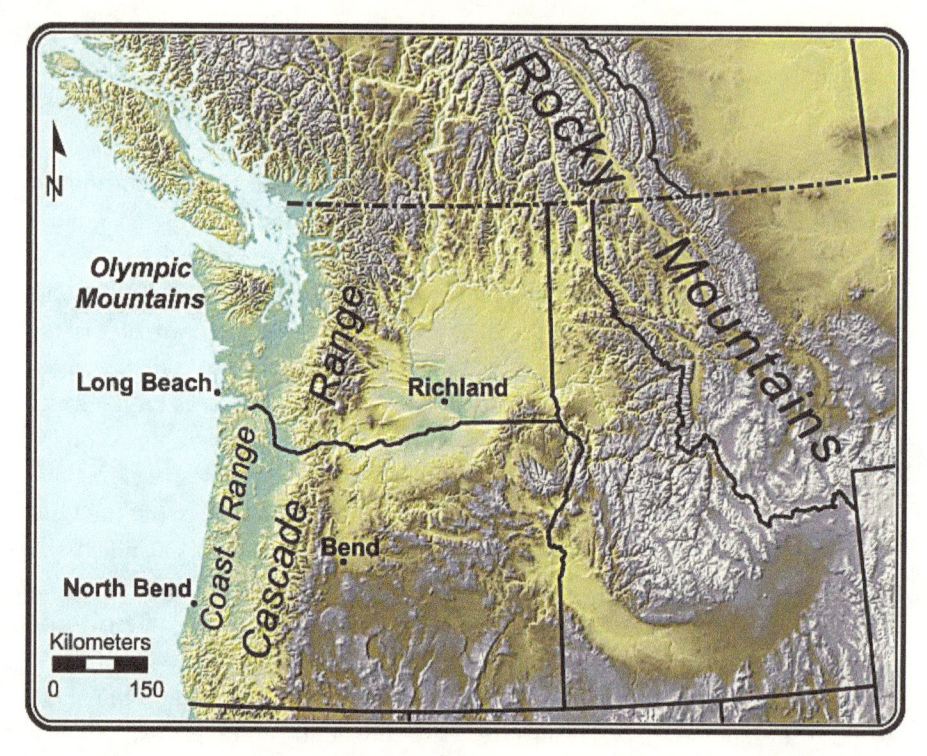

Fig. 2-3 Topographic Map of Pacific Northwest[53]

was the one place that you could fit together, share life together as an ecclesial body, but then you could also be embedded in the larger community so that your everyday lives would be seen, they would be public. There would not only be a witness, but it would also be a formative environment where the world would be interacting with you and you'd have to be learning how to grow through that." When the neighborhood becomes the contextual center for ecclesial life, it invites attentive care, drawing those who listen deeper into a social fabric of connection and care.

In a context where social life cannot be separated from the particulars of place, Cascadia's geography heightens the challenges and possibilities of religious adaptation. Buttressed by mountains in the east and water to the west, Interstate 5 provides a connective artery from Portland to Vancouver, BC. Those without religious affiliation comprise the majority of the population in the region and religious organizations occupy a marginal social position. Nevertheless, Christians who wish to collaborate can find partners across traditional boundaries of religious and denominational distinctions. The geography also introduces a silo effect in which the mountains create a barrier that restricts collaborative efforts beyond the west. Much as Douglas Todd notes, the most distinctive feature of the region "is that its rugged geography is impossible to ignore."[54] For the present study, the Cascade Mountains, which distinguish Seattle and Spokane, create the distinct cultural, socioeconomic, and religious zones from which these two hubs emerge.

For the PC, the influence of these contextual dimensions is evidenced both in the history of its founding and the particular neighborhood expressions that have gathered around their work.[55] The PC's collaborative work was catalyzed both by the experience of isolation and the realization that other experiments within the region desired connection and community. It has drawn inspiration from startup culture through its lean and decentralized organizational approach. The frequent description of the PC's work as a "movement" also reflects the region's broader future-oriented sensibility. Founders and participants share this future-oriented sensibility across the network. As one participant reflects: "This is that in-between stage. . . . We're on maybe a one hundred or a two-hundred-year curve, and we may never see what may evolve out of this, but we are in the place of figuring it out."

The work of the PC equally emerges from the particular neighborhoods where parish expressions take place. Two vignettes drawn from Vancouver and Seattle demonstrate how these broader regional trends intersect with the particularities of place. The first comes from Vancouver, where Barry Jung is practicing neighborliness. Jung, a fifty-seven-year-old former IT professional, is an area connector in Vancouver, but he is reticent to locate himself in too central a position. "This is really grassroots, Dustin," he shared, "I make myself available as opportunities come up, then I say yes." Here is how he describes what is happening in his neighborhood:

> [W]e live on the Cambie Corridor. A few years ago, the city designated that whole corridor as high density, or higher density. Mostly single-family homes, duplexes in that neighborhood. Really with any other major city, there's just been an increase in density. People moving into the cities. Really, the neighborhood is, I would say, middle income professionals. There's hospitals nearby, a cancer center nearby. So, a lot of the workers are in the healthcare area, so they're making decent wages. But they're getting moved out because people are selling their homes and building condos, and they're millions of dollars so they can't afford it. There is another sense of, I guess, a middle [income] gentrification going on in our neighborhood. . . .
>
> Then, whether this is real or not, but I sense that also there's this kind of a tension between the people that have been there and [are] established. . . . For example, some of our neighbors, they built their house in the 50s and the 60s and they've stayed there all their life and they're aging. Then there's these new condos, five, six-story condos, shiny and expensive. Already

there's this sort of otherness. Like, "It's those rich people that are moving into our neighborhood."

He transitions to the particular people and practices that draw his engagement in the neighborhood.

> We live on a very busy street. Most people don't use their front doors because there's parking restrictions in the front, so they go through their garage, and the typical story that you hear in suburb. We live in the city though, and as I was building [a garden box in my front yard], I encountered all of these neighbors, all these people walking through the front, going to work and coming home, going to the mall. I had no idea because we didn't live our life at all in the front door, to go through the front door. So we had no idea.
> And they were curious. They were asking, "What are you building?"
> "Building a garden box."
> "What are you going to grow?"
> "Growing food, like vegetables."
> "Why are you growing vegetables? People are going to swipe it."
> "No, it's for the neighbors because we have lots of gardens in the back already for us. This is really for the neighbors."
> So, it kind of piqued their curiosity. We started connecting with neighbors.

Like many others, Jung cannot tell the story of his engagement with the PC without telling the story of his own neighborhood. As Jung describes it, his movement to the neighborhood involves a form of "learning" by slowing down and "listen[ing] to what God is already doing, rather than pushing [his] own agenda" within his particular neighborhood.[56]

South on I-5 from Jung's neighborhood, Andy Carlson serves as the pastor of Awake Church near Aurora Avenue in Seattle. As one of the early experiments that catalyzed the PC, Awake Church and its sister nonprofit, Aurora Commons, are inextricable from the history of the PC. Here is how Carlson describes the relationship between their community, his neighborhood, and Seattle.

> One of the biggest things for us was opening up to how we define who our neighbor is, who that covers. And the most characteristic thing about where we are is this highway called Aurora Avenue, and that runs north and south out of Seattle. It's got an iconic history. The story of the highway, it's got all these old motels, these car lots, and sex shops. It's that place. [A] few gas stations, Jack In The Box, Taco Bell.
> I mean, you're constantly asking questions like, "What is it to be faithful...? What's the core of our identity?" Or maybe, "What can we shift and change?" And, "What do we hold dear and belong to?"... So, even when I think of when Awake first started, my understanding of the initial vision for the church was to be rooted in a place and wonder what it is to love your neighbor there.

> But what we've discovered—we kind of already knew this because many of us as part of that early community had already been living there—was that it's more than just being a transportation corridor, that there was a human element to it, like there are people that identify with that place. More so than even if we go one hundred yards in either direction of the highway. That world is different. . . . We can have our gatherings twenty blocks north of where we are right now, and it would be the same vibe, but if we went one block west or east, there would be a different vibe.[57]

Much like Jung, the history of Carlson's church and how it has changed over time cannot be separated from the particularities of the place that surrounds it, which includes a range of challenges. He continues: "As a church, we identified right away with Aurora Avenue. We weren't like, 'How can we have an awesome worship that gets people to come to church?' It was like, 'What's going on there?' Then, we try to follow the Spirit into these different spaces." Similar to Jung, Carlson describes the practices that animate their community in close relationship to the neighborhood:

> And I think our greatest capacity for that right now is as people of prayer in the neighborhood, who are able to just carry the life of the Spirit on behalf of the folks. . . . Both the people who are part of our church community and are trying to navigate the tension of Seattle world and the tension of these cultures being infiltrated by one another—like tents on sidewalks or the garbage on street corners, all that. The kind of gross stuff that the opioid crisis has brought to the surface.

In a characteristic responsive mode, the attentiveness Carlson describes emerges from sustained participation, listening to his community, and a grounding spirituality. "I long for us to . . . to be people of prayer on behalf of the folks who are actually in the midst of these difficult life circumstances," he shared. Even as the particularities of his neighborhood reflect the broader regional trends—e.g., income inequality, transience, a rapid pace of life—attention to place also shapes the regional trends through the social and cultural prism of a common life. For Jung, Carlson, and others throughout the PC, ecclesial life finds its proper form in relation to local neighborhoods. Even as the particularities of each locale shape these ecclesial expressions, the shared place-based ecclesial vision also reflects Cascadia's distinct ethos.

THE EMERGING-MISSIONAL TRADITION

Finally, the PC emerges in the wake of the Emerging Church tradition and in conversation with the missional theology movement.[58] Founders are reticent to make a direct genealogical link to either tradition or movement, preferring to note relational connections and the practice of responding to what is already emerging.[59] Nevertheless, these twin influences organize the PC's work in direct and indirect manners. The combination of observations from PC organizers with research on the Emerging Church and missional theology demonstrates the relationship between the PC and these loosely configured traditions of thought and practice.

First, the Emerging Church tradition represents a transnational reframing of Christianity characterized by an emphasis on community, hyper-local congregations, flat leadership structures, a network-based approach, missional theology, and an anti-institutional bias.[60] As Michael Clawson summarizes: "The desire for more authentic and organic forms of organization rather than the top-down businesslike models of the new paradigm, has also led those in the ECM [Emerging Church Movement] to move, however imperfectly, toward smaller, less institutionalized, and more collaborative forms of religious community with more horizontal and open-source models of shared leadership."[61] As described by practitioners and students of this "movement,"[62] the attempt to reframe Christian thought, organization, and practice[63] reflects the "adaptive ethos"[64] that drives the "religious institutional entrepreneurs"[65] of the Emerging Church. As Gerardo Marti observes: "[T]he ECM involves an earnest attempt to fundamentally redefine contemporary Christianity."[66] Although the Emerging Church as a single and clearly identifiable movement has become less cohesive, the movement remains, according to Marti and Gladys Ganiel, "one of the most important reframings of religion within Western Christianity in the last two decades."[67] Its influence has bled across the theological and organizational distinctions that once provided the occasion for its work.[68]

The Emerging Church tradition represents both an early incubator for the work of the PC and a foil as their work and organizing evolved. As an early incubator, the growth of Emerging Christianity in the early part of the twenty-first century provided an alternative to mainline thought and practice. For example, one of the early organizers for the PC notes the influence of iconic Emerging Church pastor Rob Bell on his early interest and formation in ministry. Attending seminary in Grand Rapids, Michigan, at the time, Bell's work and ministry presented a sharp contrast to his current educational setting. "I was really compelled by him and I loved what he was doing," this early organizer reflects. While other influences also contributed to the trajectory and work of the PC, Bell and others provided avenues to consider Christian thought and practice beyond the confines of conventional Christianity. Similarly, Friesen, who co-authored *The New Parish*, was a member of the Emergent Village network at an early stage in his vocational journey.[69]

At the same time, prominent Emerging Church voices within the Pacific Northwest provided a foil for the local, neighborhood-based vision that organized the PC's early work. As one interviewee observed, the controversy surrounding Mark Driscoll contributed to a "Mark Driscoll phenomenon" in which the PC's vision for neighborhood-based ecclesial expressions stood in stark contrast to Driscoll's acerbic form of mega-church Christianity. According to Friesen, "[I]n terms of the Christian world and Seattle, which is a small world [and] Seattle is a predominantly secular environment . . . people assume [Driscoll's] was the loudest voice of Christianity in the Seattle area. So, to all of a sudden be championing these small faithful expressions that weren't about a big show and absurd 'theology' or 'biblical preaching,' but actually a lived expression of Jesus in the ordinary stuff was, I think, a breath of fresh air." Much as Sparks and others noted the limits of the attractional model and the need to deconstruct pastor-centric approaches to church leadership, the Emerging Church also provides a point of contrast for the practice and early experiments with localized neighborhood expressions. If the Emerging Church provided space for early organizers to consider the possibilities of Christianity beyond received templates, the period of its popularity also demonstrated the internal limitations of this strain of Christian thought and practice.

Finally, missional theology influenced the PC's early history, structure, and animating vision. With the neighborhood as the ecclesial center, the local parish becomes the primary forum to discern and pursue the church's mission in the world. As Soerens observes in *Everywhere You Look*, "More than changing what we do, we first need to change how we see."[70] For Soerens and others throughout the PC, the requisite reframing includes how people of faith apprehend and pursue the mission of God in their proximate context. When combined with a history of connection to missional church thought-leaders (e.g., Michael Frost, Alan Hirsch, and Alan Roxburgh), these relational avenues extend the PC's organizing work. Although each figure accents distinct expressions of missional theology, they resonate together in a common missional-praxis chorus. The work of the PC, in turn, now adds its voice to a growing choir of missional wisdom. Hence, while the PC's history of engagement reflects and refines some of the "shared sensibilities"[71] that organized Emerging Christianity and missional theology, their place-based engagement reaches beyond a single silo or tradition.[72]

And it is at this point that the genealogical connection with the Emerging Church tradition begins to fray. In comparison to attempts by Emerging Church thinkers to identify the boundaries and defend the legitimacy of their movement, PC organizers are less interested in doing so. The work of the neighborhood invites a collaborative, ecumenical, and missional way of connecting and linking for followers of Jesus. The practice of neighborliness requires a posture of receiving and being received across traditional boundaries. Accordingly, as much as the Emerging-Missional traditions provide an incubator and foil for the PC's early work, their collaborative work remains a "convergence space,"[73] one that reaches beyond a single tradition or denomination by weaving the fabric of love and connection within and across neighborhoods.

CONCLUSION: WISDOM FOR ADAPTIVE CHANGE

When considered together, the OCE and PC provide critical cases to consider the forms of organizational and ecclesial adaptation that are emerging in response to the challenges faith communities face.[74] In a very short time, the adaptive vision that organizes these hubs has begun to inform kindred adaptive expressions, both within and beyond the region. The founders of these collaborative, network-based adaptations, however, do not have direct connections to one another.

Despite the differences that characterize these two sites, they share a common adaptive ethos that emerges from the ecclesial vision that guides their work and their engagement within their community. As numerous scholars of religion in the Pacific Northwest have noted,[75] an adaptive and collaborative spirit remains one of the enduring characteristics of religious life within the Pacific Northwest.[76] Killen summarizes the consequence of this insight when she observes:

> [The Pacific Northwest] is alternatively indifferent or inviting to religion, an obstacle or opportunity, a refuge or revelation. Here, more than in any other region of the United States, weak religious institutions and the absence of a dominant institutional religious reference group allow for a highly elastic religious reality. . . . The environment that renders [religious institutions] weak also provides the impetus for innovation and experimentation. . . . Creativity in religious organizations has been part of the region's religious environment.[77]

Indeed, adaptability and collaboration distinguish religious organizations across the region.[78] As other communities of faith and leaders discern how to adapt to uncertain circumstances, the wisdom found in this region—and in these two hubs—can shape how others move forward.

They do not, however, represent prescriptive catalogues for how to adapt to a shifting institutional landscape. Rather, they express practical wisdom that has the power to transform the imagination that guides ecclesial adaptation. Reflecting on his own life, Nicholas Wolterstorff observes: "The words 'wisdom,' 'imagination,' and 'power' do not describe; they point. They're the best we can do. Something like our wisdom, something like our imagination, something like our power—yet infinitely beyond."[79] As used and expanded below, the practical wisdom, imagination, and power of possibility that characterize these adaptive hubs point to a range of responses, without foreclosing the possibility of other expressions. Like patient guides on a journey, their wisdom points to the next step, bearing witness through their persistent presence, and inviting others into similar adaptive responses.

"Hope and Care in the Neighborhood" 61

1 The OCE's annual Ministry Summit in 2019

2 The PC's annual Inhabit Conference, with Tim Soerens and Christiana Rice in conversation

3 The PC's board chair, Jonathan Brooks, speaking at a gathering in 2019

"Hope and Care in the Neighborhood"   63

4 The OCE's Jerry Sittser (far left) engaged in conversation with presenters for an online event in 2020

5 The OCE's team gathered in collaboration

6 Parish leaders gathered for an outdoor meal in 2016

II

The Nexus of Collaborative Work

3

The Structure of Adaptive Change
Organizing Challenges and Values for Communities of Faith

> Well, creativity is just normal right now. . . . [Our church and other local congregations share a] practice of experimenting and developing a language and capacity as a congregation for trying new experiments and learning from them.
>
> Kevin Lind

> We just felt really fortunate to be positioned as we are, already deeply embedded in the neighborhood. . . . [I]t's just been our safety net and our people that's already very established here. So, we shifted in some ways, we went to zoom meetings pretty quickly, but we've been noticing how other people are waking up to the gifts in the neighborhood, the gifts of neighboring.
>
> Lauren Goldbloom

The cascading crises of 2020–2021 catalyzed innovation across a dynamic ecclesial ecology. When presented with a series of mounting and unforeseen challenges, the church had to adapt. Reflecting on his last year, one leader shared: "When the crisis of 2020 says you can't be in community in ways that most people think, then you're forced to adapt." Local communities of faith and those who serve them moved worship online, took worship outdoors, and relocated the center of their common life to neighborhoods. Nonprofit leaders experimented with ways to deliver their services, recruit volunteers, and raise funding. Educators delivered content across expanded or novel platforms to engage students. Medical and mental health professionals extended care to individuals and communities who hung suspended in webs of anxiety and uncertainty. These cascading crises surfaced the fragility that marks our individual and institutional lives; care also rose to respond to communities in need.[1]

Imprinted with marks of crisis and precarity, 2020 was the year of adaptation. And, as Walter Brueggemann observes, the severity of these crises "invite[s] fresh theological consideration."[2] Innovation became the *zeitgeist* of this particular moment in time. If we overlook these indelible marks, we fail to see to the conditions and wisdom that structure adaptive change.

For these two hubs in the Pacific Northwest, however, adaptation and innovation are nothing new. Their work is birthed from the womb of innovation, and wisdom born of their adaptive experience carries their work forward. Their shared vision to connect and resource individuals and communities also created an environment that promoted resilience in the face of crisis. As Laura Goldbloom, who serves as a neighborhood pastor, observes, they were already "deeply embedded in the neighborhood" and practiced at being present to the ordinary encounters that mark ecclesial existence. The particular challenges of this moment remain grave, yet a history of adaptation and enmeshment in networks created an environment that could withstand the disruption of this space.

Kevin Lind, who serves in Spokane Valley—approximately ten miles from the neighborhood where Goldbloom serves—similarly describes how a history of experimentation created a context for resilience. "Creativity is just normal right now," Lind observes. "Pretty much everything that we do is an experiment." He continues, "We've never done any of this before." Without dismissing the severity of the crisis, Lind also wonders whether their perceived stability is a byproduct of a long history of presence in this particular community. "I just wonder if part of what we're benefiting from is the long tradition and the deep roots that the church has."

The "deep roots" and "deeply embedded" basis for their adaptive responses locates their communities within a specific local and relational context. The church has always been "rooted and grounded."[3] However, the adaptive challenges faith communities face—both in the wake of the cascading crises of 2020–2021 and beyond this time—require wisdom drawn from these relational and local particulars.

The wisdom that guides Goldbloom's and Lind's adaptive responses draws from different wells, different relational networks that provide connection and care, even though they are separated by nothing more than a bus route. Nonetheless, these expressions share a similar structure that provides an adequate environment for these adaptive responses to the crises of our times. Communities of faith stand at a "hinge point," a moment where they must discern the values and actions that will sustain faith for the next generation, and take collective action.[4]

The structure that kindles wisdom for these adaptive responses can guide others who similarly stand on the edge, peering into the complexity and possibility adaptive change requires.

ON STRUCTURE

The wisdom that enables individuals and communities to adapt occurs in proximity to a structure that directs the change they pursue. "Structure" describes an organized pattern of shared partnerships, practices, and processes that nurture purpose, belonging, and stability to those joined together in adaptive change.[5] Structure includes stated values and missions that guide individuals and communities, but it also includes the implicit, unspoken, and sometimes even unrealized beliefs about individuals, the challenges they face, and the communities they inhabit. Purpose, belonging, and stability, if combined and cultivated according to the values that guide a community, create an environment to respond adaptively and remain resilient in the face of pressing challenges. When grounded in the shared purpose and belonging that constitute community, individuals are free to imagine and pursue the adaptive response their context requires.

Ronald Heifetz notes how a holding environment creates social and relational structure to contain the adaptive change such challenges require. Although Heifetz describes this in different ways throughout his work—as "community," "holding environment," and "social system"[6]—community represents both the situation where adaptive challenges emerge and the requisite condition for adaptive change to begin. Amid the confusion and uncertainty that prompt change, holding environments create containers for "conflict, chaos, and confusion."[7] A secure relational network creates space to manage the unavoidable disequilibrium that adaptive work will introduce. At a personal level, friendship serves as a holding environment to regulate the stress of adaptive work.[8] At an organizational level, organizational structures and "hopeful visions for the future" provide the cohesion required for adaptive change. According to Heifetz's framework, a holding environment "provide[s] safety and structure for people to surface and discuss the particular values, perspectives, and creative ideas they have on the challenging situations they all face."[9]

Thinking in terms of structure describes how the demands of adaptive change cross local practice, shared values, and our deepest desires for belief and belonging. "Structure" invites attention to the conditions that enable individual and collective transformation, including the institutional "conditions for life abundant" and those that diminish individuals' ability to thrive.[10] A sense of belonging in community and small groups are the primary units of transformation, but these basic social relations are always negotiated against a broader backdrop of received values and practices; structure tries to think about community in relation to the broader organizational ecology where community takes place. And relationships that are marked by shared purpose and values have the capacity to promote stability and adaptive change. Thinking in terms of structure acknowledges the transformative capacity of these relationships; it also describes how organizations—and especially those endowed with sacred stewardship—are "living realities," as Willie James Jennings observes, built on individuals' affections, joys, and desires for belonging.[11]

In order to see and understand the wisdom that guides adaptive change across these two hubs, then, we must think in terms of structure as a means to attend to formation of community, the forms of connection and disconnection that mark their collaborative work, explicit and implicit values, and the relational holding environments that structure adaptive change. As such, their work is at once an exercise in education, imagination, organization, and leadership. It aims to understand and craft the structure of a more adaptive church.

FROM ADAPTIVE CHALLENGES TO ADAPTIVE WISDOM

The development of these two collaborative centers both responds to the challenges they face and emerges from the entrepreneurial spirit of the Pacific Northwest. If, as McGonigal noted, "[t]he church has always been nimble," then local wisdom determines the particular ways churches and communities of faith meet new challenges. In these cases, the innovative ethos of the Pacific Northwest has generated sites where individuals and communities are rising to the task to adapt in the face of unprecedented challenges. The demands of these hubs' particular situation(s) represent "[a] gap between the values people stand for and the reality they face."[12] As expressed by individuals in diverse roles and institutional settings, the OCE's and PC's work emerges from a sense that existing templates and practices no longer provide what is needed to support and organize communities of faith. The felt challenges differ, but founders, key partners, and participants across both hubs express the need to adapt their organizing practices in ways that both respond to the challenges they face and preserve an ecclesial center for a common life. As one organizer of the PC observed: "The systems that have carried us for the last few hundred years are waning. Something new is on the cusp."

Ronald Heifetz's theory of adaptive change provides a conceptual framework that can enrich this account of the challenges to which the OCE and PC respond, the form of leadership they invite, and the ensuing consequences for the form of Christian practical wisdom that organizes and emerges from participation in these two hubs.[13] This framework both reflects the adaptive ethos that characterizes both sites and provides a descriptive resource for their work.[14]

These ecclesial adaptations in the Pacific Northwest, and the individual and collective imaginations that energize them, also represent a distinct expression of adaptive work that reaches beyond the structure and practices that Heifetz's account offers. Much like an individual who is multilingual, organizers and participants display a contextual dexterity, bending language, concepts, and practices according to their people's needs. They display an imagination that reaches beyond the structure Heifetz's adaptive change theory provides. While the language of adaptive change aptly describes the challenges they face, the language drawn from their communities and the Christian tradition—a deeply rooted structure—fuels their imagination and nurtures wisdom for the adaptive change they pursue.

THE PRIORITY OF VALUES

Values are the fulcrum for the change that each hub envisions and actualizes through their adaptive work.[15] Although distinct in their expression, they share a value-centric, collective effort to organize and support communities of faith around an ecclesial understanding of a common life. If the constellation of challenges that confront people of faith in the Pacific Northwest creates a context where the existing frameworks and organizational forms no longer provide an adequate structure, shared values create a temporary holding environment to craft and discern alternatives. And in this boundary space, values that animate adaptive work intersect with the educational, organizational, and leadership features that comprise communities of faith. As one participant described the animating principle of this work: "It's all about formation," before concluding with a query that links to these three features together: "How do we form the church to be the church?"

Adaptive work requires attending to a community's "deepest values"[16] and working to clarify the values that motivate individual and collective action.[17] When embedded in a structure of belonging, these values create a structure to support Christian education, organization, and leadership. Each interview invited respondents to identify and discuss the values that guide their adaptive responses. Individuals identified 198 values across thirty-nine categories. The values identified ranged from faithful presence, to philanthropy, to entrepreneurship. Table 3-1 summarizes the nine most prominent values that organize adaptive work across the OCE and PC.

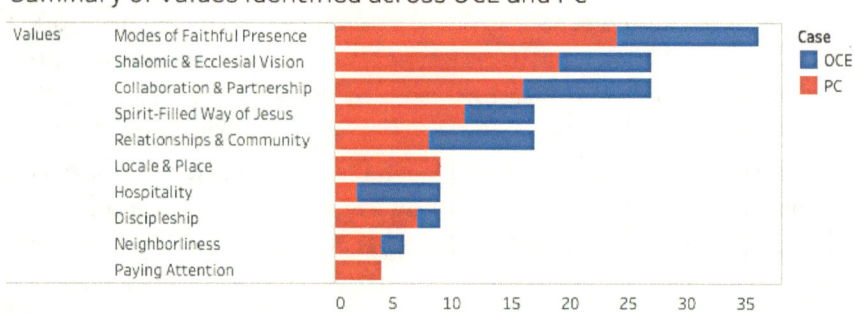

Summary of Values Identified across OCE and PC

Values	OCE	PC
Modes of Faithful Presence		
Shalomic & Ecclesial Vision		
Collaboration & Partnership		
Spirit-Filled Way of Jesus		
Relationships & Community		
Locale & Place		
Hospitality		
Discipleship		
Neighborliness		
Paying Attention		

Total Values (0–35)

Table 3-1 Summary of Values Identified across OCE and PC

The adaptive work that organizes these hubs reflects and emerges from a teleological vision of transformation. Expressed clearly by founders and participants in scripturally and theologically infused language, a pronounced "shalomic" and ecclesial vision guides this work. For McGonigal, this feature is self-evident. "This is all the outworking in *shalom*, isn't it?" he quips. The biblical theme of shalom provides a unifying scriptural-theological-teleological vision that organizes these kindred ecclesial adaptations. For the PC, seeking the welfare of the neighborhood and the broader city, as described in Jeremiah 29, is an act of neighborliness that seeks God's shalom.[18] According to one interviewee, the parish-based expressions and broader work of the PC expresses a "shalomic imagination." For the OCE, their collective and catalytic work involves "working out of shalom."[19]

The teleological vision for transformation that organizes each hub entails approaching their work as ecclesial undertaking. Frequently described as "the work of the church," these collective and collaborative enterprises seek to nurture the forms of practice and organizing that support the church in this new age. As McGonigal observes: "Living this way and doing church in this way is embedded first of all, in the model of Jesus and how he goes about his life in ministry, but then it's really what we find in Paul's letters."[20] Moreover, the "nimble adaptability"[21] that organizes both the OCE and PC emerges from an "ecclesial understanding"[22] in which the forms of partnership and presence are constitutive of the church and a way of life for followers of Jesus. Even as the ecclesial center for this collaborative work remains a priority, the challenges identified present barriers to maintaining and pursuing an ecclesial understanding of this work. As Rice observes: "We can't lose sight of the ecclesial vision of the church as a people who are coming around this vision; that, I think, is what Jesus came to show us." Although it is not the most frequently identified value, this shalomic and ecclesial understanding of the nature of their work provides a common mooring for the adaptive work that emerges around the OCE and PC. It directs both their understanding of the aims and the forms of organization that support this end.

The OCE and PC networks also express shared values for the modes of engagement, the relationship between their work and the way of Jesus, the relational and communal center for their work, and the importance of collaboration and partnership. How members of these networks engage in the individual and shared work that they undertake can be encapsulated with the idea of "faithful presence." This concept includes stated values for listening, authenticity, compassion, curiosity, thoughtfulness, truthfulness, and a commitment to serve others. Particular points of emphasis across the two cases clarify the other. For example, individuals across the PC use the language of "faithful presence" to describe how they seek to inhabit their locale and relate to those they encounter. As Sparks, Soerens, and Friesen explain, this "relational view of the world . . . means that in each situation we are listening for what our relationships require of us and responding according to our capacity."[23] This Spirit-filled mode of attending to people and place and listening for the needs and gifts within a particular community invites forms of presence (e.g., truth-telling, authenticity).

The form of faithful presence that animates these hubs expresses a mode of "being for." As James Leman explains the values that guide his work at First Church Spokane—and partnership with the OCE—he describes a vision to "be church for our neighbors." Leman continues, "[F]or our context, for the vision that God's given us, this ongoing relational willingness to be open and vulnerable with other people, I think will pay out dividends in the long run. And if nothing else, we get friends that are different than us and it's pretty cool. It's rich." Even in contexts that do not explicitly prioritize neighborhood engagement, a similar spirit of curiosity, mutuality, and hospitality distinguishes the form of being for others that guides ministry and partnership across these contexts. This represents a form of engagement rooted in a commitment to the collective well-being over self-interest. As one partner shared: "I care more about there being a kingdom of God presence in [the city where I serve] than I do about the building, or being on staff, or how that looks. I really do care more about that over my actual, even my presence within that system."[24]

High values for relationships and community, and collaboration and partnership, hang together so as to reinforce the modes of faithful presence that organize the OCE and PC and animate their shalomic and ecclesial vision. If faithful presence describes how individuals across these communities engage with their place and those they seek to serve, the values for relationships and community express how individuals pursue the relational contact that organizes and enriches each hub. Likewise, a shared value for collaboration and partnership distinguishes how leaders across these hubs express their need for one another. The value placed on relationships and community is one of the most pronounced values they share. Individuals identify this value in various ways: the value of life-on-life contact, high relational value, deep personal investment, relational fidelity, the importance of listening in community, the church as an ecosystem of relationships, and the importance of small and deep connections. Frequently paired with individuals valuing the way of Jesus, this pervasive value for relational and communal connection creates and maintains the form of social capital required for adaptive work across these collaborative networks.

The valuing of relationships and community undergirds the valuing of collaboration and partnership. This category includes stated values for connection, convening, and collective work. In many cases, the value is indexed either to the importance of the local church or a broader understanding of God's renewing work. Much as Soerens and Sparks observe, their work emerges from a commitment to "collaborat[e] for God's renewal" and a "commit[ment] to partnership." Kevin Lind expresses a similar sentiment: "Another value is definitely a value of partnership and ecumenism. The church is really willing and open to working together with other churches, to working together with other nonprofits and organizations that are trying to support our community. . . . The value of this partnership is very strong. So it's been really easy to grow the number of partners that we have. It's been really easy to see our building used even more by the community, because it's a deep value."

If, as Killen observes, collaboration is one of the distinguishing features of religious life in the Pacific Northwest, the value for collaboration and partnership across these two hubs is not surprising. What is notable, however, is the way that this value hangs together within the constellation of values that animate these two hubs. The emphasis on faithful presence, shalomic and ecclesial vision, a desire to follow in the Spirit-filled way of Jesus, a commitment to collaboration and partnership, and a high value for relationship and community, when combined, create the value-laden ethos that guides the hubs' adaptive work.

Mapping Adaptive Challenges

The challenges that catalyze the OCE and PC require adaptive, imaginative responses from participants across both hubs. The new imagination that is needed, however, can only form in and through the values that structure these communities. If the life of faith is ordered by interlocking desire, belief, and a sense of belonging,[25] individuals find an adequate structure for their adaptive response through these hubs.

Adaptive challenges are marked by the "gap," or a "conflict," between the values that will guide collective work.[26] As Ronald Heifetz notes, the adaptive challenges that confront communities and organizations represent situations without a clear solution, existing template, or identifiable organizational response. These are situations where there appears to be no "adequate response . . . [that] lack clear organizational response . . . no clear expertise can be found . . . no single sage has general credibility . . . [and] problem definition is not clear-cut."[27] In short, no one knows what to do. Organizations and those who lead them are in uncharted waters.

Such moments of challenge invite changing in ways that demand collective learning. Representing more than simple training or research, this learning requires individuals and communities to imagine and pursue new solutions to the challenges that confront them. Adaptive challenges, by their very character, demand "being and learning" more than a rote response;[28] they invite individuals to "step into the unknown"[29] in order to understand the complexity of a problem and generate appropriately complex responses. Reflecting on their experience in the pandemic, many local leaders described it as a "learning curve." As one pastor noted: "There's learning curves like that, that even almost a year in, you're still making mistakes, you're still trying to figure out what to do." And yet, this pastor and many others just like him also described how their learning enabled them to experiment in unforeseen ways. The rupture of adaptive challenges invited communities to imagine new possibilities, and from there pursue transformation.

The collective efforts that organize the OCE and PC represent an adaptive response to the challenges that confront individuals and communities throughout the Pacific Northwest. Founders encountered individuals and communities who lacked the resources, connections, and practices to organize their lives with respect to faith. For the OCE, this realization emerged through both their history of engagement with pastors and their concerted effort to maintain a listening posture. For the PC, this realization emerged from the confluence of its own experience and its encounters with parish leaders in neighborhoods. Simultaneously, these realizations invited creativity as organizers began to explore new ways to organize and support people of faith. As one leader wondered: "How do we think creatively about how the church is going to move?"

Although the organization of the PC and OCE reflect a common vision to create the conditions for creativity and innovation, they also emerge from

76   Adaptive Church

OCE Total Challenges vs. Individuals who Identify Challenges

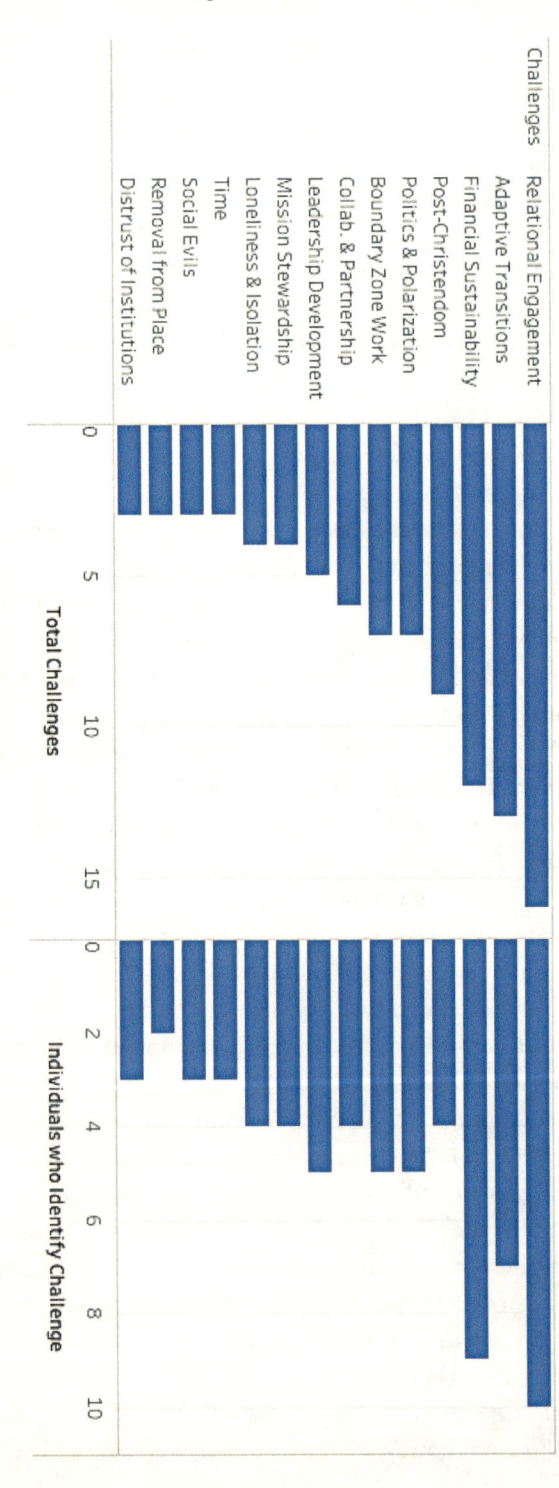

Challenges	Total Challenges	Individuals who Identify Challenge
Relational Engagement	16	10
Adaptive Transitions	13	7
Financial Sustainability	10	8
Post-Christendom	8	5
Politics & Polarization	7	5
Boundary Zone Work	6	5
Collab. & Partnership	6	4
Leadership Development	5	5
Mission Stewardship	4	4
Loneliness & Isolation	4	4
Time	3	3
Social Evils	3	1
Removal from Place	3	3
Distrust of Institutions	3	3

Table 3-2 OCE Total Challenges vs. Individuals Who Identify Challenges

a distinct constellation of challenges. Examining the factors that prompt the responses of each hub clarifies the similarities and differences between their particular expressions of adaptive work. Each interview asked: What are the challenges confronting your organization or the individuals and communities you serve? Interviewees responded with 156 distinct challenges (77 for the OCE and 78 for the PC), as summarized here.

Table 3-2 distinguishes between the aggregate challenges across the OCE and the individuals who identified these challenges. Although these values share a degree of correspondence, they are not necessarily identical. For example, individuals often identified several distinct challenges related to relational engagement. Just as it is helpful to understand the nature of the particular challenges that are shared across this hub, an awareness of situational distinctions also directs attention to the cumulative challenges that catalyze adaptation.

For individuals and leaders across the OCE, the six most common challenges are: relational engagement; financial sustainability; the broader cultural changes that founders identify with post-Christendom; political climate and polarization; what I've called "boundary-zone work," marked by liminality and uncertainty; and managing transitions within communities of faith. Individuals identify challenges related to leadership development and collaborative work, but these are not identified as frequently as those listed above. Relational engagement is both the most common challenge and has the most iterations identified across the OCE network. This category includes challenges associated with engaging within and across networks, working with congregational governing boards, and the barriers organizers face engaging an expanding network of partners and congregations. When sorted according to organizational type (e.g., hubs, nonprofits, congregations, funders), relational engagement remains a common category that is shared across these organizational populations.

In many cases, the various challenges overlap and intersect in ways that invite particularly collaborative adaptive responses. For example, after describing the politically polarized context where she serves, one pastor describes a series of interlocking challenges related to cultural change and relational engagement:

> [O]ne of the greatest challenges that we face is that we're a congregation that is over 100 years old, we've been in our location for 100 years. We have members in our congregation who have been there for 70 years, and they grew up in this place and their faith was strengthened through a Christendom model of church and community, where everybody went to church, and they continue to go to church, because that's what you do, and the

church was kind of the cornerstone for the community in terms of how things were structured and all that. We have that community of faith within our congregation, and then we have a ton of people who have come into the church—a ton is such a dramatic word—we've had several people come into the church over these last five years that I've been there and that I've been able to participate in and see.

So one of the huge challenges is, as a pastor, trying to help a congregation that's over 100 years old recognize that the culture around them has shifted, which requires the congregation to shift, and the church to change, in how it functions, and in how it lives out its mission, and those who have come into the faith community in the last five years or so already know that.

As noted here, the individuals in the congregation have different memories of the congregation and sometimes competing visions of what it is for. Nevertheless, for this particular pastor, the priority is to invite individuals to steward the mission of the congregation, even as it remains flexible to evolve in ways that still remain faithful to its central mission.

The PC, as noted in table 3-3, has distinct emphases on many of the same challenges. Much like the OCE, relational engagement is the most common challenge with the most iterations identified across the PC's network. This is followed by challenges associated with leadership development and boundary-zone work. For the PC, leadership development includes identifying and cultivating leaders

PC Total Challenges vs. Individuals who Identify Challenges

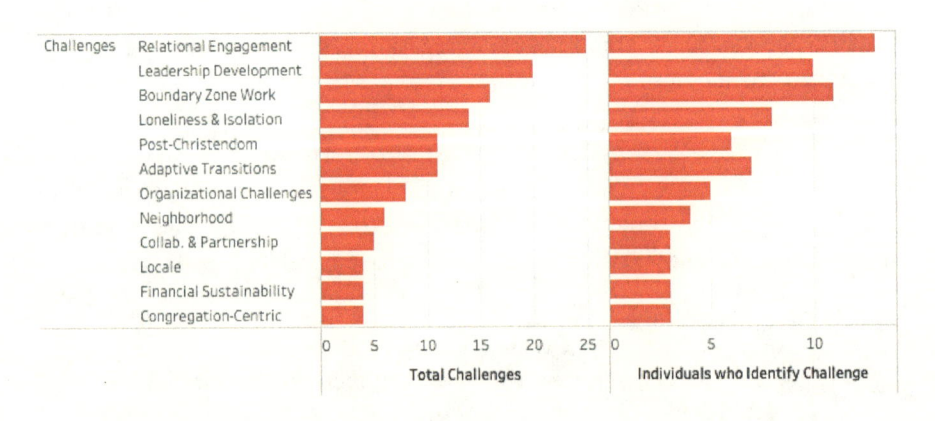

Table 3-3 PC Total Challenges vs. Individuals Who Identify Challenges

who have a vision for parish-based ministry and the value of the neighborhood. The challenges associated with boundary-zone work include the challenge of working without existing templates and in the liminal space between established organizational orders. Loneliness and isolation, managing adaptive transitions, and the challenges of post-Christendom also confront organizers and participants. Notably, even though founders identified loneliness and isolation as a prominent challenge that catalyzed their early organizing, loneliness is not identified as frequently as other challenges. In its current phase of growth and expansion, they frequently note the challenge of organizing a growing network, concerns of financial stability, and serving the broader church during a period of significant transition. That this is the case reflects the nature of the PC's adaptive challenges. The concentration of organizational challenges by interviewees most closely linked to the PC (e.g., founders, key organizers, or board members) reflects the relative prominence of this challenge within the PC during a period of rapid organizational growth.

This constellation of challenges hangs together like objects in space that are held together by invisible gravitational bonds, demanding adaptive responses. As Rice, who is both a practitioner and organizer, reflects:

> And the other thing is that because a lot of this is really tricky because there's no form, there is no structure or church structure to overlay on top of this concept of being the church in the parish, it can take on a multitude of forms. However, certain forms are a little bit more conducive to living out a proximate, integrative faith in relation to place. And often those are smaller; and oftentimes the challenges come with this [when] they have been planted or grown from a denominational plant, then finances become a challenge. So there's that, and also just loneliness and isolation becomes a challenge because oftentimes other church structures and higher church structures don't get it and don't value it and much of the fruit of it we count neighborhood transformation and people's lives being integrated and healed and changed in coming together to define belonging.

In Rice's narration, the PC's vision for a local, neighborhood-based ecclesial life moves into the boundary zone where there's no template or "church structure" to guide their particular kind of work. Rather, in this liminal space at and beyond the margins, existing church structures do not always understand this work; others do not value it. Such experiments frequently encounter organizational

Summary of Challenges Identified Across OCE and PC

Challenges	Total (approx.)
Relational Engagement	~42
Leadership Development	~25
Adaptive Transitions	~24
Boundary Zone Work	~22
Post-Christendom	~20
Loneliness & Isolation	~17
Financial Sustainability	~15
Collab. & Partnership	~11
Organizational Challenges	~8
Politics & Polarization	~7
Neighborhood	~6
Mission Stewardship	~5
Locale	~4
Congregation-Centric	~4

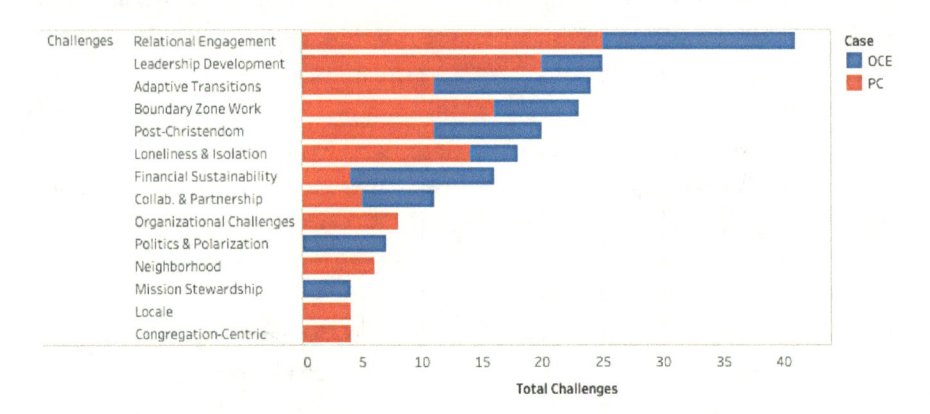

Case: OCE, PC

Table 3-4 Summary of Challenges Identified across OCE and PC

challenges as they have to explore viable financial models beyond the security of existing denominational or congregational structures.

The challenges confronting leaders and communities within these respective networks overlap considerably across network divides, too, as demonstrated by table 3-4. Of particular note is the shared concern over relational engagement, leadership development, and boundary-zone work. Notably, these challenges confront organizers and partners irrespective of their proximity to a particular denomination or tradition. For both hubs, the collective and collaborative work that organizes their adaptations involves working in the boundary space between established organizations and conventions. While organizers of the PC describe this as working without "templates," the OCE identifies the early church as an organizing template for its work. As leaders within each community seek to support individuals and communities who face a constellation of challenges within this context, the dual paradigm of relational engagement and leadership development represents both a primary focus of their work and one of their principal challenges. Individuals within both networks also identify challenges related to financial sustainability, loneliness and isolation, and post-Christendom as significant for their particular contexts.[30]

Although a history of innovation marks religious life in the Pacific Northwest, the change these challenges require is no less demanding for these communities. Even as a hopeful vision for the church beckons, inhabiting this boundary space requires a willingness to live with uncertainty. Hope and precarity are bedmates in situations that require adaptive change.[31] Beneath the constellation of challenges that confront individuals and communities, wisdom drawn from these two hubs gives witness to the hope that sustains adaptive responses.

"THEN YOU'RE FORCED TO ADAPT": COVID-19 AND THE BROADER LANDSCAPE

The acute challenges of the COVID-19 pandemic reverberated through the networks that surround the OCE and PC. While faith communities throughout the region were already adept at navigating uncertainty, the demands of this moment introduced a heightened level of uncertainty. Nevertheless, the existence of these networks created stability and resilience that enabled leaders and communities of faith to respond adaptively to the challenges they faced and the need for care across their communities.

James Leman, who serves as the pastor at First Church in Spokane, provides a representative story. Founded in the final decade of the 1800s, First Church sits between a main commuter artery in Spokane and the Spokane River. Prior to the pandemic, Leman estimates the congregation numbered between 130 and 135 on a typical Sunday, with some congregants driving from upwards of forty-five minutes away. As a Free Methodist congregation in a region marked by shifting denominational boundaries, First Church Spokane stands between an inherited tradition and the shifting composition of their neighborhood and city.

I initially met Leman in a corner booth at Petit Chat Village Bakery in north Spokane.[32] With deep roots in ministry and the Pacific Northwest—Leman grew up as a missionary kid on a reservation in Montana—Leman was coming up on thirteen years at First Church. We talked about the history of the congregation, their budding partnership with the OCE, and his vision to reconnect the First Church's mission to their local community. Leman was upbeat, even optimistic, about their expanding mission, even while the challenges facing First Church were acute. "I think we're going in the right direction, which is encouraging, very encouraging," he offered at the end of our conversation. "And I don't anticipate being the same church 10 years from now. I hope that ten years from now, not that we're not standing, sitting, passing the plate, but that we're doing that in whatever context."

I talked with Leman just over two years later, in early February 2021, this time via Zoom from our respective homes. He is hopeful and profoundly grateful for his community, but also weary. "It's been a long year with this," he shared early in our conversation. For Leman and so many others in the wake of this moment, the challenges they face are affectively inflected; they are carried like weights upon the soul, bearing silent testimony to the visible and invisible changes in their communities. To borrow language from liturgist Debbie Wong, faith leaders are in search of "Holy connection."[33] Leman could not have forecast the challenges and changes that would come when we first met in 2018, but First Church, much like many others, have faced unimaginable challenges, and their community has adapted.[34]

The pandemic introduced unprecedented challenges for Leman and other communities of faith in the region, but it did not fundamentally alter the structure of the challenges they faced. Although the story about the long-term impact of the pandemic on faith communities is still emerging, the data drawn from these hubs suggest marked continuity between the challenges that confront communities of faith in the Pacific Northwest before and after the start of the COVID-19 pandemic. When asked to identify the challenges that organize his work and ministry in our initial conversation (prior to the pandemic), Leman identified the task of getting his people to recognize the value of partnership, apathy—especially spiritual apathy—and figuring out how to prioritize time as central challenges. When I interviewed him again in February 2021 (still in the shadow of the pandemic for his context), I asked him if these are still challenges and would he identify others. With marked enthusiasm, he responded, "Absolutely. The only one that's a lot less of a challenge right now is partnership." After noting how it is much easier to make a case for the need for partnership, he notes how he would add "technology challenges" to those he mentioned previously.

Other follow-up interviews and a focus group completed in the aftermath of the pandemic expressed similar continuity. Pastors, neighborhood church leaders, nonprofit leaders, and lay leaders reported how the social-ecclesial crisis heightened the existing challenges they faced, particularly existing disconnection and polarization. As one leader observed, "Like everything else there's change in adaptation." Although the challenges remain consistent, they are now inflected through an altered ecclesial landscape. In many cases, individuals noted how COVID-19 awakened individuals to the practices they already prioritized: partnerships, relational proximity in neighborhood, local connections, and partnerships. A focus group comprised of organizers from these two hubs reported how the contextualized nature of their work crystalized the complexity of these challenges. They could not discuss the challenges they face without telling stories of the particular people and communities they serve.

Founders and participants also accentuated a marked distinction between the pre-pandemic and post-pandemic challenges: a heightened sense of fragility.

This fragility is expressed less in the catalogue of challenges individuals identify, and more in how they say it. A stutter. Hesitation. A long pause. To borrow language from Richard Osmer, there is a sense in which individuals and communities throughout the Pacific Northwest have been "brought up short."[35] As one individual observed: "So I think that COVID has shed this light on the fact that things are a lot worse than I thought. I think, I don't want to use the word 'desperate,' but 'tenuous.' I don't know." Others describe their unshakeable encounters with the challenges that confront the "homeless community" and "people on the margins" as well as the challenge of "form[ing] a community that is not centered around whiteness." In each case, these particular challenges are not new to their communities, but the social-ecclesial crisis of 2020 "pulled out a magnifying glass"—in the imagery of one participant—and surfaced the collective fragility that has always marked these communities of faith.

A Broader Landscape

Even though the challenges catalogued here are particular to the local communities that gather around each hub, they are also shared by individuals in other communities beyond the Pacific Northwest. For example, Vivek Murthy, the nineteenth and twenty-first United States Surgeon General, documented a "loneliness epidemic" rolling across communities in the United States.[36] Long before the precarity of a pandemic, individuals and communities faced the complexity of "managing transitions."[37] The uncertainty of such transitions requires individuals to move from a state of disruption, through precarity of the "neutral zone," and then into a state of stability.[38] For communities of faith more specifically, scholars of religion have discussed the emergence of what Charles Taylor describes as a "secular age," marked by the development of new conditions of belief in which, though it was once impossible to not believe in God, belief in God becomes one possibility among many.[39] This constellation of challenges has a compounding effect on the individuals in the communities of faith and faith-based organizations; over time, related challenges follow: relational engagement, leadership development, adaptive transitions, boundary-zone work, and financial sustainability. As one leader reflected in March 2021, "[I]t strikes true with my experience on the ground. . . . I've constantly heard that loneliness and isolation was top, and I think this [catalogue] much more accurately reflects what I've experienced on the ground as a higher set of priorities and challenges going into it."

THE STRUCTURE OF ADAPTIVE CHANGE

This constellation of adaptive challenges invites individuals and communities to change in ways that impact their basic dispositions, practices, and ways of organizing their common life. The change envisioned is nothing less than a wholesale transformation of the way communities structure and express their life together. Nevertheless, founders and practitioners alike recognize the complexity of the change they envision in the boundary space that marks their current existence. As Heifetz and his colleagues observe, understanding and responding to adaptive challenges requires "a healthy dose of willingness to step into the unknown."[40]

The uncertainty of the challenges that organize the OCE and PC invites individuals and communities into what Gary Gunderson describes as a "boundary zone."[41] Within these permeable social and intellectual spaces, individuals and communities find the resources they need to understand and engage the adaptive challenges they face. "Boundaries are where things come together, where the fields of relationships engage," Gunderson notes. "A boundary is exactly not where things separate, but the edge where things join: physically, as between nations; legally, as between organizations; emotionally, as between values; mentally, as between ideas."[42] These boundary spaces—where relationships, social structures, and ideas meet and mingle—represent places of creativity, possibility, opportunity, but they are also places of struggle.[43] Like estuaries where freshwater and saltwater meet, the uncertainty that marks adaptive challenges contains the opportunity that new ideas, possibilities, solutions emerge from *within* these boundary spaces. It is precisely the interstitial and relational character of boundary zones that represent both sites of immense uncertainty and possibility. Gunderson's description aptly characterizes the adaptive space that surrounds the OCE and PC:

> Boundary zones both demand and make possible a social architecture in which new relationships are possible, sustainable, and even powerful. This relational architecture is born of the complex, multilayered, persistent constellation of suffering and hope that is the reality of the boundary zone. Any living thing, if it survives more than one generation, adapts to different ecologies by developing social architecture in which it can live and thrive.... Boundary zones are the ecology in which we find life; the structure in which we are sustained and even thrive in that living is a "web of transformation."[44]

Surrounded and sustained by a tapestry of relationships, organizers across each hub are working to support the conditions for new ways of being and belonging to emerge. This ecology of relationships, each bringing a particular history and desire for belonging, contains within it the possibility for new ideas, possibilities, and structures of belonging to emerge.

For organizers and practitioners across these two hubs, their identification of the challenge of boundary-zone work both identifies a primary challenge and expresses the uncertainty of the challenges they face. Individuals describe the boundary zone in various ways—as "the edge of the edge," as a place of "suspended expectations," as moving beyond the "comfort of the institutionalized church," as trying to hold a middle ground. Emerging frequently in interviews, individuals across the PC and the OCE recognize the complexity of inhabiting this boundary-zone space, and they regularly reflect on how best to navigate this liminality.[45] "It takes a lot of savvy and thoughtfulness and just inviting people to put those differences aside and come together on the point of the gathering," Smith observes regarding the OCE's work. "But that feels like a challenge. I don't know if we always know how to do that the best." Dave Harder, who has partnered with the PC for over a decade, describes the challenge of the boundary-zone space as being misunderstood on both sides.

> When I come into a neighborhood conversation . . . I'm seen as irrelevant [because I'm Christian] . . . and it takes a lot of time to build trust. The pace in which I can come into a space as Christian really is a long game. I've now been in my neighborhood for five years, and I'm just now invited into those conversations as one who can talk, who has a voice. . . . On the other side, it's a challenge going into church spaces because they don't understand what we're doing as church in the neighborhood. . . . It's a challenge because you're misunderstood in both spaces.

Smith's and Harder's comments reflect the tensions, challenges, and uncertainty many experience in the liminal boundary spaces that surround both networks. In both cases, the boundary space can be a place of creativity and possibility, but it can also be a space of isolation, misunderstanding, and risk.

The adaptive challenges that confront individuals and communities across the Pacific Northwest require a new structure.[46] If existing forms of organization no longer support the ministry necessary for the new age, learning to see and care for bonds of connection that comprise an ecology of relations enables new structures to emerge.[47] To this end, the founders of both the OCE and PC characterize their work as an attempt to organize an alternative social structure that can support and sustain adaptive responses to the challenges communities face. For the OCE, their work involves creating a parallel institutional space alongside congregations that responds to congregations' needs rather than competing with them; for the PC, their work involves creating a "tertiary network" that does not replace existing religious structures, but enriches and strengthens them. In both cases, the challenges identified by organizers and participants invite a form of collective engagement, within and beyond the existing social architecture.

In this "hinge time" in American religious life, to borrow language from Sharon Parks,[48] the need for a new social architecture extends beyond the region. Amid the morass of uncertainty that marks this boundary space, is it possible to see beyond the current challenges we face? Are we able to organize our common life in ways that reflect the future we imagine but do not currently experience? When it feels like our world is turned upside down, how do we find hope amid an unshakable sense of collapsing possibility?

While the history and work that organizes these hubs decry technical fixes, their strikingly similar responses provide an imaginative template for the structure that organizes adaptive change. Four features constitute the adaptive wisdom that sustains their work: the power of questions; the role of authority; the organizational arrangements that enable partnership; and the centering function of place. The wisdom born of this structure provides the conditions for new ideas, relationships, and possibilities to emerge.

The Power of Questions

Across both hubs, adaptive work occurs alongside a common practice and commitment to formulating questions. For the PC, the questions "What do you see God doing in your neighborhood?" and "What gifts have you seen being leveraged in the community for the common good?"[49] direct attention to the latent possibility within a community rather than what is missing or absent. For the OCE, the questions "Is there a third way between isolationist rejection of culture and complete syncretism?" and "How do we nurture the conditions for connections to form in ways that invite us to imagine being church in the future?" invite a collaborative and teleological approach to organizing a common life. The persistence with which individuals across both hubs work to frame their questions can be captured in the words of E. E. Cummings: "Always the beautiful answer who asks a more beautiful question."[50] Similarly, questions have the capacity to direct and organize adaptive work as individuals and communities try to understand and engage the challenges that confront them. This shared practice of asking questions serve three functions in the change these hubs pursue.

First, questions provide perspective about communities' adaptive challenges. "[T]he right questions can help one get far enough above the fray to see the key patterns," Heifetz notes.[51] The right questions—and the reflective process of forming and considering them—have the capacity to provide a balcony perspective to see and understand the various factors that comprise an adaptive challenge. Although some questions serve a diagnostic function, others direct attention to the resources that already exist within a community. For example, the question "Whose problem is it?"[52] prompts reflection about who is affected by a problem and individuals' and communities' experience of loss. The Parish Collective's question "What gifts have you seen being leveraged in the community for the common good?" directs attention to the abundance of resources and gifts that already exist within a particular community.

When the founders of the PC ask what God is up to, this question invites new imaginative possibilities. A similar question is put forward by McGonigal: "What is the Spirit of God doing in our community that we're being called to participate in?" In both cases, posing and pursuing these questions requires a reframing of the vocation of church leadership and listening for the everyday stories, challenges, and gifts within local communities. As Sparks and Soerens listened to people and communities, they heard similar challenges and desires for connection. In many cases, people didn't realize there were folks in their city, in their neighborhood, or down the street seeking similar connections and ways of gathering. These and similar questions direct attention to the gifts that already exist within a community, releasing the possibility of adaptive responses and transformation.

Second, questions invite individual and collective learning in order to understand and engage the adaptive challenges that confront a community. While individuals amid uncertainty more often "want answers, not questions,"[53] privileging questions within a community or organization may be met with resistance. Forming and attempting to answer a new question is neither expedient, nor does it have a certain outcome. Nevertheless, this approach invites individuals to step into the uncertainty that marks the boundary zone between what is known and what already is. And then, the embrace of uncertainty invites consideration of new ways of thinking, working, and being together. Powerful questions, "[E]ngage people in an intimate way, confront[ing] them with their freedom, and invit[ing] them to co-create a future possibility."[54] Such questions activate and catalyze individuals to gather around the challenges they face, draw others in by curiosity, and activate individual and collective agency.[55]

Although questions have the power to catalyze and release collective activity, they cannot effect the change organizers envision apart from a structure that supports collective discernment. Like pearls cast before a crowd, they remain powerless until they are held up to the light and then tried on within a broader community. Change requires the wisdom of those who raise such questions, an environment that is able to receive them, and a delivery method that invites engagement. When these transformative, powerful questions are picked up and cherished, they begin to gleam with beauty, inviting creative care.

The structure that is able to receive questions of this kind is the type of thing that is more often felt before it is seen. It doesn't appear on an organization's website or as part of a statement of values or mission; rather, the practices that organize gatherings and unscripted encounters in the collaborative space express an "implicit curriculum" of an organizational culture.[56] For example, when I visited the conferences convened by the OCE and PC, I encountered a speaker lineup that included a diversity of perspectives and voices. Although founders never stated it expressly, this expressed a structure of hospitality, which even extended to me. And when I met with or engaged with organizers and key partners, both in interview settings and beyond, they engaged in a manner that attended with abundant curiosity to the particularity of my experience and emerging work. Even amid the bustle between conference gatherings, their attentive presence and questions conveyed and expressed support for my ongoing investigation. I felt seen in a way that extended beyond the particular history or outcomes of my work. I felt that I somehow belonged here, among both familiar and foreign people, in a way that kindled curiosity. Above all else, I was received in an abundance of care.

When questions that catalyze collective discernment are given adequate structure, they invite collective learning. The learning that occurs certainly includes acquiring additional information as well as exploring new forms of practice and being together. Across both hubs, the adaptive spirit that organizes their work is borne by a willingness to pose and sit with unresolved questions, rather than seeking a technical solution. For example, when speaking about the nature of his leadership in First Church, James Leman identifies questions as his most significant role. "I think [if] you take out the normal pastoral roles of preaching, teaching, counseling, with these types of challenges, these types of engagement, my biggest role is to ask questions that encourage people to think," he says. Similarly, this practice decenters the formal authority that is held by a single individual and provides an opportunity for collective engagement around unresolved questions. For example, when Sparks began to listen to the stories of individuals and communities in his neighborhood, it initiated a "profound awakening" in how he interacts with his community and his vocation of religious leadership. Rather than centering his voice, his experience, or his work—and, by extension, the work of the PC—he seeks to listen to those in his community and connect the individuals and gifts that reside within it. This form of listening involves attending to where "the gifts of individuals intersect with the needs of others and the community," as Soerens observes. Nevertheless, as Heifetz and his colleagues note, it is "extremely difficult" to create regular space and time for this sort of "reflection and continuous learning."[57] Individuals across both hubs clearly recognize the challenge inherent to this process, frequently noting the need to move "slowly" and to "pay attention."

Third, questions direct attention to the collaborative activity that adaptive work requires. The kind of questions that organize and direct the formation of these two hubs invite collective engagement around the needs and gifts of a community. In the case of the PC, responding to the question "What is God up to here?" cannot be answered in isolation. For the OCE, their guiding questions perpetually direct them back to the concerns of those they serve and to a practice of individual and collective discernment. In each case, questions, in conjunction with a structure to receive them, invite individuals in the community both to understand what is happening in the ordinary spaces they inhabit,[58] and to consider and discern the movement of God, thereby stitching individuals together in community and in relation to God's unfolding work in time and history. Rather than seeking static solutions, questions of this kind require a willingness to organize and gather in ways that remain open to the Spirit's work, and then respond accordingly.

The Role of Authority

The collective work that organizes the hubs represents nothing less than a subversion of the prevailing authority structures that have historically guided religious organization, education, and leadership. Authority, as presented in the adaptive leadership literature, has the capacity to direct individuals and communities to engage the perplexing, adaptive challenges that confront them. Heifetz observes: "The role of authority may seem to vanish" during periods of stability.[59] In moments of social distress or crisis, however, individuals and communities look to authority in order to understand and resolve the social pain they encounter.[60] Authority can be exercised in ways that invite collaborative and collective engagement—as frequently happens across these hubs—and it remains an inescapable dimension of social and organizational life. Authority visibly and invisibly structures communities' efforts to respond to the adaptive challenges they face, but it also has the capacity to restrict adaptive response. When left unnamed and unexamined, the structure authority provides limits the collective capacity that can pursue adaptive change.

The adaptive wisdom that guides these two hubs, in contrast, represents an individual and collective effort to locate authority in partnership and in relation to the local ministry leaders. For example, the history and ongoing leadership of each organization reflects an abiding commitment to partnership. As one OCE organizer shared when asked to explore the collaborative feature of their leadership: "I think it works because of this mutual respect that we have for each other and [we] recognize the gifts that we all bring to the table [and] we're working so hard to listen." Listening grounds their engagement with the people they serve, and a collaborative approach enables each partner to promote collective engagement around a particular aspect of their work. Expressing their agreement with the spirit of collaboration that marks the OCE's work, PC founders note their shared commitment to the work of community transformation—"[A]ll of us are giving our lives to these ideas at some level. We're in it"—before concluding, "I think the collaborative movement and future that we're moving into is really exciting. But, as it's been said many times, I think we're at a hinge point right now. I think this is an absolutely vital and crucial time for the next, at least many decades, if not centuries for the practical imagination of the church." In this boundary zone, as individuals discern how best to respond to the complex challenges they face, a common commitment to collaboration guides each community's next step. It is a way of life, one that aims to enrich the "practical imagination" of the people and communities they serve.

Each hub also relocates authority to the local ministry practitioners, who are sites and conduits of the collective transformation organizers imagine. This decision demonstrates a collective attempt to rethink and reestablish authority outside of or beyond the received structures that convey and credential authority. For example, a listening posture galvanized the OCE's early work and the PC emerged from a shared awakening to the wisdom that already existed in their surrounding neighborhoods. In gathering individuals around the challenges they face, organizers aim both to learn from and to connect the local wisdom that is emerging.

By way of illustration, scholars of religious education have distinguished between "the clerical paradigm" and "the academic paradigm" as organizing structures of American religious education and religious leadership. The clerical paradigm privileges cognitive engagement with theological disciplines—as a form of scientific inquiry—in order to train church leadership.[61] Clerical praxis is the *raison d'etre* for theological education, and local congregations are the principal site for a ministerial vocation. According to the clerical paradigm, theological education provides the requisite credentials for ministry, and authority is derivative of the minister's position and education. Christian education, organization, and leadership are structured according to credentialing of ministerial praxis.

The academic paradigm privileges academic knowledge of theology at the expense of the practical wisdom that reflects a theological way of life.[62] If the clerical paradigm organizes religious education according to clerical practice, the academic paradigm organizes education to ends that include knowledge of theology, Christian Scriptures, and dogmatics. The ability to acquire theological knowledge signifies authority, both to the educational institutions and to those who receive education in these places. Christian education, organization, and leadership are structured according to the acquisition of theological knowledge.[63]

These hubs, however, aim to locate authority beyond both the academic and clerical paradigms. Although their work includes and engages clerical practice, a shared value of faithful presence is the primary marker of their particular ministerial vocation. As one organizer observed, "I'm very rarely trying to assume authority in certain situations and trying to figure out how to empower students to be able to call authority into different situations." In other instances, a similar posture leads organizers and participants to be faithfully present in their neighborhoods and organizations (sometimes for multiple years) before they build enough trust to have a voice in decisions that impact their local communities. Communities and organizations still require the care and expertise ministry professionals extend, especially in times of crisis, but those who minister must now accrue authority by virtue of relational presence rather than institutional credentialization. Similarly, academic expertise contributes to the structure of these two hubs, but the form of education, organization, and leadership they pursue reaches beyond academic mastery. Their combined work points to and cultivates a kind of practical wisdom that is relationally and geographically indexed. As one practitioner observed: "Discipleship happens in life with people, not necessarily about what people know or how much you can teach them, but it's about how you act together and learn from one another."

Fixed and Ambiguous Organizational Arrangements

While the OCE and PC share many values and address intersecting challenges, they represent different types of ecclesial innovations that emerge from different social environments. I distinguish these as "fixed" and "ambiguous" organizational arrangements. The OCE emerged from an environment more characteristic of fixed arrangements, and the PC from an environment that was more ambiguous. While making a distinction between these different environments clarifies the conditions that enable their respective work, they are not neat categories. This distinction, nevertheless, clarifies how innovation does not emerge out of these ideal types, but more often includes a combination of fixed and ambiguous partnerships. As organizers observed when they gathered around these themes, each organization has fixed and ambiguous properties, as well as the need to learn how to navigate less familiar organizational terrain. "I think that historically we have tended to be more in the ambiguous world holistically, and that's probably where we're more comfortable, honestly. However, . . . your work has opened up worlds into more of the fixed, direct relationships," one organizer observed. When considered alongside each organization's stated value for place, these arrangements provide a unique setting that structures the social relations for certain forms of collaboration and imagination.

Organizational settings that can be described as "fixed sets" are those in which primary partners and relationships are adequately defined in order to organize and pursue a common objective. Although individuals in a fixed set of organizational arrangements continue to negotiate the priority of particular functions that direct their collective projects, the parameters and scope of the collaborative activity provide sufficient definition in order to initiate and maintain a collaborative nature. The structure of organizational arrangements matters because it establishes the condition for new paradigms to emerge. As a leading scholar of entrepreneurship, Martin Ruef, observes, in many cases a "new [organizational] form [is] hatched within existing organizational arrangements."[64] For the OCE and related ecclesial adaptations, the precise nature of the organizational arrangement informs the conditions that support an adaptive response. When pursued within a fixed set of organizational arrangements—reinforced by existing partnerships—the OCE becomes a hub for resources, information, and connection.

An ambiguous set describes an organizational setting in which identifiable partners exist, but the relationships between these partners is not clearly defined. For the PC, their neighborhood-based innovation emerged from an ambiguous set of organizational arrangements. Partners existed, but their relationships were not always clearly defined. As a result, the early work of the PC lacked a clear champion, but this also led to the formation of partnerships beyond a single institutional setting. Amorphous relational structures do not necessarily represent a disadvantage. Still, the juxtaposition between the fixed and ambiguous sets of organizational arrangements surrounding these two cases suggests their intrinsic challenges and possibilities.

With this distinction established, Heifetz's framework and these adaptive hubs can offer mutually illuminating insights.[65] One the one hand, Heifetz describes the form of "holding environments" able to support and contain the countervailing creativity and uncertainty adaptive work requires. It is helpful to consider the full definition of holding environment:

> The cohesive properties of a relationship or social system that serve to keep people engaged with one another in spite of the divisive forces generated by adaptive work. May include, for example, bonds of affiliation and love; agreed-upon rules, procedures, and norms; shared purposes and common values; traditions, language, and rituals; familiarity with adaptive work; and trust in authority. Holding environments give a group identity and contain the conflict, chaos, and confusion often produced when struggling with complex problematic realities.[66]

Amid the collective uncertainty within communities of adaptive change, relationships create a structure of connection and care. While a desire to preserve existing networks can inhibit meaningful, systemic change, leaders may also encourage the change that is required by ensuring that individuals have the support they need to navigate uncertainty. Adaptive change invites individuals and communities to step into a boundary space, relinquishing the security of certainty and predictability; if, however, individuals can navigate uncertainty in the company of others, they can begin to consider the possibility of adaptive solutions.[67]

Nevertheless, if individuals hope to begin and sustain an adaptive process, a secure relational network is required to manage the unavoidable disequilibrium that adaptive work will introduce. At a personal level, friendship creates a holding environment to regulate the stress of adaptive work.[68] At a collective level, organizational structures and "hopeful visions for the future" can provide the cohesion required for adaptive work. In its various forms, a holding environment "provide[s] safety and structure for people to surface and discuss the particular values, perspectives, and creative ideas they have on the challenging situations they all face."[69] Heifetz and his colleagues identify several practice-oriented markers of a holding environment: common language; shared values and purposes; experience working together; relationships marked by affections, trust, and camaraderie; trust in authority figures and the organizational structures; and social space that allows for the kind of collaboration, comfort, and confidentiality that adaptive work requires.[70] In each of these suggestions, Heifetz and his colleagues draw attention to the need to create and maintain an environment that acknowledges the unavoidable stress adaptive work introduces. That environment must also foster the relational bonds that are required for collaborative partnership and collective work.

And, at this point, the adaptive work that organizes these hubs provides insights to reinterpret Heifetz by demonstrating the kinds of social relations, or community, that comprise a holding environment for adaptive work. Conversations over coffee. Collaborative projects. Book clubs and reading groups. These are the kinds of ordinary, everyday encounters that create space for connections to form and collaborations to grow. When pursued over time, trust, respect, mutuality, and listening coalesce into friendship. Friendship creates the container for organizers at each hub to take the risks to pursue the wisdom of an adaptive church. Likewise, in pockets throughout these respective networks, friendship catalyzes adaptive change in neighborhoods, nonprofits, and congregations beyond these two hubs. Speaking about the forms of collaboration and connection that organizes his work in Portland, OR. James Helms shares: "These are my friends, these are my good friends, people that I'm growing in trust and love for."

Catalytic grants that supported the early work of the OCE and PC also provided a holding environment to direct and consider the required form of adaptive work. These resources and the forms of relationship and partnership they fostered created a container for the adaptive needs that organized the hubs' early visions and experiments. As founders of the PC reflect on the impact of grant funding, they note how early on "it helped us think strategically about what we're doing and why," and later provided space to reflect on the work they had been doing. Similarly, in the case of the OCE, they reflect on the value of early "formative conversations" with grant officers that both informed how they conceptualized their early work and later how they began to approach their work with congregations through a commitment to listening.

As a result, the adaptive work that takes place at these hubs cannot be separated either from the holding environment that grant funding creates or from the work of grant makers to create environments that nurture adaptive work within organizations. For example, Steve Moore, the executive director for The M. J. Murdock Charitable Trust, speaks about Murdock's work as both "convening" and working as a "catalyst." As one of the only funders within the Pacific Northwest that does not discriminate against faith-based organizations, they regularly convene thought leaders and organizational leaders from across the region, both to listen to the work taking place in their particular context and to connect them to one another.[71] The desired outcome, according to a resource offered by Murdock for nonprofits, seeks to attend to the "hidden human ecosystem" with a vision "to implement a new paradigm that filters through a holistic and human-centered lens [and] takes into account the whole of an ecology of a community."[72] Through their grants, such as those that catalyzed some of the early work of the PC and OCE, Moore observes how The Murdock Charitable Trust seeks to "nurture and enrich the educational, cultural, social, and spiritual life of individuals, families and communities."

The distinction between organizational arrangements that characterize these adaptations also introduce variations in the holding environments that organize adaptive work across these hubs. By way of example, for the OCE, which emerged from a fixed set of organizational arrangements, the primary partnerships and relationships were already defined prior to the launch of the OCE. A broader institutional holding environment supported and sustained their particular form of adaptive work. Specifically, Taylor's function as a "champion" for this early work, and his understanding for how it relates to the university's broader educational mission, created a complementary holding environment. It enabled OCE founders to consider and explore the adaptive responses to their specific challenges. Meanwhile, the PC's early and ongoing partnerships emerged from an ambiguous set and led to a range of denominational, nonprofit, and parachurch partners (e.g., UMC, Navigators). When pursued and cultivated over time, these ambiguous arrangements fostered the formation of multiple containers for adaptive work. While this multiplicity of holding environments introduces challenges, it also enriches their work through an expanded network of relationships and experiments with experiences in diverse contexts.[73]

Centered in Place

Finally, the OCE's and PC's adaptive work is centered in place. Their shared commitment to specific places structures their adaptive work in relation to the well-being of a specific locale and the social fabric that comprises a local community. The preceding features structure adaptive work in a way that creates an environment that can hold the uncertainty adaptive change requires: shared values cultivate trust and mutuality; powerful questions invite individuals to imagine new possibilities; authority derived from partnership distributes agency; and a hospitable organizational environment creates the social container to catalyze and sustain the adaptive change each hub pursues. When centered in a place, these structural features coalesce to respond to the adaptive demands of the challenges in a particular community.

Place describes the localized, contextual features that direct the adaptive change individuals imagine and pursue. The priority and centering function of place has appeared throughout this account already. It is expressed in the OCE's commitment to partner "with churches and other Christian ministries as they discern how to be the church and do ministry in the western region of the United States and around the world" and in the PC's commitment to "grow roots and weave links" among followers of Jesus who seek to foster "expression[s] of love and care in [their] neighborhood." Participants attribute a similar function to place when they describe their aim to "be present for the Kingdom in this particular place at this particular time," or note how the particulars of place invite "less programs and more listening." In time, through listening, a form of attention develops that invites individuals and communities to become "more aware of the gifts and how to apply those gifts for the betterment of the neighborhood for the betterment of the congregation."

Place structures adaptive change by giving the complex challenges that confront people of faith a particularity that makes these challenges incarnate. It literally grounds the abstract challenges that confront communities in relation to a specific location, neighborhood, or individual. For example, the challenge of relational engagement emerges in relation to a particular congregant, neighbor, or donor. Loneliness and isolation emerge from a fraying social fabric and growing polarization in communities, congregations, and families. The challenge of boundary-zone work becomes acute because of organizers' care for the people or their restless discontent with the status quo. In each situation, these adaptive challenges demand a response centered in place, coming home in a way that requires contextual and collaborative engagement in order to imagine an alternative.

"NEW WINESKINS FOR NEW WINE"

The structure that organizes adaptive work across these hubs aims to create an alternative social order that is nimble and adaptive enough to address the challenges people of faith face in the region. One organizer notes how their work is an attempt to provide "new wineskins for new wine."[74] As individuals and communities explore missional faithfulness, their work first requires imagining the new structure—the new wineskins—that can nurture and carry the wisdom of their communities. They aim to be stewards of saints. When carried forth by a supple structure that can respond to the contextual challenges they face, their adaptive work takes form in the particular communities they serve. Parish-based leaders are connected in common cause to the needs of their neighborhoods: affordable housing, busyness, belonging. Congregations link arms in the wake of an immigration crisis. When cascading crises cripple ecclesial and social life in the Pacific Northwest, local leaders display shocking resilience.

While the change these hubs pursue resembles prominent theories of adaptive work, they envision a kind of change that reaches beyond the conceptual horizon Heifetz and his colleagues offer. To extend the wineskin metaphor, their work creates a new social structure *and* invites new conceptual frames. A plurality of new wineskins is needed. To this end, the wisdom they carry offers two distinct features for communities of faith: the importance of ends and aims of adaptive change and the Christo-ecclesial basis for community. When embedded in a structure that sustains collaborative partnerships, each hub presents a social body that can support the transformation adaptive change requires for communities of faith.

End and Aims

Across both sites, a vision for individual and collective transformation directs the engagement with the challenges they face. The adaptive challenges that characterize boundary zones invite collective work that proceeds through "webs of transformation."[75] For organizers of both the OCE and PC, transformation proceeds from an ecclesial vision. Their view of the church attends to the transformation of the self, host organizations, neighborhoods, and the broader community, with each shaped by their specific geographic locale.

As partners and participants use language of transformation repeatedly across these two hubs, it is indexed to a theological understanding of the common good. For example, individuals talk about the transformation they have undergone through their connection with other members of the PC and OCE; others speak about the "mutual transformation" that takes place through their encounters within the neighborhood; several describe the mission of their organization as seeking the transformation of individuals and communities; others speak about the subtle but unmistakable transformation they have witnessed among members of their congregations. In many cases, however, when individuals talk about the transformation that has taken place for themselves or their community, they tell stories. These stories of transformation speak to the dynamic process of communal and individual change taking place across these hubs, as individuals extend beyond themselves, encounter one another, and begin to develop a new vision for themselves and their community.

When centered in place, the structure of adaptive work across these hubs can sustain the localized adaptive work they imagine. If adaptive challenges require some form of change in order for new ideas, relationships, and possibilities to emerge, the means of transformation cannot be understood apart from the end these communities imagine. Place centers adaptive work in relation to the goals and aspirations of a particular locality and community.

An explicit centering of place provides a teleological vision that a theory of adaptive work cannot provide on its own. Indeed, Heifetz identifies "values" as the fulcrum to pivot from adaptive challenges to adaptive work, but his conceptual framework lacks a sufficient account of the aims that motivate the individual and collective engagement with adaptive challenges. Rather, in his rejection of popular theories of transformational leadership,[76] Heifetz amputates teleology from his account of organizational change.[77] As a result, his theory inscribes adaptive work within a conceptual framework that lacks the internal capacity to motivate the form of problem solving, learning, and social reorganization that adaptive challenges demand. In other words, Heifetz's theory aptly describes the process adaptive work requires, but it provides an incomplete account of the conditions that sustain adaptive change.

Even if individuals and communities recognize the need for adaptive work, sustained transformation requires a vision for the common good that attends to the particularities of place. To revise Tod Bolsinger's language, once they recognize the need to "canoe the mountains,"[78] leaning into the unknown, these two hubs center their adaptive journey in relation to a specific locale. The hopeful transformation they envision does not pass over the current places they serve; rather, they aim to enrich and release the possibilities that exist already in their midst.

The collective response to the challenges that organize these hubs demonstrates how adaptive work cannot be separated from an ecclesial vision to foster the common good. The founders describe their work in relation to forms of change and transformation, but they do so at a systems level, attentive to the interrelationships among members that contribute to individual and collective transformation. Of the two cases, the PC more readily describes their work in terms of "transformation," although the OCE's work is frequently indexed to the forms of "change" it both responds to and nurtures. For example, *The New Parish*, which provides a template for much of the contextual and curricular work of the PC, outlines a vision for "how neighborhood churches are transforming mission, discipleship and community."[79] For the OCE, their mission to "develop new forms of ministry capable of effectively engaging our rapidly changing culture" reflects a teleological vision for individual and collective change. Accordingly, founders readily describe the forms of change they either envision or are seeing through their partnerships. As McGonigal shares: "The church—big C church—in Spokane is going to look different four or five years from now than it looks right now because we've got forty churches leaning into relationships with refugees.... We've got that thing going on in all six of these learning communities." When centered in place, the transformation they envision reimagines how church works and the ways people of faith interact with their local community.

A Christo-Ecclesial Basis for Community

With place as a centering structure, the social fabric that comprises a local community emerges through Christ and in proximity to an ecclesial community. Both hubs are organized around shared values for the Spirit-filled way of Jesus, relationships, and community. When combined and considered together, these values point to an understanding of community and transformation that proceeds from participation in Christ and the forms of connection and community that the Spirit brings into being. As expressed by PC organizers, their adaptive work is "center[ed] on the way of Jesus," which includes being "[f]ormed by Jesus' life, death, and resurrection, we seek to share life together as a tangible expression of Christ's body in the parish."[80] Similarly, for the OCE, their adaptive work seeks to connect and engage "followers of Jesus" across the diverse expressions of Christian faith in the Pacific Northwest. The aim, as one founder shared, is to "start reframing how we think about being followers of Jesus in this present moment." In both cases, a Christocentric vision creates the conditions for the forms of encounter, partnership, and transformation that each hub pursues. Accordingly, the adaptive work that organizes these hubs emerges from an understanding of the community both as a good in itself and as a site for transformation that extends beyond the community itself.

Although Heifetz's conceptual framework provides helpful diagnostic categories for these organizational and ecclesial adaptations, his account relies upon a pragmatic understanding of social relations. The distinguishing features of pragmatism—both in its early formulation and contemporary manifestations—present an approach that regards knowledge and human action as inseparable from experimentation and engagement with one's environment. This view contends that individuals hold a certain belief because it yields "more useful relations with the world."[81] In this sense, pragmatism not only provides a theory of knowledge, but it also provides a theory of action that attends to the educational, organizational, and relational conditions that enable (and constrain) human thought and action. Heifetz similarly identifies the need for collective engagement around adaptive challenges, but his framework lacks the internal capacity to provide an adequate social ontology to sustain the form of adaptive work and leadership he envisions. While leadership and community remain irreplaceable features for adaptive change, neither can become pragmatic to solutions to collective problems. Instead, the change that can only come from the collective work of a community requires a social ontology—an account of human relatedness—that neither constrains agency by the challenges that a collective faces nor reduces the collective to a means to address a challenge. A structure for connection and collaboration is the essential condition for beginning to explore adaptive responses, but organizers cannot instrumentalize the bonds of belonging in ways that compromise the trust that is required to imagine and pursue collective change.

In contrast to Heifetz's account, a structure that is centered in place locates adaptive work in relation to the specific aims and fabric of a local community. For the hubs introduced here, their understanding of local transformation as the end of their work and the Christo-ecclesial basis for the community they envisage sustains adaptive work and the forms of leadership they pursue.

The localized ends and aims and Christo-ecclesial social fabric that organize these organizational and ecclesial adaptations are oriented toward a form of adaptive work that picks up where Heifetz's account stops short. Each in its own way, these hubs are responding to a constellation of adaptive challenges through contextually dependent, nimble, and collaborative approaches to religious education, organization, and leadership. This form of adaptive work responds to the particular challenges individuals across each hub identify as they pursue a way of life that can sustain individuals and communities of faith within the Pacific Northwest. In the face of their complex and formidable challenges, a robust understanding of the form of community and attendant conditions that their adaptive work requires enriches the hubs' work.

CONCLUSION: RESILIENCE AND RENEWAL

I gathered fifteen leaders to consider the wisdom that is emerging from the adaptive ethos of religious life in the Pacific Northwest in March 2021. Hosted online, this gathering included organizers from the PC and the OCE, including many of the guides mentioned here, me, and various "balcony guests" whose experience and reflection could enrich our conversation and this broader study.[82] The diversity of participants' places of service displayed the breadth of religious life in the Pacific Northwest: a mainline pastor serving in Vancouver, Washington; a professor of theology from Vancouver, B.C.; foundation representatives from the Murdock Charitable Trust; organizers from the Parish Collective based in Washington and their board chair based in Chicago; organizers from the OCE based in Spokane, Washington.

We gathered during Holy Week, in the space between. For two days, the conversation moved in the boundary space between shadow and anticipation. We could not gather in person, as originally planned, but we waited, with hope, for the renewal of our communities. To borrow language from Sunia Gibbs, a pastor, artist, and creative in Portland, this gathering was an experiment.[83] Indeed, the life of faith in the Pacific Northwest and elsewhere requires a willingness to experiment. Faith communities have always had to adapt, but when the pronounced experimentation of this moment combined with the longings of Holy Week, it illumined the hope for renewal and patient presence that mark each community. Their work emerges from a hopeful vision for a more connected and collaborative church; in this moment, however, they wait, with anticipation and longing, for the transformation they envision.

The structure that organizes these hubs offers adaptive wisdom to others who hang on the edge of uncertainty, peering into the void of precarity, nurturing hopeful imagination in the space between.

As we concluded this gathering, participants began to reflect on the impact of their broader work in this particular moment. Two themes emerged consistently from their reflections and this conversation: resilience and renewal. The structure each hub provided created points of relational contact that provided ballast and mooring amid the uncertainty and demand for rapid adaptation. Like a deeply rooted tree in a storm, partners and participants found themselves shaken but not uprooted amid cascading crises. At the same time, they expand

and enrich the overall resilience of the ecology they inhabit. While each hub is far from the sole source of resilience among the people and places they serve, their presence cultivates a form of belonging that can engender the kind of resilience adaptive change requires. As one balcony guest observed, they call "us to faithfulness" and challenge "our hope."

These two hubs are also creating alternative conditions for renewal—of the kind of church, the kind of institution, even the kind of belonging that organizes communities of faith. This is a renewal more porous, more attentive to the demands of particular places, and one that distributes authority across a community of faith. It is the renewal of the ordinary. As one participant shares: "[W]e see ourselves as catalytic to a movement that is more led by ordinary people."

The kind of connective and collaborative renewal that is pursued by these hubs is not unique to them, but it does reflect the particular histories and contours of the places they steward. Their story also fosters resilience and renewal as others work to imagine and craft the structures that can sustain communities of faith into a new age. The broader story of these two adaptive hubs unfolds over the remaining chapters.

4

Anchors and Webs

Hubs as Fields, Networks, and Ecologies

The stories of these two adaptive hubs converge in a building on the southern edge of Vancouver, Washington. Rising on the banks of the Columbia River and adjacent to I-5, the Murdock Charitable Trust sits at the nexus of the two primary corridors in the region. One of the only funders in the region who doesn't discriminate against religious organizations, Murdock also occupies a central position within the ecclesial ecology that surrounds the Office of Church Engagement (OCE) and the Parish Collective (PC). Drive north and south along I-5, and one travels the path that catalyzed the Parish Collective's early connecting and convening work. Travel far enough east into the headwaters of the Columbia River, and one will eventually pass the Office of Church Engagement at Whitworth University. Just as religious life can never be separated from the particularities of place in the Pacific Northwest, Murdock's location signifies their central position within the region's broader ecclesial ecology.[1]

The air feels light and clear when I enter the Murdock office. Glass-paned and newly constructed, the office is grand in comparison to the coffee shops and academic offices where most of my interviews have taken place up to this point. In time, I learn that Murdock and these two hubs are not as different as they first appear: each serves as a connecting point for individuals and communities around them. For example, Murdock was the first company to commit to this new development, but several others followed shortly thereafter. As Steve Moore, Murdock's executive director from 2006 to 2022, shares, "People know we're not going anywhere, so we want to be an anchor institution."[2] Indeed, in each case, the work of these hubs similarly seeks to expand and enrich the vitality of local faith communities.

In the course of my conversation with Moore, he outlines a resonant vision to "resource" and "catalyze" projects across the region. Combining pastoral sensibilities with an acute desire to see individuals and communities flourish, Moore describes their work as attending to the "different parts of what it means to be a thriving or flourishing community." The desired outcome, according to a resource offered by Murdock, seeks to support the "hidden human ecosystem" with a vision "to implement a new paradigm that filters through a holistic and human-centered lens [and] takes into account the whole of an ecology of a community."[3] This connective and transformative work requires identifying individuals and organizations with the ecology that support local communities.

Adaptive change within an ecclesial ecology occurs through coordinated individual and organizational efforts. Organizations, such as the Office of Church Engagement, the Parish Collective, and the Murdock Charitable Trust, create forums that coordinate and direct collaborative efforts. Individuals attend to the local challenges and values that animate a community's common life. When connected and nourished over time, this coordinated effort redounds to impact the whole ecology of a community. As one organizer observes, the combination of challenges with the right structure might enable "something new to emerge."

Distinct organizational environments supported the conditions out of which the OCE and PC emerged, but each hub has expanded to include other organizational partners and individuals who are imbedded in other organizations. In doing so, each hub serves as an anchor within a broader web of relationships. This chapter considers the organizational features of these kindred adaptive hubs. Borrowing conceptual frameworks from organizational theory, I explore the organizational environment that surrounds these adaptive hubs. More specifically, I consider how three strands of organizational studies clarify these hubs' novel organizational form: neo-institutional theory, network theory, and organizational ecology.[4]

My account offers the first in-depth analysis of a novel organizational form of organizing religious life, which I identify as a "hub." Neither a megachurch nor a denomination, a hub is a densely networked organizational form that anchors religious life within a particular community and facilitates webs of connection across a broader ecclesial ecology. The two hubs considered in this study, provide critical cases to identify similar hub configurations within and beyond the Pacific Northwest. This novel organizational form and the kind of leadership it requires can foster a more adaptive church as other religious communities face uncertainty.

A FIELD-LEVEL PERSPECTIVE

These kindred organizational and ecclesial adaptations emerge from partnerships among individuals within these networks, but also from a broader organized pattern of activity and social relations. As noted in the previous chapters, the adaptive work that organizes these two hubs takes place within a network of trust-filled relationships that exist in varying degrees of proximity to established and emerging organizations. Neither the OCE nor the PC would exist apart from the matrix of organizations and networks of relationships that comprise them. Accordingly, a "field-level" perspective, as introduced and developed by organizational theory, clarifies the organizational setting(s) in which this adaptive work takes place.

An organizational field is defined as "those organizations that, in the aggregate, constitute a recognized area of institutional life."[5] Organizational fields represent an organized domain of social life that includes a commingling of shared values and processes of social exchange that constitute a shared field of organized meaning.[6] Organizations that share forms of connection and occupy a similar position within the broader network of formal and informal economic relationships (e.g., suppliers, resource and produce consumers, and regulatory agencies) comprise a field.[7] Still, organizational theorists' definition for an "organizational field" applies equally to the cases at hand. For example, the adaptive work that organizes each hub occurs in close proximity to congregations, educational institutions, funders, and denominational bodies. Even though the particular challenges that occasion these adaptations introduce a degree of variation across these respective organizational forms, their combination "constitute[s] a recognized area of institutional life."[8]

Attention to organizational fields invites scholars and practitioners to consider and describe the aggregate field of interconnected organizations, the means of connection between them, the shared values, and the real and symbolic boundaries of activity within a field's discrete organizations. A field-level perspective directs attention to the "to the totality of relevant actors," not individuals or discrete organizations alone.[9] This level of analysis requires attending to the composite of organizations that collectively constitute an organizational field. Furthermore, the study of organizational fields considers the structural characteristics and similar conditions that organizations share, even if they are not formally linked by partnership.[10] That is to say, even though some form of connection are indirect or unseen, structural equivalence across the conditions and forms of relationship comprise a common organizational field. As a result, a field-level approach directs attention to the aggregate of organizations that comprise a shared meaning system, the seen and unseen relations, and the forms of structural correspondence that reflect similar conditions.[11]

Analytically positioned between discrete organizations and the larger institutional constructs that give them meaning, organizational fields comprise a meso-level analysis. They attend to the social space in between, to the boundary zone of social life. They facilitate examination of both the practices that structure organizations and the larger organizational context in which social life is embedded. Accordingly, meso-level analysis has the capacity to promote "understanding of the cross-level and reciprocal effects that characterize real life in real organizations."[12] The construction of the field in this way does not draw attention to the novelty of the organizational field that the OCE and PC occupy. Rather, the novelty lies in the shifting boundaries of this field and the similar adaptive responses that are emerging simultaneously in the region.

However, the porous organizational boundaries and localized commitments that mark these adaptations complicate attempts to identify and construct an organizational field within the region. For example, if the adaptation that organizes these hubs emerges from a similar organizational field, the boundaries that define this field are difficult to identify. In both cases, the challenges that occasion these adaptations point to drastic transitions within the organizational field that has historically organized Christian thought and practice. Just as individuals across both hubs articulate a similar set of values, their adaptive work shares the premise that the existing systems of meaning and practices for organizing a common life no longer provide what is needed to meet contemporary challenges. Expressed in both hubs through the image of "new wineskins for new wine," this sentiment reflects organizers' sense for the need for new forms of organizing as well as broader transitions within the organizational field.

Nevertheless, the boundaries of this field remain difficult to identify and define beyond the adaptive hubs themselves. Although identifiable organizational actors (e.g., colleges, theological schools, congregations, foundations) have catalyzed adaptive work across these hubs, individuals with less clearly defined organizational affiliations also contribute to the shape of activity within these sites in significant ways. For example, the PC's work to connect and convene parish leaders around an ecclesial vision for the neighborhood resists a strict categorization as an organizational field. Indeed, even as some parish leaders acknowledge the role of organizations in their neighborhood work, they tend to prioritize interpersonal relationships and partner across lines of religious or confessional distinction. As James Helms, who lives in the Rocky Butte community of Portland, observes, "My life is lived as a series of overlays; I don't have much distinction between work, home life, community life. It's one life that I live, so that takes me to connect with the people around me in my direct neighborhood. . . . If we would continue to tell stories, it would include my neighbors and it would also include people in my hub. . . . For me, 'hub' is about relationship. . . . The deeper relationships, institutionally, are [interpersonal] relationships."

For Helms, the priority of friendships within the neighborhood relocates the collective activity that can transform individuals and community away from the organization to the specific locale where it takes place. Simultaneously, in discussing his engagement with the PC's endeavors, Helms begins to tell the stories of the people and friendships that surround him in the neighborhood. It is as if he cannot talk about his partners, including the PC and individuals in his neighborhood, without sharing something of the story of the lives that surround his work.

The OCE may initially appear to more naturally reflect the previous description of an organizational field, but the adaptive work that organizes and sustains it similarly emerges from the level of interpersonal relationships. Indeed, as individuals across this hub observe, the trust-filled relationships that sustain its work emerged from decades of shared life in reading groups, small groups, and other points of relational contact. In each case, an organizational affiliation provides the occasion for a relational connection, but these relational encounters extend beyond formal boundaries of a single organization or role. In both cases, the hubs' form of adaptive work involves moving across, between, and beneath existing organizations in order to create the conditions in which new forms of organizing a common life can emerge.

Established organizations within a loosely defined organizational field have provided an "anchor" to support and legitimize the work of the OCE and PC.[13] In turn, the OCE and PC have, in a very short time, begun to catalyze and anchor other forms of collective and religious life within and beyond the region. These include: local parish-based expressions across the region; church-planting networks; social enterprises; and initiatives to train parachurch ministers. In doing so, an "adjacent possible" emerges as they work to create and maintain the conditions where this type of adaptive work can take place, multiply, and affect the broader organizational field.[14] While the work within this organizational field responds to the challenges of the field's own shifting, these hubs are also creating and maintaining alternative conditions where new forms of possibility emerge. Much as Walter Powell observes, the changing boundaries of established fields introduces the potential for "quite dramatic forms of institutional change."[15]

In both cases, adaptive work in the PC and OCE occurs against the backdrop of a porous and fluctuating organizational field that provides opportunities to explore new forms of gathering, leadership, education, and organization within the region. Here, between discrete organizations and larger institutional constructs, a field-level analysis shows how the hubs' form of collective activity and adaptive work occurs in an interstitial social space between existing and emerging organizations. At the same time, however, the localized commitments that organize both hubs, and the PC in particular, resist limiting the collective activity strictly to the level of organizational interaction. The adaptive work that organizes their collective engagement with the challenges they face cultivates the conditions for localized parish expression and communities of faith. Meanwhile, the expansion of this work takes place against the backdrop of a porous organizational field. As a result, this identification of the field that creates the conditions for the hubs' adaptive work does not suggest the novelty of their organizational field. Rather, doing so locates this particular kind of adaptive work against a broader organizational backdrop. Moreover, reflecting the fluidity that has marked religion in the Pacific Northwest, the porous boundaries that characterize the hubs' organizational field signals the possibility that they represent a site of transition within the broader organizational field. In other words, the organizational landscape has shifted, and hubs represent a novel way to organize communities of faith. In order to expand this description, I now turn to network theory in order to describe and understand how connections between individual actors and organizations contribute to the adaptive responses within these two sites.

A NETWORK PERSPECTIVE

The adaptive work that organizes the OCE and PC draws heavily on a dense network of relationships and seeks to create the conditions where networks of leaders can partner together. Despite their emergence from different (and largely siloed) organizational fields, both hubs pursue a highly connective and collaborative approach, leading to a dense network of relationships and partnerships. Each hub emerges from and aims to support webs of connection and care across the region. Accordingly, network theory provides an analytical perspective that complements this account of the social conditions that occasion the hubs' adaptive work.

A network is "a system of relationships among parts."[16] The term can describe such a range of social relations, leading some organizational theorist to conclude that "network" has "become the dominant metaphor for our time."[17] Networks are not, however, a single, clearly defined category. Rather, "network" represents a flexible description that categorizes a constellation of relationships.

Although the two cases express this in different language—the OCE describes it as being a "partner" and the PC works to "weave links"—their organizing missions reflect a common vision to connect and resource networks of leaders and the communities those leaders serve. Accordingly, the work that characterizes these organizational and ecclesial adaptations yields a densely networked structure as they seek to resource and connect the work of God in their neighborhoods and communities. Each is both an anchor and a web. Founders of the PC describe it as a "tertiary network" and as a "network and platform."[18] Meanwhile, for the OCE, their work cultivates a "network of relationship" with the Ministry Partnership Network as a focal element. Hence, network theory enriches reflections about the network structure that distinguishes these two hubs and how the structure of this network directs adaptive work within them.

For these hubs, network theory offers resources to consider the enabling conditions, forms of connection, network structure, the relationship between networks, and the emergence of new organizations. Regarding conditions, a prominent organizational theorist, Walter Powell, identifies three components that enable the formation of networks: know-how, the demand for speed, and trust. When combined, these represent the "enabling conditions" that "foster the formation and proliferation of networks."[19] For Powell, networks represent a form of organization that emerges from the complementary strengths of markets and hierarchies and leads to a form of interdependence. Interdependent coordination of relationships and tasks over time promote learning and the dissemination of information such that actors can respond to variation in resources and uncertainties in the environment.[20] For Powell, know-how characterizes roles that require "either intellectual capital or craft-based skills."[21] Powell identifies cultural production (e.g., painting or music), scientific research, and mathematical analysis as examples of roles that require know-how.[22] This form of "fungible knowledge" reflects "tacit knowledge that is difficult to codify."[23] Moreover, networks are well suited to support the formation of network-specific competencies and the sharing of information, which can lead to the formation of shared values.[24]

Second, Powell identifies the demand for speed as a feature that enables the formation of networks. He suggests that corporate environments require "fast access to information, flexibility, and responsiveness to changing tastes."[25] Although Powell's assessment at this point privileges markets and corporations as the principal context of his analysis, his basic insight still merits consideration: networks enable the rapid transmission of information, learning, and resources among those who are connected to a network. They facilitate nimble responses to new information, new challenges, and changing circumstances.[26] This form of information transfer involves a form of "learning by doing" that conveys information and fosters know-how among its members.[27]

Third, trust is required for networks to form and proliferate. Powell characterizes trust as the accumulation of familiarity and reciprocity that emerges from repeated exchanges, but he neglects developing this term. Instead, he suggests that trust is likely to emerge in homogenous contexts and within institutional settings that have adequate legal and political infrastructure to support and sustain them.[28] That is to say, networks are prone to form between individuals and groups who have something in common (e.g., interests, background, ethnicity, gender, religious tradition). They also develop within institutional environments that promote the interaction between individuals, groups, and ideas.

Powell offers two key insights for the present analysis of these two hubs. First, trust is the *sine qua non* for network formation and flourishing. Second, if homogeneity has a positive correlation with trust, the formation of networks that purposefully include heterogeneity—whether it is ideological, denominational, racial, or political—require attention and care.

When considered in relation to the PC and OCE, this description brings into focus the conditions that enabled these networks to form and grow in the first place. First, the networks are built upon decades of accrued trust—both within the region and among friends. At every level of these networks, trust functions like ligaments within the body, connecting disparate parts, spanning gaps, and enabling individuals and organizations to work together. As one interviewee shared: "I think there's just a high level of respect and trust [for the founders]." Once formed, these networks permit nimble, adaptive responses and serve as sites for new connections. For example, the founders of each hub rarely speak up front at their annual events. Yet they remain active in the back of the room and during breaks facilitating and making connections. Like relational air traffic controllers, they make connections and introductions, and with each connection they enhance and expand the collective activity that organizes their work. To borrow language from Tim Soerens, who cofounded the PC, they try to be the "connecting tissues." The result is a network of interconnected faith leaders and communities rooted in their respective contexts. They can respond nimbly when challenges or opportunities arise. In contrast to the economic logic that guides Powell's account, the nimble and adaptive responses that take place in these hubs are locally determined. Examples include organizing faith communities to support immigrant communities after the 2016 presidential election, creating alternative social spaces amid soaring real-estate markets, and gathering individuals in a single room where fifteen different languages are spoken for a common meal. In each case, these adaptive responses require connection and trust in order to coordinate local and collaborative work. And, finally, the animating aims of the network that has formed around each hub requires know-how. The adaptive challenges identified in chapter 3 require more than rote skill or technique; rather, individuals across these hubs observe how a reframing of their imagination is required to pursue religious leadership and faithful presence in their neighborhoods and communities. The form of know-how that is embedded in and emerges from these two hubs moves beyond Powell's description of "either intellectual capital or craft-based skills."[29] It requires a form of Christian practical wisdom.

Furthermore, network theory also offers resources to consider the different forms of connection that comprise the networks that have formed around these hubs. Specifically, network theory distinguishes "strong" and "weak" ties—or the connections between actors within a network. Strong ties represent close connections with "frequent and close contacts."[30] In many cases, strong ties are relationships in which individuals have many connections in common. Strong ties are typically based on trust,[31] include friends, and are frequently the product of a relationship's long duration. Weak ties, in contrast, represent looser forms of affiliation and are less likely to share common connections, but still play a vital role within a broader network. Weak ties are akin to acquaintances and normally require less emotional investment.[32]

Nevertheless, weak ties represent points of contact between otherwise unconnected parts of a broader network. These types of connections within a network provide "vital bridges between disparate clusters that would otherwise not be connected at all."[33] Weak ties are also frequently channels for information[34] between disparate parts of a network and contribute to the formation of collective memories.[35] While homogeneity characterizes strong ties, weak ties are less likely to require (and promote) homogeneous forms of connection.[36] As such, weak ties often provide the connective tissue between disparate members and contribute to the transfer of information between actors and organizations. If the trust that characterizes strong ties provides the cohesion required for durable networks, weak ties—such as acquaintances and other informal relationships—provide the connections required to form and expand networks beyond homogeneous groups.

Strong and weak ties form the webs that surround these adaptive hubs. In addition to the friendships that supported the founding of each hub, the hubs' early organization took place around existing strong ties across the region. As Beck Taylor, who played a key role in launching the OCE, observes: "[I]t's hard to imagine that [the OCE] would've gotten off the ground but for the amazing relational capital that both Terry and Jerry brought to the endeavor." In both cases, the "relational capital," which is to say strong ties, that predated the OCE and PC created the conditions for their formation and expansion. Moreover, their programmatic dimensions strengthen ties by providing additional points of connection between members within this network. Whether expressed in the PC's vision to "weave links" or the OCE's language of "thick relationships," the adaptive work that organizes these hubs builds and strengthens ties between individuals, organizations, and communities that are either estranged or entirely disconnected from one another.

At the same time, weak ties play a critical role within both hubs by connecting disparate networks and facilitating the transmission of information, ideas, and practices. In both cases, each hub depends upon the strength of these weak ties. As an adaptive response to the fragmented and isolated state of leaders, organizations, and communities, organizers seek to connect and coordinate these disparate individuals and communities. Considered together, these individuals become bridges for information, ideas, and connections to move between separated and siloed sectors of the region. As a result, individuals and ideas begin to connect and flow between Vancouver, B.C., Seattle, Tacoma, and Portland. Nonprofits in Spokane begin to link up with churches and community leaders. A network of church planters has cross-pollinating conversations with thought leaders at a local university. A national parachurch ministry begins to resource its leaders to attend to the needs of particular neighborhoods.

While individuals may still note the importance of friendship for the connections linking disparate parts, this level of connection lacks the relational redundancy that characterizes strong ties. These connections also have the fragility that comes from distance or infrequent interaction. In many cases, the organizers of each hub stand at the nexus of multiple, non-redundant networks that engage large numbers of individuals, but nevertheless remain siloed from the others. When they are connected and coordinated within these hubs, these weak ties have a multiplying effect. For example, World Relief has expanded access to volunteers and support through its connection to the OCE and parish-based leaders across the Pacific Northwest are beginning to gather and learn from one another. As a result, through this combination of strong and weak ties, each hub serves as a network of networks in which the PC and OCE engage in a form of adaptive work that connects and coordinates individuals and communities.[37]

Third, network theory aids in assessing the structure of each network and how the webs of connections contribute to each hub's adaptive work. Specifically, network theory identifies the key actors (or nodes) that bear some relationship to one another, and the various forms of relationships (or edges) that comprise a network. A brief introduction to key analytical distinctions in network theory enables us to visualize the networks that are emerging around these hubs, and then to assess the network's structures. Network analysis attends to individuals, groups, organizations, the various patterns of relation between them, and the different patterns of connection across these levels. For example, network theory identifies three units of analysis: the dyadic (or pair), the actor, and the group.[38] The dyadic level attends to the relationship between two individuals, the actor level considers the capacity for an actor (an individual or an organization) to achieve desired outcomes, and the group—or network—level considers the structure of the network and the actors that comprise it. For

OCE Partners Network Visualization

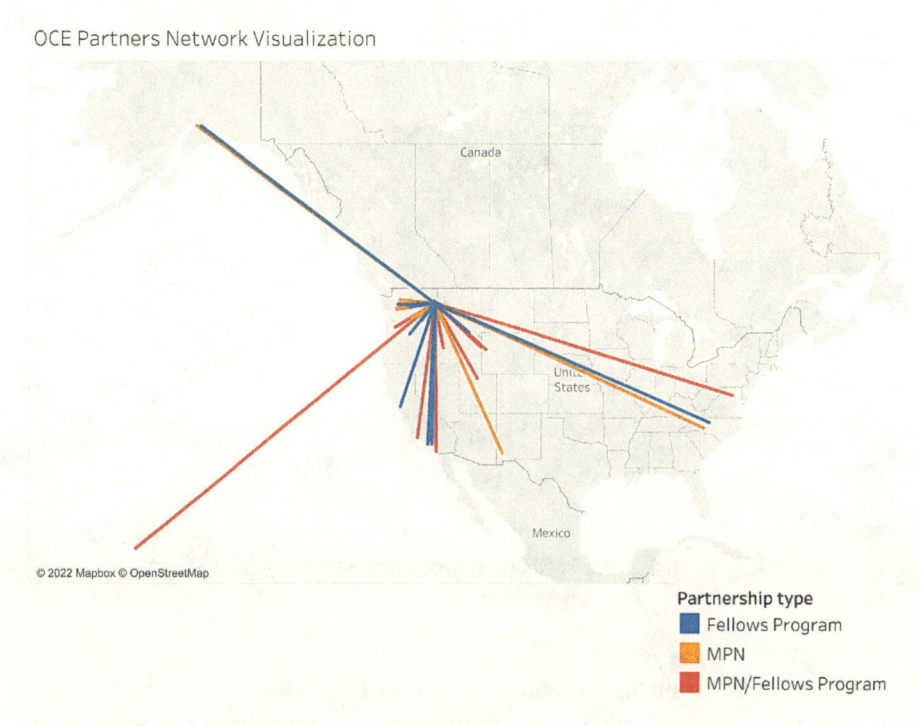

Partnership type
- Fellows Program
- MPN
- MPN/Fellows Program

Fig. 4-1 OCE Partners Network Visualization (National)

each approach, a primary descriptive and analytical task for network theory is to identify and describe the forms of connection that link one node—an individual, actor, or group—to another. Network theory also helpfully notes how different kinds of connection comprise connection between individuals and groups. The identification and construction of a network requires determining the forms of interaction that comprise some form of connection within a network of relationships, and considering how a particular form of connection interacts with other actors. Hence, social analysis—and, as I argue in the second half of this book, practical theology—requires attending to and describing the various patterns and forms of relationship that comprise a given network.

When employed in relation to the present cases, network analysis provides resources to visualize the webs that have emerged around these two hubs.

OCE Partner Visualization

Partnership type
- Fellows Program
- MPN
- MPN/Fellows Program

Fig. 4-2 OCE Partners Network Visualization (Regional)

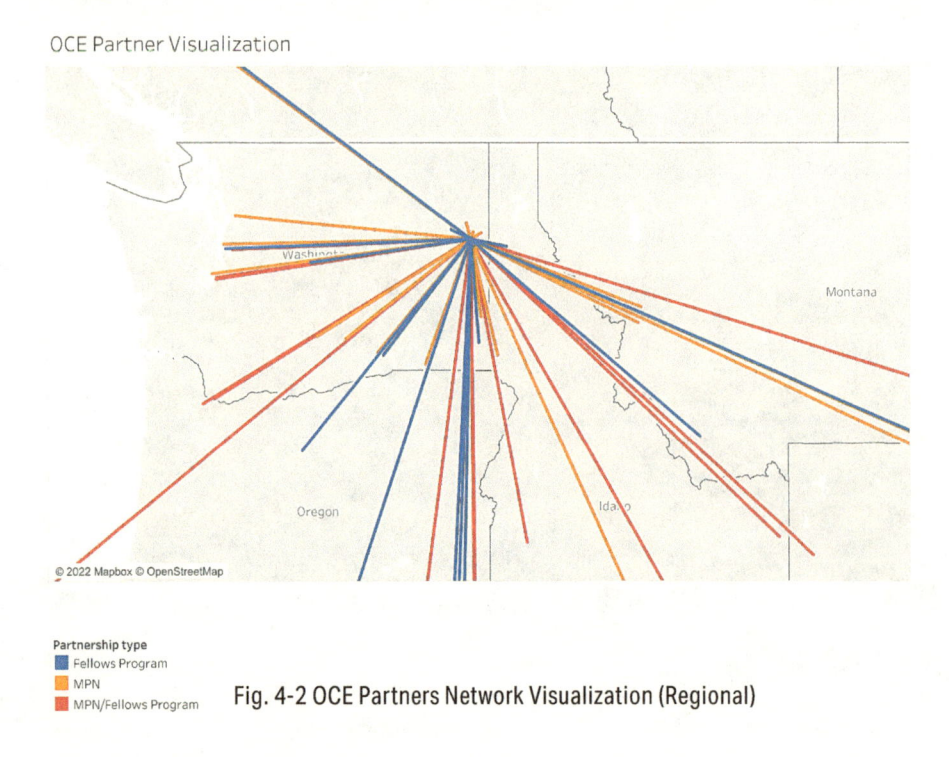

Network visualization, in turn, provides a means to consider the network structure that organizes adaptive work within them. As noted in previous chapters, each hub has organized a network of partnerships around the challenges that reflect each hub's particular location in the Pacific Northwest. For the OCE, this has yielded a network of partners that remains primarily regional, but also includes partners beyond the region. For the PC, this has produced a dense network of regional partners and has begun to reproduce similar clusters in other domestic and international regions where individuals desire more localized expressions of an ecclesial life.

For example, OCE data from the 2018–2019 Ministry Partner Network and Fellows Program provides data to visualize the formal partners that have gathered around the OCE's work. Figures 4-1, 4-2, and 4-3 provide three different perspectives for this visualization. The blue represents partners through the Fellows Program, the red represents partners through the Ministry Partner Network, and the green represents partners that have fellows and are members of the Ministry Partner Network. As noted here, the OCE's network of formal partners is concentrated in the Pacific Northwest, but it also includes domestic

OCE Partner Visualization

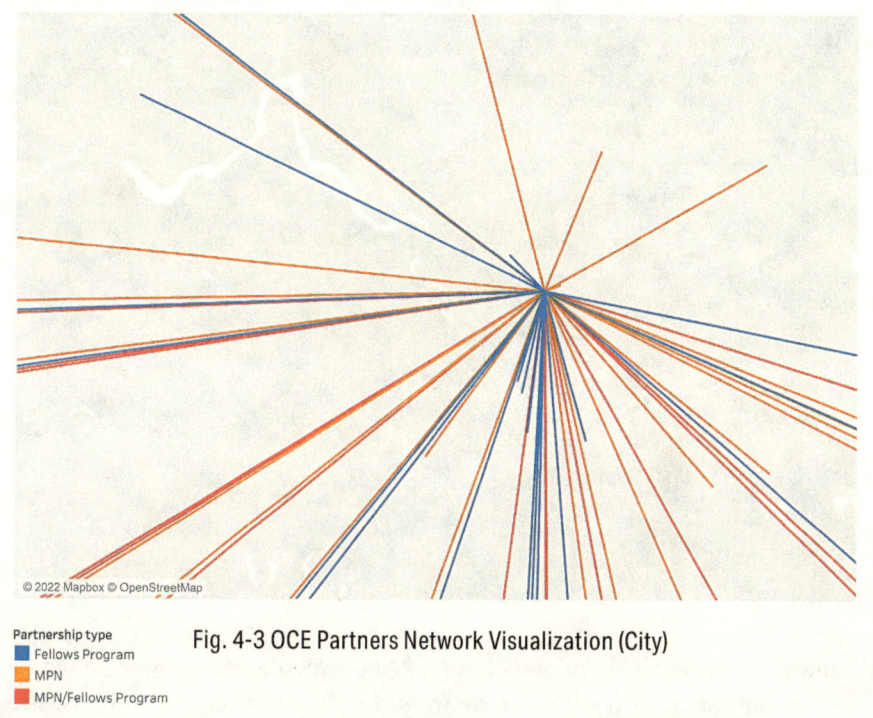

Fig. 4-3 OCE Partners Network Visualization (City)

Partnership type
- Fellows Program
- MPN
- MPN/Fellows Program

and international partners beyond the region. At the regional level, as depicted in figure 4-2, the concentration of partners comes into sharper focus. The OCE has a cluster of partners in Southern California—which is not surprising given the connections between OCE founders and Fuller Theological Seminary in Pasadena—and a handful on the East Coast and in Hawaii and Alaska. Still, the majority of its partners remain regional.

Indeed, as Taylor shared when asked about the partnerships that organize his work, there seem to be different "spheres" of partnership, expanding from partnerships within the city, to partnerships within the region, to partnerships at a national level.

Regarding the city as a primary sphere of partnership, figure 4-3 presents the constellation of formal partnerships that have gathered around the OCE's work. The adaptive work that organizes the OCE's work emerges from its particular location in Spokane, where it seeks to support the conditions for local congregations and ministries to join together in partnership.

At each level, the formal partnerships presented here represent a combination of resource exchange, relational engagement, and the formation of

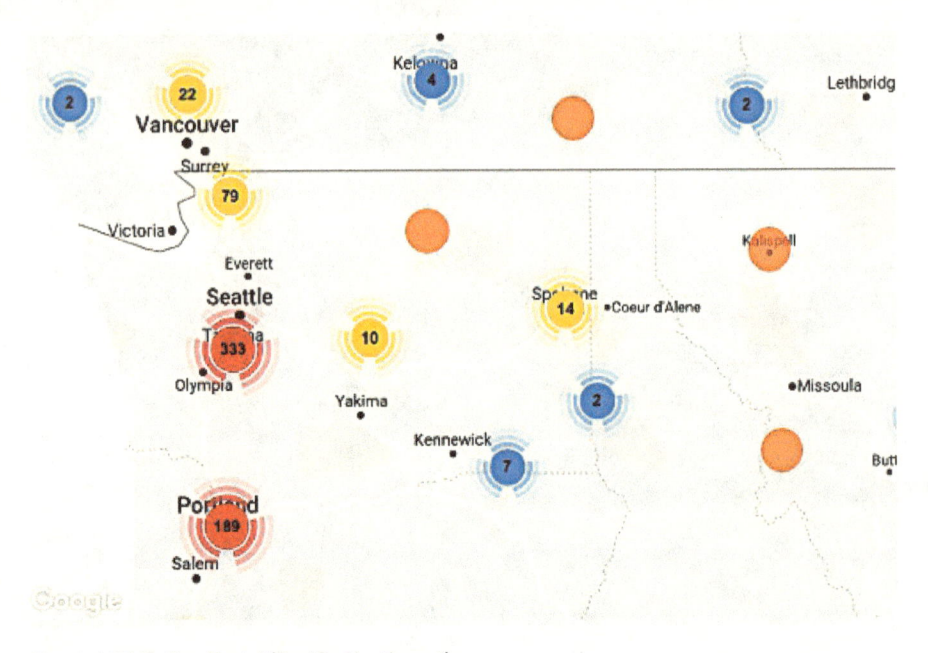

Fig. 4-4 PC Online Portal (Pacific Northwest)

connections through shared relationships and experiences. These include: the cost to join the Ministry Partner Network; funding that fellows and host sites have to raise in order to receive a fellow; and relational engagement between the OCE and Partners and host sites. In the case when all three are present, visualized by the green lines, these "thick relationships" represent clusters of partnership where the OCE and partners are joining together in shared adaptive work.

For the PC, network visualization similarly provides a means to depict and understand the network of relationships and partners that is gathering around their vision to relocate ecclesial life to the neighborhood. The PC's vision to "grow roots" and "weave links" includes a networked vision that reflects their efforts to create a "network and a platform." With this intention in view, individuals can digitally link with other parish-based expressions and discover other practitioners within and beyond their own region through a free, online portal, as presented in figure 4-4. While their online portal provides an on-ramp for practitioners to identify and connect with other practitioners in their region, their recent membership program introduces a second avenue for partnership.

The PC is cultivating an international network of parish practitioners. Although this work remains geographically clustered in the Pacific Northwest, similar hubs of localized, collaborative activity are appearing in Canada,

Australia, and the United Kingdom. In each case, these expanded partnerships emerge from and involve relational engagement between the PC's organizers and local practitioners within a region. Without detracting from the significance of their global organizing work, the form of partnership visualized here represents a network that prioritizes interpersonal connections. Individuals can join the PC portal at no cost (apart from providing an email) and membership rates range from $29 to $99 per month. These separate initiatives provide avenues for individuals to access and expand their partnerships, but interpersonal connections remain the focus. Thus, the primary form of connection visualized here represents a loose form of affiliation. When compared to the network that has organized around the OCE's work, the PC network includes more linkages dispersed across a wider geography, but the majority of these connections represent connections to individuals (rather than congregations or organizations). Accordingly, they have a lower barrier of entry to engage with this network. This comparison does not provide a basis to draw conclusions about the respective merits of either network, but it does provide a point to consider the different kinds of networks that organize the respective hubs' adaptive work.

The structure of these specific networks comes into sharper focus when a macro view of each network is considered alongside a qualitative assessment of the partnerships that surround each site. Through semi-structured interviews, I asked, "Who are the key individuals or organizations that you consider partners for your work?" Figure 4-5 provides additional insight into the relational structure that organizes these hubs. With the PC on the left and the OCE on the right, this visualization preserves the west-east orientation from the previous visualizations. Responses from the founders of each hub confirm that founders have no direct connection to the other at the time of our initial interviews. Indeed, they are connected, but intermediary organizations provide bridges between the founders of one hub and the other. Although these hubs have some connections in common, their structure and organization largely remain siloed from the other. Further, the networks visualized here represent the relational forms of partnership that organize this collective work within the region. In some cases, individuals' responses do represent some form of formal partnership at the organizational level (e.g., Navigators), but the identification of an organizational partner was frequently followed by mentioning a specific individual within that organization that is the primary connection. Hence, the kinds of connections presented here are relationally inflected points of contact, each of which has its own history and context.

PC   OCE

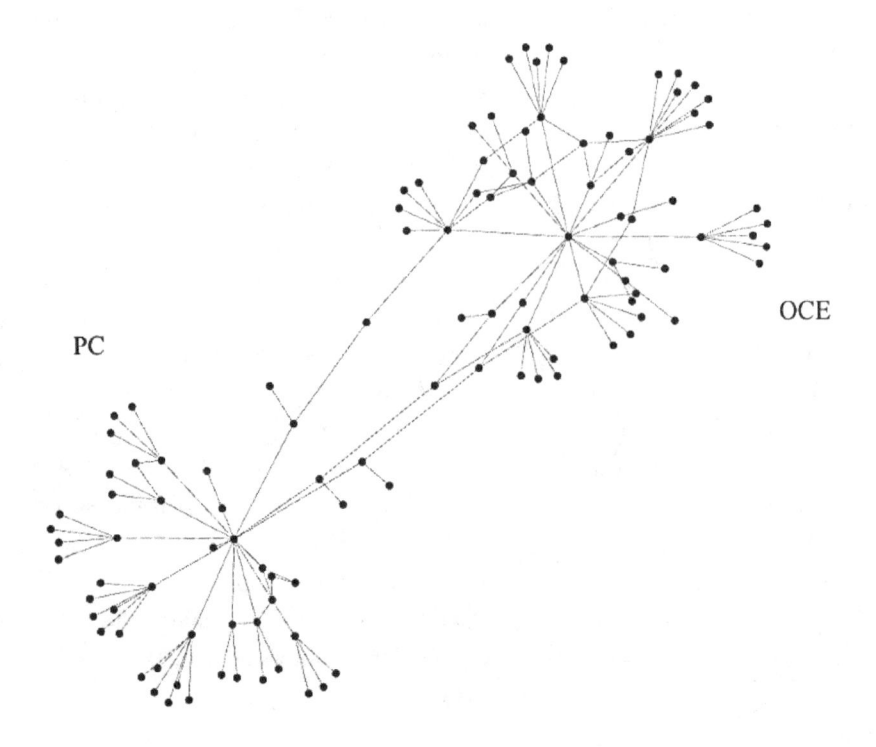

Fig. 4-5 OCE and PC Relational Network

Beyond the siloed character of this visualization, four of its features briefly merit note. First, each hub represents a network of networks. Several nodes identified in each network represent extensive networks of their own that engage individuals and communities reaching far beyond the organizing work of either hub. These include: V3, Thresholds, The Northwest Church Planting Network, and World Relief. The relational connection to these networks exponentially multiplies both the number of individuals and organizations that gather around these adaptive hubs and the kinds of partners they engage.

Second, these siloed networks are connected by various intermediary organizations. Specifically, The Murdock Charitable Trust, Whitworth University, and Young Life represent nodal points within this network, providing potential means to link the adaptive work that takes place in one hub to the other. The diverse organizations that bridge the gap between the OCE and PC should not be overlooked. One is a charitable foundation, another is a Christian college, and yet another is a parachurch ministry. As noted at the beginning of this chapter, the diversity of organizations that provide potential bridges between one network and the other reflects the broader organizational field in which this shared kind of adaptive work takes place.

Third, interviewees identify both individuals and organizations as partners. While the network above primarily presents organizational partners, participants frequently identify a specific relational connection to organizational partners. When viewed in this light, there is a higher concentration of individual connections within the PC's network than in the OCE's. This concentration reinforces the point that they represent different kinds of networks, but also directs attention to the priority of these direct, interpersonal connections within the overall network. Networks are never organizational partnerships alone; rather, the strength of the network, especially regarding networks that engage in adaptive work, hinges on the individual relational connections that bind it together.

Fourth, the average number of partners interviewees identified is 3.6. With some individuals identifying more than three and some fewer, the mode is two. While these figures could be read as points of statistical comparison, they may also reflect the standard capacity of individuals within these networks to recall the specific partners that organize and support their work. Admittedly, each individual could identify additional partners if given more time or prompting. However, if these figures in fact represent the limits of respondents' ability to recall the individuals or organizations that serve as partners for their work, it suggests the priority of these primary partnerships, only heightening their importance.

Finally, this visualization provides a means to consider a final feature of these networks: they create the contexts for entrepreneurial activity and the emergence of new organizational forms. Due to the structure of networks—which includes both strong and weak ties—individuals and organizations within a network have access to resources, relationships, and information that they otherwise would not possess. Across both networks, the relationships and partnerships that have formed around them have enriched individuals and communities, frequently affirming and encouraging the work that local leaders are doing. As a result, participation in networks positively correlates to individuals' ability to pursue innovative and entrepreneurial activities. Aldrich and Ruef express the impact of social networks on entrepreneurial activity in terms of "resource mobilization."[39] Indeed, the PC and OCE have the capacity to facilitate the transfer of existing ideas, resources, relationships, and information. If, as noted in the first chapter, new organizations are often "hatched within existing organizational arrangements,"[40] the OCE and PC serve as an ecclesial and organizational gestation space where new practices and new forms of religious organizations can emerge. Similarly, through their efforts to resource and connect local leaders and communities, they are working to create the social conditions in which ecclesial entrepreneurs consider, explore, and resource innovations and entrepreneurial ideas. While this kind of religious and organizational entrepreneurship can occur within any network, these kindred organizational and ecclesial adaptations reflect the distinct entrepreneurial ethos of religion in the Pacific Northwest.

Nevertheless, it is not just the presence of networks that incubates new ideas and organizational forms. As Niall Ferguson notes:

> Networks are important not just as transmission mechanisms for new ideas, but as the sources of the new ideas themselves. Not all networks are likely to foster change; on the contrary, some dense and clustered networks have the tendency to resist it. But the point of contact between diverse networks may be the place to look for novelty. The question is what the nature of the point of contact is.[41]

Networks do not necessarily foster new ideas and promote innovation. Even though they have the capacity to foster change, they do not all function in this way. The nature of the contact between individuals or other actors within a network is the decisive point of analysis. As described above, the trust-filled relationships and diversity of partners that characterize these networks create a generative context to foster and explore new ideas and partnerships.

While network analysis has the capacity to identify the actors within an overall system and consider the various relations between them, the metaphor of a "network" reaches its limit when one attempts to describe the relationship between actors and the changes within the overall system. It is one thing to describe the structure of relationship within a network, but a different metaphor is required to describe the dynamic process of change within the broader system of meaning and relations: that of ecology. Functioning as an anchor and a web, each hub exists within a shifting ecology of resources, partners, and organizations.[42] To address this need, this final section considers how insights from organizational ecology offer resources to attend to and describe the ecclesial ecology that supports and surrounds the OCE and PC.

AN ECOLOGICAL PERSPECTIVE

An ecological approach describes the dynamic structure of these hubs and locates their adaptive work within a broader network of relations—or organizational ecology—that sustains change within and beyond these hubs. A field-level approach draws attention to the overlapping organizational fields that create the context for the adaptive work that occurs within these two sites. A network approach, on the other hand, demonstrates the dense network of relations that represent connective, trust-filled sinews, supporting the conditions to imagine, pursue, and organize collective responses to the challenges individuals face. Nevertheless, these two approaches lack explanatory capacity to consider how the relationship between the broader field of organized religious life and the network of relationships contributes to the precise organizational form these collaborative hubs represent. Accordingly, this final section introduces an ecological perspective and considers how insights from this approach can contribute to this account of these twin sites.[43]

An ecological approach is a theory of organizational change. As introduced by Michael Hannan and John Freeman, organizational ecology examines groups of organizations—which are frequently described as "populations"—over long periods of time in order to understand the conditions that support the formation of new organizations and the disbanding of existing organizations. As Hannan and Freeman observe, the animating question that drives this approach is "[H]ow does change in larger systems affect the forms of organization in society?"[44] By attending to the constellation of changes that take place in their surrounding organizational environment, this approach is well suited to consider "conditions under which transformation occurs"[45] as well as the priority and practice of leadership during organizational transition or uncertainty.[46] As Hannan and Freeman write: "[E]cological analysis is appropriate when organizations are subject to strong inertial pressures and face changeable, uncertain environments."[47] Organizational change is a process of adaptation to factors that are extraneous to organizations, not a strategic process that leaders within organizations guide.[48]

Organizational ecology also explains why some organizations become resistant to change. It suggests that, once established and legitimized, organizations develop inertia such that change within an organization becomes successively more difficult as an organization ages. That is to say, organizations are comprised of human systems and—much like living organisms—possess an organic quality that is adaptive but also becomes resistant to change the longer they exist. Like an acorn that takes root and sprouts into a sapling, organizations' organic qualities leave them vulnerable during their early stages, but it also makes them very difficult to uproot and replant once they mature. Accordingly, this approach suggests that change readily occurs either early in an organization's life cycle or by introducing new organizational forms into the surrounding organizational ecology.

As anchors and webs, each hub exists within a dynamic ecology of relationships and seeks to catalyze change across the organizations they serve. They aspire to be nimble and adaptive, but each emerges from a particular organizational environment. Organizational ecology clarifies the novel organizational form organizers at each hub foster. First, an ecological approach identifies organizational forms in order to consider the relationship between individual organizations and the broader field of similar organizations. For organizational ecologists, the organizational form "gives a unitary character"[49] to organizations that share common features. For the specific population that serves as the focus of this study, research in sociology of religion typically distinguishes between theological schools, Christian colleges, congregations, and faith-based nonprofits. While the adaptive work across both hubs complicates these designations, this description of organizational forms directs attention to the similarities and distinctions among organizations and partners across these two hubs.

The identification of organizational boundaries provides a second means to clarify the structure of organizational forms and consider the relationship between organizational change and a broader organizational ecology. Respondents' descriptions of the mission of their work or organization suggest the presence of at least six organizational clusters across these two fields:

- a congregational form that seeks to serve those who have been gathered together in a faith community;
- an educational form that seeks to educate individuals and communities;
- a resourcing form that seeks to support and resource individuals and communities;
- a parish form organized by a commitment to local community and practice;
- a connectional form that links ministry leaders and communities of faith;
- a service form that seeks to engage individuals and communities in benevolence toward marginalized communities.

While the organizers of these hubs explain their work in relation to each of these six forms, the priority of the local parish-based or congregation-based expressions remains the central emphasis of their work. Meanwhile, the individuals and organizations that have gathered around this work tend to emphasize one of these missional commitments.

As organizational forms emerge, evidence of successful collective action and a common expertise strengthens them. Just as the repetition of collective action at longer-running organizations contributes to the preservation of organizational boundaries (e.g., admitting students, conferring degrees, hosting regular worship events), new avenues for collective action also change the existing boundaries within this field. In both cases, some early form of successful collective action contributed to each hub's growth: a successful grant application, convening a group of parish leaders, a city-wide gathering in Spokane in response to a perceived crisis in immigrant communities, annual conferences that resource and support ministry leaders, and the multiplication of parish-expressions and conferences in domestic and international sites. As each hub grows, organizers' ability to continue successful forms of collective action at each point of growth will be required to continue its particular form of adaptive work.

Shared expertise also reinforces emerging organizational boundaries. The adaptive work that organizes these sites requires both technical expertise and practical wisdom. In their discussion of the nature of their collaborative work, the chief organizers of the PC draw attention to a shared practice of connecting with individuals within their specific communities. Although each individual brings different forms of technical expertise to this work, they share an understanding of the craft required to create conditions where individuals and communities encounter one another. A similar feature characterizes the team that organizes the OCE's adaptive work. In each case, these teams have the technical ability to organize and accomplish the tasks that their work requires (e.g., submitting grants, teaching, hosting conferences, connecting in partnerships). But technical competency alone cannot achieve their stated mission if it is separated from the practical wisdom that directs and animates it. The form of leadership that emerges from them requires practical wisdom to direct this work.

Two external factors also contribute to the establishment of new organizational forms. First, legitimization from other powerful actors within populations of organizations enables individuals to identify discrete organizational forms. Partnerships with existing educational institutions (e.g., Whitworth University and The Seattle School of Theology & Psychology) conferred a degree of legitimacy during the early stages for each innovative hub. Similarly, grants from regional and national foundations supported the formation and expansion of these sites. These awards both validate the work of the OCE and PC and provide forums for their leaders to meet and engage with other grant recipients. Finally, partnerships among individuals within and beyond these organizations and writing about the work that occurs within them provide additional legitimacy to their work and organization.[50]

New organizational forms also emerge when they begin to be taken for granted in the minds of actors within an organizational field. As demonstrated in the chapters up to this point, these hubs share a densely networked, collaborative structure. They are organized by a mission to partner with individuals and organizations with the hope of resourcing, connecting, and revitalizing local forms of Christian witness and practice. In doing so, these sites draw upon and emerge alongside existing organizational forms, but they also represent a point of transition within this broader organizational ecology. Admittedly, the networked, multiorganizational, and collaborative character that marks these hubs can cause some confusion and ambiguity. Are they parachurch organizations? Are they a subsidiary of a host educational institution? Are they simply networks of churches?

Rather than pressing them into existing organizational forms, however, it is better to consider the possibility that they represent a novel form of organizing Christian communities in response to the adaptive challenges they face. Indeed, as participants and partners across these two hubs share about the organizing work of the OCE and PC, they utilize similar language to describe the organizing mission of these two adaptive hubs. They are "bridge" spaces that seek to "connect" and "resource" individuals and communities, nurturing the conditions that enable dually ecclesial and organizational adaptations. They are marked by "relational fidelity" and a commitment to the well-being of local faith communities, neighborhoods, and the network of relationships that have gathered around their work. And, demonstrating a form of Christian practical wisdom, each is "rooted in a tradition that affirms the good"[51] and engages in this collective work "for the sake of others."[52]

The OCE and PC represent a novel form of organizing religious life, a hub. As an anchor, each hub grounds religious life within a particular place. As a web, each hub fosters the types of connection that support local religious life. Emerging from the Pacific Northwest's entrepreneurial ethos, each hub resources local leaders to respond adaptively to the challenges they face.[53]

Further, the OCE's and PC's work occurs in proximity to shifts within the broader ecology, including the demise of existing organizations and the introduction of new organizations. This includes the death or disbanding of several theological schools in the region—including Fuller Theological Seminary's Seattle Extension Campus—and the addition of new programs or institutions into the theological education space.[54] Nevertheless, the catalog of challenges that organizes these hubs suggests that these adaptations do not emerge principally in response to changes in the organizational environment, but in response to the challenges that confront local communities of faith and ministry leaders. According to the organizers and partners, these particular adaptations do not principally reflect small shifts in the organizational population, but an attempt to reimagine the practices of organization, education, and leadership that nurture communities of faith and their local expressions. As Dave Harder observes: "Our consumer models of church are dying and dying quickly, and the only way forward is for us to reconsider how we be the church in the neighborhood. . . . Our colonial, Christendom idea of church, where church as a way of belief, church as building, church as institution, is non-existence; we have to get back to this Jesus way of creating that space of inclusion and love in the neighborhoods where we live." And, as McGonigal, the OCE's director, similarly notes: "Everybody recognizes that there are challenges, that we don't control these factors," and then queries, "How do we imagine being church in the future?"

Thus, these densely networked, collaborative centers that have emerged out of and alongside existing religious organizations in the region are disrupting and reshaping the broader organizational ecology within the Pacific Northwest. Although established organizations have provided organizational space and resources to support and catalyze the formation of the OCE and PC, their development extends beyond a single catalyzing organization. Moreover, the common connective, linking, and resourcing work that organizes these hubs redounds to existing organizations. If, as organizational ecologists note, the inertia that governs established organizations also shows that change prompts the introduction of new forms or new actors, the organization and growth of these hubs has the capacity to disrupt and invite similar forms of adaptive work in the ecclesial ecology.

A final feature of these hubs merits note: leaders' agency during periods of change and uncertainty.[55] If organizations principally change in response to variation in their broader ecology and then increasingly resist structural and strategic changes as they age and accrue legitimacy, organizational leaders have to work within a limited range of changes they can implement. This restricted ability manifests itself in various ways. The organizational form itself can limit change by "constrain[ing] the choices available for any organizational members, including managers."[56] Second, the finite resources within an organizational ecology limit leaders' ability to execute change. Further, the existing allocation of resources and "pattern of competition" narrows the scope of possible changes.[57] Just as species and professionals that survive selection processes come to occupy a narrow niche that provides adequate resources and incentives to support their life and work, organizations find a niche that both supports and constrains leadership within them. The calcified pattern of competition restricts a leader's ability to initiate and execute organizational change. Finally, the limits of human rationality constrain leaders' ability to identify the range of possible changes.[58] As Herbert Simons, one of the fathers of organizational studies, observed, an unlimited rationality would make administrative and organizational studies "barren."[59] Consequently, the range of organizational changes that are both known and realizable is constrained by the organizational context in which a leader serves.

Nevertheless, the time surrounding organizational founding and uncertainty grants leaders expanded capacity to make change. Leaders have an opportunity to implement changes earlier in the life cycle of organizations because there remains some fluidity in the organizational structure and collective process. Boundaries are still forming, specific patterns and practices are not yet taken for granted, and an organization has yet to settle into a specific niche. In the period before the organizational structures have calcified and a broader organizational ecology has fully adapted to a new organization, leaders are less constrained by the givens that restrict their ability to identify and implement change.

Leaders also play an integral role during periods of transition and in moments of uncertainty. Hannan and Freeman express the implications of their theory in this way:

> If the odds of survival run against organizations with a particular variant, this does not mean that an organization choosing that variant is doomed. But it does mean that managerial skills matter a great deal in such circumstances. If there is a time when managerial acumen does not matter, it is when the dice are loaded so heavily in favor of the organizational variant in question that it could hardly fail.[60]

Leadership within organizations that occupy a favorable position within the broader ecology requires a different form of practical wisdom as compared to those that occupy a marginal or transitional position. In moments of change, leaders have the capacity to organize the work and collective activity within a community in ways that address the challenges they face. As leaders across these organizational and ecclesial adaptations work to support the conditions for "new wineskins for new wine" they are trying to reimagine the forms that support and sustain communities of faith. Moreover, as individuals gather around these innovative centers in the Pacific Northwest, their work represents a transitional phase within a broader ecclesial ecology that invites and requires a particular form of leadership in order to support the conditions in which adaptive change occurs.[61]

CONCLUSION

Before transitioning to the second half of this book, it is necessary to acknowledge several potential questions that may emerge at this point in the argument. Specifically, what is the common story across these two adaptive hubs in the Pacific Northwest? Is this a story of outposts of resistance amid undeniable decline of religion in America? Is it a story of the changing of the guard among (primarily) Protestant Christianity in which a missional vision eclipses its mainline forebearers? Is it a story of the signs of renewal through more densely connected and localized ecclesial expressions? Is it a story of the Spirit of God crossing boundaries and connecting communities in unwieldy and unexpected ways? Is it the story of the future of the Church?

The evidence presented here provides partial support for each conclusion, but these narratives would offer, at best, only a partial account of the broader story. At worst, they would offer a crass generalization about highly complex communities. Instead, here is the through line: this is a story about the Christian practical wisdom that supports and sustains adaptive work as individuals and communities reimagine the practices of organization, education, and leadership that order a common life. In the face of the challenges that confront communities of faith, collaborative hubs are emerging—each with their own history and context—that share a vision to support the conditions where individuals and communities reimagine church.

III

A Practical Theology for an Adaptive Church

5

Reimagining Church
Pastoral and Ecclesial Imagination for Adaptive Change

On a crisp and clear Saturday morning in Seattle, I find myself wandering the neighborhood around Pike Place market. It is the second day of the PC's Inhabit Conference, and, courtesy of construction blocking a main intersection—and possibly the swirl of conversations I have been having—I am struggling to find an out-of-the-way, specialty coffee shop where I am scheduled to meet Dave Harder. After climbing a narrow stairway that bottlenecks before turning 180 degrees, I pass a whiskey bar and then finally find my way to Storyville Coffee, and spot Harder near the coffee bar.

He wears white Converse shoes, a light blazer, and thick-rimmed glasses; his hair is cropped close along the sides and neatly styled on top. He combines the classic and the cutting edge. While we talk over coffee, I realize his appearance reflects his mode of theological engagement and the ecclesial vision that organizes his work. Serving at the edge of established religious organizations, Harder works to combine the best of the Christian tradition with presence in cities and neighborhoods. A fire burns in a stove behind me. Looking through a wall of windowpanes, I can see the Olympic Mountains clearly across Puget Sound. I later find myself thinking: "If there is such a thing as the quintessential Seattle experience, this must be very close to the ideal."

Harder, who is Canadian and has a long history of relationship with Tim Soerens and Paul Sparks, speaks passionately about the need for "new metaphors" and "new ways to imagine what this may become." Reflective of the broader values that organize adaptive work across these two hubs, Harder notes the importance of the Jesus way, relationship and community, presence, and creativity and imagination. When asked to clarify the final value, he notes: "A lot of my shifts theologically have come from the wisdom of my place. And wisdom has come from community . . . [a] communal way of learning. . . . I bring a story, a way, a history, a tradition, and so do they; and if we can have this reciprocity—this giving and receiving—in community I grow in wisdom." Several of these themes speckle this narrative already (e.g., imagination, wisdom, community, learning). Yet with imagination, Harder expresses the way in which the other elements are intrinsically, and necessarily, related within the broader account of adaptive work. Specifically, even as the adaptive work that distinguishes these hubs involves distinct individual and collective efforts to respond to the challenges communities face, the OCE's and PC's founders also share a common understanding of their work as an ecclesial enterprise. More specifically, they have a common understanding of their ecclesial organization, education, and leadership as a dynamic expression of the practices required to cultivate and release imaginative faculties. Just as each hub pursues the forms of possibility and meaning that new forms of communion and gathering require, these existing and emerging collaborations comprise gestation spaces for adaptive and collective work. In its most condensed form, their shared work reflects a vision to "reimagine church."[1]

Before proceeding, a brief note is required about the rhetorical shift between the conclusion of Part II and the beginning of Part III. While the first half of this project has largely sought to describe the structure and practice of adaptive change across these two hubs, the argument now shifts to consider the ecclesial imagination that is embedded in these particular collaborative hubs, which includes the conditions that enable this kind of ecclesial innovation to be done more faithfully. For some, the final statement may evoke suspicion and ire. Although an ostensibly interdisciplinary approach guides the argument up to this point, it proceeds on a descriptive register, with the concerns of theology largely (and purposefully) concealed. Admittedly, the statement above is of the kind that cannot be proven.[2] The teleological vision and explicit ecclesial center that grounds these kindred adaptations invite—and, I think, require—moving beyond a descriptive register. Accordingly, this chapter and the chapters that follow explicitly engage theology in order to show how this kind of Christian practical wisdom works.[3] This form of engagement points to the imagination and possibility that directs adaptive change in light of the reality and promises of God. Combining these field-driven concepts with insights drawn from the Christian tradition, I theologically redescribe the Christian practical wisdom that nurtures an adaptive church.

This chapter has three parts. The first part introduces and reviews Craig Dykstra's account of ecclesial and pastoral imagination in order to constructively engage the exercise of imagination at play across these hubs. When considered in relation to the insights from organizational ecology that concluded chapter 4, this provides an occasion to consider the properties of the dynamic ecclesial ecology that organizes adaptive change across these two hubs. Specifically, this ecclesial ecology both constitutes the places and serves as a prism that nurtures and directs the imaginative faculties adaptation requires. Third, and finally, this chapter concludes by using the sites' work to constructively extend Dykstra's account to consider the conditions that foster pastoral and ecclesial imagination.

REIMAGINING CHURCH: PASTORAL AND ECCLESIAL IMAGINATION

Individuals across the PC and OCE share a common understanding of their collective work as an act of (re)imagination. Organizers and participants across both hubs express the imaginative activity variously as "shalomic imagination," as "reimagining church," as "collective imagination," and as "parish imagination." Still, the precise meaning of these phrases frequently remains obliquely defined. Rather, they gesture toward a way of seeing and being that includes the self in relation to others, or the need to come to see oneself—and others—in this new manner. Organizers' and participants' ecclesial innovation occurs on the edge "between the familiar and the emergent,"[4] and crafts new forms out of the relationships and resources at hand. Like an artist, their work requires imagination, even if they cannot provide a full description of this category.[5]

In this absence, Dykstra's essay "Pastoral and Ecclesial Imagination" describes a form of presence that resonates with the organizing practices of these two hubs. Importantly, it also provides a conceptual framework that directs attention to the conditions that enable organizational and ecclesial adaptation. For Dykstra, "imagination" describes a way of seeing and being filled with "the capacity to perceive the 'more' in what is already before us." As he explains, "It is the capacity to see beneath the surface of things, to get beyond the obvious and the merely conventional, to note the many aspects of any particular situation, to attend to the deep meaning of things."[6] The imagination Dykstra describes includes a mode of being that requires attention to the affective, trans-historical, somatic, and communal ways of being in and with the world.[7] The result is an understanding of imagination as an integral component of individual, social, and ecclesial life. An "integrating process" is required to apprehend the "linkages between ourselves and our world," and to discern how God's entanglement with(in) or world renews our imaginations.[8]

The primary focus of Dykstra's account, however, is not a general theory of imagination, but a situated understanding of the conditions that contribute to the flourishing of communities of faith and their leaders.[9] Dykstra identifies the "symbiotic" relationship between pastoral and ecclesial imagination, which—when nurtured over time and in the context of a community—enable individuals and communities to live in light of the reality and promises of God.[10]

> Pastoral imagination and ecclesial imagination live, if they live at all, in a perpetual and dynamic process of mutual interdependence. They are symbiotic. They are caught up with each other in a virtuous circle.... The church's ecclesial imagination is the essential condition for fostering and shaping the pastoral imagination. At the same time, pastoral ministry, undergirded and guided by a truly rich pastoral imagination, is an essential condition for the continual fostering and shaping of the church's ecclesial imagination.[11]

Pastoral and ecclesial imagination exist in an inseparable "spiral of mutual influence, encouragement, and empowerment."[12] Pastoral imagination describes the entirety of how a pastoral leader "see[s] and interpret[s] the world,"[13] including "specific capacities of mind, spirit, and action" obtained through ministry and required for ministering well.[14] Moreover, this formation and exercise of pastoral imagination requires a form of "practical know-how."[15] Theological education certainly fosters this kind of know-how, but it finds its final form and expression in service of an ecclesial community.[16] As Dykstra observes, imagination takes form over time and is nurtured by "learning humanity," a "disciplined spiritual life,"[17] and formation through Christian practice.[18]

Reflecting the form of thought and practice that organizes these two hubs, Dykstra also demonstrates how pastoral imagination can only be received as a "gift" and requires a practice of listening.[19] This kind of Imagination emerges within educational, social, and ecclesial settings that enable leaders to see the "more," to see the spaces within the communities they serve that shimmer with divine presence and possibility.[20]

The formation of a sufficiently flexible pastoral imagination cannot be separated from ecclesial imagination. According to Dykstra, ecclesial imagination "is the way of seeing and being that emerges when a community of faith, together as a community, comes increasingly to share the knowledge of God and to live a way of abundant life—not only in church but also in the many contexts where they live their daily life."[21] Ecclesial imagination envisions a way of seeing and being—reflecting what we have described as practical wisdom—that arises from and through the social relations that texture a community of faith. The form of community Dykstra describes emerges in response to God's activity in time and history and through participation in Christ. Organized by his understanding of "a way of life abundant,"[22] Dykstra's work proceeds on the premise that there is a way of life that is emerging from the "uneasiness" of "times of yearning."[23] Pursued over time in the company of others, amid the quotidian reality of human existence, this way of life invites individuals to receive God's gift by "liv[ing] for the sake of others, and indeed for the sake of all creation."[24] Ultimately, the reality and promises of God orient ecclesial imagination, leading to a faith-filled expression within both the congregational setting and the extra-ecclesial places where faith is formed and practiced.

Although several others have adopted Dykstra's conceptual framework and applied it to study theological education, pedagogy, and pastoral practice,[25] existing research emphasizes pastoral imagination. Granted, Dykstra devotes the majority of his essay to describe pastoral imagination, but he clearly—and repeatedly—states how pastoral and ecclesial imagination exist in a symbiotic relationship.[26] An exclusive focus on pastoral imagination ironically overlooks Dykstra's fundamental insight. He does not argue for a distinct form of pastoral imagination that can be segmented and studied, but that the formation and flourishing of pastoral imagination occurs alongside and through the places where ministry is practiced. Just as pastoral imagination nurtures ecclesial imagination, ecclesial imagination supports the conditions where pastoral imagination forms and flourishes over time.[27] Like a double helix, the two are inseparably intertwined. The growth of one enriches the other; if either diminishes, communities of faith and those who serve them will weaken.

The adaptive change that organizes the OCE and PC exemplifies Dykstra's insight. As Harder notes, his work proceeds along a "communal way of learning." He understands his work as inseparable from "place" and the "giving and receiving" that marks his community. And, importantly, this individual and collective form of learning represents a form of "wisdom." In one way or another, the ecclesial adaptation across both of these hubs reflects Dykstra's fundamental insight, but in ways particular to each hub's adaptive aim.

For the OCE, its work proceeds on the premise that the congregation represents the fundamental building block for faith formation, religious leadership, and the ecology of extra-ecclesial institutions.[28] Although their work involves "reimagining church," the OCE's programs and partners largely preserve an understanding of the congregation as a discrete social setting and the pastor as an identifiable role within a congregation. Nonetheless, their work also aims to reestablish historic connections between congregations and church-related institutions, accentuating the embeddedness of congregations—and pastoral ministry—within a network of partnerships. As the founders note, their work simultaneously seeks to be a "bridge" and "catalyst." They aim to create and maintain the conditions such that older partnerships can be renewed and new ones formed. With partnership as an organizing commitment, they are able to craft conditions that enable what Kathryn Tanner calls "non-rivalrous forms of social coordination."[29] They understand this collaborative work as a way to "reimagine church."

Similarly, the PC's founders and participants use the language of "imagination" to describe the scope and aims of their work, but for them, imagination functions with a slightly different ecclesial referent.[30] As noted in previous chapters, their work proceeds on the premise that it is necessary to rethink the way church works in relation to its place. As Harder noted: "[T]he only way forward is for us to reconsider how we be the church in the neighborhood.... Our colonial, Christendom idea of church, where church as a way of belief, church as building, church as institution, is non-existence." And, for many individuals within this network, attention to and presence in the neighborhood initiated a "slow conversion" to see the neighborhood as the ecclesial center where worship and church take place.

This final claim merits some clarification. While the PC's founders understand the center of ecclesial existence in relation to a definite locale, they do not seek to supplant the local church. Indeed, as Sparks, Soerens, and Friesen observe: "The life of worship is more than what you do together at your Sunday gathering; it encompasses the whole of your collective lives together.... The local church learns to rely on the Spirit's movement in every situation as a way of being faithfully present to the relationships in your context."[31] As Sparks describes it, this simultaneously social and pneumatic movement requires an "ecological imagination" in order to see how individuals and communities, organizations and institutions, and neighborhoods and congregations are interconnected. In this sense, this description of the neighborhood as the ecclesial center preserves an essential position for local congregations within neighborhoods, but it also reorients and refocuses ecclesial life in relation to its place. Soerens states the consequences forcefully: "[W]e need to see a revolution happen in how we imagine what it means to be human; and we feel like that's the point of the actual local church." While this move to the neighborhood does not entirely ignore existing congregations—quite the opposite is true—the primary site where the imaginative transformation takes place is not the congregation, but the neighborhood. Moreover, as Harder noted at the beginning of the chapter, discipleship in the neighborhood initiates various forms of unlearning that a place-based ecclesial existence requires. The result is an understanding of the need, both, to reimagine the practice of church, including its forms of gathering, and to cultivate a "new imagination for connecting the particular to the universal, the local to the global."[32] The result is a "movement" of activists and organizers, pastors and parish leaders, megachurches and mainliners, academics and parachurch workers, each of whom seeks to reimagine the church in the neighborhood.

Nevertheless, these hubs and the range of pastoral vocations that characterize them constructively extend Dykstra's conceptual framework. For example, despite the distinct accents that characterize these hubs, they share an understanding of the need to reassess and reimagine the paradigms that direct pastoral vocations and broader ecclesial life. For the PC, an early catalyst for their work was coming to recognize the hollowness of approaches to church growth that elevated pastoral charisma.[33] Emerging in the shadow of iconic megachurch pastors and out of the experience of personal and pastoral burnout, their individual and collective work sought to understand what it means to be a pastor in and for a community rather than over a community. Jessica Ketola's narration of her journey reflects what many individuals who have gathered around the PC's adaptive work share:

> I was raised in the church, and my parents were pastors. I had gone through a phase where I . . . was really longing for a way forward for the church. . . . [The Leadership in the New Parish program] gave me a new imagination for how to be the church today and it resonated with me deeply because so much of my critiques of my own experience in the church was that there was so much incongruence. . . . [I]t felt like everything that felt disconnected or incongruent or dualistic in some of my other church experiences could come home in this setting where love has to meet the ground, love is fleshed out every day; there are no hit and runs in the neighborhood. These are people you are going to live with on a daily basis, so the way you live out your faith and the way you engage is very respectful of that because you're in relation and you're in proximity.

As Ketola describes her journey, she notes how this introduction to the new parish paradigm not only resonated deeply with her, but gave her a place that called forth her own pastoral vocation. She had been serving in church and nonprofit settings for many years, but it was not until she began to pursue faithful presence in her neighborhood that she began to understand her vocation as leading a neighborhood-based church.[34] For Ketola, as for many others, presence in the neighborhood calls forth a particular kind of imagination. Service in this context came after some formal ministry experience for multiple individuals. It also incorporates wisdom drawn from other forms of knowledge and experience. When combined and brought to bear in relation to the needs and gifts of a particular neighborhood, this "parish imagination" looks for ways to "entangle your daily life in collaboration together as the whole body of Christ in the neighborhood."[35]

Similarly, the OCE's work shifts the primary locus of theological training from a pastor-centric model to a congregation-centric model. As McGonigal notes, their work began with a commitment to listen to congregations, believing that "[congregations] will tell [us] what it is they want and need."[36] While their work remains attentive to the needs of local pastors, it also seeks to enrich the entire congregation by resourcing and connecting members who surround pastoral ministry. Reflecting Dykstra's narration of the "symbiotic" relationship between pastoral and ecclesial imagination, the OCE's work simultaneously seeks to strengthen pastoral ministry and local congregations.[37] For example, Mike McKay, who serves as a lay leader at First Presbyterian Church in Missoula, Montana, notes how the primary impact of the OCE has been through the Academy of Christian Discipleship. Courtney Arntzen, who serves as the associate pastor at Mike's church, makes a similar observation, noting "the way that [participants in the Academy of Christian Discipleship] converse with each other has shifted, and their excitement about being in Scripture and studying.... Sometimes we get to actually witness, as a whole community, somebody comes from not being a part of a community of faith for over twenty years." She continues, "It's been amazing to see some of these individuals who have taken this, and whose lives have been transformed."

In other scenarios, pastors identify the timeliness of this approach, noting the importance of supporting pastoral leadership by enriching congregational life. Still, the impact they observe remains indexed to their relationships and the potential for the OCE to enrich their work in the years ahead. As James Leman notes:

> I think, if anything, it's helped shape more of what we're going towards in the coming months. This idea of the neighborhood impact team. If all we had was this vision of be[ing] church for our neighbors, I would sit there, and scratch my head as to, "We have no idea how to do that. We don't even know what our neighbors' needs are." But, because we know that the OCE is having inroads into areas that we wouldn't normally be able to have inroads into, the effect on me is more of a willingness to [say], "Okay, let's develop a team that works closely with the OCE, that also fits directly under the things we're looking to do, and [explore] how do we strategically partner in that."[38]

The network of relationships that exists within the OCE invites cooperation between pastoral leadership and the local congregation. When combined with the OCE's network of support, this collaborative process unleashes new forms of ministry within the local congregation and broader community. As a result, when asked what else is needed to support the future of their work, participants in the OCE identify various needs for additional resources, leadership development, prayer, partnership, but a common thread is the need for a new imagination. This movement requires learning how to see, learning how to talk, learning how to listen.

Although OCE participants are less likely to use the term "imagination" than those connected to the PC, their collective work similarly involves reforming and renewing an ecclesial imagination. In this way, Dykstra's work effectively identifies the symbiotic relationship between a pastor and a given community and the imaginative interplay that emerges through their interaction. The formation of this kind of pastoral and ecclesial imagination involves a way of seeing and being that has the capacity to "see beneath the surface of things"[39] as a community of faith—and those called to serve them—come "to share the knowledge of God and to live a way of abundant life."[40]

ECCLESIAL IMAGINATION WITHIN AN ECCLESIAL ECOLOGY

The interplay of pastoral and ecclesial imagination in these hubs reintroduces a previous theme: the relationship between the adaptive change and a dynamic ecclesial ecology. This ecology, which includes congregations, Christian colleges, theological schools, nonprofits, funders, theological schools, and parish-based expressions, possesses a dynamic quality that is constantly evolving in response both to internal pressures and the changing composition of this ecology. These kindred organizational and ecclesial adaptations express a novel form of organizing Christian communities in response to adaptive challenges. And finally, in moments of cultural and ecclesial rupture, leadership has a heightened capacity to make change during the early stages of an organization and periods of dynamic change within a broader ecology.

In my earlier description of the ecclesial ecology that surrounds these hubs, I used "ecology" descriptively in order to consider the dynamic network of relationships that distinguishes hubs. This early use incorporated interpretive insights from organizational theory to consider the structure of these hubs. If, however, the attempt to reimagine church within this ecology requires pastoral and ecclesial imagination, that is to say, requires the individual and collective ability to see the "more" within this ecology, the exercise of this imagination and the evolution of this ecclesial ecology are conjoined. More specifically, the ecology represents the variegated spaces in the Pacific Northwest where this kind of imagination is on display. It also shows how engaging in these various places might influence the form of pastoral and ecclesial imagination required for this kind of adaptive change.[41] Functioning simultaneously like a "place" and a "prism," this ecclesial ecology both contributes to the formation of a particular kind of imagination and directs its expression.[42] As such, "ecclesial ecology" describes the constellation of identifiable forms of organized, ecclesial life, such as congregations, theological schools, Christian colleges and universities, philanthropic centers and nonprofits. But it also includes experiments and expressions of "creative deviance" that take place in the boundary spaces between existing and emerging orders.[43] The interaction between hubs and a broader field of social life creates the organizational and ecclesial backdrop for adaptation and change. As other communities discern and build collaborative partnerships, these connections across an ecclesial ecology enrich and sustain the dually imaginative and adaptive change they pursue.

ECCLESIAL ECOLOGY AS PLACE

This ecclesial ecology serves as a place that contributes to the formation of the ecclesial imagination that is required for this kind of adaptive work. According to individuals across both hubs, participation in various aspects of this ecology contributed both to the formation of their faith and the development of their imagination for this kind of adaptive work. As Ben Katt, who appeared in a previous chapter, notes, his experience preceding his catalytic work with the PC included a series of experiences within Christian higher education, denominational settings, theological education, an internship in the Pacific Northwest, and a stint as a church planter. Although he experienced dissonance within some of these spaces, they also provided resources, relationships, and training that contributed to the eventual formation of the PC. His participation in these various places serves as a "pipeline"—they channel resources to pursue work and ministry.

Alongside the training and formation that take place in educational and congregational settings, the family of origin also has the capacity to calibrate how individuals approach and understand their work. For example, when asked about how she approaches her engagement within the OCE network, Abby Leman notes: "[M]y dad was a systems thinker, so I was raised in that. . . . He was very, very influential in shaping who I was."[44] In another instance, a parish leader describes how her family cultivated a passion for others to "encounter God" and "experience unconditional love." Representing an early and formative holding environment for many individuals, family offers the language of faith and a willingness to trust amid uncertainty.

The supporting organizational contexts similarly catalyzed and contributed to the particular adaptive change organizers envisioned and pursued. In the case of the OCE, Whitworth provided an institutional space that supported the respective work of the two founders for multiple decades, but it also created a context for friendships to form. For the founders of the PC, participation within the various places that comprise this ecology provided avenues for friendships to form, while also serving as a foil. When combined, this ecology stirred imagination to consider other forms of possibility.

Connected in a Common Life

Dykstra's work, once again, enriches this account of the places that contribute to the formation of pastoral and ecclesial imagination within an ecclesial ecology. As Dykstra notes, the life of faith—and the form of pastoral and ecclesial imagination that are constitutive of it—are "communal before they are individual."[45] Even as faith depends on an "experience of the Mystery of God," it "takes place in fellowship" marked by a "living, moving, dynamic existence that takes place in the environment of the Spirit."[46] Accordingly, particular "places" curate faith formation and imagination: congregations, family, higher education, theological education, and religious language itself.[47] The formation of pastoral and ecclesial imagination quite literally takes *place*.

Dykstra does not provide an extensive theoretical introduction for his use of "place" nor does he explicitly discuss the interrelation of the places he identifies.[48] However, the sequence and description he provides present a vision of the social tapestry that contributes both to formation in the life of faith and to the adaptive vision that characterizes the hubs' attempts to "reimagine church." This simultaneously ecclesial and ecological description proceeds from the conviction that communities include "people who are intersubjectively related to one another across time and space by a body of convictions, language patterns, and practices that they hold in common."[49] A pattern of faith formation that pursues a "way of life abundant" invites individuals and communities to respond to God's ongoing work in time and history.

The individual and collective imagination that guides an adaptive church reflects an ability to see the virtuous form of connection that definitively marks the life of faith. It attends to an interconnected life of faith, one that involves moving in and through these various formative places, always utterly dependent on the work of God through the Spirit. Such an understanding of the interrelation among these places (i.e., congregations, family, higher education, theological education, and religious language), reflects what has been described as the "living human web."[50] Reflecting the intersubjectivity that grounds ecclesial imagination, supporting virtuous forms of connection requires "conditions" that enable and sustain this type of formation and encounter.[51] Just as pastoral and ecclesial imagination emerges in and through these places, its exercise includes the capacity to see the "more" in the various interconnected places where faith and community are nourished and may flourish.

As such, pastoral and ecclesial imagination find their form and substance in relation to a dynamic ecclesial ecology.[52] Communities of faith, pastors, and people of faith "participate in and connect with . . . a living ecology of institutions and organizations that nurture increasing strength, vitality, and fullness in the whole."[53] To live well in this ecology requires both the cultivation of pastoral and ecclesial imagination and cultivating the places where this symbiotic form of imagination is formed. As José Humphreys, who spoke at the PC's Inhabit Conference in 2019, similarly suggests, "Our world consists of micro systems such as individuals, families, and religious systems. These micro systems are connected to larger systems like schools and communities, and macro systems like economies and governments."[54] For these hubs and other similar experiments, their work reflects an ecological vision for ecclesial life and social change.[55] A sufficiently flexible pastoral and ecclesial imagination concerns itself with how to inhabit this ecclesial ecology with grace and gratitude.

When considered ecologically, the forms of individual and collective imagination that organize adaptive work across these hubs emerge from and find their expression within the ecology's interconnected places. For the hubs themselves, their work reflects, and emerges from, the collective engagement that pervades the ecclesial ecology. Grounded in and attentive to an ecclesial vision for their collective work, these hubs emerge from a history of partnership and collaboration between congregations, theological schools, foundations, nonprofits, Christian colleges and universities, and local faith expressions. Although the organizational configurations may differ, the individual and collective intersubjectivity that constitutes these places creates the conditions of possibility for collaborative and imaginative work. As Sittser notes, the OCE's work emerged from a conviction that "there's an older model, an older ecology of relationship that's been lost in historical memory, where [the college] was the college of the community and pastors were on the board of trustees and students attended local churches and there were all kinds of connections." Although the work of the OCE does not seek a bygone era, their work proceeds from an understanding of the interrelatedness of local congregations, theological institutions, educational centers, nonprofits, and new church movements.

In a similar way, the PC's animating vision proceeds first from an understanding of the "ecclesial center" and then works to explore the conditions and forms of connection required to resource and support churches in the neighborhood. Although they acknowledge they weren't using ecological language at the time, Sparks reflects on how the neighborhood comprises a "primary ecology" for social and ecclesial life. "Human beings need this contact where they can be known, where they can fit together, where they can learn how to carry out the fundamental dimensions of life," he notes. This work requires a form of mutuality and sharing between partners that enriches the work of the other. Speaking of the importance of partnership, Sparks notes how a network of local and translocal connections sustains their work. Specifically, these include: connections to other practitioners in close proximity; what he calls "guides," who have been doing this kind of work for some time; a connection to someone who has a strong regional vision for parish-based work; connections to other ecclesial or parish-based expressions; and partners who specialize in a focused niche that is helpful to someone in the parish.[56] Sparks indicates that the PC's work seeks to promote the conditions where diverse kinds of connections can "resonate together." As he notes: "We would look at ourselves as one—hopefully an anchor—but one network among hopefully many that are arising or will arise."

The result is the formation of hubs that enable individuals and communities to live in light of the reality and promises of God. As one participant notes, the OCE includes "interdependent networks of individuals and organizations that support one another in both direct and indirect ways." And, as another observes, partnerships between denominations, nonprofit organizations, seminaries, and publishers support and extend the PC's organizing and connecting work. In both cases, the OCE and PC represent more than strategic partnerships or coalition building. Rather, their work seeks to renew and reform the ecclesial imagination that sustains the life of faith, especially in a time of significant change.

Ecclesial Ecology as Prism

Just as each adaptive center emerges from and enriches the ecclesial ecology, participation within it redirects the imaginative capacity that informs their work. In this way, the ecology also serves as a prism for the formation and performance of this particular kind of adaptive work. Like light shining through a triangular prism, the imaginative work that takes place across this ecclesial ecology refracts through the forms of encounter that occur throughout the hubs. For example, organizers of both hubs note how their vision and experience across the ecclesial ecology shaped their adaptive vision: they have served as pastors, teachers, small business owners, and members of faith communities. More significantly, however, in listening to the needs of their communities they came to consider and imagine the need for an adaptive and imaginative space.

Individuals across the PC express this shared sensibility when they talk about the need for new "forms." Josh McQueen, who serves at Overlake Christian Church in Redmond, Washington, describes the absence of and need for new organizational forms to enrich the life of faith. As the Communities Ministries Pastor in a megachurch that averages 2,000 to 2,500 worshipers on a Sunday, he identifies busyness, isolation, and fragmentation as challenges which discourage people from viewing church as "an organizing principle of life." In response to these challenges, he invites people within his community to serve as parish pastors, believing that there is need for alternative ways to conceive of and act as a community of faith within their particular context. He observes: "There has to be some way, for people who are willing, to give them a form to live into. For us, there is this sense that we lack the forms that are strong enough to help pull people away. If we can create the forms that allow people to live into something that is meaningful and beautiful, there are people that want that and are willing to make sacrifices." Across both hubs, work that enriches the ecclesial ecology seeks to give people and faith leaders a form that "allow[s] people to live into something that is meaningful and beautiful."

Nevertheless, in so far as this ecology serves as a prism for the (re)formation of imagination, its distinct relational and pneumatic character contributes to the renewal of individuals, communities, and religious organizations. Frequently described as "kingdom work" across the hubs, a common form of ecclesial and collective engagement connects the ecclesial ecology that surrounds each hub. Each hub emerges from a dense network of trusting relationships. In OCE founders' words, it seeks to build both interpersonal and institutional connections, thereby fostering the "thick" relationships required for collaborative and imaginative work. Moreover, interpersonal relationships link the constellation of partners that surrounds each hub. At every level—from neighborhoods, to discrete organizations, to cities, to the region, to international partnerships—the points of contact across the ecclesial ecologies that sustain these hubs represent an individual and ecclesial intersubjectivity. A porous and fluid "we" expresses the collective nature of their work, bespeaking and inviting the reimagination of the church.

Organizers and participants also note the centrality of the Spirit to their adaptive and collective work. Speaking to the organizing vision for the OCE's Summit, Mindy Smith observes how they are "pay[ing] attention to how it's forming and what God's doing in that." Given the disparate components of the event (and the OCE's broader organizing work), she identifies a need to pay attention, with the hope "that the Holy Spirit will bind those things together." Similarly, the values that organize the PC's local engagement and leadership across parish expressions proceed from a commitment to be faithfully present. As Rice observes, this includes being "present to God, but also the presence of the Spirit, listening to the Spirit."

The pneumatic dimensions of both hubs can neither be quantified nor fully explained; yet it remains an inescapable dimension of each hub's organizing vision. The Spirit is the precondition for faith formation and the adaptive work each hub pursues.[57] As co-laborers within a broader ecclesial ecology, this dually adaptive and imaginative work requires the activity of the Spirit. One of the OCE's partners expresses this when he shares:

> I mean the X-factor, which we don't write about a lot in academic journals and stuff, is that there is the Holy Spirit, right? I mean, there is just something that's been happening in Spokane that is a work of God, and I think an example is the fact that there's a lot of different churches here, or Christian organizations or Christian leaders, who are really, truly friends with each other, and truly care about the same things, and are going the same direction, and that's very uncommon. So, there's just something that the Spirit of God is doing here.

Or, as another leader succinctly expresses it: "The Spirit is on the move."

Such an appeal to the Spirit raises interpretive and methodological challenges. Is it the Spirit that is at work in these settings? If so, how does one determine the relationship between the Spirit's work and the adaptive work that guides these communities? The emergence of these hubs should be explained neither solely as the work of the Spirit nor as a product of organizational phenomena.[58] Rather, these appeals require an understanding of the relationship between the Spirit and the various places that constitute this ecclesial ecology. In each instance the pneumatic dimension requires one clarification: although interviewees describe the Spirit as a critical actor, other social or organizational relationships provide a setting to apprehend the Spirit's work. As one leader notes after describing the Spirit's animating work, such an awareness directs attention to "our interdependence with all the things that it means to live a placed and rooted life." In other words, rootedness and attention to place are conditions to perceive and respond to the Spirit's enlivening work.

The interpersonal and pneumatic dimensions of these hubs provide prisms that (re)direct the pastoral and ecclesial imagination so as to enrich the broader ecclesial ecology. This prismatic quality of an ecclesial ecology enables its members to engage in networks of relationships that enrich existing communities and organizations and enable the formation of new forms of gathering. For example, Jonathan Brooks, who serves as a PC board chair in addition to serving as a pastor in Chicago, describes the impact of the diverse, collaborative perspectives that characterize the PC and its events. Specifically, after noting the experience of hearing and engaging with parish-based practitioners across various contexts, he observes how this has impacted his local organizing work: "The beauty of the Parish Collective, to me, is that when you're in a space full of people from different contexts who are all doing different work, it begins to spark your imagination for things that you may not have even thought about in your own context." Attention to the ecclesial ecology also invites wonder. As James Leman notes, when he attends to the surrounding ecclesial ecology in Spokane, it evinces the "richness" that congregations, nonprofits, and educational institutions possess and their complementary interrelationship. "I look at this sort of ecology, and I'm able to see the beauty that each one would bring."

The forms of encounter and partnership that characterize each hub promote boundary-crossing engagement. Crossing boundaries invites individuals and communities to see the beauty of these connections and then to reimagine the patterns of life required to enrich ministry and life together in a particular place. Much as Dykstra notes, the pneumatic, ecclesial, and interpersonal dimensions of this work are intertwined—each connected and supporting the other, creating the conditions for imaginative work to take place.

In other cases, the partnerships that surround these adaptive hubs provide occasions for individuals to engage across the ecclesial ecology. For example: a megachurch commissions part of its pastoral team to consider how their work can enrich neighborhood-based expressions; community foundations partner with parish leaders to support the needs of their communities; megachurch pastors and church planters meet regularly for conversation around shared texts; congregations throughout Spokane partner to care for refugees in their city. In each case, boundary crossing collaboration weaves these disparate elements into an ecclesial whole.

McQueen provides one example of how this form of collective work expresses ecclesial imagination. When asked to describe his engagement with the PC, McQueen notes how his pastoral work at a megachurch and his parish work in his neighborhood are interrelated. When asked to identify the partners that support his work, McQueen notes the relational and organizational connections: "Yes, for sure, Tim, Dwight, and Paul—the three guys that are sort of responsible for the genesis of Inhabit—the Parish Collective for sure, the Inhabit Conference itself, The Seattle School; those have been really catalytic in terms of being able to connect us to something that feels like there's a movement happening and it feels like there were resources available." And then, following this relationally inflected triad of partners, McQueen describes the value of stories from other parish expressions, noting how "just knowing this is happening in Boise, Idaho, Portland, Oregon, and on the East Coast, and Canada; it's just refreshing to be part of the conversation." For McQueen, his congregational and parish context intersects both with the PC and a broader ecclesial ecology.

Congregations also provide a social container to form and express ecclesial imagination. For McQueen, his congregation serves as a holding environment that supports his pastoral work to catalyze neighborhood expressions and equip parish pastors. For example, in collaboration with a colleague, McQueen works to invite individuals from within their congregation to serve as pastors within their neighborhood. As a result, McQueen's work now includes personal experiments with intentional community and localized ministry and a program to identify, connect, and release people from their congregation to serve as parish pastors in their neighborhood. The work of the PC has certainly enlivened and encouraged his ministry, but McQueen also identifies the impact of an expanded network of thinkers and practitioners, including his local congregation. As he shares: "[T]his particular church has been open to this conversation around parish ministry, around proximity and neighborhoods and forming communities around those values." He continues: "[W]e've had the blessing of our church leadership, both our staff and senior staff and most of our elders." As McQueen demonstrates, the PC and OCE connect individuals and communities across multiple holding environments. Through partnerships, events, and relational engagement, they connect otherwise disconnected members of an ecclesial ecology. Each hub's role as a connector, convener, and resource enriches local congregations and parish settings—the ecclesial center—and enlivens disparate attempts to reimagine church.

These ecclesial adaptations represent places and prisms for the formation of the pastoral and ecclesial imagination required to "reimagine church." While each hub organizes in response to the challenges that confront communities, bearing a sober witness to the limits of existing forms and paradigms for leadership, organizers do not dismiss the manifold gifts that exist within the ecclesial ecology. Rather, they see the "more" within ordinary places, including congregations, nonprofits, neighborhoods, and educational institutions, and seek to open individuals and communities to the possibilities that exist through the renewal of this ecclesial ecology. Organizing for adaptive work reimagines church through a collaborative effort. Collaboration connects and resources both communities of faith and those who serve them, but it is ultimately God who enlivens and makes this form of imagination grow. In each case, an abiding sense of God's presence and care for particular communities marks the wisdom that catalyzed—and sustains—the OCE and PC.

Finally, although the distinctive characteristics of these hubs occupy different positions within the ecology, their work of connecting, collaborating, and resourcing emerges from within and returns to the vitality of this ecclesial ecology. To return to Dykstra's language, the work that organizes these two hubs reflects an ability to see the "more" in the places, neighborhoods, and partnerships that organize communities and the life of faith. Moreover, while this work cannot proceed apart from the enlivening, quickening, and connecting activity of the Spirit, interpersonal contact throughout this ecology comprises the condition of possibility both for the formation and the renewal of this collective, ecclesial imagination. To borrow language from partners across both hubs, this work involves an attempt to get people "in the room," and then nurture the organizational and ecclesial conditions that enrich the broader ecclesial ecology. To the extent that this common attempt to reimagine church requires pastoral and ecclesial imagination, its exercise emerges from a dynamic ecclesial ecology. On the other hand, a shared attempt to reorient the conditions for developing individual and collective imagination in the first place is the principal, and potentially most disruptive aspect of their work. In the wake of fragmented and siloed communities of faith, each hub seeks to reconstitute an ecclesial form of intersubjectivity by creating alternative social structures and attending to the Spirit's movement. They do so in order to connect, resource, and catalyze the imagination required to sustain the life of the church.[59]

PASTORAL AND ECCLESIAL IMAGINATION FOR ADAPTIVE CHANGE

It is precisely at this point that the adaptive work that organizes both the OCE and PC begins to extend beyond existing paradigms in practical theology. Insofar as Dykstra illumines the sites' adaptive work, the attempts to "reimagine church" press for a more porous understanding of the pastoral vocation and the ecclesial environment. These hubs share an imaginative task to see and pursue ways of being church beyond conventional templates. While both hubs engage existing local congregations, they also seek to nurture the conditions where new forms of gathering, new forms of association, new forms of leadership, and new ways of being church beyond the walls of a congregation take place. To use Dykstra's language, this dimension of their work accents "the many contexts where [communities of faith] live their daily life."[60] At the same time, the adaptive work that organizes these hubs presses further, suggesting that these "many contexts" are not just extra-ecclesial spaces, but are, in fact, places where individuals and communities can come to know and love God.

The work of the PC, in particular, accentuates this point. Karen Reed describes her experience moving into her neighborhood and rooting herself in that place as a "slow conversion." After serving as an urban missionary through her denomination, Pentecostal Assemblies of Canada, for nine years, she now finds that the people in her neighborhood, many of whom are not religious, enrich and enliven her imagination. As she notes: "I have actually found more commonality in conversations around place-making, around attentiveness to the built environment, around the social capital, around having a good connection.... I have more commonality with my very-far-from-God neighbors that are engaged on these things and thoughtful on these things than my suburban pastor friends that are not even thinking about these things." Ongoing engagement in the neighborhood and connection to place-based experiments that have no connection to the church "sparked my imagination," she notes. She recalls, "That exposure really helped challenge and shape my imagination for another way of living into my faith." The conversion that has taken place for many in this network is not merely coming to recognize that the church can and should attend to the neighborhood. Rather, the neighborhood *itself* is the principal site where "church" finds its form and intention.

The connecting and convening work of both hubs emerges from an ecclesial center, but it acknowledges and attends to the porous boundaries of the ecclesia. According to this vision, the (re)formation of ecclesial imagination taking place involves blurring the distinction between "church" and its "many [other] contexts." Developing imagination entails seeing these places instead as sites where the community of God finds abundance in an encounter with one another and a broader communion.

The forms and formation of pastoral imagination on display across these two hubs do not represent a single, clearly identifiable pastoral vocation, but a range of pastoral vocations that require a similar form of imagination. As described above, the conventional pastoral paradigm initially inhibited Ketola from pursuing her pastoral vocation. However, when she came to understand how her presence in the neighborhood invited her whole self—combining her passion for the arts, spiritual direction, and hospitality—she came to understand her work as a pastor in and for her neighborhood. Although the OCE's work initially appears to primarily engage pastors of local congregations, their work uncovers and supports a wider range of pastoral vocations within and beyond communities of faith. For example, Abby Leman, who is a non-ordained, female leader in a small church, began to find ways that her varied personal and professional experiences could, when combined, enrich her service to her community. With a B.A. in theology, a master's degree in counseling, and exposure to the theory and practice of organizational leadership, Leman describes her introduction to the OCE as coming home. "It made sense to me, because it was more of a systems approach, though they didn't call it that," she notes. "It excited me because I do my best work with space for spontaneity and adaptability." Much as with Ketola, Leman's engagement with the OCE called forth her gifts and experience, inviting her to bring them to bear on the needs of her particular community. In a similar manner, the work of the summer fellows extends well beyond the standard pastoral vocation. Only one of the fellows interviewed for this research served in a congregational setting; the others worked in nonprofit and advocacy organizations. Nevertheless, the work of these former fellows demonstrates a common attention to and valuing of the connections across diverse kinds of organizations and the role the OCE has played in supporting their work. As one fellow shares: "[The OCE] connect[ed] me to other folks, who connect me to other folks."

When considered in relation to the challenges and values that organized these adaptive hubs, the pastoral and ecclesial imagination on display in these two hubs expands beyond Dykstra's framework. While each of the hubs—in its own ways—retains connections to local congregations, they also emerge from and seek to enrich the formation of imagination beyond an understanding of the congregation as the primary site of ministry and gathering. Embedded in a dynamic ecclesial ecology that both constitutes the places and prism where this imagination forms and flourishes, the hubs' work releases latent imaginative possibility that redounds within and beyond the region. Like spring poppies, classic and cutting-edge expressions of pastoral and ecclesial imagination are springing up in communities across the region. Reflecting the dynamic interplay of varied attempts to reimagine the church, each hub's adaptive work attends to the conditions where communities of faith cultivate the forms of imagination and leadership required to live in light of the reality and promises of God.

Questions for an Adaptive Church

The adaptive work that organizes the hubs' attempts to reimagine church raises two critical questions for an adaptive church. First, what is the relationship between the distinct kinds of pastoral and ecclesial imagination embedded in and emerging from each hub? Their adaptive work surfaces the shared imaginative faculties contributing to these attempts to reimagine church. Yet, the particular locations, histories, and networks of each hub have the capacity to promote an imagination that excludes the other. For example, the OCE's primary emphasis on the congregation may invite individuals and communities to dismiss local parish expressions as subsidiary forms of ecclesial life. Similarly, for the PC, the identification of the neighborhood as the principal site for the renewal of imagination may invite a cavalier dismissal of existing forms of organization, education, and leadership that supports people of faith. The existence of these two densely networked hubs within discrete silos appears to corroborate this possibility. These similar attempts to reimagine church contain within them the capacity to evolve so as to prevent individuals within one from seeing the other, replicating the very siloed and fragmented practice of church they originally sought to avoid.

Nevertheless, this description of the relationship between a broader ecclesial ecology and the imaginative landscape that surrounds these hubs provides a means to consider how their shared attempts to reimagine church need not remain in isolation from the other. If the ecclesial ecology supporting and surrounding these hubs includes a variegated organizational and ecclesial space, this ecology includes both known and unknown actors.[61] The work of each hub emerges from different segments of Christian thought and practice in the Pacific Northwest. At the same time, their collaborative and adaptive work reaches toward the other in an attempt to draw upon the practical wisdom that the other possesses. Like the crew of a racing sailboat, actors' imaginative work across this dynamic ecology simultaneously attends to the cultural and pneumatic winds and responds to the movements of others within the ecology. Even if unnamed, the imaginative and adaptive work that occurs at one point of this ecclesial ecology draws upon the work of others, even those who remain obscured from the imaginative vision that directs this work. The result is a form of individual and collective work that enriches both the local expression of communities of faith and the collective imagination that constitutes this interrelated ecology of organizations and institutions.

Second, these reflections raise the question about the conditions that cultivate the imagination required for ecclesial-ecological adaptive work. This account of the imaginative landscape that supports and surrounds these two hubs has attempted to show how this kind of Christian practical wisdom works. But it also merits noting how communities of faith and those who serve them do not always function in ways that attend to and support the flourishing of an ecclesial ecology. Rather, the adaptive work that organizes these sites emerges from a shared understanding of a need for new imagination—new forms, new wineskins, new paradigms—that enrich communities of faith and contribute to the common good. I turn to these needs in the chapters that follow.

For the time being, however, the need for this type of imagination remains both a precipitating and an ongoing requirement for ecclesial and imaginative work. For example, Sparks and Soerens talk about the necessity to develop "connective leaders that have this ecological imagination." Sittser talks about how this work must be "owned and shared by our community of churches, locally and regionally." Katt laments the "poverty of emerging leadership" and the need for "innovative, holistic, mission-minded people." Others talk about the importance of "connections" and the "long slog" required to "nurture imagination" in people, which offers a "taste of another way of being." In each case the needs and challenges are unique to a particular context and community, and the precise expression of this kind of imagination will vary. Nonetheless, the Christian practical wisdom that organizes and emerges from these adaptive hubs invites a similar form of pastoral and ecclesial imagination. That individual and collective imagination is able to see the broader ecclesial ecology and consider the forms of engagement that nourish it. It remains open to the possibility that, in the quotidian movement and encounter within this ecology, the Spirit of God continues to move. This form of imaginative work requires "stereoscopic attention to both the specific moves of personal and communal living and the all-encompassing horizon of faith."[62] Such a faith-filled encounter between personal and communal life provides the condition of possibility for an encounter with God, communion with one another, and forming the individual and communal imagination required for adaptive work on the edge of certainty.

CONCLUSION

These kindred attempts to "reimagine church" reach toward a social and ecclesial horizon, but have yet to bring the future they imagine into a present reality. In their present form, they both occupy the "not yet" that characterizes organizational and ecclesial innovation, seeing and hoping for an alternative future reality, but unable to fully inhabit this vision in the present. Nonetheless, their strikingly similar response to the challenges that confront individuals and communities supports the formation of a strikingly similar organizational form. This form emerges from and alongside existing structures. It represents an attempt at a new and compelling vision for ecclesial life. As Dykstra concludes in a co-authored essay: "Perhaps an alternative metaphor is just beyond our horizon. If the past is any indication, the churches may well borrow again from institutional patterns alive in the larger society. . . . We can be sure, however, that the fashioning of new patterns of organizational life from whatever materials are at hand will require a good deal of imagination, care, and even courage."[63]

Each hub's stated aim to "reimagine church" reflects a larger imaginative tapestry that sustains faith formation and ecclesial adaptation. While Dykstra's understanding of pastoral and ecclesial imagination provides a robust framework to understand and critically engage these two hubs, their work in turn expands and enriches his concepts. The synthesis of this conceptual and adaptive work with the concluding description of ecclesial ecology provides both an organizational and a theological account of the social and pneumatic conditions that enrich an adaptive church. The expression of this pastoral and ecclesial imagination within a dynamic ecclesial ecology helps individuals and communities see the "more," and to discern the movement of the Spirit in their midst. An adaptive church of this kind invites those in their care to live in light of the reality and promises of God, placing their lives in locality and renewing pastoral and ecclesial imagination through prismatic participation in the life of faith.

6

Adaptive Church

Patterned Practice for a Way of Life

Addressing a friend's son on the occasion of his baptism, a thirty-eight-year-old pastor-theologian writes: "By the time you grow up, the form of the church will have changed considerably."[1] As he reflects elsewhere, his work as a pastor and a theologian has sought to understand and support "the variety of new ecclesial forms of community" through service, scholarship, and political engagement.[2] Although this pastor does not attempt to presage the future of the church, he insists on the need for and inevitability of change within and for the church. Rather, as he pointedly claims throughout his work: the church and the forms of ministry that support it are changing.

These words could easily come from either hub, yet they come from Dietrich Bonhoeffer in 1944, predating the PC and OCE by nearly sixty-five years.[3] They also call to mind an earlier period of social and institutional upheaval, when God's self-revelation and commissioning of people as a church turned the "world upside down."[4] Although separated by time and space, Bonhoeffer, the story of early Christian communities, and these hubs share a fundamental concern: discerning and pursuing the forms of witness and organization required for a "new age." An ecclesial form of engagement organizes the adaptive change they pursue, drawing wisdom from their local community and a broader history of adaptive practice.

Each hub locates their work in continuity with Christians throughout history and especially with other ecclesial renewals. These previous movements pattern their kindred practice. Like the musical key for improvisational music,[5] a broader tradition of adaptive expression and the witness of local ecclesial entrepreneurs combine to fuel the imagination their adaptive work requires. Although not always acknowledged by practitioners across these hubs, their work draws wisdom from a deep well of missional innovation.[6]

This chapter engages in *theological redescription*. Theological redescription aims to "redescribe objects, actions, situations, and contexts in ways that reveal hidden meaning, modes of oppression and misrepresentation, with a view to offering a fuller and more accurate description that highlights alternative understandings and previously inconceivable options for theory and action."[7] Even when organizers and participants are unable to provide a full account of their activity, Scripture and Christian tradition provide a means to redescribe their work in light of the reality and possibilities of God.

The patterned practice of an adaptive church combines the disparate threads of this argument into a single account of the conditions that renew the ecclesial imagination. The whole theological reflection thus far not only leads to the discussion of an adaptive church, but is possible and meaningful from the perspective of the patterned practice of an adaptive church.[8] With Bonhoeffer and Luke-Acts as guides, I theologically redescribe the life together that emerges in and through these hubs. This ecclesiological form of thinking—as Bonhoeffer describes it—is characterized by relation, belonging, and possibility. Moreover, as other leaders and communities of faith consider how to be(come) a more adaptive church, this chapter presents the conditions that enable the transformation of individuals and communities. While moments of ecclesial rupture invite renewed reflection about the forms of connection that organize the life of faith, the formation of early church networks demonstrates how virtuous patterns of connection have always distinguished a formative and transformative way of life. And yet the way of life that emerges remains inescapably bound to an ecclesial understanding of a common life. The dense network of partnerships and collectives that have emerged around and through the OCE and PC represent an ecclesial understanding of the patterned practices that enable and sustain an adaptive church.

A WAY OF LIFE FOR THE PACIFIC NORTHWEST

Individuals identify the transformation that has taken place through forms of everyday encounter that occur through the OCE and PC, and within the broader community. For example, reflecting the discussion of ecclesial imagination in the previous chapter, Kevin Lind talks about how his congregation, Opportunity Presbyterian Church in Spokane Valley, Washington, has experienced a transition from a pastor-centric to a congregation-centric approach to discipleship. When asked what has contributed to this change, he initially struggled for words, but then began to piece together the various factors. In his words: "There was a lot of conversation last year in our small group about authenticity and really being real and getting to know people on a deeper level that I think was missing in the more academic setting. So it's interesting that the university made us less academic as a church, but it really did. It brought people together in a way . . . especially last year when we met in our home." After noting how the annual OCE Summit and curricular offerings invited them to look for "ways to join what God's already doing [in the community]," he begins to describe the collective effect of their engagement with the OCE: "That was an earth-shattering type of journey to go on. And so I think the people that went through that then kind of became formed together as a stronger group of disciples trained to help each other grow and challenge each other. . . . There's also a shift of just people being busy for the church to be the church." When asked moments later to describe the practices that have contributed to this change, he uses language that echoes Bonhoeffer's own life and work. "You know just the basic practices really that help shape what we're reading and reflecting on Scripture together and through, like, prayers of intercession for each other that were real, and not just whose aunt was sick; sharing life together." For Lind and others, this form of encounter—with Scripture, with the Word and work of God, with a common life—contributes to a form of individual and collective transformation.

Karen Reed describes the forms of individual and collective transformation that have occurred through her pursuit of faithful presence in Vancouver, B.C. Speaking about the forms of connection that have emerged over her last nine years in Vancouver, Reed notes how this kind of slow, connective work frequently takes place beyond the professional sphere that typically organizes collective life. She notes: "I've had leadership titles my whole life, [but] I no longer have business cards and even when I speak I don't use any of those because it's intriguing to me that 'neighbor' and 'homemaker' are two roles that have never been professionalized; not like 'pastor', pastor's been professionalized."[9] She then concludes by describing the need for presence and practice that requires a form of knowledge that experts do not possess. "Just like a family," she says, "you can't approach a family that way in how you structure relationships and in how you even nurture your life together; and it's a very messy, intuitive, relational work that is not done by experts." Reed demonstrates how the way of life that emerges in and through a neighborhood invites and conveys a form of wisdom. Indeed, the way of life that is emerging in and through these adaptive hubs requires a form of practical wisdom. This form of individual and collective *phronesis* emerges in proximity to the places that contribute to the formation of pastoral and ecclesial imagination, but its aim and animus reach beyond a professional sphere.

The individual and collective effort to reimagine church through these two hubs includes and directs attention to the conditions that order a common life. As organizers of both hubs suggest, their convening and collaborative work attempts to craft structures where individuals and communities come to transformative encounters with one another, a broader community, and the ongoing work of God. For example, reflecting on the history of the PC, Sparks first observes how it began with a longing for "new imagination," only to note how this reflection led him back to his neighborhood. He shares: "Throughout the Scriptures [I] kept finding that the local expression of church, number one, was one of shared life. So, there was a learning how to fit together gifts, hopes, challenges; learning how to bear each other's burdens; learning how to, you know, forgive each other; learning how to grow agency and collaboration and relationship." Simultaneously, for Sparks, this was followed by the realization that this "shared life" was "always in the midst of the larger community." As he notes, this realization prompted further reflection about the ecclesial body in relation to the neighborhood: "The neighborhood was the one place that you could fit together, share life together as an ecclesial body, but then you could also be embedded in the larger community, so that your everyday life was seen, they would be public. There would be a certain, not only a witness, but there'd also be a formative environment where the world would be interacting with you and you would have to be learning how to grow through that." This "way of life" is "centered on the way of Jesus" and seeks to "share life together as a tangible expression of Christ's body in the parish."[10]

The work of the OCE is patterned after the historic witness to a common Christian life and supports the conditions for individual and collective transformation. As Sittser notes in *Resilient Faith*, his work about early Christians and the early Christian way of life was marked by a distinct—if not also peculiar—social witness that led to the transformation of individuals, communities, and cities. He writes: "Early Christians believed that the church embodied a new *oikoumene* [or household], only of a very different kind from Rome's. . . . There was something profoundly audacious about this claim. The Christian movement was at this time small and marginal, considering the size and sophistication of the empire. Yet the leaders of the church claimed that the church constituted a new *oikoumene*, though it had little to show for it."[11] For Sittser and the broader OCE, this claim directs their connecting and collaborative work: the Christian way offers a third way between grasping for power or cultural assimilation. The transformative power of the early Christian movement lay in the alternative sociality it offered. The work of the OCE includes supporting the conditions for the forms of encounter that Lind described above, thereby renewing the individual and collective imagination required to reimagine church. Embedded in every aspect of their programming and organizations—from the Academy of Christian Discipleship, to Summit, to their Fellows Program—the OCE seeks to support communities that can identify and pursue this third way.

While both hubs share an interest in the early Christian movement and other periods of ecclesial renewal, the most striking point of commonality is how their contextual engagement and understanding of the history of Christian witness combines to catalyze adaptation.[12] Sittser expresses this succinctly when he writes: "Our cultural memory of the past might actually be keeping us from seeing the changes happening before our very eyes and from adapting creatively to them."[13] Or, as Sparks observes, the kind of adaptive work that organizes their engagement requires asking, "how do we live together and how do we order our loves?" In this "hinge time," the call of people of faith in the Pacific Northwest (and beyond) provide patterned practices to support and renew an adaptive church.

THE LIFE TOGETHER OF AN ADAPTIVE CHURCH

Bonhoeffer provides an initial pattern to theologically redescribe adaptive practice. His description of the priority of relation, belonging, and possibility outlines the conditions of organizational and ecclesial change that characterize these expressions of adaptive church. The adaptive work that characterizes these two hubs both works within and expands the adaptive patterns Bonhoeffer's life and work provides.[14]

LIFE TOGETHER AS RELATION

Bonhoeffer's early work and these adaptive hubs direct attention to three forms of relation: the concrete, historical instantiation of community; the reality of sin and broken community; and the transformation of community and organization. When taken together, these three elements provide a means to understand how relationality is the prime condition for ecclesial and organizational adaptation.

First, for Bonhoeffer, if Christ exists as community, the community that emerges through participation in Christ similarly assumes a concrete, historical form. "Community is a concrete reality,"[15] writes Bonhoeffer, and "the church is not merely ideally, but actually present in history."[16] The attendant account of community "grows out of the concrete situation" for Bonhoeffer, and bears expression in space, time, and history.[17] In response to God's self-revelation, the *sanctorum communio* that the Holy Spirit brings into being takes place and shape in and through the concrete, historical realities that characterize human existence. This leads Bonhoeffer to characterize the *communio* as the "objective spirit"[18] even as its concrete and historical character rests "upon the Word"[19] and the Holy Spirit.[20] As he summarizes: "Human community comes into being where community with God is a reality."[21] "Belonging" provides the nearest contemporary category for Bonhoeffer's description of the priority of relations for *communio*. The form of relations Bonhoeffer envisions emerges in and through Christ, recasting belonging for those who are gathering together in and through Christ.

The form of community that emerges in Christ is a dependent community that does not exist apart from Christ and the relationships that come through Christ. As Bonhoeffer writes: "A Christian comes into being and exists only in Christ's church-community and is dependent on it, which means on the other human being."[22] This form of being, which emerges in relation to Christ and to one another, constitutes both the *communio* and the reconstituted selves that come into being through their participation in Christ and this dependent form of community. Bonhoeffer's description of the dependent community reflects a form of double participation, presenting the construction of human identity both in relation to Christ and in relation to community.[23] In a similar manner, the form of relation Bonhoeffer envisions creates the means by which belonging emerges, in and through Christ, which rejects the corporate/individual dichotomy. These relations instead provide a means by which individuals can be conjoined and recast through participation in Christ.

Nevertheless, the concrete, historical form of community Bonhoeffer narrates also bears the marks of sin and broken community—or broken relations. "The *peccatorum communio* continues to exist with the *sanctorum communio*," writes Bonhoeffer.[24] Further, the individual and collective culpability, which follows from participation in Adam, produces a common social and ontological result: isolation. The self, which properly exists by virtue of participation in Christ and in relation to another, becomes fragmented and dissociated. "'The humanity of sin' . . . consist[s] of nothing but individuals."[25] Moreover, sin fragments the individual and collective self that Bonhoeffer envisages in Christ.[26]

For Bonhoeffer, community is held together and renewed by the practices that allow it to be remade in Christ. Embodied, collective practices—such as prayer, solitude, communal reading, and singing—order the individual and collective life of those in community. Rather than abstract ideals, practices for Bonhoeffer represent concrete instantiations that point to the reality inaugurated in Christ. These practices hang together and presume the Christological, scriptural, and ecclesial bases presented earlier in his work. Through the practices of a community gathered in Christ, the individual and collective person is remade and renewed.[27] Any effort to foster community, however, occurs in proximity to fractured relations. The community that emerges in and through Christ is held together and renewed by the practices that allow it to be remade anew in Christ.

> [T]he *sanctorum communio* continues to fall again and again, it comes into being anew, passes away, and comes into being once more. . . . Yet for the *sanctorum communio* this movement, its repentance and faith, revolves around a fixed point: the word is what causes the church to break up into the community-of-the-cross, and through the word it is "built up" to become the Easter-Community. The community of saints as the community of penitent sinners is held together by the unity of the body of Christ.[28]

In Christ and in the community that is gathered in and around him, the individual and collective person is remade and renewed. The relations that emerge in Christ reconstitute an individual by incorporating them into a collective; without diminishing the reality of this basic social unity, in Christ, in which the individual and the collective are renewed. This is the bedrock insight of Bonhoeffer's account of relations.[29]

Admittedly, interviews and engagement across these hubs make it difficult to determine the degree to which individuals or communities understand their work in this manner. Although there is a distinct commitment to the priority of partnership, collaboration, and presence, the specific theological rationale for this interconnected form of life is rarely given a full-throated articulation. Further, even though founders frequently borrow and incorporate insights from resources that are not explicitly theological (e.g., Peter Block's work on community) to organize their individual and collective reflection, the rationale for this eclectic borrowing similarly remains unspecified. While these observations do not fault or discredit this form of engagement—in fact, the spirit of this work resembles Bonhoeffer's own interdisciplinary engagement—this absence does point to the potential value of Bonhoeffer's insight. Specifically, insofar as individuals seek a collaborative and connective form of life, this connective and adaptive capacity is derivative of the nature of God and proceeds by means of participation in Christ and in the community; Christ brings it into being. For those who hope to pursue a common life that supports and sustains adaptive expressions of church, Bonhoeffer presents a patterned adaptive practice that describes the transformative potential for relation. He also presents a sober assessment of the reality and fracture that marks social existence.

LIFE TOGETHER AS BELONGING

The priority of relations introduces the second defining feature of this kind of adaptive work: the conditions that enable a life together to be a form of *communion*, or belonging. In his earliest work, *Sanctorum Communio*, Bonhoeffer describes the conditions that enable the transformation of community and organization according to the form of belonging that emerges in and through Christ. Bonhoeffer develops his account of the "structure" (*Struktur*)[30] that characterizes the "empirical church" according to his assessment of basic forms of social relation: community (*Gemeinschaft*) and organization (*Gesellschaft*).[31] With Ferdinand Tönnies' typology as a template,[32] Bonhoeffer presents community (*Gemeinschaft*) as the form of living together in which, through Christ, individuals learn to be *with* and *for* each other.[33] The relational ties that characterize community take place in concrete space and time, while the church-community Bonhoeffer envisages is also not entirely constrained by it. In Christ and through the Holy Spirit, "[t]he structural being-with-each other of church communities and its members acting-for-each other . . . is what constitutes the specific sociological nature of the community of love."[34] The structure of community is already determined in Christ.[35] It takes shape only through the form of life that emerges as individuals-in-community learn to relate to one another as beings who are for each other. The church is a community that "is at once already completed and still in the process of growing."[36]

Bonhoeffer argues the objective reality of the church—and the form of community that it comprises—includes the characteristics of a *Gesellschaft*. The community brought into being by the Word cannot exist apart from the "structure" from which community can emerge. "In a historical perspective, the church consists of many individual congregations, and an organization [*Organisation*] that encompasses them. . . . Unless it is equated completely with the organization [*Organisation*], the 'empirical church' seems to be merely an abstraction, or the statistical composite of all individual congregations."[37] Expressing the collective character of a *Gesellschaft*, the church also creates the possibility of assembly, whereby individuals gather and encounter each other in Christ. Indeed, the offices of the church, the administration of the sacraments, and the liturgical rites that organize a community of faith share many characteristics of a *Gesellschaft*. For this reason, Bonhoeffer concludes: "It would appear that the image of the church as an organized type of social formation can be classified sociologically under the concept of organization [*Gesellschaft*]."[38]

The relations inaugurated by Christ transform the basic social structures that pattern belonging. Bonhoeffer uses *Gemeinschaft* and *Gesellschaft* to describe the structure of the church, while also understanding these two categories to be transformed and remade through the individual and collective remembering that occurs in Christ. In the "empirical church brought about by the Spirit . . . community [*Gemeinschaft*], organization [*Gesellschaft*] and association of authentic rule [*Herrschaftsverband*] are truly most closely intertwined."[39]

At the same time, these basic sociological types are recast and transformed. "[C]hurch is a form of community *sui generis*," writes Bonhoeffer, "in it the basic sociological types of organization, community, and association of authentic rule are combined and transcended [*überwunden*]."[40] If Christ existing as community becomes the basis of the church, for Bonhoeffer, the social relations that emerge in Christ and through community are the relational and social loci that have the capacity to remake the individual and collective person.[41] As a result, "the person comes into being only when embedded in sociality,"[42] such that "community and individual exist in the same moment and rest in one another."[43] The individual, the community, and the hope of transformation cannot be separated from engagement with the social structures that surround individuals-in-community.

When reconsidered in relation to Bonhoeffer's description of belonging, his understanding of the conditions that enable a life together reframes the adaptive work of the OCE and the PC. Specifically, this patterned understanding of the interrelationship between *Gemeinschaft* and *Gesellschaft* and their transformative capacity presents the social poles that ground and animate adaptive work across these hubs. In both cases, the OCE and PC emerged in response to the perceived fragmentation of community and the perceived need for alternative social structures to support communities of faith during a time of change. Notably, both have responded by nurturing forms of *Gemeinschaft* and *Gesellschaft* in order to support and sustain the renewal of pastoral and ecclesial imagination. While one may argue that the PC's localizing efforts place an emphasis on *Gemeinschaft*, and that the genesis and ongoing work of the OCE occurs in proximity to *Gesellschaft*, it is an error to exclusively associate either hub with a single form. Rather, each hub pursues a form of collective work that reflects their understanding of the absolute dependence of forms of community and organization on one another. For the PC, this is expressed in organizers' personal commitments to the local communities they serve; in recent attempts to organize learning communities as a focal site of learning and formation; in their understanding of the need for partner organizations; and in their ongoing work to fashion adaptive organizational structures that can support and sustain parish-based expressions. Similarly, for the OCE, the inseparability of community and organization is expressed in organizers' history and ongoing engagement with local faith leaders; in the location of their office within and in relation to various established organizations; and in their formation of learning communities that are organized by focal concerns. In both cases, the common adaptive work that characterizes the OCE and PC moves between these two forms of social structure, seeking to organize and support the common life required to nourish communities of faith and leadership throughout these interconnected places.[44]

Similarly, the PC's and OCE's ongoing engagement at each level has the capacity to contribute to individual, collective, and institutional transformation.[45] As Friesen suggests, the PC's work includes various forms of "transforming relationship" that create the conditions for individuals and communities to imagine and pursue an alternative way to organize a common life.[46] Similarly, the work of the OCE has led organizers and participants to observe the transformations happening through collaborative forms of engagement. As McGonigal reflects on the OCE's partners' diverse perspectives and experiences, he concludes: "God is doing something in terms of the melding of those relationships in ways that could never happen if we tried to sit down and have a conversation about 'what's your theology?'" Clifford Green aptly summarizes the consequence of this individual and collective transformation for Bonhoeffer and the adaptive work that organizes these hubs:

> The transformation of human life brings people from the periphery of life to its center, from a fragmented existence to an integrated life, from otherworldliness to historical life in the world, from an episodic regression to a faith which informs their whole life, from subjective inwardness to responsibility in public life, from dishonest and humiliating apologetics to meaningful acceptance of reality, from individualistic self-preoccupation to "existing for others."[47]

The work of these hubs aims to support the transformation of human life. Emerging from the edge of uncertainty and disconnection, they work to craft a more interconnected and integrated life. In their most basic form, they invite individuals and communities to exist for others. When combined, such encounters between God and humanity, in Christ, and the attendant encounters between the individual and community, through participation in Christ, has the capacity to transform the social structures and imaginative horizon that organize a common life.[48]

Life Together as Possibility

Bonhoeffer's description of life together as possibility provides a final element of the patterned practice of an adaptive church. His understanding of the conditions of possibility recasts his account of the priority of relations and the structure of belonging. For these organizational and ecclesial adaptations in the Pacific Northwest, Bonhoeffer clarifies the ontology and the ecclesial pattern of thought that directs and sustains them.

Bonhoeffer describes revelation as the irreplaceable condition for faith and faith formation. The church provides the requisite unity of human action and knowledge in which humankind receives the revelation of God. Revelation comes only through the Word and where individuals participate in a community in which God's self-revelation can be apprehended:

> The "church" is, therefore, not a human community [*Gemeinschaft*] to which Christ then comes or not, nor is it a gathering of such persons as those who (as individuals) seek Christ or think they have Christ and now wish to cultivate this common "possession." The church is rather the community of faith created and founded upon Christ, in which Christ is revealed as the δεύτερος ἄνθρωπος, as the new human, or rather, as the new humanity itself.[49]

Combining themes that appear throughout his work, Bonhoeffer describes the interrelationship between church, community, Christ, and the new humanity that emerges in and through Christ. Bonhoeffer then continues, "Only in the community itself . . . [can revelation] be understood in its real, existence-affecting being."[50] Bonhoeffer contends that one learns to receive the other and pursue a mode of life marked by being-for-each-other only in the context of church-community.[51] Simultaneously, only in such a pattern of relations can one apprehend the faith to see oneself as received in Christ and have one's life marked by the reality that God is for us.[52]

When considered as such, the transformation of community and organization in Christ becomes the condition of possibility for revelation and the formation of a community of faith. Revelation requires a form of "Christian sociology"[53] that is also "ecclesial knowing,"[54] which finds its proper form and function in relation to ecclesial community. Within this form of "ecclesial thinking and knowledge" social structure is the condition of possibility for faith and formation; this structure is secondary in importance to revelation.[55] Moreover, for Bonhoeffer, the possibility of life together depends upon the reality of encounter with God and with one another in community, not on the durability of a single institution. "[A]ny system of human beings, who are not eternally in the truth, is an untrue system and must be shattered so that the true system may become possible."[56] The result is an understanding of both ecclesial community and organization as the social condition for transformative encounters, which may transform the very structure that enables individuals and community to encounter one another under the Word.[57]

These three features of Bonhoeffer's theology—the priority of relations, belonging, and the nature of possibility—express the "ecclesiological form of thinking" that patterns the OCE's and PC's attempts to reimagine church. For Bonhoeffer, the possibility for transformation occurs in response to the reality of God's self-revelation in Jesus Christ and the connecting work of the Holy Spirit. Still, transformation can never be separated from the concrete social existence and forms of practice that constitute a community of faith. Furthermore, even as Bonhoeffer identifies the church as a *sui generis* social form that can only be apprehended from within, this form of thinking and the reality of the church remain provisional. Nevertheless, these conditions of possibility emerge from and reflect an ecclesial imagination grounded in the reality of God and the possibility of personal, collective, and social transformation in and through Christ and the church.

Bonhoeffer's thought also clarifies the conditions of possibility for the transformation these adaptive hubs pursue. The adaptive work that takes place across this ecclesial ecology resonates with Bonhoeffer's conceptual framework; meanwhile, Bonhoeffer's insight provides a theological redescription for the adaptive work that marks them. Coded throughout my research as the "power of possibility," the adaptive work of these two hubs reaches toward an ecclesial horizon illumined by the infinite possibility emerging from connection and encounter, and which may enrich and enliven people of faith and the places they inhabit. Assuming a plurality of forms and expressions, this theme of possibility pulses, like life-giving blood through the veins, through these adaptive hubs, animating their organization and the work of their partners and participants. Indeed, while formidable challenges confront individuals and communities throughout the region, they are trusting in and seeking to discern God's ongoing work through the concrete, quotidian realities of human existence.

A single illustration cannot capture the sense of pregnant possibility within these expressions of adaptive church. One can only point to it. Nevertheless, the animating sense of possibility that provides the bedrock for these adaptive hubs is expressed in comments by their founders. For the OCE, McGonigal shares: "I think for all the lament of the deterioration of the church and lack of church attendance—you know all the statistics—I view this as a tremendous moment of opportunity. If the church can pivot to an understanding of a third way approach to being in the world and doing ministry . . . I think it's a blessing that power is being stripped away from the church." In a similar manner, for the PC, Soerens observes how their "working hypothesis is that the density of the neighborhood can release new levels of possibility." Noting how "possibility is key here," Soerens locates the form of possibility in relation to an ecclesial understanding of the placed nature of ecclesial existence, which invites attention and presence in the neighborhood.

A similar pattern of thought and speech emerged when organizers from both hubs gathered for a convocation in March 2021. Growing in prominence throughout our two-day gathering, like a thunderhead that blossoms in the summer sun, the power of possibility began as hopeful expectation and became a realizable vision for connection and collaboration. It is expressed in the cadence of the conversation, moving from measured articulation to naming concrete avenues for ongoing reflection. This power of possibility then crystalized as participants identified the pressing matters for reflection and work: the need to reimagine how authority is exercised in ecclesial structures, the urgency of conversation about the future of church buildings for languishing and financially precarious congregations, the need for different discipleship and training structures for a rising generation of people of faith, and spaces that honor the creative vocation of ecclesial entrepreneurs beyond existing credential structures. Expressing a hopeful vision for possibility that does not deny the reality of challenges, one organizer reflected, "I think this issue of entrepreneurial innovation is an idea whose time has come. Whatever church is going to be post COVID, it's not going to be what it was before.... So, I think this is one of the key elements of the takeaway from this conversation that really needs to be nurtured, thought about and to create some other incubators. And I don't know exactly what that would look like and what the resources for that would be." Or, as another organizer noted, the conversation gave rise to a hopeful vision to consider "what's possible for the church in a particular region." When considered together, these hubs point to and express a patterned practice that could enrich similar expressions of adaptive church.

HUBS AS A NETWORKED WAY OF LIFE

The transformation of individuals and communities envisioned through these hubs represents an understanding of these features—relations, belonging, and possibility—within a broader way of life.[58] Reflecting during a gathering of ecclesial entrepreneurs, Soerens shares, "I think what we have in common across this group, is that we have all—at least in some way—given our lives to this work." The way of life that is envisioned and modeled by these hubs emerges out of and alongside the alternative social structures they craft. The proximity of these experiments to dense networks of social relations and common purposes contains a possibility for formation and transformation. And the formation of dense networks of social relations represents the "practical dynamics within which world-changing occurs," in early and contemporary communities of faith alike.[59]

Each hub locates their work in continuity with earlier periods of Christian renewal. Much as with Bonhoeffer, a close reading of the decisive turn in the story of the early church provides a second point of theological redescription and contemporary reflection. Acts 11:19–13:4, which recounts the formation of early-Christian networks around Antioch, will guide the theological redescription of these hubs.

If the narrative trajectory of Luke-Acts presents "one continuous story,"[60] the story of the early Christian networks (at Antioch and beyond) in Acts 11:19–13:4 situates the early church in Luke's larger narrative. More specifically, it presents the proclamation of the repentance and forgiveness of sins to all nations (Luke 14:47) and gives social expression to early Christians' claim that Jesus is Lord.[61] In its narration, this story presents the impact of God's self-revelation as creating a "world upside down" in which the former patterns of social and religious life are drastically reoriented—including social networks.[62] Such a reading locates the contents of these sections very near to the center of the narrative world of Luke-Acts.

The scenes depicted in 11:19–26 and 13:1–4 disclose the inverted world order encountered by Christians. The Holy Spirit comes upon (ἐπέπεσεν)[63] Cornelius and his household and they receive baptism (10:1–48), altering the existing boundaries of belonging. Some scholars read Cornelius' conversion as the high point of the first major section of Acts, but this conclusion overlooks the significance of the narrative that follows.[64] Kavin Rowe notes how the conversion of Cornelius is a "fundamental" feature of the Luke-Acts narrative, but "it simply does not follow that the founding of the church in Antioch is less so."[65] Following Rowe, attention to four aspects of the church in Antioch demonstrates the formation and significance of networks for the early Christian way of life.

Precarity and Uncertainty Catalyze Connection

The formation of the church in Antioch emerges, in part, due to the precarity and uncertainty of their situation. The stoning of Stephen in Jerusalem (7:54–8:1) initiated a "severe persecution" that "scattered" (διασπαρέντες) believers as far as Antioch. The third-largest city in the Roman Empire and the capital of Syria,[66] Antioch was a hub of cultural and political activity.[67] Such dispersion leads to the mingling of peoples, ideas, and dialects that come to encounter one another only through their displacement. Following the proclamation of Jesus as Lord by unnamed evangelists (11:20),[68] the Antioch church begins to form.

Place serves as a defining marker of their identity. Although the identity of these actors remains concealed, the narrator tells us everything we need to know; their place and relational presence authenticates their words. And, much like religious life in the Pacific Northwest, their words and the power of God turn their listeners to the Lord (11:21).

The conditions surrounding the rise of the Antioch community were severe. Luke uses the word θλῖψις to introduce this persecution that opens the scene in 11:19. The figurative use of θλῖψις is often translated "persecutions" in the New Testament.[69] At two later points in Acts, Luke places the same word in Paul's mouth when he encourages communities suffering under persecution. According to the Pauline theological grammar found in his epistles, θλῖψις includes a mimetic identification with Christ's own suffering (cf. 2 Corinthians 1:4, 6; 1 Thessalonians 1:6–7; Colossians 1:24).[70] If the narrative in Acts is read in this way, the affliction of believers that leads to their dispersion suggests a mode of ecclesial and social life that cannot be separated from the mode of Jesus' own life.

The precarity and uncertainty caused by persecution expresses a common feature across this narrative in Luke-Acts, Bonhoeffer's life and work, and these two adaptive hubs in the Pacific Northwest. Individuals and communities are acted upon in ways that dimmish their agency. As the narrative recounts, "those who were scattered" (διασπαρέντες) become the container where early Christian networks introduce a revolution in belonging. In the liminality on the edge of uncertainty, these early Christians engage in an early church struggle as they determine the way of life that can sustain them.

God-Established Early Christian Networks

Amid this uncertainty, God is the agent who constitutes the Antioch community. With subtle artistry, Luke presents the theological epicenter of the Antioch community in three distinct characterizations of God. First, the proclamation of the Jesus as Lord represents the central claim of the believers when they arrive in Antioch. As developed in the earlier stages of his narrative, such a proclamation identifies Jesus with the God of Israel (Luke 10:25–42).[71] Turning to the Lord (11:21), in this sense, involves regarding Jesus as the one true God. When Hellenists turn to the Lord, it is taken as sign of the "grace of God" (11:23).[72] Luke's description of this event presents a second characterization of the founding of the church in Antioch. The same God who sends an angel to Mary in Nazareth (Luke 1:26), cares for the grass and faithful alike (Luke 12:28), and raised Jesus from the dead (Acts 2:24; 3:15; 3:26; 4:10), is associated with the emergence of the community and Antioch. Finally, when Luke describes Barnabas' arrival, he characterizes him as "a good man, full of the Holy Spirit" (Acts 11:24). Notably, Barnabas becomes one of the primary teachers in Antioch (11:26) and he is later sent out by the Spirit (13:4). These three descriptions of the "Lord," "God," and "the Holy Spirit" depict the Lord God, in the fullness of the divine, trinitarian being, as the primary actor that constitutes the Antioch community.

God's activity in time and history invites individuals-in-community into a particular way of life. Much as Bonhoeffer notes, the life of faith is only apprehended through a participatory relation, participation in Christ and participation in the structures of belonging God calls into being. God's activity as the lifeblood of community releases individuals to be for one another amid the virtues and fractures of humanity. This is the same pattern that marks the Christo-ecclesial center for each adaptive hub, the PC and the OCE. Their work responds to what they discern God is already doing to transform the particular communities and organizations they serve. "It's the Holy Spirit at work," one organizer from the PC shared in a two-day gathering. The OCE organizers placed a similar accent noting how "churches have been totally surprised by just simply paying attention to that, what God has done—we all would say spirit-inspired work—to create some new forms of ministry and some new partnerships and to give people who did not otherwise feel any sense of power, the empowerment to really move forward and do some marvelously creative things." Even in the boundary zone of uncertainty, the narrative of Luke-Acts and the story of these two hubs identify God's ongoing work as the prime adaptive agent.

Strengthening Networks amid Uncertainty

Gathering and teaching over a sustained period of time strengthens this new network amid uncertainty. As Luke narrates, "So it was that for an entire year [Saul and Barnabus] met with [συναχθῆναι] the church and taught [διδάξαι] a great many people" (Acts 11:26). At this point, the narration leaves many lingering questions in the mind of the reader. How often did they meet? Where did they gather? What practices informed their common life together? What did they teach? Luke's narration does not disclose such specificity; rather, it notes their presence and longevity: Saul and Barnabas remained in Antioch for a year and met with the believers gathered there. Luke also does not specify who teaches, leaving open the possibility of a collaborative form of instruction that involves mutual engagement between the learners and the teachers as well as between the co-teachers.[73] Given this possibility, such an account resists technocratic conceptions of teaching in which formation involves the transmission of knowledge and values from a teacher to a pupil.[74] The social reality of the Antioch church becomes inseparable from its pedagogy as the politics of this new social reality represent the site that discloses the content of the evangelical message.

Such an ecclesial vision suggests the formation of a relationally saturated network around the new reality that is inaugurated in Jesus. To use Edward Farley's language, Luke's narration presents the "ecclesial existence" that constituted the early Christian community.[75] It is fitting, then, that the followers of Jesus who proclaim that Jesus is Lord are actually called Christians (Χριστιανούς) (Acts 11:26) only at this point in the story. It is as if one needs to follow three-quarters of Luke's story before one can begin to understand what it means to be associated with Christ. Those who are called Christians are heirs of this story, and the teaching (διδάξαι) bears witness to this story.[76] The story's contents reorient the world early Christians find themselves in and press for a radically new form of sociality in which they gather through the common call of Christ.[77]

Amid times of transition and uncertainty, teaching enables individuals and communities to find their way forward when their world feels like it's been turned upside down. Organizers for both the OCE and PC are teachers, writers, caretakers of their communities, and champions for the local wisdom that can reorient a common life. To return to the language Dykstra introduced, their work aims to enrich and renew the ecclesial imagination that sustains the life of faith in the Pacific Northwest. While their primary teaching often occurs outside of the classroom—in coffee shops, sidewalks, and living rooms—they also serve as guides for the many individuals whose imaginations are stirred by their wisdom and work. The patterned practice enumerated by Bonhoeffer's work also includes relational presence through teaching. Indeed, Bonhoeffer's proximity to "the church struggle" drives him back into the life of spiritual formation and training pastors for a future church. While Luke-Acts does not disclose the content of the teaching that catalyzes these early-Christian networks, wisdom drawn from these moments in the narrative provides guides for the way of life that emerges from them.

Expanding Networks of Connection and Care

Antioch comes to represent a wider network of churches connected by the proclamation of the word of God.[78] Scholars often identify Acts 12:25–13:3 as a "Lukan suture" that connects the unfolding narrative with the previous Antioch account in 11:30.[79] Paul is a connector-convener across communities. Luke repeatedly observes that Paul's missionary journeys leave from, include, or return to Antioch (Acts 14:26; 15:22–23; 15:30; 15:35; 18:22). Luke also positions the Antioch community at a central point in his work, presenting the emergence of a network of churches that share common connections with and through the Antioch church. Paul's missionary journeys (Acts 13:4–28:31) and writings further serve to create an informal network of associations in which early Christianity emerges.[80] Diverse descriptions are used to characterize Paul's role—that of a broker or a connector[81]—yet the function remains much the same: Paul provides relational connections across otherwise disconnected communities.

The narrative of Acts suggests these interconnected communities emerge from and reflect a form of existence that is consistent with Luke's gospel message. The impetus for Paul and Barnabas' missions emerges through worship and at the direction of the Holy Spirit. The Spirit's intervention, according to Luke, includes a call, a work to which the Spirit calls, and commissioning by a community. Throughout Paul's journeys, the proclamation (καταγγέλλω) of the "word of God" becomes that which binds communities of faith together (13:5).[82] The combination of the Spirit's commissioning and the proclamation of the word of God becomes that which both founds local churches and begins to knit them together within a wider communion.

The life of faith assume a similar form for these adaptive hubs in the Pacific Northwest. Connection and care crystalize their adaptive work in response to God's call upon their lives. Organizers pursue a particular way of life, one marked by curiosity, hospitality, and restless discontent with the status quo. Even as they innovate in order to organize and educate the communities they serve, God remains the primary agent who catalyzes their adaptive work. The wisdom born of God remains the soul and substance of an adaptive church; this is the hope for renewal of an ecclesial imagination within a shifting ecclesial ecology.

The emergence and growth of these hubs reflects the patterned practice we read in Luke-Acts: they emerge from precarity and uncertainty; training and formation (over an extended period of time) strengthen this new network amid such uncertainty; the Holy Spirit provides a source of ecclesial cohesion, honoring the particularity of place and a breadth of expressions; Christian networks emerge, even when the world is turned upside down, drawn forth by the word and work of God.

ECCLESIAL NETWORKS AND A CHRISTIAN WAY OF LIFE

In Luke's telling and for these hubs, their networked expression embodies an interconnected way of life. More than a strategic attempt in a shrinking religious marketplace, each hub reflects an abiding vision to be with others in a way that expresses a holistic way of life. For Luke, the patterns of interconnectedness within early Christian communities inform a way of life, or a "habit of being," that orders both individual and communal forms of existence.[83] The early Christian way of life, in the narrowest sense, is located within local church communities. However, to separate these communities from the broader networks of interconnections overlooks a central element within the narrative arc of Luke-Acts. For Luke, God's self-revelation in Jesus not only founds a local ecclesia, but introduces a form of ecclesial existence in which members from different communities are interconnected by the gospel message, apostolic teaching, and practices of the faith. For Luke, a networked form of ecclesial existence both displays the truth of the gospel message and constitutes a site for Christians to pursue their distinct way of life. For contemporary communities, the life of faith reflects a similar form. Knowledge of God and formation in the practices that inform the Christian faith are tightly bound to the networked communities Christians inhabit.

At this point, returning to Acts 12 offers two insights about the form of life facilitated by networks for early and contemporary Christians alike. First, the rise of networks demonstratively performs Luke's repeated affirmation about the Lordship of Christ, which lies at the center of his account. Falling between his descriptions of the Antioch church's founding and the emerging ecclesial networks, Luke places a brief excursus about the persecutions experienced by other believers. Similar to other decisive transitions in his narrative, Luke situates the theo-historical significance of the church against a larger historical backdrop. Whereas God opposes Herod (Acts 12:23), the word of God continues to "advance and gain adherents" (12:24). The contrast produced by Luke's narration not only presents the emerging Christian community as calling into question the prevailing social (and political) order of the Roman world, but also affirms the priority of the Lord God over competing claims to one's loyalties.[84] For Luke, Christianity not only represent a *rival* tradition, but in fact a *stronger* tradition than those presently available in the Greco-Roman world.[85]

Networks also create an extended social matrix in which Christians pursue the way of life that proceeds from and informs their particular claims about God, the created order, death, morality, and humanity. A given way of life cannot be separated from the wider social and theoretical framework that gives it meaning.[86] In Acts as well as for these adaptive hubs in the Pacific Northwest, networks permit a range of Christian practices and express the expansive social horizon in which a way of life is pursued. For example, Luke-Acts offers insight about the practices of benevolence, prayer, and hospitality that characterized Christian communities. Much as Bonhoeffer notes in *Life Together*, these patterned practices order individuals in community.[87] When the Antioch community heard of the need experienced by believers in Judea, they sent relief according to their ability (Acts 11:27). During Peter's imprisonment, the church prayed "fervently to God for him" (12:5) and upon his deliverance he returns to the church (12:12–17). Similarly, these communities across the Pacific Northwest extended care and hospitality during the COVID-19 pandemic, creating space for connection, hospitality, and belonging. As one pastor in Seattle reflected, they endeavor to be "aware of how do we still care and sense needs as they are arising and just be on the lookout for folks."[88]

Through participation in networks of connection and care, individuals find belonging in a wider communion characterized by benevolence and hospitality. The extension of generosity and hospitality to other communities, along with the commissioning of individuals to those other communities, expresses an expansive theological vision. This vision, which Luke locates at the literary and theological fulcrum of his work, expresses an ecclesial existence in which participation in a community binds an individual both to local members, but also to unseen individuals who have received a similar proclamation and gift of the Spirit. The existence of such early Christian networks, which is characterized both by association and moral obligation, expresses the cosmic scope of the gospel message and the connection in a common way of life. This patterned practice demonstrates how the formation of networks around these hubs in the Pacific Northwest invites individuals into a similar way of life. While separated by time and distance, the story of these hubs' adaptive work re-grounds ecclesial existence in the particular communities and organizations they serve. The patterned practice of Bonhoeffer's work, the narrative in Luke-Acts, and these two hubs provide an "imaginative spark" for an adaptive church.[89]

ADAPTIVE CHURCH: FRAGILITY AND SOCIAL ANALYSIS

This theological description offers one final clarification about the patterned practices that distinguish an adaptive church. Even as these hubs are organized by a shared understanding of possibility, they are marked by an inherent fragility. Three aspects of this fragility merit note: the fragility of sin, the fragility of uncertainty, and the countervailing fragility of diversity and homogeneity. Bonhoeffer and Luke-Acts provide a lens to reinterpret the inherent fragility that marks these expressions of adaptive church on account of sin, uncertainty, and the countervailing fragility of diversity and homogeneity.

SIN

Bonhoeffer's writings and Luke-Acts accent the inherent fragility on account of sin. The fragility caused by sin stretches as one continuous thread from Bonhoeffer's early work (e.g., *Sanctorum Communio, Act & Being, Creation and Fall*) through his pastoral and pedagogical writings (e.g., *Life Together, Discipleship, Letters from Finkenwalde*) and into his academic writings and correspondence from the end of his life (e.g., *Ethics, Letters and Papers from Prison*).[90] Bonhoeffer's understanding of sin exists in a dialectical relationship to his broader account of soteriology, in which Christ is the actualizing agent and animating person for the church.[91] Bonhoeffer's assessment of the conditions that enable a life together contains a sober assessment of the fracture of personhood and collective humanity, as well as a hopeful vision for the reconstituted forms of a common life that emerges in and through Christ.[92] Accordingly, as he later develops this theme in *Life Together*, he notes how Christians "no longer seek their salvation . . . in themselves, but in Jesus Christ alone."[93] Bonhoeffer then quickly follows by noting how Christ renews and reconstitutes the form of humanity required to encounter oneself and one another in and through community.[94]

Luke-Acts similarly displays how sin fractures human community and introduces an inherent fragility into efforts to recraft a common life. Jesus teaches his disciples to pray "forgive us our sins" (Luke 11:4); Jesus tasks his followers to proclaim "repentance and forgiveness of sins" (24:47); Peter invites those gathered on the day of Pentecost to repent and be baptized so that "your sins may be forgiven" (Acts 2:38); and Paul's journeys from Antioch carry the proclamation of "forgiveness of sins" (Acts 13:38). The accent in the narrative, however, is the way sin fractures the human community God calls into being. The word and work of Jesus reincorporates those who are far off, those who are cast off by community, back into a community of belonging. For Jewish and Gentile hearers alike, the proclamation of forgiveness of sins is an invitation to belief and belonging. This particular way of life is marked by a sober assessment of the characteristic fragility of all forms of sociality, but also offers a hopeful vision that, through Christ and the quotidian quality of human existence, God opens up the possibility to know one another and ourselves.

The theme of sin appears sparsely in the interviews, published materials, and conference content. With only two passing references to "sin" throughout interviews with OCE and PC constituents,[95] readers may be tempted to dismiss this insight as trite. The fragility of sin should not be discarded too quickly; rather, it offers a critical corrective to a potential error in this theological redescription. The practical wisdom that distinguishes these hubs' adaptive work is organized by a pervasive understanding of the power of possibility. Yet an account of their latent possibility must be conjoined to a countervailing understanding of human fallibility, including an understanding of the deleterious fracture of sin on collective work and community alike. The fragility of sin, according to Bonhoeffer and Luke-Acts, complements the Christological and ecclesial center that organizes the practical wisdom required for adaptive work. The power of possibility does not express the endless horizons for human creativity. The adaptive possibility of these hubs is not only limited, but it is also fractured and fallible. When God is the prime agent of the adaptive work in a community, the power of possibility emerges *in spite of* fractured human community, not as a derivative of infinite human potential. Grappling with the reality of sin, human fallibility, and fractured community in this way governs the hubris of unbridled adaptation and innovation. Indeed, even as a host of challenges and the reality of God combine to foster infinite possibilities, the forms of possibility that emerge in and through adaptive work must always proceed mindful of the propensity to err, and the capacity for sin to lead to broken community and isolation.

Uncertainty

The fragility on account of uncertainty marks the adaptive work of the OCE and PC and other emerging organizations. This theme appears throughout these two hubs. Chapter 3 provided an initial discussion of this theme, noting how boundary-zone work represents a prominent challenge across these hubs. Boundary-zone work entails the challenge of working without existing templates in the liminal space between established organizational orders. Beyond the uncertainty that individuals across these ecclesial ecologies identify, the very organization and ongoing existence of the OCE and PC reflect the fragility of uncertainty. "There's no promises of permanent employment here," McGonigal notes, "It's grant funded and revenue funded unlike anything else in the institution. If you're willing to live with that uncertainty, you're welcome here. If you want security, this is not the place to be." In a similar manner, the history and ongoing organization of the PC exemplifies fragility. Started without the temporary stability of grant funding and without a definite organizational home, the first decade of the PC's work was uncertain on multiple fronts. Accordingly, speaking about the history of partnership, Soerens notes: "It is possible, but not probable, that without their investment into making these learning communities happen, we might not still be around, just because of our fragility, financially speaking." In both cases, although the uncertainty that individuals identify across these hubs is inherent to this kind of adaptive work, that uncertainty also constitutes a persistent fragility intrinsic to these expressions of adaptive church.

Bonhoeffer's work and Luke-Acts recasts the inherent fragility of uncertainty that characterizes these hubs in relation to God's ongoing activity in time and history. In each case, individuals find belonging in a reconstituted community that God brings into being. Although the individuals remain actors, with agency, in this unfolding narrative, their way of life responds to what God is already doing. Reflecting on Advent, Bonhoeffer notes how waiting extends throughout the entirety of Christian existence: "The time of Advent is a time of waiting, though our entire life is a time of Advent, a time of waiting for that final time when a new heaven and a new earth will emerge."[96] The waiting that marks Christian existence offers a corrective to the "impatient age" that hastily seeks "fulfillment" beyond the gift of God's historic and ongoing sustenance.[97] Consequently, writing from prison in 1943, where he was facing his own uncertain future, Bonhoeffer expressed the practical consequence of this practice: "[A] prison cell like this is a good analogy for Advent; one waits, hopes, does this or that—ultimately negligible things—the door is locked and can only be opened *from the outside*."[98] Indeed, for Bonhoeffer, the absolute dependency that characterizes human existence—in relation both to God and to one another—entails that one can only receive what one most wants and needs by waiting for God's gracious in-breaking in time, history, and community.

The story of Luke-Acts is also one of uncertainty, but more than anything, it is a story of God's entanglement in human community. Even when the story appears to hang by a thread, God acts through the mundane realities of human existence: when people of God subsist under a king who claims divine authority, Jesus is born, inaugurating a very different order of authority; when Jesus, the long-anticipated messiah is crucified, God raises him from the dead; when those called by Jesus fear for their lives following the resurrection, the Holy Spirit binds them together in an unexpected community; when Peter sits imprisoned—much like Bonhoeffer—an angel of the Lord releases the chains and sends him back to work (Acts 12:6-11). The uncertainty of human existence is illumined by Luke's narrative as a site of divine encounter. Without minimizing the precarity of uncertainty, Luke recasts the perceived isolation of uncertainty as spaces to reimagine belonging; the story invites readers to see anew how we all belong to God and how we belong to one another, even in the very places of abandonment. This work of God turns the world upside down precisely in the place of uncertainty, and then invites a people into a way of life.

Bonhoeffer and Luke-Acts once again offer a resonant description of the theological rationale that guides adaptive work across these hubs. While neither hub displays a spiritual quietism that refrains from action, they also display a clear understanding of how their individual and collective work remains absolutely dependent on God and on relationships to others. While communities of faith face manifold challenges, God is already at work in local communities. The Spirit of God continues to go forth, inviting people into an unexpected community. Evidence of this understanding appears throughout this research: in the description of the Christological and ecclesial center that guides this work; in the repeated identification of the Spirit as an operative agent; and in an abiding commitment to friendship and collaboration. It is a responsive mode of existence, one that listens to what God is already doing, and works to create the conditions where individuals and communities can respond to God's gracious call upon their lives. Even as the frailty of uncertainty marks an adaptive church, the reality of God imprints possibility in the relational matrix of ordinary human existence. As Bonhoeffer and Luke-Acts suggest, the frailty of uncertainty marks adaptive work in a way that presses those who pursue it into a posture of absolute dependence, on one another and on God's gracious fulfillment, in and beyond time.

Diversity and Homogeneity

These expressions of adaptive church are marked by the countervailing fragility on account of diversity and homogeneity. A defining feature of these hubs is their ability to connect and convene individuals and communities. Their abiding commitments to partnership, collaboration, friendship, and presence have supported the creation of spaces where individuals from a broad organizational, denominational, and ideological spectrum gather and encounter one another. As Jonathan Brooks noted in the previous chapter, their collective witness has the capacity to contribute to the vitality of the broader ecclesial ecology. It can do so by renewing the pastoral and ecclesial imagination within the hubs' communities.

At the same time, the history and ongoing organization of these hubs is marked by a persistent and unmistakable homogeneity. Homogeneity is particularly apparent in terms of race and gender. Of the thirty-eight individuals who were interviewed across these hubs, thirty-five identified as white, Caucasian, or Anglo-Saxon, and twenty-seven identified as male.[99] This identification is reflected in the organizers of each hub as well. Even though each hub has recently sought to incorporate more diverse leadership, they were both forged out of gendered and racially homogenous dyads or triads. Indeed, there was more racial diversity in the composition of the annual events organized by the OCE and PC, but it still skewed heavily to one side. For example, I estimate that the OCE's Summit was about 90 percent white and attendance at PC's Inhabit Conference was majority white, even though there was greater racial diversity in terms of speakers and leadership throughout each event.[100] Admittedly, founders and the animating commitments of each hub demonstrate a concerted attention to racial diversity in their ongoing collaborative work. For example, this is reflected in the plenary topic for the OCE's Summit in 2019—The *Imago Dei* and Race—and the purposeful organization of the speakers and presenters during the PC's Inhabit Conference, which foregrounded female and minority perspectives, and the configuration of board leadership.

The presence of such diversity and homogeneity has the capacity to introduce a further form of fragility into these adaptive hubs. For example, even as scholars of entrepreneurship note how diversity in terms of age, gender, race, networks, and skill sets offer distinct strategic advantages for entrepreneurial activity, they also observe how entrepreneurial groups tend to form in ways that do not reflect a strict strategic calculus. The vast majority of entrepreneurial efforts have more homogenous features "than the prescriptive ideal envisioned by strategic approaches to entrepreneurship."[101] Although diversity of partnership could expand the potential reach of their collaborative efforts, in practice, shared entrepreneurial efforts are more often marked by homogeneity. Social and historical factors can explain the concentration of homogeneity in entrepreneurial efforts. Trust—which is frequently accrued through more than a decade of relationship—provides a means to overcome the "liability of newness" that characterizes diverse entrepreneurial teams.[102] Hence, even as the structure of the teams that have catalyzed and sustained the OCE and PC reflect the homogeneity that characterizes other entrepreneurial efforts, this homogeneity can also inhibit the reach of their work. Conversely, as both hubs seek to incorporate and nurture a greater diversity of perspectives within their organization and in their partners, the accrual of trust required for this kind of work represents a prominent challenge.

The Christo-ecclesial vision of Bonhoeffer's work and the boundary-crossing narrative in Luke-Acts similarly attend to the tension between diversity and homogeneity. For Bonhoeffer, the reconstituted ecclesial body, as the church, recasts the particulars of human existence. As Michael Mawson observes, Bonhoeffer locates individuals as "person(s) who already stand in concrete, living relationships with God, others, and reality."[103] However, arguments and potential for discord also continually exist amid this reconstituted community.[104] In a similar manner, the new community that is described in Luke-Acts is more often a community of discord than of harmony. Even as the Spirit of God binds people together in an unexpected community, the story recounts how individuals debate the terms of boundaries, partnerships, and particularity: the disciples are reluctant to receive Saul, until they receive Barnabas' testimony (Acts 9:26–27); Jerusalem Christians initially criticize Paul for sharing the word of God with Gentiles (11:2) and later question the practices that mark them as people of God (15:1); and Paul and Barnabas separate based on disagreement over who should accompany them on their journeys (15:36–41). As Willie Jennings aptly notes, these encounters press those who are called to follow Jesus into the "risk of trust."[105] Even if God has called us into a new community, can we trust that others will honor and care for fragile parts of our lives? As we move together in mission, can we preserve trust, especially when we face seeds of discord? As we consider the personal and professional risks that adaptive work requires, have we accrued enough trust to move in partnership?

For Bonhoeffer, Luke-Acts, and these adaptive hubs, crafting a community marked by homogeneity and diversity is part of the frailty of an adaptive church.

This fragility of an adaptive church surfaces two unresolved questions about the structure of the community of the hubs and their adaptive work. First, even as the pursuit of collective activity requires gathering diverse individuals and communities around their adaptive challenges, are there limits to the forms of diversity that can sustain an adaptive church? As Bonhoeffer, Luke-Acts, and the witness of these hubs suggest, the wisdom required for an adaptive church demands care and caution. While the challenges that confront communities of faith require collaboration, these partnerships can only form out of mutual trust. Trust is the precondition for the type of connection and belonging that marks an adaptive church, and the transformation an adaptive church envisions can only move at the speed of trust. In order for diversity to shape the ecclesial imagination that nourishes adaptive church, leaders and the broader community can also only move at the speed of trust. And for individuals and communities who have historically held positions of power and prestige, the partnerships that distinguish an adaptive church require a willingness to be received at the table of another, without demanding to set the table or eat first. To borrow language from Patrick Reyes, this posture requires trusting "you will be taken care of" and "learning to see that we can all eat."[106] Adaptation does not always entail activity; it invites patient presence as well. Insofar as individuals are unwilling to move at the speed of trust and pursue partnership with a posture of mutual hospitality, there will be limits to the forms of diversity that can enrich an adaptive church. Above all else, this particular frailty of an adaptive church demands patience, a willingness to wait, and trust.

Second, for communities whose collective work is animated by a Christo-ecclesial vision, how might the process of adaptive work also support the conditions for the boundary-crossing, collaborative, and pneumatic work that reflects belonging? Indeed, Bonhoeffer's own biography demonstrates how his encounters across boundaries of race and class in Harlem contributed to the formation of his Christo-ecclesial vision. That vision took shape in proximity to the "perspective of marginalized people."[107] The narrative arc of Luke-Acts moves in proximity to the discarded and dismissed: the poor, women, sinners of every stripe, Gentiles. In short, all are invited into this unexpected community where belonging restructures human relations.

Nevertheless, the countervailing fragility of diversity and homogeneity that characterizes these hubs resists an absolute defense of diversity or homogeneity as the precondition for an adaptive church. Rather, the unresolved character of this feature of the hubs' adaptive work demonstrates the need for practical wisdom to attend to the forms of diversity and homogeneity that can sustain adaptive work in light of the reality and promises of God. Their ongoing work aims to attend to pervasive divisions that mark communities of faith. Their leadership expresses their commitment to move at the speed of trust. And the local divisions within the communities they serve introduce ongoing fractures into the community created by the adaptive work they pursue. Even as each hub envisions and aims to support spaces of belonging, neither has fully achieved the connection and community they envision. Rather, they hang suspended, waiting on the ongoing work of God and listening to the needs of their communities, held together by the hope of an ever creative and connective God.

CONCLUSION

The challenges that faith communities face in this hinge time demand a way of life that imagines and sustains an adaptive church. For many communities of faith, the world has been turned upside down. With ruptures reverberating through an ecclesial ecology, communities of faith and those who lead them have to adapt. The church has always had to adapt. The community called by God is changing: this is the backdrop to the story of Luke-Acts and Bonhoeffer's life and work. To rephrase Bonhoeffer's words to a newly baptized child: "By the time [we] grow up, the form of the church will have changed considerably."

The patterned practice of an adaptive church creates structures for connection, belonging, and possibility. When crafted over time in the company of others, these expressions embody a way of life that continues a patterned practice of an adaptive church. For early Christian networks, Bonhoeffer, and these adaptive hubs alike, this patterned practice anticipates a reality that has not been fully realized. However, they are sustained by the hope of God's ongoing entanglement in time and history.

Amid a "great unraveling" in American religious life,[108] this way of life acknowledges the complex challenges that confront local communities of faith, but it also bears forth wisdom from the womb of belonging. These hubs kindle hope for a new day. In continuity with Bonhoeffer, Luke-Acts, and courageous Christian witness, the hope carried by these hubs is not for the return to power, position, or privilege. While these organizations recognize the decline of Christendom as a challenge, they also receive it as a gift. Their work embodies an interconnected, Spirit-filled, Christo-ecclesial way of life, practicing and performing the patterned practice of an adaptive church. To borrow a description from one focus group participant, they provide "a more spacious" imagination about what is possible. Their work invites us to "understand, know, and live the gospel on the ground in the midst of all that, call[ing] us to faithfulness and challeng[ing] our hope."

The patterned practice of an adaptive church leaves one question unanswered: What kind of practical wisdom is required to support and sustain the conditions and way of life that an adaptive church requires? Although Bonhoeffer and Luke-Acts point to the form of wisdom this way of life requires, they stop short of detailing its character.[109] The way of life that distinguishes the OCE and PC expresses a form of wisdom that can nurture and sustain practical wisdom.

As individuals and communities attempt to discern how the form of church has changed, and then adapt accordingly, they need Christian practical wisdom in order to pursue the conditions where individuals and communities are free to imagine and pursue an adaptive church. Chapter 7 combines the work across the previous six chapters to provide an account of the Christian practical wisdom that distinguishes an adaptive church.

IV

A Theological Paradigm for a Changing World

7

"We're Better Together"

Wisdom, Presence, and Leadership for Adaptive Change

In a cozy, book-lined office, I meet Doug Strong, the Dean of the Seattle Pacific University's school of theology. It is 2017 and this is my first research trip to the region, and I have not yet begun to focus on the OCE and the PC. Nevertheless, our conversation follows a similar pattern as my interviews across The Office of Church Engagement (OCE) and The Parish Collective (PC). When asked what else he needs to pursue the mission of his organization more faithfully, he observes: "I could use many, many more voices that articulate what the new Christianity for the twenty-first century is going to look like." He continues, "I need people—theologians, biblical scholars, and pastors—to help us see what that new vision is." Echoing the opening scene for this book, Strong expresses a need for new vision to support and sustain a Christian common life in a "new age." He continues by describing the need for "spaces and places for the collaboration to occur; where we can interact, support each other, resource each other." There is, in the language introduced by this book, a need for a more ecological ecclesiology that attends to the conditions that support a more connected and collaborative common life.[1]

The day I meet with Strong is October 31, 2017, which marks both Halloween (or All Hallows' Eve) and Reformation Day. This year commemorates the five hundredth anniversary of Martin Luther nailing his Ninety-Five Theses to the door of Castle Church in Wittenberg.[2] Strong's description of the need for new vision, voices, and spaces strikes a chord on this particular day. After speaking with Strong, I cross wood and carpeted floors and then pass through glass-paned doors to exit the building. Built in 1893 and recently updated, this structure is the university's oldest building and its construction evokes memories of the establishment of many institutions of religious higher education and theological education across the Pacific Northwest. Crossing a manicured lawn, peppered by the early leaves of fall, I recall institutional indicators that the religious heritage that inspired the founding of this institution persists: a congregation of the founding denomination sits across the street from campus; this building, which houses the theology department and seminary; and a campus-wide chapel service, which is offered weekly in the sanctuary of the adjacent congregation. As I reflected that afternoon in my notes: "With this conversation, I feel like a whole new landscape has opened up."[3]

The practical wisdom of an adaptive church presses into the need Strong and others have identified. Through collective, collaborative, and imaginative work, they nurture the conditions that enable individuals and communities to reimagine church. Nevertheless, both hubs face the challenge of identifying and preparing leaders to support and sustain the adaptive work they envision. As Ben Katt, who has a long history with the PC, observes: "There's a poverty of emerging leadership. There are few emerging leaders, in terms of innovative holistic mission-minded people, that are going to come through our traditional leadership pipelines in our denominational system." The adaptive work that these kindred hubs pursue requires a particular kind of leadership, one that reflects the requisite form of Christian practical wisdom necessary to support and sustain it.

The vision and work that organize these organizational and ecclesial adaptions gesture toward—even constitute in some cases—a response to the leadership deficit within and beyond the Pacific Northwest. Specifically, these hubs reflect and require leadership that enables individuals to respond to the challenges they face. This form of leadership, which pursues a mode of being with individuals and communities, requires Christian practical wisdom in order to be able to explore and support the conditions that mark an adaptive church.

PRACTICAL WISDOM FOR ADAPTIVE CHANGE

This book began by describing the need for Christian practical wisdom in order to respond to challenges that communities face. This chapter considers this practical wisdom for leadership within and through an adaptive church. The next chapter considers the forms of practical wisdom that can sustain this kind of adaptive change in other communities.

Christian Practical Wisdom

Much like the cable that guides hikers up a steep summit, Christian practical wisdom has provided a guidewire for this argument. This concluding section, however, clarifies the form of Christian practical wisdom that organizes and emerges from these adaptive hubs. Specifically, six aspects of Christian practical wisdom support and sustain leadership and ongoing adaptive work in and for this new age. By way of review, Christian practical wisdom is

> morally attuned, rooted in a tradition that affirms the good, and driven toward aims that seek the good. It is . . . open and adaptive to new situations. It is nimble and at times even self-critical. Most of all, this knowledge is practical, grounded in ordinary experience, and learned over time in the company of others and for the sake of others.[4]

Six features distinguish this definition: Christian practical wisdom is morally attuned; it seeks to discern the forms of virtue and ways of life that contribute to the flourishing of individuals and communities. Although there will inevitably be some disagreement about the moral framework that guides individual and collective practice, Christian practical wisdom seeks to respond to the reality and promises of God by discerning the good for those whom God calls into community.[5] Second, it emerges from a tradition that affirms the good. As noted in chapters 1 and 2, the adaptive work that organizes these adaptations arises from disparate segments of the Christian tradition. Their work engages in boundary-crossing forms of collaborative activity. The host traditions that catalyzed this work—and the attendant institutional configurations—share a desire to seek the good of individuals and communities. Third, Christian practical wisdom is nimble and adaptive. The adaptive work that organizes these hubs exemplifies Christian practical wisdom's nimble and adaptive character. In response to the challenges communities face, each hub seeks to discern appropriate adaptive responses and the pastoral nimbleness that carrying out such ministry requires. As individuals and communities engage in adaptive work, they need practical wisdom in order to negotiate the potential and the real tension between faithfulness to a received tradition and faithful innovations that one's context invites or requires.[6]

Fourth, and as a consequence of the third feature, Christian practical wisdom is also self-critical. Marked by a spirit of humility, wisdom imparts a willingness to consider the limitations, internal contradictions, or fallibility of one's own thought and practice, and that of one's community. Christian practical wisdom requires believing that we know only in part, and may be in error. Fifth, Christian practical wisdom is also grounded in ordinary experience and oriented toward praxis. Christian practical wisdom requires "affirm[ing] the wisdom and detail of these experiences as constitutive aspects of the theological enterprise."[7] If it has not been stated clearly throughout this argument, it merits repeating: attention to the quotidian, contextual, collaborative work that characterizes the OCE and PC is constitutive of the theological reflection that takes place in them and in response to their work. Sixth, and finally, Christian practical wisdom is learned in the company of others and for the sake of others. The Christian practical wisdom alive in these adaptive hubs cannot be learned alone or acquired through self-interested means; it comes through participation in the life of a community. It is frequently expressed in service to others. As noted in the previous chapter, the transformation organizers pursue requires proximity to others and a local community.[8]

As communities discern how best to pursue and support collaborative partnerships, this chapter considers the Christian practical wisdom that sustains leadership for an adaptive church. The first part discusses leadership as a form of "being with." The second part identifies six expressions of leadership that support adaptive work across this ecclesial ecology. The third part considers how the practice of leadership described in this chapter complements existing paradigms in leadership theory and practical theology.

LEADERSHIP AS BEING WITH

The leadership that animates these hubs reflects a consistent posture of "being with." As noted in chapter 3, periods of social and organizational change invite (and require) leadership. More specifically, the adaptive work organizers pursue through the PC and OCE models a posture of being with individuals and communities in light of the reality and promises of God. Providing a corrective to the limitations of Heifetz's account, this posture of "being with" reflects an explicit teleology, considering individual and collective action in relation to God's ongoing activity in time and history. Further, leadership across each hub pursues a posture of being with others—both individuals and collectives—according to a Christo-ecclesial social ontology, seeking to understand and honor the individual and collective transformation through belonging. Without dismissing the complexity and urgency of adaptive challenges, this posture situates leadership in relation to a teleology and a social ontology sufficient to sustain the individual and collective change adaptive work requires.

Describing leadership as "being with" reflects the shared language across these two hubs, but this framework also draws on insights from beyond their particular work. For example, the PC's organizers identify "the personal practice of faithful presence" as the essential precondition of leadership in and for parish renewal.[9] Rice and Frost, whose work supports the PC, similarly describe leadership as a midwife. Like a midwife, leaders create and maintain the conditions where the Spirit, communities, and individuals co-create adaptive responses to the challenges they face.[10] Reflecting on the history of their work, Friesen describes a similar posture. "I think one of those core practices, or it may not have been a practice as much as it is a bit of a posture or a framework, might be that the church isn't an end in and of itself, but it exists for the flourishing of the place it's in."

The OCE similarly cultivates a posture of "being with." Decades of friendship and relational engagement throughout the region predated the OCE's formation. Once formed, the OCE's founders pursued a listening mode in attending to the needs of local congregations and thickening the connections that are required to support and renew a dynamic ecclesial ecology. Jerry Sittser, who serves as the OCE's senior fellow, provides a fitting metaphor in *Resilient Faith*, his book on the early Christian period: "Authority in the early Christian period functioned like a circulatory system, a vast network of arteries that circulated the gospel blood."[11] Similarly, organizers and participants pursue a way of life that prioritizes relational engagement and that has a history of collaborative connection within and beyond the region. Various expressions of this posture occur across the OCE's network. Reflecting on his own practice of leadership, one participant notes, "It's not complicated, well-thought-through leadership. It's visceral relationship leadership." Similarly, as one of the conveners reflects on his own vocational journey, he notes: "I just felt like even though I might have to give up some nimbleness, I actually value being with more." As he later notes, "We're better together."

Leadership as "being with" seeks the transformation of communities and organizations by cultivating the conditions that invite individuals to join together as co-creators in light of the reality and promises of God.[12] Promoting neither quietism nor passivism, this posture assumes the agency of individuals as actors (for good and for ill) through an active form of being with individuals, communities, and the ongoing activity of the Spirit of God. Leadership as "being with" reflects an absolute dependence—on one another and on God—as the means and medium for the transformation that adaptive work requires. This posture both reflects God's Trinitarian being and Jesus' own way of being in and with the world.[13] Ultimately, it draws hope-filled perseverance from the broader *communio*, or structure of belonging, as an actor in the change God is working in the world and through an adaptive church.

Six Modes of Being With

Six modes of "being with" express the practical wisdom required to support adaptive work within a dynamic ecclesial ecology: the Caretaker, the Catalyst, the Champion, the Connector-Convener, the Surveyor, and the Guide. Leadership across these hubs rarely occurs in isolation. Rather, organizers and participants display complementary expressions that support adaptive change through their collaboration.[14] Further, the combination of different modes of leadership

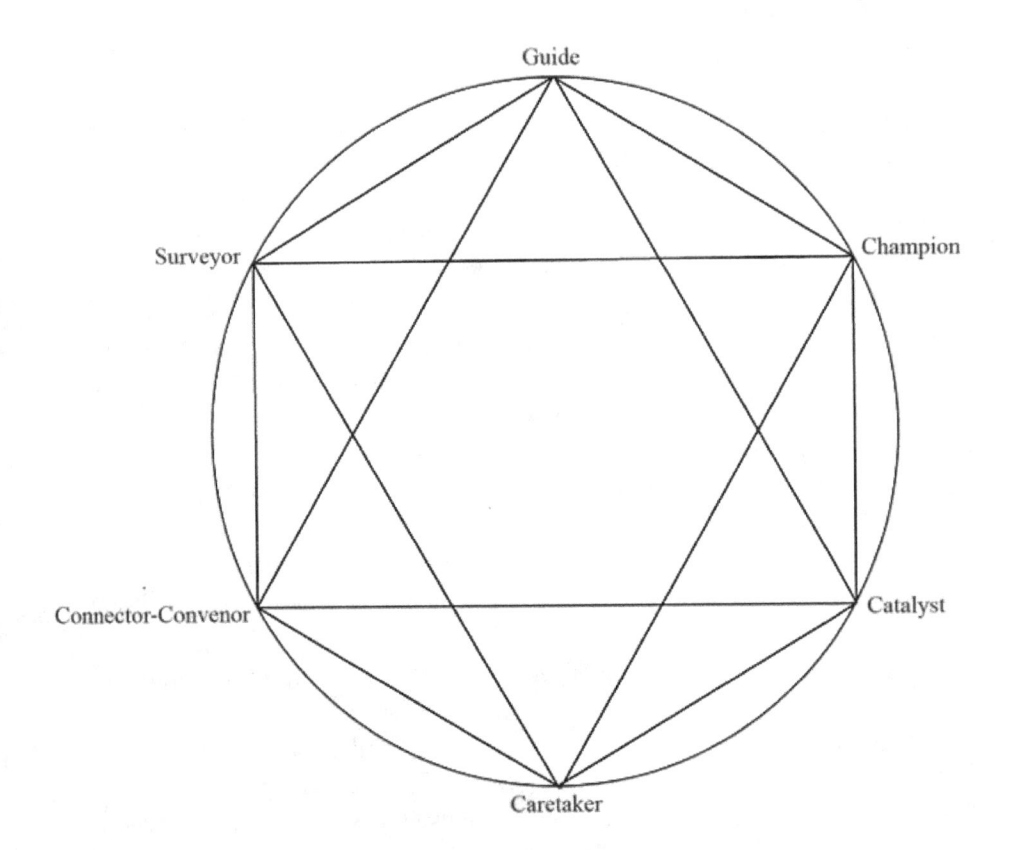

Fig. 7-1 Six Modes of Being With

across the PC and OCE highlights different kinds of teams that support adaptive change. As developed and considered in relation to these kindred organizational and ecclesial adaptations, these modes of leadership cluster in a pattern of complementary relationships, as visualized in figure 7-1.

The descriptions below introduce each of the six modes of leadership and then consider how three patterns of partnership (teams, centers and ranges, and polarities) organize adaptive work within the Pacific Northwest's ecclesial ecology. Each description identifies the defining features of each mode, describes two organizing practices, and offers a metaphor for how individuals express this mode of being with in relation to the communities they serve.

Caretaker

The Caretaker holds the hopes, dreams, and pains of a community, seeking to create the conditions where they are transformed through an encounter with God and community. This form of leadership emerges from a profound care for individuals and their collective well-being and affirms the abundance of the resources that exist within a given community. Frequently serving their community behind the scenes, leaders of this type manage the day-to-day activities required for a common life. This mode of "being with" includes administrative competence, but it requires much more than managerial technique. Rather, it reflects a way of inhabiting a space and being in relation to others that maintains the conditions for ongoing change. Caretakers shape the specific details that enable connection and transformation to happen. As one individual describes the intention that directs her leadership in a community: "I touch, I frame, I shape, I set up, I choose." Both local leaders and senior administrators expressed leadership through "being with" in the mode of a Caretaker.

The two organizing practices for this mode of being are *presence* and *setting the table*. The practice of "presence" reflects individuals' application of relational fidelity and commitment to the collective's well-being. In some cases, this practice is expressed in their commitment to a definite locale or neighborhood; in others, it is expressed in care for the connections across disparate parts of a broader ecology. Reflecting a Caretaker's commitment to presence, an organizer in one hub describes the importance of listening, service, and humility. Speaking of the practical consequences, he notes: "You're always welcome at this table, but if you don't want to come to the table unless you're going to require us to push that partner away from the table, then we really can't collaborate together because that violates the very spirit of who we are." The practice of presence dovetails with the practice of "setting the table," which creates and maintains the conditions that support the flourishing of individuals and communities. Although this second organizing practice includes logistical matters of staffing, partnerships, and collaboration, it also can include literal meals. Reflecting on her own leadership, one parish pastor notes: "And so I think leadership, first, is remembering, like, who's at the table, how is power being shared, whose voices are here, which is a much slower way to grow the church. To get other voices involved in saying let's figure out what this can look like." After noting how this commitment is expressed in formal and informal settings, she summarizes: "It's a lot of setting the table."

Meanwhile, like an organizational midwife, Caretakers pursue a form of "being with" that creates and maintains the organizational conditions for individual and collective flourishing. Caretakers are attentive to the complex interplay among an organizational setting, the individuals who comprise a community, and the Spirit's generative work. The wisdom borne by Caretakers pursues a collaborative response to the changing needs of individuals and communities. As one individual summarizes: "We just hold space and we just watch it emerge and we just see the stories emerge." Moreover, Caretakers' work is dynamic, constantly evolving to respond to the changing composition and needs of the community they serve. Displaying prudent attention to the new things that others—namely the Spirit—are bringing into being, they cultivate signs of life when they emerge.[15] With their words, work, wisdom, and winsome presence, Caretakers create and maintain the organizational conditions in which meaningful encounters occur.

Catalyst

Located counterclockwise of the Caretaker, the Catalyst is an entrepreneur who inhabits the edges of organizations and institutions. An innovator in a position or organization, she is a spark for the change that impacts the broader ecclesial ecology. These individuals are starters, but not necessarily sustainers. Reflecting on a Catalyst in one of these networks, a colleague shared: "She loves to start things, get them going, and then set them free to somebody else who's going to maintain them." Indeed, the work of the Catalyst involves liberating ideas and individuals in ways that enrich the organizations and the communities that individuals inhabit. Catalysts often express discomfort with established organizations and professions, but they are far from mavericks. Rather, they are constantly ideating in proximity to others, and are frequently creating the conditions for others to do the same. Moreover, when located in proximity to a Champion, the Catalyst's capacity to take risks, innovate, and create expands exponentially. Across both hubs, the work of Catalysts redounds to the broader ecology by infusing new ideas and innovations into the network of relationships.

The Catalyst's organizing practices are *innovating* and *ideating*. As expressed by organizers and participants across each hub, Catalysts pursue the practice of innovating in order to alter the conditions that support a life of faith. For Catalysts in each hub, the work of innovation represents more than a creative bent; it is a missional imperative. Responding to the challenges that confront communities of faith, Catalysts carry the entrepreneurial spirit that animates attempts to reimagine church. As one Catalyst observed: "I almost feel like my calling is to change the mind of the church." Consequently, Catalysts pursue a second organizing practice: ideating. If innovating expresses Catalysts' drive to explore ecclesial innovations, ideating represents their ongoing attempt to refine and alter expressions. As illustrated in the history and organization of each hub, Catalysts' work represents an ongoing attempt to ideate around the challenges they face. Emerging from sustained engagement with local communities and according to an ecclesial vision, Catalysts' ideation expresses a willingness to take risks and experiment for the sake of a community. Further, when given an adequate holding environment, Catalysts' ideation nimbly refines ideas, practices, and programs in response to the evolving needs and composition of a community.[16]

An ecclesial entrepreneur provides a fitting metaphor for this mode. Ecclesial entrepreneurs occupy existing roles of religious leadership (e.g., pastors, priests, chaplains), as well as a host of adjacent roles (e.g., parachurch workers, nonprofit professionals, social workers, activists).[17] As expressed by Catalysts, ecclesial entrepreneurship is ecclesially rooted innovation that catalyzes change based on a restless discontent with the status quo and a hopeful vision for the transformation of individuals and communities. This kind of rooted-and-renovating work involves "liv[ing] into the tensions of going for something we don't see," as one Catalyst observed. Catalysts do not pursue forms of ecclesial entrepreneurship simply for the sake of novelty. Rather, these individuals ideate, innovate, and collaborate in proximity to their place and for the sake of the common good.

Champion

The Champion's mode of "being with" energizes and elevates the adaptive work taking place at diverse points across an ecclesial ecology. Champions are not possessive of resources or potential, they leverage their position and privilege for the sake of others. Reflecting the Champion's mode of "being with," one individual described her leadership in these terms: "I feel like a lot of my role of leadership is trying to release leadership as opposed to trying to take it, if that makes sense, and trying to invite other people into positions of leadership they might not have before." While the Champion's mode of "being with" clarifies the purpose and process of adaptive work—frequently through questions—their fundamental orientation reflects a commitment to the individuals and communities they serve. Champions express their leadership by "coming alongside" and "holding and creating space" for others' work and ideas. Champions elevate individuals and adaptive work. Though this mode does not require formal authority, positions of authority enhance a Champion's reach. As a result, the Champion's distinct mode of "being with" enables and maintains the environments for adaptive individuals and communities to form and mature.

Two practices characterize the Champion's work: *elevating others* and *telling stories*. These practices reflect the Champion's mode of "being with" in distinct ways; in many instances, however, these practices are intertwined. Reflecting on his own form of leadership, one Champion notes: "Leadership is primarily influence in connection, so those are the two things that we're trying to do.... [Y]ou do that by casting vision on stories, by elevating stories. So, in some of us who are in leadership, one of the advantages and privileges that we have is that we know more broadly what's going on." The Champion elevates others' work and ideas in order that a broader community can learn from these creative expressions. At the same time, Champions tell stories. Exemplified by the Parish Portraits that occur throughout the PC's Inhabit Conference, storytelling champions the work of others and affirms this kind of slow, adaptive work. In many cases, a Champion's ability to identify and tell stories casts light on overlooked components of the ecclesial ecology. For the individuals engaged in the day-to-day work of an adaptive church, the Champion's ability to be with individuals in this way conveys a sense of being seen, heard, and valued. When pursued and expressed over time, these two organizing practices validate adaptive work that is already taking place and stimulate similar expressions in other communities.

The metaphor of a "player-coach" expresses the Champion's mode of leadership. As described in *The New Parish*, a player-coach combines wisdom that comes from lived experience with the ability to encourage and inspire at critical junctures. In contrast to a disengaged expert who is removed from "the game," the player-coach "not only has played many games before but is in the game right now."[18] Individuals who inhabit this role possess a form of wisdom, which reflects an understanding of the skills and experience of their team, and comes from knowing how to play the game. When considered as an expression of the Champion's mode of being, this metaphor accentuates the Champion's relational embeddedness, which cultivates and requires wisdom. When expressed over time and in the context of a community, this particular form of practical wisdom enlivens adaptive work in and for a dynamic ecclesial ecology.

Connector-Convener

The Connector-Convener, located clockwise from the Caretaker, pursues being with individuals and communities by tending the connective sinews of the ecclesial ecology where adaptive change takes place. These individuals, who are acutely aware of pervasive disconnection, understand the importance of shared texts and context, and they work to provide mediums for individuals to meet and connect. Connector-Conveners also place a high value on the importance of personal relationships and possess emotional intelligence and interpersonal skills. Reflecting on a key Connector-Convener in this ecology, someone shared: "[He] has this endless capacity to hold information and people." While there is an abundance of Connector-Conveners across these two networks, this mode of being reflects more than an ability to make introductions. Rather, the work of the Connector-Convener reflects years of relational engagement in diverse contexts and depends on an unshakeable sense that "we are better together." Carrying in their minds a relational rolodex, Connector-Conveners have a sense for the stories that comprise a community and ways to gather people in order to make meaningful connections. Organizations create a platform for an expanded mode of convening, but the practical wisdom for how to convene people well is borne by particular individuals within an ecology.

The Connector-Convener mode may initially seem to represent two separate modes: one that connects and one that convenes. However, these expressions represent a single mode of inhabiting a dynamic ecclesial ecology. Those who express this practical wisdom understand how connections alone are insufficient for the transformation they envision. An adaptive church requires rebuilding the connections that enable collaborative work, but a sense of belonging emerges when people are purposefully gathered together. Like the downstrokes and upstrokes of a cyclist turning a bicycle's pedals, the interlocking work of connecting and convening builds and strengthens the connective sinews that initiate and sustain adaptive change.

The practices of *asking questions* and *listening* express the Connector-Convener's distinct mode of leadership. In each case, these practices represent active postures of being with individuals and communities. In listening, Connector-Conveners affirm the dignity, value, and contributions of individuals in and to a community. They are also listening for where and how the Spirit of God is moving in and through their midst. Expressed by organizers and participants across these hubs, this practice of listening permeates the connective and collaborative work that organizes each hub. As one Connector-Convener notes, this practice is indexed to a local community and the relational connections that comprise it: "[I] mak[e] those connections and listening; I do a lot of listening as a leader," she states, before breaking off into a long chuckle. She then continues, "Listening to people's stories, to what the Spirit might be up to." Similarly, Steve Moore, who directs the M. J. Murdock Charitable Trust, one of the chief convening organizations in the region, identifies listening as a central practice of their grantmaking efforts. "[I]t grows out of listening; it grows out of figuring out a pathway forward. It's not always real clear what that pathway forward is; [you] figure out who are some people or some groups that are really doing great work, and then try to put gasoline on that, and multiply and duplicate it."

Listening dovetails with the practice of asking questions, which seeks to understand and explore the gifts, challenges, passions, and pains that animate a person's life. Connector-Conveners ask questions in order to open space for new ideas, imagination, connections, and possibilities to emerge; their questions "create the space for something new to emerge."[19] Expressed in an invitational rather than critical spirit, this practice invites those who respond to offer the gifts of their perspective and wisdom. Further, connection to specific localities and communities of faith disciplines the practice. When employed in the context of trust-filled relationships, the practice of asking questions directs attention to the personal and collective transformation that adaptive change requires.

When listening and asking questions are paired, they enable Connector-Conveners to nurture and enhance the connective tissue within an ecclesial ecology. A central Connector-Convener summarizes the close relationship these two practices share: "The gift of listening and asking questions is in itself a way of learning. . . . Every question must be genuine, but I am also aware that the listening process and the questioning process help people learn to see, and listen, and ask questions for themselves." Citing the importance of the work he has done to understand "ecology," he then observes how he's developed a sense for what "good connections look like." He notes: "You start to get the feel for what things need to fit together." Reflecting a form of *phronesis* that emerges in relation to place, relationships, and a broader tradition of thought and practice, this "feel for what things need to fit together" directs Connector-Conveners' engagement with the communities they serve. When combined with other expressions of leadership, this posture enhances the relational connectivity required for an adaptive church.

The metaphor of a conductor clarifies the practical wisdom that directs the Connector-Convener's distinct mode of being with individuals and communities. Like a conductor directing an orchestra, the Connector-Convener has know-how that enables her to gather and coordinate diverse voices, experiences, and perspectives. Their work requires considering both the individual contributions and the collective potential before them. As Sparks, Soerens, and Friesen note, a conductor "seeks to facilitate the flow, to awaken presence, to help all parties enter in fully aware of their unique limits and responsibilities. . . . The person in this role understands leadership as an active way of being, not a static position of authority."[20] Where this metaphor falters, however, is in the centrality and visible position that the conductor occupies. Much like a conductor, Connector-Conveners can support good and beautiful expressions of community; nevertheless, the practical wisdom they bear frequently takes place "off-stage." It is frequently expressed in the time between conference events, in coffee shops, or on the streets of a neighborhood. Like a conductor standing before her orchestra pit, Connector-Conveners express a form of practical wisdom that reflects intimate knowledge of the community they serve and the complementary gifts that reside within it. Connector-Conveners catalog the ways these gifts resonate with one another. They enable individuals to gather and encounter one another in ways that enhance collective well-being. Their leadership, however, principally points to others and supports the conditions where others resonate together independent of a Connector-Convener. Through gathering and connecting of individuals and communities Connector-Conveners envision a future where others have the wisdom to navigate the relational matrix of an ecology on their own.

Surveyor

The Surveyor pursues a mode of "being with" that first attends to the system of connections and ideas that comprise an ecclesial ecology, then seeks to translate insights for the good of the community. It is common for Surveyors to have some academic training, but this posture is not exclusively expressed by academics. Rather, this mode of "being with" is borne by organizers and participants who have the ability to think at the systems level, noting the connections between individual parts and the whole. These individuals frequently have wide-ranging interests and experience. As one Surveyor notes, they are well suited for a "think tank" environment. Nevertheless, their connection to local communities and faith leaders disciplines their work in a way that grounds it in the lived realities of people of faith. Reflecting their expansive interests, Surveyors are attuned to the entire ecclesial ecology, attending both to the center and the margins. Accordingly, these individuals inhabit this ecology as collectors and translators of information, frequently inviting feedback from multiple sources. They then work to translate ideas, concepts, and information for the good of the community. Reflecting more than thought leadership, this form of "being with" informs and enriches the vision that directs adaptive change within communities of faith.

Surveyors are less common across these hubs than are Connector-Conveners. Nevertheless, this mode of "being with" is expressed in two practices: *investigation* and *translation*. First, Surveyors' investigation seeks to explore and understand the patterns, connections, and concepts that are the material of a common life. Investigating includes sustained engagement with ideas and scholarship; curiosity pervades Surveyors' mode of "being with," directing their attention and eliciting wonder. However, Surveyors' investigation is relationally directed. As a Surveyor summarized: "I think part of it is just like being present, being curious."[21] This form of investigation is certainly directed toward conventional communities, practices, and resources, but it also includes attending to what is happening at the boundaries or on the margins. The work of Surveyors, in this regard, includes attending to the broader social and historical landscape in which particular adaptive expressions arise. Surveyors then work to translate the insights that emerge from their engagement, with other ideas and within the ecclesial ecology, in order to enrich faithful action. As one Surveyor notes, he understands his vocation as being a bridge between the church and the academy. "I would say my central calling is to be a bridge between the world of the academy, the world of ideas, great texts, great ideas, and the world of ordinary people and the church," he shares, "And so I have to kind of live in both worlds."[22] Surveyors live in both worlds, move between them, and work to craft the conditions that place concepts and communities in conversation, to the benefit of intellectual and local communities alike. And, as this Surveyor notes, the work of translation requires wisdom. "So, you've gotta negotiate that world and live in that world, but figure out how to distill it, and so you can communicate to a larger world that needs to learn from these ideas and adapt them and grow in a wisdom."

The organizing metaphor for Surveyors' work, a community librarian, clarifies the phronetic dimension of their leadership. Like a community librarian, the Surveyor trades in concepts and texts; thinkers and ideas are like friends to them, assuming a life of their own and filling the Surveyor's idle thoughts. Surveyors know the texts of varying bodies of knowledge and have the ability to guide others as they explore the relevance of various texts and concepts in the face of a challenge. Discussing the form of leadership his work requires, one Surveyor observes: "[Leaders are] like a librarian in that they are resourcing people to live into their sense of call or mission, like their place, in the way that's uniquely them. Like what's the research question that a people, that they're trying to live into. The librarian can't answer that for them. They can't tell them what to do." In this way, Surveyors support and serve communities by directing exploration, but their engagement is based in relationship with a discrete community and particular relationships. Much like a community librarian, they display a form of practical wisdom that combines thorough knowledge of information with an intimate understanding of the complexities of their people's lives and their surrounding community. The antithesis of an isolated researcher, Surveyors study and steward both texts and contexts. When embedded in a particular community, Surveyors have the ability to offer a word on point, combining their knowledge and wisdom to speak to the needs, questions, and challenges of those they serve.

Guide

The final form of "being with," the Guide, reflects a posture of coming alongside individuals and communities amid their uncertainty. Mentors, spiritual directors, and life coaches express certain aspects of this form of "being with." However, the Guide's mode of "being with" bears something more. Guides have a perspective that enables them to see the whole—to occupy a balcony space—and well-worn wisdom about the conditions that can start and sustain adaptive change. They have the imagination to see the "more" in the ecology and all of its constitutive parts. Guides have connections to communities of faith, but their practical wisdom supports adaptive change in communities beyond their own geographic locale. This individual is not prescriptive, but offers guidance about the next step. Often removed from the spotlight, this figure is not always self-evident, but remains essential to the adaptive work that takes place across this ecology. To borrow language from one careful reader of culture and communities, Guides combine a range of skills and experiences; they are "a sage, supporter, and a saint."[23] Expressed both at the local level and in senior positions of administrative leadership, this form of "being with" is anchored in a profound care for the flourishing of individuals and communities.

A Guide's posture reflects two organizing practices: *coming alongside* and *discerning the next step*. The first practice, "coming alongside," reflects Guides' ardent commitment to the well-being of individuals and communities. They provide support that enables action without being overly prescriptive. As one Guide notes, "I'm always really reminded of the importance that leadership is this alongside posture. . . . I want to sit back and watch people live and thrive and [do] what they intend to contribute to the world, and nobody needs to know that you have a part in that." Accordingly, Guides come alongside individuals and communities, journeying with them and enabling them to take appropriate action. The Guide's work includes a second practice: "discerning the next step." While the Guide's mode of being entails relational fidelity expressed through the practice of "coming alongside," the Guide also supports faithful forms of action. Their practice enables individuals and communities to discern the next step. While Guides stop short of prescribing the outcome of adaptive change, they provide insight and direction at critical junctures in the life of an individual or a community. Other members of the ecclesial ecology, not the Guides themselves, identify the impact of a Guide's practice and posture on their adaptive work. From the practical wisdom of local parish leaders to senior administrators in philanthropy, the well-worn wisdom of Guides enables individuals and communities to discern and then take the next step. While the outcome of this kind of "being with" rests with local communities, words and wisdom from Guides provide the courage to keep going. Reflecting on the early work that contributed to the writing of *The New Parish*, the authors observe: "Without the miracle of support, collaboration and guidance from the growing web of partners and practitioners experimenting in parishes, we would not have made it this far."[24]

The practical wisdom that animates the Guide's posture is embodied by Virgil from *The Divine Comedy*. Identified as a guide throughout the text,[25] Virgil exhibits a patient presence that reflects a Guide's distinct form of practical wisdom. Like Virgil, the Guide journeys with individuals and communities from peril to beatitude. Along the way, Virgil both interprets the stages of a journey and cautions about potential hazards. Virgil offers advice where needed and correction when his charge, Dante, is at risk, but there are also moments where Virgil's knowledge and experience are depicted as limited. A thoroughly human figure, the Guide offers their best, well-worn wisdom, even as they continue their own journey. Over time, Dante becomes less reliant on his Guide. Further, an exemplar of wisdom, Virgil's own journey provides the basis for the guidance he offers. Virgil's words and work emerge from alongside, enabling Dante to take the next step, and pointing him to the ultimate source of human flourishing. As their journey concludes, Dante finds himself in the company of Beatrice, who personifies wisdom, virtue, and grace. And, at this point, Dante's guide, Virgil, departs.[26] In a similar manner, the Guide inhabits the ecclesial ecology as a patient presence, simultaneously working alongside and going before, in a way that enables individuals and communities to take the next step on their adaptive journey.

These six modes of "being with" reflect the interrelated expressions of leadership that sustain an adaptive church within a changing ecclesial ecology. The formation and leadership of hubs requires more than a single form or posture of leadership; it invites a complementary combination of different modes of being with individuals and communities. Table 7-1 summarizes these six modes of leadership.

Mode of Leadership	Organizing Practices	Metaphor
Caretaker	Presence Setting the Table	Organizational Midwife
Catalyst	Ideating Innovating	Ecclesial Entrepreneur
Champion	Elevating Others Telling Stories	Player-Coach
Connector-Convener	Listening Asking Questions	Conductor
Surveyor	Investigation Translation	Community Librarian
Guide	Coming Alongside Discerning the Next Step	Virgil

Table 7-1 Summary Table for Six Modes of Leadership

These diverse expressions of leadership share a common feature: they all require and cultivate a form of wisdom. Expressed in various ways in the examples used above, practical wisdom reflects a somatic and social form of knowledge; it emerges from individuals' engagement with various contexts and traditions, and it is borne by practice. It is a kind of knowledge into which one is constantly being formed. The inseparable connection between local communities and leadership entails that the acquisition of this wisdom is never final or finished; it constantly evolves in response to the changing texture, composition, and community one serves. As one local leader notes: "It's a deeper wisdom; you know, it develops an intuition in me that I'm able to then lead out of that, with that intuition." Over time, the fabric of relationships and the place one serves cultivates a form of wisdom.

PARTNERSHIPS FOR ADAPTIVE CHANGE

Attending to these six modes surfaces the different expressions of leadership that organize the OCE and PC, but it also demonstrates how leadership for an adaptive church is never exercised alone. Rather, these six modes demonstrate a complementary pattern of collaboration. Specifically, three patterns of partnership sustain each hub's adaptive work: leadership teams, ranges and centers, and forms of complementary polarity.

LEADERSHIP TEAMS

While the OCE and PC share a collaborative leadership structure, their leadership teams include people who operate with different modes of "being with." For example, the organizers of the OCE combine the Caretaker's, the Surveyor's, and the Champion's modes of being with. McGonigal exemplifies the practical wisdom of a Caretaker, Sittser leads as a Surveyor, and Taylor serves as a Champion for this work. Each one supports and sustains the OCE's adaptive work by making their distinct contributions to the collaborative effort. Frequently described as a "team," each contributes in ways that enhance the collective activity. While each member has the ability to play multiple roles and demonstrates a range of capacities, each leads out of their respective center.[27] This assessment does not suggest that these leaders cannot or do not exhibit other capacities; rather, this particular team demonstrates the complementary capacities that support their distinct kind of adaptive work.

The team that organized and now sustains the PC's adaptive work likewise reflects a triad of complementary leadership capacities. Their team combines the Connector-Conveyer's, the Catalyst's, and the Guide's forms of being with individuals and communities. For example, Sparks identifies, attends to, and connects individuals and communities engaged in parish-based work. Emerging from his practice of walking neighborhoods, he has developed an acute sensitivity to the kinds of connections that can sustain neighborhood work and an ability to listen for and see the people engaged in it. Soerens demonstrates a catalytic capacity to start, resource, and connect forms of ecclesial entrepreneurship.

While he frequently connects and convenes individuals, his primary mode of being with reflects that of a Catalyst. Furthermore, the early work of the PC required identifying and finding individuals who could guide their work. Over time, they identified individuals beyond the region who could serve as mentors and guides (e.g., Peter Block and Walter Brueggemann), but their early work identified and learned from ordinary Guides who were already doing this work in the neighborhood. The growth of this movement and recent attempts to sustain it have required identifying additional guides. They have learned with and from individuals who have the capacity to help them navigate their adaptive journey. Finally, Christiana Rice, who recently joined the organizing team, pursues a form of being with that reflects the Guide's distinct form of practical wisdom. While Sparks and Soerens similarly provide guidance for individuals throughout this network, Rice's combination of skills and experience complements Sparks' and Soerens' primary modes of leadership.

The differences between these two teams illustrate how different kinds of leadership support adaptive change amid fixed and ambiguous organizational settings. The adaptive work that organizes these hubs occurs within different organizational configurations: a fixed set of organizational arrangements (OCE) and an ambiguous set of organizational arrangements (PC). In a fixed set the primary partners and relationships are adequately defined in order to organize and pursue a common objective. In an ambiguous set, identifiable partners exist but the collaborative activity is centered in a shared concern, and the specific relationship to and among these partners is not clearly defined.

The distinction between fixed and ambiguous organizational settings brings to the surface the kinds of teams that sustain an adaptive church in each context. In the case of the OCE, its team supports adaptive work in a fixed organizational setting. In such a context, where primary partners and relationships are already defined, the work of a Caretaker, Champion, and Surveyor sustains their work. Adaptive work in this context takes place within the bounds of an existing organization and attendant set of relationships. While the OCE seeks to strengthen and rekindle relationships that have been lost, their work, nonetheless, takes place in proximity to an established organization: the Caretaker attends to the conditions that care for both what already exists and what is emerging; a Champion nurtures and maintains a holding environment within a fixed organizational setting for this kind of adaptive work to take place. For the OCE, the senior office holder played this role, but a Champion's primary contribution to adaptive change is not their formal position, but the credibility to champion it. Even within a fixed organizational setting, a Champion supports this work by creating and maintaining space within existing structures and partnerships where adaptive, entrepreneurial activity can take form and flourish. The Surveyor supports adaptive work within a fixed organizational setting by tending to the constellation of resources and relationships that sustain that work. The Surveyor's role, at this point, requires taking stock of existing resources and relationships and those that exist beyond the fixed set. For example, Sittser's work as a Surveyor involves demonstrating how the work and wisdom of the early Christian tradition enriches contemporary thought and practice. It also includes engaging with individuals and communities beyond the mainline tradition. The contribution of the Surveyor, in this way, contributes to the team in a fixed setting by infusing the work with information and imaginative resources.

The specific configuration of the PC supports adaptive change within an ambiguous organizational setting. While this configuration lacks the clear boundaries of a fixed set, the organizing and adaptive work in which it engages has a clear center: the renewal of ecclesial life in the neighborhood. To this end, their team, which includes a Catalyst, a Connector-Convener, and a Guide, pursues adaptive work in the absence of clear boundaries. The Connector-Convener identifies and connects individuals engaged in common forms of adaptive work. In the absence of clearly defined organizational boundaries and partners, the wisdom of the Connector-Convener links isolated individuals and communities and then convenes them around a shared purpose. The Catalyst complements the team by ideating and innovating beyond the boundaries of conventional thought and practice. As Soerens' leadership demonstrates, the PC is working to imagine alternative structures, practices, and conceptual frameworks that can reground church in the neighborhood. Although he is in no way the sole Catalyst in this network, Soerens' leadership reflects the Catalyst's practice of ecclesial entrepreneurship, pursuing ecclesially rooted innovation that catalyzes change based on a restless discontent with the status quo and a hopeful vision for the transformation of individuals and communities. Combining practical wisdom drawn from ministry and entrepreneurship, the Catalyst supports entrepreneurial adaptive work by tending to the relationships, resources, and partnerships that can sustain this collective effort. Centered in attention to place and church in the neighborhood, the work of the Catalyst in ambiguous organizational settings requires moving within, across, and beyond established organizational boundaries.

Finally, the Guide plays a critical role on a team in an ambiguous organizational setting. The Guide offers well-worn wisdom about the course this team should pursue and the appropriate next step. At critical junctures, the PC's organizing team has leaned on the practical wisdom of Guides. For example, their early work emerged alongside the wisdom of parish-based practitioners; the growth of their network drew wisdom from missional, theological, and organizational guides; their recent attempts to sustain this work draw wisdom from Guides within and beyond the organization. At each critical stage, the Guide comes alongside and leads from within as individuals and organizations discern the next step. While the Guide reiterates the centrality of the organizing mission, he or she also contributes to the collective effort to imagine and pursue new ways to organize a common life. Identifying the need for leadership that draws wisdom from midwives, one Guide similarly observes: "Midwives never take the credit, they always say that they just attended the process." Leading with patient presence and a hopeful vision for what an adaptive church can be(come), Guides invite individuals and communities to imagine what is possible on the other side of uncertainty.

The leadership teams for the PC and OCE, then, reflect different configurations of roles that pursue adaptive change, yet these two configurations also overlap. To return to the image with which this chapter opened, these teams represent distinct and complementary ways to pursue adaptive work in response to the challenges communities face.

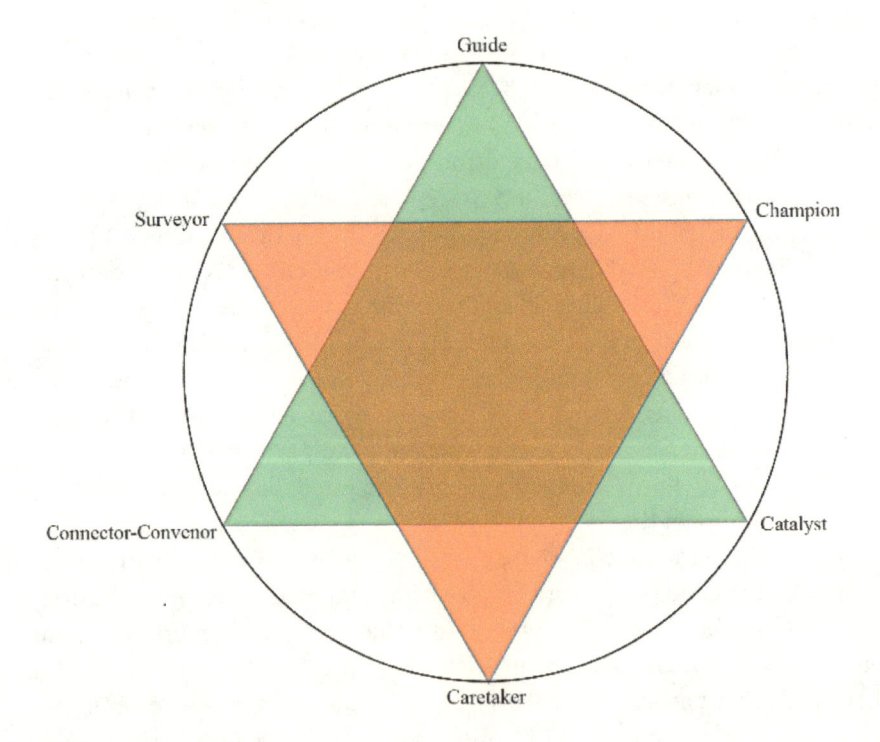

Fig. 7-2 Leadership Teams

While each team has its distinct features, the teams share features as well. For example, the OCE engages in catalytic, entrepreneurial activities that seek to reimagine church. It draws heavily on the practical wisdom of Guides within and beyond the organization. Its formal leaders employ various forms of connecting and convening in pursuing their adaptive work. Similarly, the PC's work is supported and sustained by the practical wisdom of Surveyors within and beyond the network. This work also requires Champions.[28] Finally, the sustainability of the PC depends on Caretakers who can attend to the growing network and organization that surrounds its work. Individuals across both teams demonstrate a nimble versatility that enables them to play multiple roles. Much like an athlete who can support her team by playing multiple positions, leadership teams require wisdom and the ability to lead through multiple modes of being.

The versatility of individuals on both teams should not obscure a fundamental insight: the different environments out of which an adaptive church emerges require a team that can lead amid the uncertainty they encounter. The fixed organizational setting requires a team that can work within the boundaries of an established organization, even as it works to redefine the boundaries that can expand their project. The ambiguous organizational setting requires a team that can catalyze, connect, and convene disparate individuals, communities, and organizations around a central concern. The work that takes place where these forms of "being with" overlap comprises a generative, liminal space of imaginative possibilities.[29] In this boundary space—where different teams and forms of organizing adaptive work intersect—this convergence offers generative conditions for new patterns and practices to emerge.[30]

Centers and Ranges

An adaptive church also requires complementary modes of leadership. For individuals across these hubs, their particular expression of a single mode frequently includes a range of adjacent expressions. For example, the Caretaker's mode of "being with" includes its adjacent expressions: the Connector-Convener and the Catalyst. The distinction between centers and ranges describes this pattern. "Centers" express the central mode of "being with" that grounds individuals' engagement with a community and their contribution to a team that pursues adaptive work. "Ranges" describe the breadth of individuals' mode of being with the individuals and communities they serve. Individuals across both hubs display a central mode of leadership, but they are also capable of operating in other closely related modes.

The exterior hexagon in figure 7-3 visualizes the connections between each mode and its adjacent neighbors.

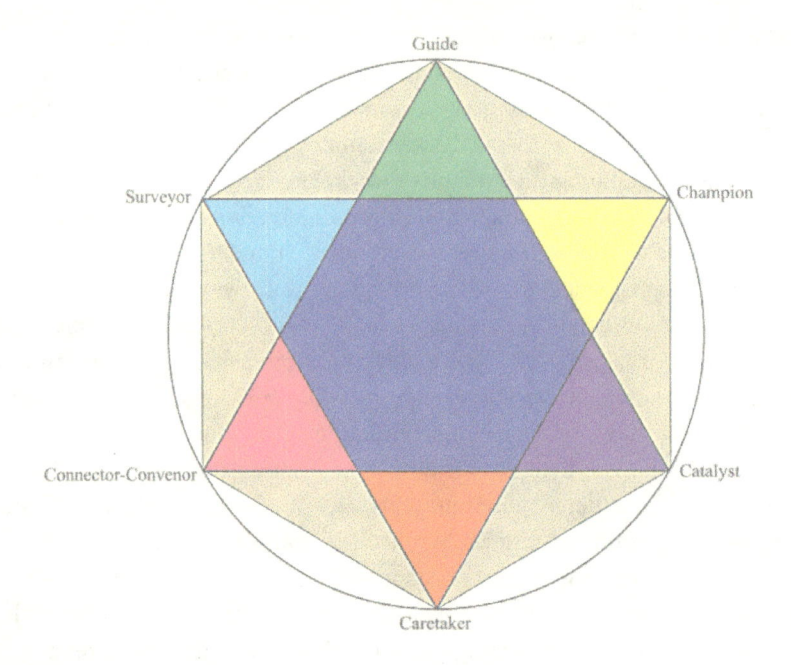

Fig. 7-3 Centers and Ranges

For example, the practical wisdom of the Caretakers includes both the ability to connect-convene and to catalyze change within the community they serve. This work, as pursued by individuals across this ecology, is grounded in a commitment to care for and nurture the community where one serves. As one pastoral leader notes: "I really think, in terms of pastoral leadership, that, ideally, I'm investing in other staff members, and a small group of people who have been identified as leaders in some capacity throughout the congregation, and that there is a diversity in that. . . . I really believe in a ripple down leadership model of investing time and energy in a few people really well over a course of a long haul, while continuing to encourage them to also invest in a few people over the long haul." As she continues later, the work of leadership in her context emerges from "a commitment to sticking with people for the long haul" in hopes that small and incremental changes can shift the culture of the broader community. She concludes: "You're looking for shifts of inches rather than 180 degrees, and those little shifts of inches can actually change the church trajectory of the community of faith together." As exemplified in her work, a Caretaker's leadership involves both connecting-convening individuals and supporting the conditions for catalytic change.

In a similar manner, the Connector-Convener draws upon adjacent modes of "being with." The M. J. Murdock Charitable Trust exemplifies this interrelationship. Emerging from a vision to "serve individuals, families and communities across the Pacific Northwest," they pursue their work by "build[ing] relationships for the common good."[31] As described by Steve Moore, Murdock's executive director, their grantmaking is "trying to nurture and strengthen the ecosystem." In doing so, however, they pursue their work through a form of connecting-convening that reflects and draws upon adjacent expressions. Through regular convening and ongoing collaboration with leaders and institutions from across the region, they listen to the needs of their constituency. Like a Surveyor, this information gives them perspective about the whole, which they then translate to support individuals and communities. Like a Caretaker, the animating concern for their work is the well-being of the communities they serve. As a result, Moore describes his leadership in a way that is centered in the wisdom of a Connector-Convener, but also includes adjacent expressions: "[We] try to listen deeply or listen closely to the burdens or challenges of the heart that leaders face and to have ways and programs that might provide what would address those particular needs."[32] As expressed by a similar Connector-Convener, this leadership includes "get[ting] all of their ideas, thoughts, stories in the room together for the sake of having a dialogue and to learn from another through those very experiences."

The Surveyor likewise draws upon adjacent expressions. One Surveyor regularly gathers pastors from across the region, and these connections provide insight about local communities of faith. Perpetually attending to individuals and the broader "system" they inhabit, as one Surveyor notes, they are constantly collecting information and insights from those they serve. Others may also describe them as Guides, as their perspective and understanding of the whole enables them to encourage others to take a particular step.

The Catalyst's mode of ecclesial entrepreneurship is expressed in proximity to adjacent modes of leadership. Even as their ideating and innovating takes place on the boundaries of established organizations or orders, they catalyze change precisely because they care for individuals and communities. Frequently pursued by individuals who are connected to their neighborhoods and local community, their catalytic work is an expression of neighborliness and a hopeful discontentment with the status quo. These ecclesial entrepreneurs frequently start and support the programs, businesses, and kinds of change that can enrich a broader ecclesial ecology. In each case, the innovation emerges from and returns to specific people-in-communities. Described elsewhere as a "system entrepreneur," the wisdom of the Catalyst enables them to "connec[t] to community, civic, and church sectors, as well as to anchor institutions . . . all while retaining credibility and connection to the community."[33] Catalysts also champion the work of individuals and communities they serve. As described by one Catalyst, who attends to the conditions that support catalytic work within this ecology, his work expands the collective capacity to catalyze change: "Our primary work is not the culture change of other institutions, but it is an invitation that we now feel confident to receive," he notes. "[I]t's kind of classic inside-outside change work. . . . We're on the outside leaning in, and I feel like the dust we're able to kick up and then mold from is interesting and unique."[34] Reflecting the ecclesially rooted nature of their leadership, Catalysts are Champions of their communities, of other catalytic efforts, and of those who share hope-filled visions for transformation.

The Champion's mode of "being with" similarly draws upon adjacent expressions. Like the Guide, this individual has a balcony perspective that enables him to consider how the components of a system or organization fit together. Drawing upon a combination of lived experience and authority within a community, Champions pursue their work by coming alongside those they serve, enabling them to take the next step. As one Champion shared: "Just personally being able to come alongside and give my personal support to the work that they're doing, I think, has been important for them, and it's been important for me." This individual describes his contribution in terms of a "champion's perspective"; however, the practical wisdom that informs his work also reflects adjacent modes of leadership. Organized by their commitment to the well-being of the communities they serve, Champions support the kinds of adaptive change that enrich their community. For example, this particular Champion also notes how "[he's] a big believer in kind of entrepreneurial thinking, thinking outside of the box, thinking about new ways to do things." As he continues to describe his contribution to their team, he notes—in a characteristic Champion mode—the importance of asking questions: "I feel like my job is always to be asking questions." The implied purpose of these questions is to clarify and enrich the collective work of the organization he serves in order to "more faithfully live into its mission." Hence, drawing upon the wisdom of adjacent expressions, the Champion pursues her work by offering guidance and catalytic energy. Pursued from an alongside posture, the Champion contributes to the collective well-being by elevating and telling the stories of her community.

Finally, the Guide draws upon adjacent expressions in her effort to come alongside individuals and communities. Like a Champion, her work elevates others in a self-effacing manner. Guides have the relational knowledge to tell the stories, gifts, and burdens of the individuals and communities they serve while also holding the individual and community from a posture of abundant care. Through their relational journey with individuals and asking questions, they champion the work others are doing. Guides come alongside individuals and communities, but their work primarily elevates the work of others, and then points those they serve to the next step on their journey. Like Surveyors, their posture provides insight and stories about the lived experience of varied individuals and communities. When combined with their diverse knowledge and experience—which Guides tend to possess—these connections yield experiential insight about the broader landscape where they serve. Ultimately, Guides translate insights and information to the particular individuals and contexts where they serve, moving back and forth between local communities and the broader ecclesial ecology. Through their work and practical wisdom, Guides come alongside individuals and communities, championing their work and locating their combined effort within a broader ecology. Their mode of "being with" emerges from alongside and seeks to enable individuals and communities to discern their next step.

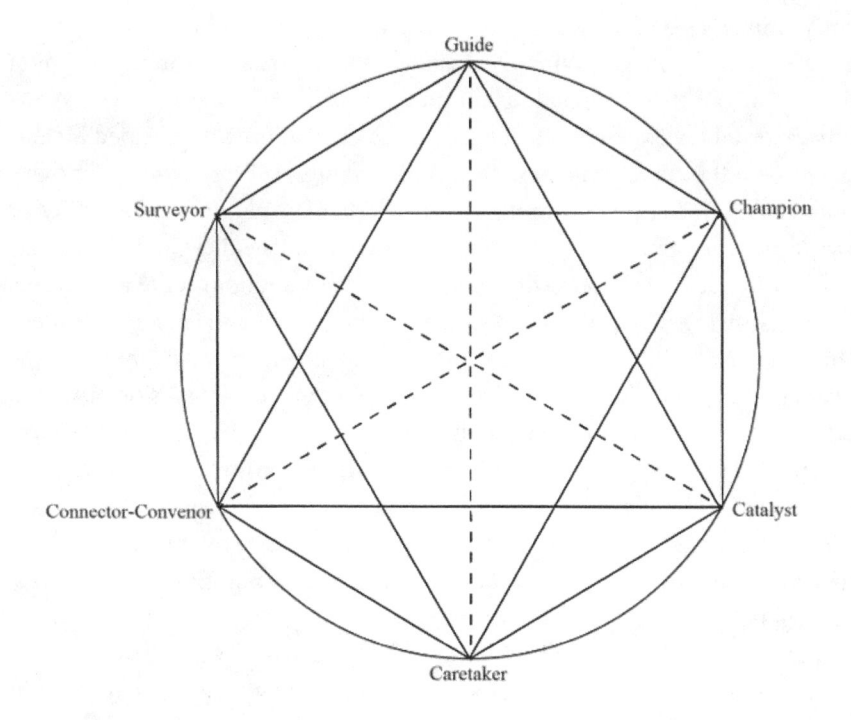

Fig. 7-4 Polarities

Polarities

Leadership from a particular center also bears a reciprocal relationship with the mode of "being with" that occupies the opposite position. Like the relationship between magnetic poles, I describe this pattern as polarities. For example, Caretakers and Guides, Connector-Conveners and Champions, and Catalysts and Surveyors frequently join in partnership. Or, individuals with one central mode also display a polar expression (e.g., a Caretaker also serve as a Guide). These relationships take shape as polarities along three axes: the axis of care; the axis of connection; and the axis of change. Partnerships along these axes link the adaptive work that takes place within one sector of an ecclesial ecology to the broader whole by organizing adaptive work around a common concern and complementary expressions of being with. Figure 7-4 visualizes this relationship.

A few examples illustrate how these relationships play out across these hubs. First, McGonigal, who exemplifies the Caretaker's practical wisdom, pursues a form of leadership that exists in close proximity to the Guide. After more than twenty years of pastoral and college ministry, McGonigal has served as a guide for many; early conversations with a program director at the Lilly Endowment, John Wimmer, also informed his leadership in the OCE. As McGonigal reflects on the history of the OCE, Wimmer's imprint is unmistakable. Through ongoing conversation, a history of relationship, and a mode of coming alongside, Wimmer supported the conditions that enabled the OCE to form and helped McGonigal discern the appropriate next step. As McGonigal reflects: "John Wimmer's admonition to me at the beginning is part of what has permeated the values of how we run the office and that is we are always in a listening mode." Simultaneously, the Caretaker's mode of "being with" enables him to serve as a Guide. McGonigal's work with pastors and students, for example, comes alongside them as they discern faithful forms of life and work. As one former student who now serves as a local pastor observed: "I've known Terry McGonigal since I was [a student]. . . . As soon as I showed up here [in Spokane], my first phone call was to Terry." Whether expressed through spiritual direction, coaching, or mentoring, the work of Guides and Caretakers proceeds along an axis of care. Hence, each form of leadership exemplifies a complementary form of practical wisdom; when combined, they nurture the fabric of care in communities, organizations, and neighborhoods.

The Catalyst's and Surveyor's modes of "being with" attend to the conditions that enable change within a broader ecclesial ecology. Although leadership through each mode expresses a particular form of "being with," Catalysts and Surveyors frequently lead in partnership with one another. If Surveyors attend to the broader social and historical landscape in which particular adaptive expressions take place, this work brings them into conversation and relationship with Catalysts. In one instance, a Surveyor and a Catalyst note how they have been journeying together in friendship for decades. Speaking of the Surveyor, a Catalyst shares, "I'd consider him in the circle of some of my best friends. . . . We've known each other a long time."[35]

Individuals whose leadership is grounded in one mode also express the polar mode. For example, Surveyors have the capacity to serve a catalytic role within a broader ecclesial ecology. Through their work, words, and practical wisdom, they shape the conceptual and material conditions that organize a common life. As one Surveyor notes, "I'm sort of the catalyst for the think tank part of our [work]." Catalysts also draw upon and lead in proximity to the Surveyor's work and wisdom. In their hopeful discontentment with the status quo, Catalysts ideate and innovate in order to initiate change in and for the local communities and organizations they serve. This form of leadership draws upon and constructively extends an expansive range of contextual and scholastic knowledge, but the aim always returns to the local community. As a neighborhood leader notes, she understands herself as a "catalyst and instigator." She reflects:

> I feel like part of my call is to be an interpretive reporter and try to figure how to keep wise and how to keep the challenge of how to articulate things that I have been so immersed in . . . trying to find language [like] that is very challenging to know what will spark people to lean into another way of being, because I'm really talking about a wholesale change. This is not tweaking. I'm trying to change the conversation away from the ecclesial-centric dialogue and as the crisis has continued, as modernity is collapsing . . . I want to hear [pastors and community leaders] ask the question, "What do you think God is up to in all this?"

This form of catalytic work involves translating and developing concepts, in proximity to local communities, in order to energize the change a Catalyst envisions. When expressed as conjoined and complementary sensibilities, Surveyors' and Catalysts' practical wisdom energizes adaptive work within and for a broader ecclesial ecology.

Finally, Champions' and Connector-Conveners' leadership share an axis of connection. Just as Connector-Conveners tend to the connective sinews that comprise the ecclesial ecology, Champions elevate the individual and collective work of those around them. At the same time, each frequently draws upon the practical wisdom that the other exemplifies. For example, even though Connector-Conveners have immense capacity to hold relationships and convene individuals around a common concern, a Champion is uniquely situated to elevate a Connector-Convener's capacity to pursue the connective work an adaptive church requires. Similarly, even as a Champion has the ability to elevate others and tell stories about the transformation of individuals and communities, the Champion relies upon Connector-Conveners to organize the collective work that is required. If a Champion pursues a mode of "being with" that resembles that of a player-coach, the Connector-Convener contributes to this work by identifying and getting the right people on the team.

Individuals who exemplify one mode of "being with" also share features of the other. For example, a senior leader at a national parachurch organization identifies his hope to foster "a more organic leadership." In a characteristic Champion's mode, he conducts his work with a broad perspective that enables him to tell the stories of individuals and communities, but it also includes expressing "influence in connection." This form of leadership includes "connecting in leadership" with local leaders and "elevating" their work. The Connector-Convener's leadership includes championing the work of individuals and communities and telling stories that bear witness to the hopeful work that is popping up in everyday lives and communities. Like conductors for an adaptive church, they carry the everyday stories from their communities and release them to harmonize with collaborators across an ecclesial ecology. When gathering, Connector-Conveners work to craft the conditions that enable everyone to participate and champion the work of individuals and communities by centering their stories. This intentionality in gathering supports the conditions where new life, new work, and new imagination emerges. Champions' and Connector-Conveners' practical wisdom is conjoined by a common attention to connection and combines to identify, connect, convene, and elevate individuals engaged in adaptive work.

Partnerships across these three polarities enable individuals to connect the adaptive change that takes place in one part of an ecology to another. Each of these polarly interrelated modes of leadership is borne from a different mode of being with individuals and communities. These three axes—and the various forms of leadership they reflect—overlap and intersect in meaningful ways, but they are not identical with one another. Rather, like magnetic poles that ground and center collective work, care, change, and connection encompass and hold together, in complementary ways, the collaboration adaptive change requires. When considered in relation to the particular individuals and localities that invite leadership, leadership across these six modes supports an adaptive church in the varied organizational settings where innovation takes place. No single expression is superior to another; nor can one be expressed apart from the others. When combined and coordinated, however, leadership across each

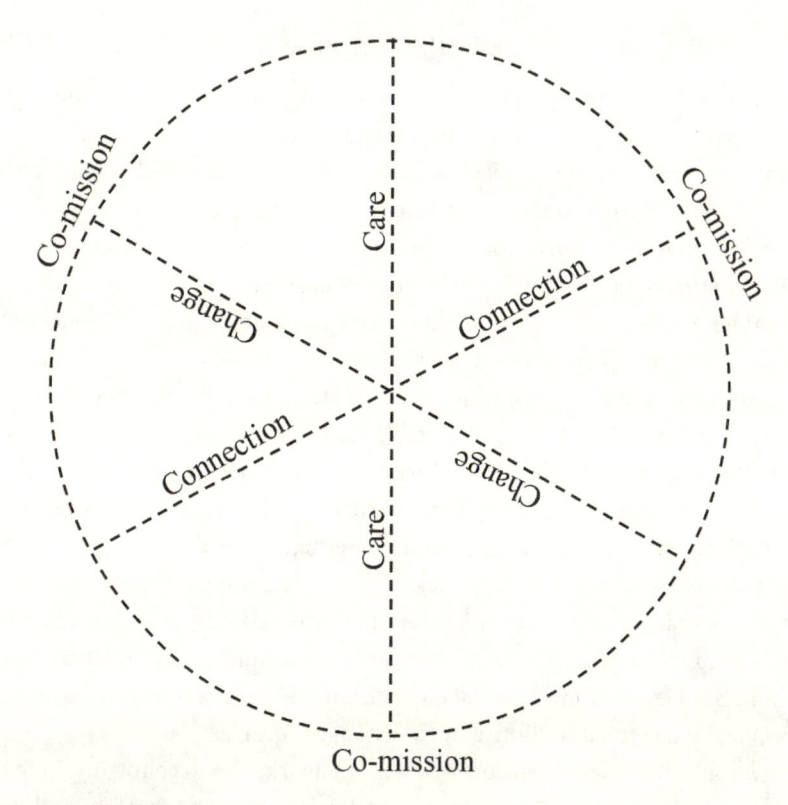

Fig. 7-5 Axes of Leadership

axis can ripple through the broader ecclesial ecology. To borrow a phrase from Sam Wells, this form of "being with" that responds to God's way of being with the world, invites individuals and communities to engage in virtuous collaborations, a form of co-mission, where individuals join together, with one another and with the Spirit, to imagine and pursue ecclesial entrepreneurship.[36] The practical wisdom that guides this type of collaboration creates the container for the other three to enliven an adaptive church through connection, care, and creativity. Like the shape of a double helix, these four features hang together in a virtuous pattern of inner relation. Complementarity enriches the adaptive work that takes place across these hubs, and the absence of individuals who possess any form of practical wisdom in turn diminishes the overall nimbleness of organizational and ecclesial adaptation. When pursued in relation to others and the broader tradition of Christian thought and practice, these interrelated expressions of Christian practical wisdom support an adaptive church within and for the broader ecclesial ecology.

ADAPTIVE LEADERSHIP AND PRACTICAL THEOLOGY

Before concluding this chapter, it is necessary to note how this paradigm of leadership structured as six interrelated forms of practical wisdom contributes to prominent theories in the adaptive leadership and practical theology literature. First, for models of adaptive leadership, it elaborates the basic relations that organize and energize adaptive change. Second, for theories of leadership in practical theology that define leadership solely in terms of servant leadership, this account identifies a wider range of expressions. Hence, my description advances both the study of leadership and its practice within communities of faith.

First, the model developed here clarifies the basic relations that organize and energize adaptive work. As noted in chapter 3, Heifetz's conceptual framework provides a helpful diagnostic tool to understand the challenges that confront communities of faith in the Pacific Northwest. His account, however, has two limitations: an implicit teleology and a pragmatic social ontology. Accordingly, his account of adaptive change lacks the internal capacity to nurture the relationships that ecclesial innovation requires. The result is an account of adaptive leadership that rightly identifies the need for adaptation and practices that sustain it. But Heifetz stops short of considering the practical wisdom that sustains specifically the collaboration adaptive change requires.

As a contextual extension of Heifetz's work, the account presented here accentuates the *phronetic* dimension of leadership that supports and enables adaptive change. Indeed, as Sharon Parks has shown in her extended case study of Heifetz's teaching methods, leadership can be taught. Nevertheless, my account suggests the *sine qua non* of leadership for adaptive change does not depend upon a particular curriculum or form of competence; it requires *phronesis*.[37] Insofar as leadership can be taught, leadership education requires a form of practical wisdom—a way of being in and seeing the world—that enables individuals and communities to understand and respond adaptively to the challenges they face. In the cases presented here, the exercise of leadership reflects an ecclesial and Christocentric understanding of the conditions that enable individuals and communities to pursue a form of adaptive work. In doing so, these organizational and ecclesial expressions engage and pursue a way of life that offers a robust teleological vision and a social ontology to sustain their adaptive work. As the OCE and PC respond to the challenges they face, the formation of Christian practical wisdom can quicken the exercise of adaptive leadership. Such work requires attention to the broader ecclesial ecology in which adaptive work takes place and the conditions that enable organizations and communities to adapt to the challenges they face. When sustained by complementary expressions of "being with," this form of practical wisdom supports the conditions for adaptive expressions to emerge and redound within a broader ecclesial ecology.

This constructive extension of Heifetz's account raises two critical questions: (1) Does this account merely baptize Heifetz's conceptual framework within a theological grammar? and (2) Do individuals and communities consciously understand and describe their work in these terms? In response to the first question, this work draws insights from Christian thought and practice because Christianity is the tradition for these two hubs. As Heifetz and those who have followed him rightly note, the exercise of adaptive change requires a moral level of reflection, including how deeply held values may both energize and inhibit collective action.[38] The descriptive and constructive work presented here similarly interprets the adaptive work that organizes these hubs within a traditioned moral discourse. As such, it attends to the conditions and conceptual frameworks that contribute to the transformation of individuals and communities. Although this account identifies resources that can enrich Heifetz's conceptual framework, and offers a corrective to the two previously mentioned limitations in Heifetz's theory, it does not claim that adaptive change exclusively takes place within or in relation to the Christian tradition. Rather, my argument demonstrates how reflection within a particular tradition can enliven the kind of adaptive work Heifetz envisions. Other traditions of thought and practice may contain a different reservoir of resources, which may similarly enliven the collective action adaptive work requires.

In response to the second question, my descriptive and constructive work faithfully extends the pattern of thought and practice alive in these adaptive hubs. Although leaders and participants across these hubs do not provide a fully developed articulation of the conditions, imagination, and conceptual frameworks that organize their work, my analysis has attempted to remain critically faithful to their work.[39] Much as John Swinton and Harriet Mowat advise, it seeks "to reflect critically and theologically on situations and to provide insights and strategies that will enable the movement towards faithful change."[40] In a similar spirit, my description and analysis attempt to offer back to these communities—and those who journey with them—a resonant pattern of thought and practice that can enrich their ongoing efforts.

This work also offers a corrective to prominent accounts of leadership within the practical theology literature that reduce leadership to a single mode or expression. For example, Richard Osmer's *Practical Theology: An Introduction* presents a four-fold model of practical theological interpretation: the descriptive-empirical task, the interpretive task, the normative task, and the pragmatic task.[41] This four-fold approach has equipped a generation of pastoral leaders and scholars with a straightforward paradigm for understanding and evaluating the integrated tasks of pastoral leadership and practical theology. For Osmer, servant leadership distinguishes the pragmatic task. This form of leadership seeks to "influence the congregation to change in ways that more fully embody the servanthood of Christ."[42] Osmer's work, and similar developments of the servanthood motif, rightly locates leadership in relation to a central biblical theme.[43]

Osmer's account and related approaches, however, reduce leadership to a single mode of being present with individuals and communities. Admittedly, individuals across both hubs describe the work as a form of "service."[44] Nevertheless, their leadership exemplifies diverse and complementary expressions, with service as one of many ways that work together to support change. The common feature across these variegated expressions is proximity to an ecclesial center and a shared form of Christian practical wisdom that guides their work. Through connection and collaboration across a dynamic ecclesial ecology, leadership through these six modes cultivates the connections and imagination needed to enliven pastoral and ecclesial imagination. As these two and other kindred expressions of adaptive church emerge and evolve, a nimble, adaptive, and collaborative form of leadership is required to nourish and enliven the adaptive work of individuals and communities.

What emerges across these two hubs is not a single mode of leadership; rather, it is a rich tapestry of complementary expressions. Leadership for an adaptive church requires a "choreography," attending to the gifts and challenges within a community and open to the ongoing work and wisdom of the Spirit of God.[45] Above all else, it requires an ability to see and pursue change in relation to a broader communion of witness, joining in partnership with those who have come before and those who will come after, in order to adapt to the crises of complex challenges. Leadership across these six modes exemplify interrelated forms of wisdom that, when expressed in partnership with others, enable communities to pursue the organizational and ecclesial adaptations that sustain their common life.

CONCLUSION

Leadership in and for an adaptive church requires nothing less than Christian practical wisdom. While existing paradigms capture certain features of the leadership that animates these hubs, there remains, as Strong noted at the beginning of this chapter, a need for "many more voices that articulate what the new Christianity for the twenty-first century is going to look like." In this present boundary space, where the templates that organize religious life are changing and uncertainty pervades, leadership is needed to support the conditions where individuals and communities pursue faith-filled ways of being. If the Pacific Northwest indeed serves as an incubator and laboratory for religion in North America, these six modes of leadership exemplify ways of leading that can enrich similar adaptive expressions. When formed and expressed in ways that release imagination across an ecclesial ecology, these complementary modes of leadership enable individuals and communities to live in light of the reality and promises of God.

8

A Moment of Renovating Virtue
Adaptive Possibility beyond Certainty

> There are in our existence spots of time,
> That with distinct pre-eminence retain
> Renovating virtue, whence . . . our minds
> Are nourished and invisibly repaired;
> A virtue, by which pleasure is enhanced,
> That penetrates, enables us to mount,
> When high, more high, and lifts us up when fallen.[1]
>
> William Wordsworth

> And in a hopeless world, there is hope and all things are possible. New things are possible. . . . [N]ew things that we never thought were possible are now possible.
>
> Jessica Katola

Driving north through Spokane neighborhoods lit only by porch lights, I pass familiar sites and streets. I recall what an Uber driver shared on an earlier trip to the region: "I rarely come out this way; it's not really on the way to anything." The two-lane street toward Whitworth and the OCE traffics in ordinary life; winding through neighborhoods, passing parks, churches, and car dealerships. Located beyond the bustle of the city and tucked within a neighborhood, the OCE sits beneath ponderosa pines. Exiting the vehicle, the stillness and darkness enfold me. The space and tranquility feel pregnant with possibility. "The Spirit brooded over the waters,"[2] writes the author of Genesis. Even before there was light and life, creation was brimming with the possibility of an ever-creative God.

Breathing deeply in the silence, this place feels both familiar and curious. I first came to this region and walked beneath these trees twelve years ago, drawn by a love for the western Rockies and by curiosity. Like many others who have come to the Pacific Northwest, I came to the region because I sensed that a different type of question is possible on the far side of the Rockies. Now, standing beneath these trees on my last research trip to the region, I find that I've returned, still trying to ask a different question. "I know this place," I think to myself. I know this space, many of the people throughout the region, and the possibilities to which it points.

Yet, the place also feels foreign and curious. I recall a similar night in Seattle only a few months earlier. After leaving the PC's Inhabit Conference gathering for the evening, I took the ten-minute ferry ride across Elliott Bay toward Alki Beach, where I was staying. As I exited the ferry, the stillness of the night enfolded me, but darkness was nowhere to be found. The city's luminescence danced on the waves and then raced toward the heavens, reminding any spectators of the promise of this global city. In neighborhoods and streets beneath and beyond Seattle's skyline, the PC is inviting individuals into an ordinary, everyday, placed ecclesial existence. This slow, patient posture sees the possibility for a more rooted life together, one that brings more life-giving forms of connection, and begins restitching structures of care and connection.

Remembering that night in Seattle, I consider how the striking similarities and fundamental differences between these two adaptive hubs make what once felt familiar more foreign and what once felt foreign more familiar. "It is no longer clear to me who 'my people' are," I later note. "If I had to choose, I think it would be impossible. My thought, my reflection, my imagination have become so entangled with and emerged alongside both [organizations] that it is difficult, at least in my mind, to separate one from the other."[3]

In this particular spot of time, standing in the shadow of the ponderosa pines, I encounter an imaginative luminescence amid a familiar darkness. Their work and wisdom kindle a way of seeing and being that attends to the adaptive possibilities that support an adaptive church. As existing structures fracture in this hinge time, these two hubs and similar expressions beyond the region offer a template for Christian organization, education, and leadership beyond certainty. The wisdom of an adaptive church requires taking these three together; new structures of belonging require all three: organization that promotes encounter, education that supports transformation, and leadership that protects the conditions for this essential and fragile collective work.

To borrow language from William Wordsworth, the work of these hubs offers other communities of faith a "renovating virtue." As Wordsworth puts it:

There are in our existence spots of time,
That with distinct pre-eminence retain
Renovating virtue, whence . . . our minds
Are nourished and invisibly repaired;
A virtue, by which pleasure is enhanced,
That penetrates, enables us to mount,
When high, more high, and lifts us up when fallen.[4]

Composed in mid-nineteenth-century France, during a period of cultural and institutional transition, Wordsworth describes latent possibilities in "spots of time" that "nourish" and "repair." And, as Wordsworth notes, this virtue can "lift us up when fallen," inviting our communities to imagine and pursue the incarnate possibility that God has imprinted on our ordinary existence.

In so far as the stories of this volume offer "renovating virtue," an adaptive church requires something more than rebuilding or remodeling existing structures. It requires renovation of a collective imagination. Grounded in place and connecting around the challenges communities of faith face, these hubs are crafting and recrafting how individuals see and inhabit an ecclesial ecology. Their work displays renovating virtue in its finest form.[5] Without denying the cataclysmic challenges individuals and communities are currently facing, an adaptive church sees renovating possibilities within and on the other side of uncertainty.

POSSIBILITY BEYOND CERTAINTY

As participants in a dynamic ecclesial ecology, other leaders are invited to participate in the (re)connective work God is doing in and through communities of faith. The time covered by this work included unshakable encounters with the limits of individual and collective life. We were brought up short by crisis and collective vulnerability.[6] A sober assessment of the fragility and unsustainability of the structures that have historically guided religious organization, education, and leadership regulates the power of possibility that pulses through these hubs. Rather than sliding into disenchantment or despair, their work weaves together the local, institutional, and regional connections that create spaces of belonging. Hub-making kindles the power of possibility for individuals in the midst.[7]

And it is precisely in the space when individuals across these hubs find their limits, that it invites them to imagine the ongoing work and wisdom of God. When I first met Jessica Ketola, she was working as a neighborhood pastor in Richmond Highlands, north of downtown Seattle. She described her work as "liv[ing] into the tensions of going for something we don't see." Several months later, now in the belly of the pandemic, she acknowledged the unmistakable encounters with limits.

"The move towards more embodied local expressions of the church that actually can live this thing out on the ground is so important right now," she shares. "And we are limited in that and that feels really hard, that the thing that we really love to do is be present to people. But I still am so convinced that God is at work, even though really, in the natural, I mean, there's not a lot to be super excited about." We are limited, and yet, Ketola is convinced God is at work, even when there is not much to show for it. This conjunctive imagination, the ability to see the "more" in the limited spaces that mark an ecclesial ecology, invites participants across each hub to imagine the ongoing work of God.

The renovating virtue that marks an adaptive church expresses what is possible when individuals renew the connections, between individuals within a local community and between individuals and the organizations they inhabit, that sustain the life of faith. With clarity and candor, Ketola describes the hope that permeates the possibilities she sees in this moment: "And in a hopeless world, there is hope and all things are possible. New things are possible. . . . [N]ew dreams and new things that we never thought were possible are now possible." New things are possible. Amid the uncertainty that marks the life of faith, the story of these hubs kindles a hopeful imagination that sees what is possible on the edge of certainty. Faith communities have always carried the wisdom of an adaptive church, but this particular "spot of time"—to borrow Wordworth's image—draws forth this wisdom for a new age. As individuals explore what is possible beyond certainty, they invite others to do the same. And, as other communities determine how best to "cross over" from the uncertainty they face, their work can kindle possibility beyond certainty.[8]

Contrary to approaches to practical theology that conclude with prescriptive conclusions, this renovating virtue invites individuals to consider the forms of possibility that emerge beyond certainty.[9] Their work invites those within them—and others who intend to imitate their work—to leave behind the certainty that prescriptive or pragmatic conclusions provide. Instead, their work kindles questions. And in this boundary zone, marked by the uncertainty that catalyzes an adaptive church, individuals are finding the wisdom they need to respond to the invitation that this work extends. As one leader reflects: "What's possible in this moment?" What is possible when communities of faith explore renovating virtue? What is possible when faith communities and those who lead them step beyond certainty?

ADAPTIVE POSSIBILITIES

This final chapter considers how these hubs and a broader ecclesial ecology nurture and sustain possibility beyond certainty.[10] I have primarily focused on these two hubs in the Pacific Northwest because they are critical cases for the wisdom that nurtures a more adaptive church. The practical wisdom they exemplify is able to enrich religious organizations, education, and leadership beyond the region. The first section identifies the adaptive possibilities for the OCE and PC, as they work to sustain their kindred expressions of adaptive church. The second section considers the adaptive possibilities for individuals in six interrelated sectors that support adaptive change within a broader ecclesial ecology. Finally, the third section identifies the invitation this work extends to other leaders and communities of faith.

Adaptive Possibilities: OCE and PC

The OCE and PC represent different approaches to the challenges that confront communities of faith, yet they developed strikingly similar ecclesial innovations. The OCE emerged in a fixed set of organizational arrangements, and the PC came from an ambiguous set of arrangements. Nevertheless, they share an overlapping series of adaptive possibilities as they advance their ecclesial adaptations. Just as the practical wisdom that guides these teams intersects in multiple ways, the adaptive possibilities that distinguish the next phases of their work overlap as well. Three shared adaptive possibilities characterize this work.[11]

1) Financial Stability and Community Ownership

As each hub considers how to sustain its ongoing work, they must navigate the tension between financial stability and community ownership. The financial stability of an ecclesial life is a catalytic challenge and remains a primary concern for founders across both hubs. Expressed in terms of the "right financial model" or as "self-sustaining," the organizing concern of each hub remains much the same: the need to identify and explore the economic models that enable adaptive change within, alongside, and beyond established institutional structures. The hubs established a runway through grants, in the case of the OCE,[12] and earned income through consulting and projects, in the case of the PC.

These early sources of funding provided time and space to explore, test, and refine the programs and structures that organize their work. The expansion of and positive response to their work, however, now require considering the long-term financial models beyond the startup stage. The OCE is exploring how to endow portions of its work, which would enable it to avoid becoming reliant on funding from the university. For the PC, recent grants have expanded their internal capacity and provide a resource-rich context to explore sustainable financial models. In both cases, the question of financial stability remains an adaptive possibility.

Nevertheless, the question of financial stability cannot be separated from the need for community ownership. As one organizer noted when asked what else is needed, financial stability only resolves part of this adaptive possibility: "Well, not more money. . . . It has to be owned and shared by our community of churches, locally and regionally." Indeed, the vision that drives this work is not just to provide resources and services; rather, each hub seeks to catalyze collective action. Organizers also identify the need "to develop connective leaders that have this ecological imagination that . . . want to live under this same risk." While founders' early work connected and resourced local leaders, they now hope to promote community ownership at the local and regional level. In both cases, the adaptive possibility of sustainability includes both financial stability and community ownership; one cannot be achieved apart from the other.

2) Leadership Succession and Relational Capital

These hubs face a second adaptive possibility: leadership within a network structure that requires high levels of trust and relational capital. Both hubs emerged in proximity to founders' dense networks of relationships, accrued from decades of service and friendship in the region. As each hub grew, organizers' combined networks connected each hub to leaders and other communities across the region; a high level of trust and friendship thickened collaborative partnership. This feature now presents a challenge as organizers consider the forms of leadership necessary to support and sustain this work into its next phases.

Each hub encounters this challenge in ways unique to its history. For the OCE, the age of the founders creates "an opportunity for sustainable leadership succession planning," as one advisor notes.[13] The relational character of their leadership requires transferring not only formal authority, but trust, understanding of the network, and relational capital. With Sittser's and McGonigal's retirements in 2021, the OCE has initiated a process to transfer leadership to the next generation. As of this writing, Mindy Smith is the newly appointed Interim Director of Church Engagement.

The PC, in its own way, is beginning to consider this question as well. After more than a decade of catalyzing, connecting, and organizing work, founders are attending to the risk of "founder syndrome." While their ages vary,[14] they also identify a need to attend to the shape of leadership that follows their work. Sparks and Soerens reflect: "We've had some very good conversations about will we be doing this 'til we are seventy-five each—that's not ideal. I think that's a central leadership tension." Noting the need to cultivate more diversity of leadership— "We're two white guys," they share—they are also working to support the forms of leadership that reflect the diversity of parish-based leadership.[15]

Leadership succession and the transfer of relational capital require attending to the tension inherent to adaptive change. On the one hand, leadership for this form of collaborative and collective work requires relational capital that accrues from a history of service and engagement in a particular place. On the other hand, the growth and expansion of such adaptive hubs may require a different form of leadership, and attendant practical wisdom, than what was required to launch these organizational and ecclesial adaptations. As the OCE and PC consider the next phases of their work and organization, each must, in its own way, cultivate and connect leadership for the next stages.

3) Institutionalization and Innovation

These hubs face the adaptive possibility of establishing institutional structures that preserve a culture of innovation. On the one hand, each emerged within and alongside existing institutional structures. Without entirely disregarding existing institutional templates, each sought to support the conditions to "reimagine church," attending to organization, education, and leadership that provide structures of belonging. Organizers also had to learn how to "dance well with institutions" and support the conditions to reshape existing structures through their engagement with and within a particular hub.

Founders and key organizers across both hubs identify the need to consider institutionalization and innovation. For example, Rice notes the urgency for more structure to the PC's work: "[I]f we don't get our shit together with organizational system and structure, there is no way that we can hold this together well." Smith similarly describes the OCE's current work: "[It] feels exciting just to be in the building stage, but it does feel like, 'Okay, we still got some more work to do on this house to get it stable.'" Acknowledging the catalytic efforts that were required to initiate and launch each hub, each must now consider the patterned practices that can sustain their work.

Each organization also faces the challenge of forming nimble structures that enable leaders to see and respond to the ongoing evolution of their work. This adaptive possibility for each hub provides an occasion to learn from and engage other organizations who express different forms of an adaptive church. In each case, organizers' engagement around these adaptive possibilities requires a form of creativity that resists technical solutions. "I think what we're really trying to focus in on is how do we make this familiar church that people all think they know and understand?" Smith observes, "How do we make it strange and unfamiliar and interesting again in a way that there's some curiosity? And how do we think creatively about how the church is going to move?" As these and similar organizations consider how to reimagine church, they will need to attend to the tensions these three adaptive possibilities present. In doing so, the places of encounter between siloed communities, practices, and concepts become sites to explore the practical wisdom that can sustain an adaptive church beyond certainty.

Adaptive Possibility: Ecclesial Ecology

Other individuals and communities, within and beyond the Pacific Northwest, are engaged in experiments that address the challenges confronting local faith communities. Their work displays what Shannon Hopkins and Mark Sampson describe as a "forest imagination" that emerges from a "new language of connectedness."[16] Innovating on the other side of uncertainty, these hubs weave interconnection, stitching individuals, communities, and ideas together in ways that transform a broader ecclesial ecology. As expressions of adaptive church emerge, they can learn from others experiments and entrepreneurs within the broader ecclesial ecology.

These adjacent possibilities express a shared desire for the renovating virtue that marks an adaptive church.[17]

The next section, then, considers the conditions that enable individuals and communities to cultivate expressions of adaptive church through six interrelated roles within a broader ecclesial ecology. The wisdom born of an adaptive church illustrates how new possibilities emerge as individuals link arms in collaborative activity. These adaptive possibilities express the interconnected practical wisdom in which additional expressions of adaptive church can form and flourish.

Pastors

Pastoral wisdom and imagination are the lifeblood of an adaptive church.[18] Even as individuals work to reimagine congregations' practices, local churches form individuals and communities into a particular way of life. Like the ballast amid turbulent waters, pastors' patient presence provides a place to stand amid uncertainty. While pastoral leaders interviewed across this project display a contextually centered wisdom, they share a fundamental orientation: hope. Without hope, communities lose the ability to imagine and pursue the changes that can renew an ecclesial ecology.

Pastors face three adaptive possibilities as they nurture the hope that sustains an adaptive church. First, pastors nurture a sufficiently supple ecclesial imagination through language drawn from the well of Christian thought and practice. Pastors are stewards and instructors in the language that guides communities of faith; they also model, introduce, and expand the language so as to invite consideration of the adaptive possibilities of life in relation to God. Their presence and proclamation bend imagination toward hope. Without hope, communities of faith flounder; when nourished by hope, however, individuals-in-communities can take the risks an adaptive church requires. For example: Starting a new initiative at the tail end of an accomplished career. Making a bet on the need for a neighborhood-based ecclesial life. Stepping outside of denominationally funded churches. Extending hospitality to the refugee and the homeless person. Becoming a chaplain to a community. Buoyed by hope, each decision points to the possibility of an adaptive church.

Pastors are also able to invite their congregations to consider how to organize their common life beyond a pastor-centric model. If, as argued throughout this project, pastor-centric approaches might inhibit ecclesial imagination, pastors release adaptive capacity by reforming the practices that guide their communities. Modeling a response to the adaptive challenges that confront communities of faith, each hub points to the creative and faithful alternatives that exist beyond a pastor-centric model. The process to shift a congregation away from a pastor-centric imagination does not follow a clear strategy or timeline. The wisdom that guides these hubs, however, suggests the need to listen for the gifts and callings of individuals in a local community and create space for collective discernment. Crises of various forms can also catalyze this change. When supported by structures of belonging, communities of faith can explore the adaptive possibilities beyond a pastor-centric model.

Third, pastors create holding environments for similar organizational and ecclesial adaptations to form and flourish. Congregations have the capacity to provide the stability, resources, and relational connections that adaptive change requires; they provide a fixed set of organizational arrangements, including established partnerships, resources, and facilities, that can catalyze, incubate, and launch adaptive expressions of church. As anchors within a broader ecclesial ecology, congregations can become hubs for experimentation that takes root and flourishes beyond the walls of a single congregation. Pastors are able to champion efforts to innovate at and beyond the edges of familiarity in communities of faith, and they can connect and convene individuals and communities around the challenges they face. Leading as stewards of saints, pastors can catalyze conditions for an adaptive church in and through their particular congregation.

Christian Educators

Educators enrich the broader ecclesial ecology by cultivating the practices, conceptual resources, and institutional structures that sustain an adaptive church.[19] "Christian educators" describes theological educators, but it also includes educators and administrators in other roles who contribute to the formation and flourishing of people of faith.[20] In this particular spot of time, Christian educators, in various capacities and institutional settings, contribute to what Charles Foster calls a "catechetical culture"[21] by engaging two adaptive possibilities. First, Christian educators are required to design educational institutions stable enough to incubate new ideas and flexible enough to respond to the needs of those they serve. As anchors within a broader ecclesial ecology, the long-term stability of Christian educational institutions enhances the adaptive work that can enrich the places students serve.[22] Simultaneously, these institutions must remain nimble enough to respond to and support the local needs of communities of faith and those who lead them. This practice of cultivating educational institutions that are stable and nimble—and it does represent a single practice—requires reorienting the educational model for theological education. Rather than expecting individuals to come to a host institution, it invites educators to take the wisdom and resources of a host institution to a local community. It requires a community-centric approach to education. This shift does not diminish the value of institutional spaces that cultivate knowledge and learning. It does, however, advance a posture of being with individuals by enriching local expressions of an adaptive church.

Second, Christian educators also cultivate an adaptive and entrepreneurial ethos within educational institutions. The imagination that fuels new expressions of ecclesial life emerge in proximity to theological education. As disciplined reflection within the Christian tradition meets localized adaptive challenges, new vision emerged for the adaptive possibilities beyond certainty. Each hub provided a container, marked by creativity, friendship, and hopefulness, that displays these adaptive possibilities for a broader ecclesial ecology. Educators' ability to carve out formative and transformative spaces of belonging demands a willingness to take the risk of alternative vision for education. As one leader noted, it requires "stepping into the unknown." Those who lead educational institutions must cultivate, promote, and reward efforts to innovate within and beyond a single school or seminary. This hospitable posture toward innovation extends beyond permitting employees to experiment within the terms of their given role; it requires a willingness on the part of educational institutions to be *for* a community by inviting the adaptive possibilities of local innovators into its midst. At its best, theological education is a gestation space for faithful ideas, practices, and communities that enrich the broader ecclesial ecology. Yet in order for these fragile forms to grow, they require a holding environment and connections to like-minded ecclesial entrepreneurs. As educational institutions develop the porous organizational boundaries that mark an adaptive church, they must also learn how the wisdom they need already surrounds them in local practice. Although this form of adaptive change requires stepping into a boundary zone of uncertainty, they will also encounter the adaptive possibilities that lie beyond the certainty of organizational and disciplinary boundaries. And in this spot of time, the challenges that confront communities of faith invite Christian educators and institutional leaders to take this risk.

Lay Leaders

The vitality of an adaptive church is carried by the vision of the laity. For example, when asked what else is needed, one pastor in Seattle identifies the need for lay engagement: "I think for people to take risks. . . . I would urge folks who feel like they have any capacity whatsoever to consider giving themselves to something rather than just thinking of church."[23] The collective, creative activity that characterizes adaptive work cannot start or be sustained apart from lay leadership.

Lay leaders support and sustain adaptive work within a broader ecclesial ecology through three adaptive possibilities. First, they can engage in the day-to-day life of a local congregation, neighborhood-based ecclesial expression, or related ecclesial innovation. An adaptive church requires wisdom drawn from people of faith within the local communities, and their particular engagement invites more than participation or committee work. This adaptive possibility includes more than tacit engagement: it invites leaders to regard local wisdom and experience as integral to the future of ecclesial life in their community.

Lay leaders' wisdom can sustain an adaptive church by actively supporting the ecclesial life within their particular place. They also extend the educational efforts to expand the ecclesial imagination of their particular community. In both cases, the work of the OCE and PC invites people of faith to reimagine their understanding of both faith and the broader community. As other lay leaders pursue other expressions of adaptive church, they can cultivate practical wisdom by reading widely, across theology and Scripture, but also well beyond these areas. Like community libraries of the texts and contexts, lay leaders can bring their local wisdom into the center of an adaptive church.

Lastly, lay leaders provide stability for local congregations and experiments in adaptive church. Pastors and congregations have the capacity to nurture adaptive experiments that can enrich and expand the vitality of a broader ecclesial ecology. Expressions of adaptive church are also appearing beyond congregational spaces. In both instances, financial and organizational fragility mark the congregations and experiments working to imagine a more adaptive church. Lay financial support certainly provides stability for communities to organize and support their common life; but lay leaders are also needed to provide stability through their presence within a community of faith. Like the lifeblood of the ecclesial ecology, local lay leaders tether an adaptive church to a particular place and release the adaptive possibilities of collective action. Lay leaders, in turn, are invited to see an adaptive church as the organizing principle of their life, to come to see themselves as individuals-in-(a particular) community.

Nonprofit Ministers

Nonprofit ministers build and strengthen the boundary-crossing connections that nourish an adaptive church.[24] Partnerships between hubs and nonprofits enrich the work of both in mutually beneficial ways; each hub connects nonprofits to an expanded network of partners, and nonprofits extend the hubs' contextually grounded work. To this end, three adaptive possibilities for nonprofit ministers can support an adaptive church.

First, nonprofit ministers can articulate an ecclesial understanding for how their ministry is connected and contributes to a broader ecclesial ecology. An expanding range of vocations of religious leadership marks the shifting landscape of religious life in North America. Research beyond the Pacific Northwest similarly finds that a growing percentage of graduating seminarians serve in capacities outside of pastoral ministry, and frequently in the nonprofit sector.[25] Ministry in nonprofits provides an expanding platform for ministry, but it also requires an ecclesial understanding of the relationship between a particular nonprofit organization and a broader ecclesial existence. There is, in other words, a need to articulate the ecclesiology of nonprofit organizations.

Second, nonprofit ministers are uniquely positioned to work for the good of the particular place where they serve and live. The importance of a particular cause or need can energize efforts to support a nonprofit's work, but nonprofit ministry does not necessarily require attending to the particular place where one lives and works. As more nonprofits embrace remote-work policies in the wake of 2020–2021, individuals serving in this sector must consider the relationship between their organization's mission and their local community. This adaptive possibility applies equally to each of the six interrelated sectors, yet the nature of nonprofit ministry, which addresses a felt need for a specific community, invites renewed attention to the place nonprofit ministers inhabit. As nonprofit ministers serve across communities and contexts, they may attend to God's localized work, seeking the well-being of the places they inhabit.

Finally, nonprofit ministers may incubate similar adaptive expressions by cultivating a vision for relational ministry. In multiple instances across these hubs, individuals developed a vision for relational ministry through previous experience in or service through parachurch or nonprofit ministries. When linked and nurtured through these adaptive hubs, individuals express a value for the partnership and collaboration that defines an adaptive church. Nonprofit ministers may similarly foster a relational posture that enriches an ecclesial ecology and equip others to care for the connection that an adaptive church requires.

Philanthropists

Philanthropists' position grants them a balcony perspective to attend to the activity of disparate parts. This perspective combined with financial and relational resources enables them to connect, convene, and catalyze adaptive expressions. Philanthropists are needed to support and contribute to additional expressions of adaptive church through two adaptive possibilities.

First, philanthropists nurture the conditions for individuals and communities to gather in response to the challenges they face. As illustrated by these hubs, a Christo-ecclesial understanding of a common life organizes transformation of individuals and communities in and through an adaptive church. Without diminishing individual or organizational particularity, a more connected common life will emerge as individuals reach across organizational boundaries, denominational identities, and the logic of scarcity that inhibits collaboration. "Innovation happens at the engagement of difference," one organizer observed.[26] Nevertheless, silos persist, even between those who pursue similar adaptive change—such as the two hubs profiled here.

Philanthropists and philanthropic organizations can address the need to connect across silos by virtue of their power to convene. Reflected during a two-day gathering of leaders from the region, Murdock's Senior Program Director for Enrichment, Kimberly Thornbury, observed: "It does feel like a privilege to have the power to convene, and do that well, and [to] build relationships to create these spaces." As other philanthropists continue their connecting and convening work, there remains an ongoing need to foster the conditions where individuals and communities of faith can engage across differences. When nurtured by the practical wisdom of Connector-Conveners, these gatherings have the capacity to catalyze, sustain, and enrich an adaptive church.

Second, philanthropists are able to strategically support and resource teams to address the challenges that confront individuals and communities. Insofar as these cases provide templates for adaptive work, the OCE and PC demonstrate the catalytic potential of collaborative leadership for an adaptive church. As philanthropists identify and support collaborative teams, they can consider three avenues for strategic funding: (1) Funding to support collaborations that address the needs of their local communities. One organizational leader shared in March 2021, "I think the collaborative movement and future that we're moving into is really exciting. But as it's been said many times, I think we're at a hinge point right now. I think this is an absolutely vital and crucial time for the next, at least many decades, if not centuries for the practical imagination of the church." As other organizations and leaders join this "collaborative movement," philanthropists have an opportunity to prioritize collaboration in the structure of their awards and their funding decisions. (2) Funding to resource similar teams at each stage of their innovation cycle. As other individuals build and extend collaborative networks, they will encounter both similar and contextually specific challenges. Philanthropy can address this need by funding resource centers and specialists to support the collaborations that support an adaptive church. These individuals can serve as Guides, Champions, and Surveyors, providing support for the catalytic and connecting-convening work that addresses the needs of local communities. And (3) funding that nurtures friendship across an ecclesial ecology. The relational networks that enable nimble and adaptive responses to crises develop over years; they cannot be forced or fabricated by programs. Trust is the essential relational property of a vibrant ecclesial ecology, and friendships marked by trust allow individuals-in-community to take the risks an adaptive church requires. While funding friendship will not promote an expedient change, this slow strategy supports the structure of belonging that bends collective imagination toward hope.

Ecclesial Entrepreneurs

Ecclesial entrepreneurs contribute to the broader ecclesial ecology as restless creatives imagining and creating new expressions of ecclesial life. They occupy conventional roles within an ecclesial ecology, but they also reside on the margins of institutions and in the boundary spaces between existing and emerging structures. As demonstrated through the stories of these two hubs, their hopeful discontent fosters an imagination for what is possible when people of faith receive the wisdom of an adaptive church. Two adaptive possibilities can sustain their ongoing work: staying alive and remaining engaged with existing institutions.

The creative, entrepreneurial work ecclesial entrepreneurs pursue requires constant attention to the forms of support that sustain their work. As expressed by individuals across each hub, their work at and beyond the edges often introduces fatigue, uncertainty, and burnout. They face the ongoing challenge of "staying alive" amid the adaptive change they pursue.[27] The precarity of adaptive change requires attending to the practices, connections, and restorative spaces that sustain leadership amid uncertainty.[28] Although this particular challenge is not unique to ecclesial entrepreneurs, their exposed position within the ecclesial ecology requires regular attention to the conditions that enable them to remain creative, connected, and hopeful. Representing more than a personal responsibility, caring for these ecclesial innovators is also the work of other individuals, partners, and organizations who learn from and benefit from their work. Partners and other communities of faith can acknowledge ecclesial entrepreneurs by listening deeply to them and receiving their work as a vital contribution to a broader ecology of faith. If ecclesial entrepreneurs can remain active and engaged, their creativity and the catalytic work they pursue will enrich the vitality of the broader ecclesial ecology.

Second, ecclesial entrepreneurs' ongoing engagement with existing institutional structures and forms of Christian practices also enriches their work. Even as a hopeful discontent energizes ecclesial entrepreneurs, they must constantly negotiate the tension between existing and imagined forms that organize a Christian life. As ecclesial entrepreneurs navigate this narrow edge, they traverse the fluid boundary between hopeful discontentment and anti-institutionalism.[29] This adaptive possibility requires resisting the false dichotomy between institutional engagement and institutional distrust. While a degree of discontentment can energize their work, meaningful engagement with and within existing structures can also sustain their work. This conjunctive imagination, at its best, marks ecclesial entrepreneurs' work, creating space for new forms and practices to emerge in proximity to existing organizational forms. When enlivened and infused by the (re)imaginative work of the people of God, ecclesial entrepreneurs' restless discontent can crystallize a collective vision, one that expands in virtuous forms of creativity, that reorients the horizon for what a community can imagine in and through an adaptive church.

AN INVITATION

The adaptive possibilities that distinguish an adaptive church are open to individuals and communities regardless of location, profession, or denominational identity. The six interrelated sectors discussed here identify how individuals and communities explore and cultivate the conditions wherein existing and future organizational and ecclesial adaptations can take root and grow. Together, the adaptive possibilities across these six sectors clarify one final feature: the ability to initiate, join, or contribute to an adaptive church is not restricted to a single role or profession. Rather, a porous and capacious "we" describes the collective that coalesces around the challenges that confront local faith communities. Adaptive change that enriches the broader ecclesial ecology is not the exclusive work of a pastor, a professor, a nonprofit minister, or any other professional. The work of reimagining church is not restricted to a few; it is the collective work of a community of faith, one into which we are each invited during this particular spot of time. As one individual shared: "We're better together."

The local, collective work that nourishes and sustains an adaptive church is also never finished. Rather, it continues amid the everyday realities that characterize faith.[30] In moments of uncertainty, as leaders and communities of faith weigh the adaptive possibilities, the ordinary encounters and challenges that characterize Christian existence carry an invitation: together, "we" can receive the wisdom of an adaptive church. This wisdom is always a gift, for it comes only in the company of others, and it is expressed for the sake of others. Even amid uncertainty, communities can receive this recreative gift. When born in structures of belonging, sustained by hope, and enlivened by the Spirit of God, an adaptive church invites communities of faith to respond to the current challenges they face by (re)imagining what is possible.

In this distinct spot of time, a renovating virtue sustains leaders and faith communities who gather around a hopeful vision for an adaptive church. Like these other communities of faith, the OCE and PC will have their own history; they will face future challenges; current organizers or participants will move into other forms of service; and there may come a time when each hub has served its purpose and will cease to exist. These cases and this broader story stop short of offering a prescriptive solution to the many challenges that confront communities of faith; instead, each hub points to the Christian practical wisdom that enables individuals and communities to live in light of the reality and promises of God. As individuals, communities, and scholars consider the conditions, practices, and distinguishing features of an adaptive church, some features of their work will resemble these two hubs, but the particular context(s) and contributors will direct their work in unique ways.[31]

The wisdom and resources that enable individuals to reimagine church in this way already exist within the broader ecclesial ecology; that wisdom needs only to be uncovered, given space to grow, and connected within a more adaptive church.

Appendix A

Naming

Networks, Data, Methods, and Names

NAMING NETWORKS

This research occurred in proximity to preexisting relationships and networks within and beyond the Pacific Northwest.[1] As Natalie Wigg-Stevenson observes, theological inquiry invites qualitative research done "*in* Christian community *as* Christian practice."[2] I did not have any direct exposure to either the OCE or PC prior to my research. However, I was familiar with the OCE's host institution, Whitworth, as an alumnus. Further, a personal network of relationships, within and beyond the region, placed me in relational proximity to founders, organizers, participants, and funders across the PC and OCE.

My work and relationship with both hubs surfaced the question of belonging. "It is no longer clear who 'my people' are," I reflected at a late point in my research. As Wigg-Stevenson suggests, theological inquiry in proximity to community and as Christian practice invites a form of "reflexive ecclesiology," one that considers the intersubjectivity inherent to theological inquiry and ecclesial community.[3] My theological and empirical work occurs in proximity to these communities of practice, even as their concerns and questions further clarify my research. An "ecclesiological form of thinking,"[4] as Bonhoeffer observes, can only be pursued "from within."[5] Although distance restricted my time in the

PC   OCE

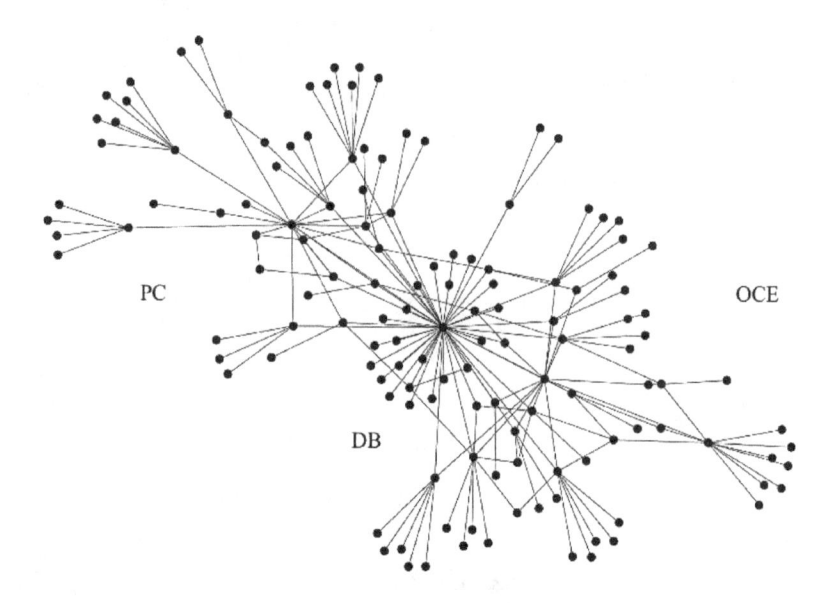

DB

Fig. A-1 Reflexive Ecclesiology Network

region, my research and relational proximity uniquely enabled me to study these two expressions of adaptive church.

My research, presence, and participation introduced an additional actor into the Pacific Northwest's ecclesial ecology: myself. I sought to acknowledge and understand how my presence, interests, questions, and writing impacted each hub and the communities they serve. In time, I realized the history and growth of each hub is largely siloed from the other. The founders of one hub did not have direct access to the other at the time of my research. Although intermediary organizations represent shared partners, with the capacity to translate resources and insights from one part of the ecology to the other, these organizations did not serve a bridge-building function between these two hubs. As founders from each hub began to inquire about the other, I realized my work and presence involved translation and bridge building.

Figure A-1 locates me in relation to individuals and organizations across these hubs. With the PC and the OCE located on the left and the right, my position within this broader network, illustrated by the label "DB," provides the connective center between them.

My presence bridges a gap, providing a convergent space for collaboration, community, and change. My description also renders each hub's work intelligible to the other, and to others beyond the region. In sum, my research within and across each hub provides a medium for resources, insights, and relational capital to move between disparate sectors of an ecclesial ecology.

NAMING DATA

Semi-structured interviews are the primary archive of this project's data. Interviews ranged from one hour to two and a half hours. Whenever possible, I completed interviews in person. I recorded each interview and transcribed it using a transcription service (Rev) or transcription software (Dragon Naturally Speaking). I coded each interview using an inductive and deductive coding schema. Every interviewee received and signed an informed consent form indicating how I could use their information. In all but one case, interviewees agreed to be identified in my writing.

Individuals across both hubs have written extensively about their work, in print and online. This literary archive provides insight about founders, key organizers, and the broader pattern of thought surrounding their work. I am the first researcher to provide a full description of the kindred organizational and ecclesial adaptation they pursue. However, writings from other researchers and journalists identify the novelty of each expression, providing an external assessment of the OCE and the PC.

My research also reflects site visits and research trips throughout the region. I attended each hub's annual conference. My participation in these events provided insight about how founders and current organizers pursue the connective and collaborative work they envision. I also traveled throughout the region, meeting with leaders and practitioners. I completed visits to Boise, Idaho; Bellingham, Washington; Portland; Seattle; Spokane; Tacoma, Washington; and Vancouver, Washington.

I also convened organizers from each hub for a two-day digital gathering. Co-hosted with the M. J. Murdock Charitable Trust, this gathering included three leaders from each hub and seven invited balcony guests. Balcony guests represented thought leaders from within and beyond the Pacific Northwest who could enrich our conversation in contextually specific ways. Guided by Heifetz's description of the need for balcony perspective, balcony guests were invited to observe the conversation about this research and interactions between participants—from above, on the balcony—and contribute when invited into the conversation. The two-day conversation was transcribed and treated as a focus group for analysis.

Founders from each hub received a full copy of an earlier version of this research, my dissertation, and discussed my preliminary findings during the two-day gathering. When possible, I also invited organizers to attend events in their region where I was presenting or discussing my work. After attending a national gathering where I presented my research, one organizer expressed appreciation for the invitation and the sense that I "get" their work.[6] While I alone am responsible for the findings and constructive account offered here, I developed this work in ongoing conversation with the individuals who practice the practical wisdom of an adaptive church.

NAMING METHODS: PRACTICAL THEOLOGY AS CONVENING

As an actor within this broader ecology, my presence, research, and writing promote more critical and faithful action.[7] As described by Swinton and Mowat, practical theology represents a form of action research, "encourag[ing] controlled and focused change using the knowledge and expertise of those involved in the research setting."[8] Just as each hub supports the transformation of communities and organizations, my research promotes "transformative action" through engagement with and alongside their work.[9] At its best, practical theology convenes disciplines, contextual guides, and communities of practice in a virtuous pattern of collective discernment.

I came to realize critical and faithful action principally requires a new social architecture, not only new paradigms or conceptual frameworks. Virtuous connections create the container for collaborations that can reshape a common life. If the wisdom of these hubs points to the power of convening, my work should do the same.

To this end, I convened organizers and balcony guests as the final phase of this work.[10] I followed best practices for focus group facilitation and organizational research.[11] Appendix E summarizes the questions that guided our conversation.

Organized around the primary findings from my work and guided by questions for collective engagement, the conversation progressed from leaders at each hub introducing their respective work to each hub wondering about the possibilities for collaboration. "Are there ways that we can collaborate in those [same geographical spaces] to strengthen the distinct work that each of us is doing and support the other?" one organizer wondered. To which another participant responded: "I think working together, we can do something pretty amazing."[12] Even in a digital space, the conversation provided a container for connections that could generate virtuous collaborations. Our gathering "provid[ed] a more spacious language," one participant observed.

NAMING NAMES

Individuals across both hubs generously supported this project. They offered their time, provided feedback on early drafts, and made introductions to individuals within their networks. They also extended trust, allowing me to study and write about their work. Organizers across both hubs acknowledged how my research could add legitimacy to their organizations; they also noted the fragility and unfinished character of their adaptive work. My research is a byproduct of their service in the region, and I remain grateful for the chance to learn from and alongside their collective work.

My account identifies each organization and attributes comments to interviewees. Due to the public nature of each hub, it is not possible to anonymize their work. Further, the limited number of religious organizations in the region precludes any attempt to anonymize these organizations without erasing critical features of their history or context. Put simply, the Christian practical wisdom each expresses cannot be separated from the particularity of their work. The conditions required for adaptive church resist anonymity. I attribute comments to founders and key organizers, but not always to participants across these hubs. In an effort to protect individuals' local work and ministry, I do not always attribute comments to participants, especially when they describe their community of faith or local context. I also intentionally do not attribute responses to interviewees in chapter 7, "We're Better Together," which identifies six modes of leadership for adaptive work. Beyond my description of each hub's team, I do not identify individuals with a particular mode of leadership. I obscure identities at this point to avoid placing individuals within a particular mode, potentially compromising their local work and ministry. In instances where individuals changed positions or roles in the time since our interview, I identify them according to their place of service at the time of this research.

Appendix B

Interviewee Phase and Date

Due to the nature of this study, it is not possible to maintain strict anonymity for either the individual participants or the affiliated organizations. With relatively few religious organizations within the Pacific Northwest, it is not possible to provide a thorough description of the activities and characteristics of each organization without enabling individuals who are familiar with the region from being able to identify them. Accordingly, my informed consent process asks participants if they "can be quoted and identified in [my] report." In all but one case, interview participants agreed to be identified, and all but one participant in the final focus group agreed to be identified. Accordingly, with the permission of my study participants, I identify participants and attribute quotes to specific respondents. Individuals' affiliation at the time of the interview is listed below. In some cases, study participants have since transitioned to new positions.

Phase	Name	Hub	Date
I	Bill Pubols	N/A	October 30, 2017
I	Douglas Strong	N/A	October 31, 2017
I	Cary Paine	N/A	November 1, 2017
I	K. Scott Connolly	N/A	November 2, 2017
I	Beck Taylor	N/A	November 3, 2017
II	Dwight Friesen	PC	September 28, 2018
II	Craig Detweiler	PC	October 5, 2018

Phase	Name	Hub	Date
II	Gerald Sittser	OCE	October 8, 2018
II	Robert (Bob) Savage	OCE	October 8, 2018
II	Kevin Lind	OCE	October 8, 2018
II	John Williams	OCE	October 8, 2018
II	Terry McGonigal	OCE	October 8, 2018
II	Carter Hudson	OCE	October 9, 2018
II	Rob Fairbanks	OCE	October 9, 2018
II	James Leman	OCE	October 10, 2018
II	Kathryn McInturff	OCE	October 10, 2018
II	Andrew Goodwin	OCE	October 10, 2018
II	Anonymous	N/A	October 19, 2018
II	Mindy Smith	OCE	October, 23, 2018
II	Beck Taylor	OCE	October 23, 2018
II	Mark Finney	OCE	November 2, 2018
II	Elizabeth Leman	OCE	November 5, 2018
II	Mike McKay	OCE	November 9, 2018
II	Courtney Arntzen	OCE	November 14, 2018
II	Robert Moore III	OCE	January 1, 2019
II	Tim Soerens	PC	February 4, 2019
II	Paul Sparks	PC	February 4, 2019
II	Steve Moore	OCE/PC	February 5, 2019
II	Kirk Lauckner	PC	April 25, 2019
II	Rich Jones	PC	April 25, 2019
II	Barry Jung	PC	April 26, 2019
II	Andrew Carlson	PC	April 26, 2019
II	Josh McQueen	PC	April 27, 2019
II	Dave Harder	PC	April 27, 2019
II	Anna Golladay	PC	May 3, 2019
II	Benjamin Katt	PC	May 6, 2019
II	Karen Reed	PC	May 8, 2019
II	Christiana Rice	PC	May 14, 2019
II	Lauren Goldbloom	PC	May 15, 2019
II	Jonathan Brooks	PC	May 21, 2019

Phase	Name	Hub	Date
II	Al Engler	PC	June 4, 2019
II	Jessica Ketola	PC	June 6, 2019
II	James Helms	PC	June 25, 2019
III	Josh McQueen	PC	December 14, 2020
III	Jessica Ketola	PC	December 15, 2020
III	Lauren Goldbloom	PC	December 15, 2020
III	Mike McKay	OCE	December 15, 2020
III	John Williams	OCE	December 17, 2020
III	Kevin Lind	OCE	December 17, 2020
III	Andrew Carlson	PC	December 17, 2020
III	Courtney Arntzen	OCE	December 28, 2020
III	James Leman	OCE	February 18, 2020
III (focus group)	Tim Soerens	PC	March 30–31, 2020
III (focus group)	Paul Sparks	PC	March 30–31, 2020
III (focus group)	Jonathan Brooks	PC	March 30–31, 2020
III (focus group)	Terry McGonigal	OCE	March 30–31, 2020
III (focus group)	Jerry Sittser	OCE	March 30–31, 2020
III (focus group)	Mindy Smith	OCE	March 30–31, 2020
III (focus group)	Steve Moore	OCE/PC	March 30–31, 2020
III (focus group)	Kimberly Thornbury	OCE/PC	March 30–31, 2020
III (focus group)	Thad Austin	Balcony Guest	March 30–31, 2020
III (focus group)	Jason Byassee	Balcony Guest	March 30–31, 2020

Phase	Name	Hub	Date
III (focus group)	Jeff Grubbs	Balcony Guest	March 30–31, 2020
III (focus group)	Kyle McManamy	Balcony Guest	March 30–31, 2020
III (focus group)	Matt Overton	Balcony Guest	March 30–31, 2020
III (focus group)	Sharon Parks	Balcony Guest	March 30–31, 2020
III (focus group)	Anonymous	N/A	March 30–31, 2020

Appendix C

Phase I Interview Guide

PART I

DEMOGRAPHIC INFORMATION

1) Institution name:
2) Institution type:
3) Respondent's name:
4) Respondent's title:

PART II

RELATIONSHIPS WITH AND AMONG CHRISTIAN COLLEGES AND UNIVERSITIES

1) In the last two years, which Christian colleges and universities in the Pacific Northwest would you identify as your primary partners?[1]
2) Are there other colleges and universities (either regionally or nationally) that you would identify as your primary partners?
3) Of those included above, on average, how regularly did you have contact with representatives from these institutions? Contact can be meetings, phone calls, or emails.
4) What facilitates your interaction(s) with the institutions listed above?
5) What goes through your mind when building relationships with individuals from Christian colleges and universities?

Relationships with and among Theological Schools

6) In the last two years, which theological schools in the Pacific Northwest would you identify as your primary partners?
7) Are there other theological schools (either regionally or nationally) that you would identify as your primary partners?
8) Of those included above, on average, how regularly did you have contact with representatives from these institutions? Contact can be meetings, phone calls, or emails.
9) What facilitates your interaction(s) with the institutions listed above?
10) What goes through your mind when building relationships with individual theological schools?

Relationships with and among Christian Study Centers

11) In the last two years, which Christian study centers in the Pacific Northwest would you identify as your primary partners?
12) Are there other university-based, religiously affiliated educational organizations (either regionally or nationally) that you interacted with during this period of time?
13) Of those included above, on average, how regularly did you have contact with representatives from these institutions? Contact can be meetings, phone calls, or emails.
14) What facilitates your interaction(s) with the institutions listed above?
15) What goes through your mind when building relationships with individuals at university-based, religiously affiliated educational organizations?

Relationships with and among Congregations

16) In the last two years, on average, how regularly do representatives from your organization have contact with local congregations?
17) Which three to five congregations would you identify as your primary partners?
18) What facilitates your interaction(s) with the congregations listed above?
19) What goes through your mind when building relationships with individuals from congregations?
20) *Question only for congregations*: In the last ten years, have any of your members attended a Christian college or seminary?
21) *Question only for congregations*: Where did your pastoral staff receive their undergraduate and theological education?

Relationships with and among Foundations

22) In the last two years, who are your three to five largest foundation supporters and how regularly do you have contact with representatives from these foundations? Contact can be meetings, phone calls, or emails. You may respond N/A if this does not apply to your organization.
23) In the last two years, approximately what percentage of your external funding comes from individual donors? How is your approach to potential individual donors similar or different to your approach to potential foundation donors?
24) *Question only for foundations*: How do you identify prospective grantees? If you do not have an open call for proposals, what avenue(s) or networks enable you to identify new prospective grantees?
25) What goes through your mind when building relationships with individuals affiliated with foundations?
26) Are there connections to other organizations or individuals that we haven't talked about that are important to the ongoing life and work of your organization? If so, which ones?
27) Are there other things that you think I should know about your organization or organizations like yours, specifically as it pertains to your partnerships, collaborations, and identity as a religious organization?

PART III

Religious Leadership

28) What are the challenges confronting your organization? Do you think these challenges are shared across similar organizations?
29) What goes through your mind when you think about the network or ecology of partners and organizations that surround yours?
30) How do you decide which connections to maintain, which new ones to form, and which ones to discontinue?
31) How do you narrate the mission of your particular organizations and how does your connection and collaboration with other organizations contribute to fulfilling the mission described above?
32) What is needed for you and your organization to either continue to fulfill or more faithfully fulfill your particular organizational mission?
33) Would you be willing to put me in touch with some of your primary partners that we have discussed today?

PART IV

DEMOGRAPHIC INFORMATION

34) Respondent's gender:
35) Respondent's race (please indicate if you identify by more than one race):
36) Age:

Appendix D

Phase II Interview Guide

PART I: INTERVIEWEE INFORMATION

1) Organization name:
2) Respondent's name:
3) Respondent's title:
4) How long have you served in your current position?

PART II: MISSION AND PARTNERSHIP

5) How would you describe the mission of your particular organization? If you do not currently serve in an organization, what type of mission do you hope to support through your work or service?
6) What are the key events in the life of your organizations and ministry that have shaped your understanding of this mission or your vocation? (Ask follow-up questions to clarify and explore further as needed)
7) What are the key events in your life and education that have prepared you to pursue and support this work or this vocation? (Ask follow-up questions to clarify and explore further as needed)
8) Who are the key individuals or organizations that you consider partners for your work or vocation?
9) For partner organizations: How has your work with OCE or PC enabled you to pursue your mission?

10) What other forms of organized associations, gatherings, or practices facilitate your interaction with the individuals or institutions listed above?
11) How would you describe the relationship between the broader network of organizations and your specific organization or work?
12) What goes through your mind when you think about the network or ecology of partners and organizations that surround yours?
13) How do you decide which connections to maintain, which new ones to form, and which ones to discontinue?

PART III: ADAPTIVE CHALLENGES AND ADAPTIVE WORK

14) What are the challenges confronting your organization or the individuals and communities you serve or will serve?
15) From your perspective, do you think other individuals and organizations face a similar challenge within their context?
16) You identified [IDENTIFY A CHALLENGE OR SET OF CHALLENGES] as a pressing challenge for your organization or the communities you serve or will serve. Can you explain the source and nature of this challenge?
17) What other factors have contributed to the shape of this challenge within your organization and the communities you serve or will serve?
18) What has worked well and what has not worked as well as you or others sought to engage this challenge in your context?
19) What are the values that guide your engagement with the challenges you identified? Do you think individuals share these values across your organization and/or the community you serve?
20) From your perspective, what is the function of leadership in relation to the challenge(s) you've identified?
21) In an ideal scenario, what would it look like to address this challenge within your organization and community?

PART IV: ORGANIZATIONAL LEADERSHIP AND LEADERSHIP DEVELOPMENT

22) What practice and partnerships would you identify as most integral to your service and leadership?
23) How have you or others attempted to shape the work and structure of your organization in ways that engage the challenges that you described above?
24) How have you or others attempted to cultivate community in ways that engage the challenges that you described above?

25) For the OCE, PC, and funders: In your work with religious leaders, how does your organization seek to train and support them to address the challenges that are unique to their context(s)?
26) For the OCE, PC, and funders: Are there focal practices or values that guide your training of religious leaders?
27) For the OCE, PC, and funders: How do you hope your support and training of religious leaders will impact the organizations and communities they serve?
28) For the OCE and PC: Could you walk me through a typical class or event that includes the religious and community leaders you serve?
29) For students, pastors, or partner organizations: How has your work, education, or organization been impacted through your engagement with OCE/PC?
30) For students, pastors, or partner organizations: How has your engagement with OCE/PC connected you to other individuals or organizations that are pursuing a similar ministry or vocation?
31) For funders: How has your work with other grantees been impacted through your engagement with OCE/PC and the individuals and communities they serve?
32) What else is needed for you, your organization, or those you serve or will serve to either continue to fulfill or more faithfully fulfill your/their particular organizational mission?
33) For the OCE and PC: Would you be willing to let me attend some of your training sessions with religious leaders?
34) Would you be willing to put me in touch with some of the partners we have discussed today?
35) Is there anything else I need to know about you, your work, or your partnership with the OCE/PC?

PART V: DEMOGRAPHIC INFORMATION

36) Respondent's gender:
37) Respondent's race (please indicate if you identify by more than one race):
38) Age:

Appendix E

Phase III Interview Guide

PART I: INTERVIEWEE INFORMATION

1) Please share your name and where you serve.
2) When we last met you served at [ORGANIZATION NAME], have you changed jobs since we last met?
3) If you have changed, what is your new role?
4) What factors contributed to your job change?

PART II: CHALLENGES, VALUES, AND PARTNERSHIP

5) When we talked last time, you shared about [DESCRIBE MISSION OF ORGANIZATION]. Has this changed at all?
6) You also shared about some of the challenges that you and your community face. For example, we talked about [SHORT LIST OF CHALLENGES]. Have the challenges you face changed since we last met?
7) If so, what has changed?
8) What new challenges do you face?
9) You also shared about some of the values that guide you and your community. For example, we talked about [SHORT LIST OF CHALLENGES]. Have the values that guide you and your community changed since we last met?
10) If so, what has changed?
11) What new values guide you and your community?

12) We also talked about some of the partners that support your work. From your perspective today, who are the key individuals or organizations that you consider partners for your work?

PART III: AFTERMATH OF SPRING 2020

13) There's no question it has been a tumultuous spring and summer for religious organizations and communities of faith. I'm especially mindful of the COVID-19 crisis, economic uncertainty, and collective unrest following the deaths of George Floyd, Breonna Taylor, and Ahmaud Arbery. What have the last six to eight months been like for you and your community?
14) Can you tell me a story of a particularly memorable challenge for you and your community?
15) What new challenges have surfaced in the last few months?
16) To whom have you turned?
17) In retrospect, what resources do you wish you had?
18) Where have you turned for creativity and hope?
19) Can you tell me a story of a new life that has emerged for you and your community?
20) What has leadership looked like for you in this particular moment?

PART IV: CONCLUSION

21) Is there anything else I need to know about you or your work?

Appendix F

Two-Day Focus Group Gathering

This gathering will explore four themes that intersect with the adaptive work each hub pursues. A pair of questions indicates how each theme may organize our conversation.

> **Catalyzing Conditions:** What types of organizational and relational conditions catalyzed your early connecting and convening work? What types of organizational and relational conditions do you seek to cultivate to catalyze similar work among those you serve?
>
> **Connection:** What makes for meaningful and durable connection? What types of connection(s) do the leaders you serve need in order to pursue their work?
>
> **COVID-19:** How did your organization respond to the challenges following COVID-19? What unexpected lessons did you and those you serve learn in the wake of COVID-19?
>
> **Community:** What unique gifts does your work offer to other communities and organizations? How can other communities and organizations offer their unique gifts to support your work?

The conversations during this gathering encompassed approximately six hours of conversation and engagement. With the permission from participants, I recorded our conversations and later transcribed this material.

Appendix G

Informed Consent Form

All participants in each phase of research received and reviewed informed consent information, as summarized in the template below. Participants in Phase III had the opportunity to review and complete an electronic version of these informed consent materials.

<u>INFORMED CONSENT:</u>

Thank you for your interest in a study of Adaptive Challenges and Practice of Religious Leadership across Ecclesial Educational Institutions in the Pacific Northwest. I hope that the findings from my research will provide you and similar religious leaders with a better understanding of the changing landscape of religious organizations and the practices that support religious leadership in the region.

If you agree to participate, I will ask about your organization, the relationships between your organization and other religious organizations, the challenges religious organizations face, the practice of religious leadership, and how your organization supports religious leaders and the communities they serve. Some of the survey and interview questions may ask about your personal opinions and experiences with the relationships between your and other organizations, the experiences and practices that have shaped your understanding of leadership, and how your work at your organizations supports communities and religious leaders in the region. Please only share what you are comfortable with and feel free to let me know if you would like to skip any questions.

I would like to discuss your organization in the findings from this study. With your permission, I also may like to share specific comments you have made and attribute them to you. However, please let me know if there is anything you would not like me to share and/or if you would not like to be identified by name. If you agree, I would like to audio-record our conversation so that I can focus on what we talk about instead of taking notes. I anticipate our conversation will last between an hour and an hour and a half. If you would prefer not to be recorded, that is fine and I will take handwritten notes instead. With your invitation, I would like to attend educational events supported by your organization to develop a better understanding for your work.

Please understand that your participation in this study is voluntary and you can stop participating at any time. I can also send you my research findings after my research is complete. I anticipate holding onto your responses indefinitely.

Please do not hesitate to contact me at [email] or [phone] if you have any questions about your participation in this study. You may also contact my research advisor, Dr. Mark Chaves, at [email]. For questions about your rights as a participant in this study, you may contact the Duke University research ethics committee at 919-684-3030 or campusirb@duke.edu.

Because this represents a larger research project, if you express interest (below) I may contact you about another research project in the future.

If you agree to participate in the study, please sign below and indicate how I can use your information (we can revisit these options after the interview is over).

- I can be quoted and identified in your report.
- I can be quoted but do not want to be identified in your report
- My interview can be audio-recorded
- I am interested in being contacted about additional phases of this study

Participant Signature: _____

Participant Name: _____

Date: _____

Notes

ACKNOWLEDGMENTS

1. Murdock, however, did not provide funding for Phase II of my research. This phase pivoted to examine the ecclesial ecology that supports and surrounds the OCE and PC, which includes Murdock.

INTRODUCTION

1. Matthew Kaemmingk, personal communication, January 15, 2019.
2. Erin Martin, email correspondence, November 27, 2017.
3. Anne Lamott, *Traveling Mercies: Some Thoughts on Faith* (New York: Pantheon Books, 1999), 41–42.
4. See Mark Chaves, *American Religion: Contemporary Trends*, 2nd ed. (Princeton, N.J.: Princeton University Press, 2017).
5. This description is modified from an essay that appeared in *The Presbyterian Outlook*. For the full essay, see Dustin Benac, "Theological Education for a New Age," *Presbyterian Outlook*, September 25, 2018, https://pres-outlook.org/2018/09/theological-education-for-a-new-age/.
6. See Amos Yong, *Renewing the Church by the Spirit: Theological Education after Pentecost* (Grand Rapids: Eerdmans, 2020). As Yong observes: "A fundamental realignment is occurring: North American denominational structures are giving way to dynamic networks connected by ministries, charisms, and relationships" (17). See also Brad Christerson and Richard Flory, *The Rise of Network Christianity: How Independent Leaders Are Changing the Religious Landscape* (New York: Oxford University Press, 2017).
7. Patricia O'Connell Killen and Mark Silk, eds., *Religion & Public Life in the Pacific Northwest: The None Zone* (Walnut Creek, Calif.: AltaMira Press, 2004).
8. For example, numerous Christian colleges, Roman Catholic institutions, and theological schools have closed in the region within the last five years. A partial list includes: Moody Bible College's Spokane campus (2018); Marylhurst

University (2018); Fuller Theological Seminary's Northwest campus (2019). The closing of these institutions has also catalyzed the establishment of new institutions and collaborations within the region. For example, a contingent of faculty from Moody Bible College's Spokane campus established Great Northern University in Spokane, Washington after Moody closed its campus in the Pacific Northwest; Claremont School of Theology entered into a partnership with Willamette University to provide expanded access to theological education in the region.

9 See Pew Research Center, "In U.S., Decline of Christianity Continues at Rapid Pace: An Update on America's Changing Religious Landscape," October 17, 2019, https://www.pewforum.org/2019/10/17/in-u-s-decline-of-christianity-continues-at-rapid-pace/; Chaves, *American Religion*; Lyndon Shakespeare, *Being the Body of Christ in the Age of Management* (Eugene, Ore.: Cascade, 2016).

10 David King, "The Surprising Financial Strength of American Congregations," *Insights Newsletter*, January 28, 2020, https://philanthropy.iupui.edu/news-events/insights-newsletter/2020-issues/january-2020-issue-2.html; Centre for the Study of Christianity and Culture, "Churches, COVID-19 and Communities: Experiences, Needs, and Supporting Recovery" (University of York, March 2021).

11 Edward Farley, *Theologia: The Fragmentation and Unity of Theological Education* (Philadelphia: Fortress, 1983), 16. I have intentionally used "template" to describe how the stories of these hubs can resource other communities; while some concepts and practices are translatable to faith communities beyond the region, others are not.

12 Mark Silk, "The Pacific Northwest Is the American Religious Future," *Religion News Service*, June 4, 2019, https://religionnews.com/2019/05/31/the-pacific-northwest-is-the-american-religious-future/.

13 See appendix B for a full list of interviewees and interview dates.

14 While the Pacific Northwest has smaller Hispanic and African American populations as compared to national averages, the region remains a space where people of faith must gather amid tangled religious and racial histories. The story of religious life in the Pacific Northwest, as Patricia O'Connell Killen and Mark Shibley observe, includes higher American Indian and Hawaiian/Pacific Islander populations as well (Patricia O'Connell Killen and Mark Shibley, "Surveying the Religious Landscape: Historical Trends and Current Patterns in Oregon, Washington, and Alaska," in Killen and Silk, *Religion & Public Life in the Pacific Northwest*, 27).

15 Various other definitions have been offered for "hub." For example, taking cues from network theory, Niall Ferguson defines a hub as "individuals in social networks with high degree centrality, betweenness centrality or closeness centrality" (Niall Ferguson, *The Square and the Tower: Networks, Hierarchies and the Struggle for Global Power* [New York: Penguin, 2017], 28).

16 See Christopher Scheitle, *Beyond the Congregation: The World of Christian Nonprofits* (New York: Oxford University Press, 2010) for an overview of recent research in this field. As Mark Chaves has argued, religious nonprofits represent an underexplored area of inquiry (Mark Chaves, "Religious Organizations: Data Resources and Research Opportunities," *American Behavioral Scientist* 45 [2002]: 1523–49). The most pressing question for scholars of religious organizations, according to Chaves, is "what difference does religion make to organizational behavior?" (1523–24). An adequate assessment of this question, however,

requires an interdisciplinary approach that combines social scientific methods with insights from the humanities.

17 Thad Austin, "Collaborative Partnerships: Christian Ministry in a Post-pandemic World," in *Crisis and Care: Meditations on Faith and Philanthropy*, ed. Dustin Benac and Erin Weber-Johnson (Eugene, Ore.: Cascade, 2021), 54.

18 Douglas Todd, introduction to *Cascadia: The Elusive Utopia: Exploring the Spirit of the Pacific Northwest*, ed. Douglas Todd (Vancouver, B.C.: Ronsdale Press, 2008), 1.

19 Patricia O'Connell Killen, "Memory, Novelty and Possibility in This Place," in Todd, *Cascadia*, 66.

20 Patricia O'Connell Killen, "Introduction—Patterns of the Past, Prospects for the Future: Religion in the None Zone," in Killen and Silk, *Religion & Public Life in the Pacific Northwest*, 13.

21 E. J. Klemme, in *The Pacific Northwest Pulpit*, comp. Paul Little (New York: United Methodist Book Concern, 1915), quoted in Killen, "Introduction," 9.

22 Seattle Times Staff, "The Unchurched Northwest," *Seattle Times*, October 11, 2005, https://www.seattletimes.com/opinion/the-unchurched-northwest/.

23 Christopher James, *Church Planting in Post-Christian Soil: Theology and Practice* (New York: Oxford University Press, 2018), 17.

24 Silk, "Pacific Northwest Is the American Religious Future."

25 Killen, "Memory," 85. Killen stops short of identifying how the four new understandings she identifies—human maturity, anthropology, a way of conceiving community, and a practice of a social life—collectively represent a form of practical wisdom.

26 The language of "new age" reflects an earlier use in my introduction.

27 Jason Byassee, foreword to *Christian Witness in Cascadian Soil: Coworkers with God in the Land of Hiking, Hipsters, and Hand-Crafted Lattes*, by Ross Lockhart (Eugene, Ore.: Cascade, 2021), ix.

28 Sunia Gibbs, "Everything Is an Experiment," in Benac and Weber-Johnson, *Crisis and Care*, 127–31.

29 And then Killen concludes: "Cascadia is the 'nurse log' for a new understanding of human maturity, a new anthropology, a new way of conceiving community, a new practice of social life" (Killen, "Memory," 83–85).

30 James, *Church Planting in Post-Christian Soil*.

31 News Tribune Editorial Board, "Yes, Tacoma's Historic Churches Can Be Rescued. Let's Celebrate This Success Story," *News Tribune*, April 6, 2021, https://www.thenewstribune.com/opinion/editorials/article250450861.html?fbclid=IwAR3GVlAK-zF4LDAmzVnHFiH7XKT87K7c1lRVM02-rrT-KMdG4r2JpVE1cT0.

32 Jason Byassee and Ross Lockhart, *Better than Brunch: Missional Churches in Cascadia* (Eugene, Ore.: Cascade, 2020).

33 Bonnie J. Miller-McLemore, "Introduction: The Contributions of Practical Theology," in *The Wiley-Blackwell Companion to Practical Theology*, ed. Bonnie J. Miller-McLemore (Malden, Mass.: Wiley-Blackwell, 2012), 7.

34 In the years following Craig Dykstra's essay "Reconceiving Practice," a substantial body of literature has emerged that seeks to describe and enrich a way of life for people of faith. For examples, see Craig Dykstra, *Growing in the Life of Faith: Education and Christian Practices*, 2nd ed. (Louisville: Westminster John Knox,

2005); Dorothy C. Bass, ed., *Practicing Our Faith: A Way of Life for a Searching People*, 2nd ed. (San Francisco: Jossey-Bass, 2010). After more than two decades of theological conversation about the formation and importance of Christian practice(s), Lauren Winner's *The Dangers of Christian Practice: On Wayward Gifts, Characteristic Damage, and Sin* ruptures existing discourse according to her account of the "characteristic damage" inherent to all forms of human life, including Christian practice (Lauren Winner, *The Dangers of Christian Practice: On Wayward Gifts, Characteristic Damage, and Sin* [New Haven, Conn.: Yale University Press, 2018], 1). Even as Winner's work challenges the uncritical privileging of Christian practices, she also seeks to promote more faithful forms of witness and practice by acknowledging and attending to the dangers inherent to Christian practice.

35 As Miller-McLemore writes: "[P]ractical theology's academic importance rests on its value for, or its relationship to, the life of everyday faith" (Miller-McLemore, "Introduction," 9).

36 Miller-McLemore, "Introduction," 11. Christian Scharen and Aana Marie Vigen's edited volume *Ethnography as Christian Theology and Ethics* (New York: Continuum, 2011) identifies the "blurring" of the disciplinary boundaries between practical theology and ethics that characterizes qualitative research across these fields (xvii). Miller-McLemore's assessment also reflects similar appraisals offered by Pete Ward in *Introducing Practical Theology: Mission, Ministry, and the Life of the Church* (Grand Rapids: Baker Academic, 2017) and David Roozen and James Nieman's edited work *Church, Identity, and Change: Theology and Denominational Structure in Unsettled Times* (Grand Rapids: Eerdmans, 2005).

37 Miller-McLemore, "Introduction," 14.

38 On practical theology as an interdisciplinary field, see Miller-McLemore, "Introduction"; Richard Osmer, *Practical Theology: An Introduction* (Grand Rapids: Eerdmans, 2008); Ward, *Introducing Practical Theology*; John Swinton and Harriet Mowat, *Practical Theology and Qualitative Research*, 2nd ed. (London: SCM Press, 2016). On organizational studies as an interdisciplinary field, see Paul Adler, introduction to *The Oxford Handbook of Sociology and Organizational Studies: Classical Foundations*, ed. Paul Adler (Oxford: Oxford University Press, 2009); Jeffrey Pfeffer, *New Directions for Organizational Theory: Problems and Prospects* (New York: Oxford University Press, 1997); Mary Jo Hatch, *Organizations: A Very Short Introduction* (Oxford: Oxford University Press, 2011). Clare Watkins has characterized research at this intersection as "organizational ecclesiology" (Clare Watkins, "Organizing the People of God: Social-Science Theories of Organization in Ecclesiology," *Theological Studies* 52 [1991]: 689–711).

39 See chapter 5 for a full discussion of this definition.

40 Following insights from organizational studies, the ecclesial ecology represents a meso-level analysis. Analytically positioned between discrete organizations and the larger institutional constructs that give them meaning, organizational fields call for a meso-level analysis that jointly examines the practices that structure organizations and the larger organizational context in which social life is embedded. Accordingly, as Smith et al. note, meso-level analysis has the capacity to promote "understanding of the cross-level and reciprocal effects that characterize real life in real organizations" (D. Brent Smith, Benjamin Schneider, and Marcus Dickson, "Meso Organizational Behavior: Comments on the Third Paradigm," in *The*

Notes to Pages 8–9 261

Sage Handbook of Organization Studies, 2nd ed., ed. Steward Clegg et al. [London: Sage, 2006], 161.

41 Swinton and Mowat, *Practical Theology and Qualitative Research*, 261, emphasis in original. In their concluding discussion they argue that practical theology can exist within and contribute to the broader scholarly enterprise if it is understood as a form of action research.

42 Bent Flyvbjerg, *Making Social Science Matter: Why Social Inquiry Fails and How It Can Succeed Again* (Cambridge: Cambridge University Press, 2001), 4. Although Flyvbjerg does not work within theological studies, his language aptly characterizes how attention to practical reason directs practical theological engagement with qualitative methods. As my colleague Erin Weber-Johnson and I have argued, a contextual, interdisciplinary, and *phronetic* approach is necessary to attend to the Christian practical wisdom that organizes communities' responses to the challenges they face (Dustin Benac and Erin Weber-Johnson, "Ecclesial Imagination for Organizational Transformation: Hospice Care, Midwifery, and the Ordering of a Common Life," *Practical Theology* 12, no. 2 [2019]: 158–74). This emphasis is consistent with a renewed interest in *phronesis* within theology, ethics, and philosophy. For examples, see Oliver O'Donovan, *Self, World and Time*, vol. 1 of *Ethics as Theology* (Grand Rapids: Eerdmans, 2013); Alasdair MacIntyre, *Ethics in the Conflict of Modernity: An Essay on Desire, Practical Reason, and Narrative* (Cambridge: Cambridge University Press, 2016).

43 Although Randy Maddox characterized practical theology in 1991 as a "discipline in search of a definition" (Randy Maddox, "Practical Theology: A Discipline in Search of a Definition," *Perspectives in Religious Studies* 18 [1991]: 159–69), scholarship over the last two and a half decades has provided greater clarity to the field's organizing concerns and methodological commitments. Nevertheless, considerable variation persists within this field. Among others, these include definitions offered by John Swinton and Harriet Mowat, who define practical theology as "critical, theological reflection on the practices of the Church as they interact with the practices of the world" (Swinton and Mowat, *Practical Theology and Qualitative Research*, 7); Richard Osmer, who defines practical theology according to its descriptive, interpretive, normative, and pragmatic tasks (Osmer, *Practical Theology*); Dorothy Bass and Craig Dykstra, who present practical theology as a "movement," drawing simultaneously from academic, ecclesial, and practical modes of reflection, that is ordered by the pursuit of "life abundant" according to the eschatological reign of God (Dorothy C. Bass and Craig Dykstra, introduction to *For Life Abundant: Practical Theology, Theological Education, and Christian Ministry*, ed. Dorothy C. Bass and Craig Dykstra [Grand Rapids: Eerdmans, 2008]); and Pete Ward, who defines practical theology broadly as "any way of thinking that takes both practice and theology seriously" (Ward, *Introducing Practical Theology*, 5).

44 Miller-McLemore, "Introduction," 14.

45 Kathleen A. Cahalan, "Unknowing: Spiritual Practices and the Search for a Wisdom Epistemology," in *Christian Practical Wisdom: What It Is, Why It Matters*, by Dorothy C. Bass et al. (Grand Rapids: Eerdmans, 2016), 319–20.

46 Bass et al., *Christian Practical Wisdom*, 5.

47 The empirical focus of my research defines "Pacific Northwest" as Washington, Oregon, and Idaho. Although other studies include or exclude Alaska, Montana, and Idaho, my tristate designation reflects a common approach. See Killen, "Introduction," 10, 14. This approach provides boundaries to organize the preliminary investigation, but interviews within and beyond the region demonstrate the variation within the region and how individuals beyond this tristate designation identify themselves as members of the Pacific Northwest. For example, Courtney Arntzen, who serves as in Missoula, Montana, still locates herself within the Pacific Northwest. Given this diversity of perspectives, Timothy Egan provides an apropos definition: "The Pacific Northwest is simply this: wherever the salmon can get to" (Timothy Egan, *The Good Rain: Across Time and Terrain in the Pacific Northwest* [New York: Alfred Knopf, 1990], 22).

48 Bonnie J. Miller-McLemore, "Disciplining: Academic Theology and Practical Knowledge," in Bass et al., *Christian Practical Wisdom*, 177.

49 Bass et al., *Christian Practical Wisdom*, 5.

50 L. Gregory Jones, dust jacket cover, Benac and Weber-Johnson, *Crisis and Care*.

51 The extended case study methodology has precedent both within practical theology and social scientific research. As outlined and described by Robert Yin in *Case Study Research and Applications*, case study research requires empirical inquiry of "a contemporary phenomenon" in which the "boundaries between the phenomenon and context may not be clearly evident" (Robert Yin, *Case Study Research and Applications: Design and Methods*, 6th ed. [London: Sage, 2018], 15).

52 The three forms of data and analysis reflects the importance of "triangulation" in qualitative research, which uses multiple, complementary sources to substantiate the description and constructive proposal that organizes this project. For helpful discussions of triangulation, see Royce Singleton and Bruce Straights, *Approaches to Social Research*, 5th ed. (New York: Oxford University Press, 2005), 431–34, and Uwe Flick, *Managing Quality in Qualitative Research*, 2nd ed. (Thousand Oaks, Calif.: Sage, 2018), 87–88.

53 Sylvia Frey and Betty Wood, *Come Shouting to Zion: African American Protestantism in the American South and British Caribbean to 1830* (Chapel Hill: University of North Carolina Press, 1998), 139. Although Frey and Wood's description guides a historical project, their language provides a fitting description of the relationship between these two cases.

54 Silk, "Pacific Northwest Is the American Religious Future."

55 Ronald Heifetz, *Leadership without Easy Answers* (Cambridge, Mass.: Harvard University Press, 1994), 22.

1 "THE CHURCH HAS ALWAYS BEEN NIMBLE"

1 The presentation of the Office of Church Engagement (OCE) first reflects the sequence in which I completed research; it does not signal the priority of this template over the Parish Collective (PC).

2 Mary Oliver, "When I Am among the Trees," in *Poetry of Presence: An Anthology of Mindfulness Poems*, ed. Phyllis Cole-Dai and Ruby R. Wilson (West Hartford, Conn.: Grayson Books, 2017), 44.

3 Charles Goodrich, Kathleen Moore, and Frederick Swanson, introduction to *In the Blast Zone: Catastrophe and Renewal on Mount St. Helens*, ed. Charles Goodrich,

Kathleen Moore, and Frederick Swanson (Corvallis: Oregon State University Press, 2008), ix.

4 Linda Sharman, "The Seeley Mudd Chapel—Making a House a Home," *Whitworth Alumni Magazine* 48, no. 1 (1979): 1.

5 Whitworth University, "The Campaign for Whitworth," *Whitworth Today* 87, no. 2 (2018): 5.

6 See appendix A for an extended discussion of my position in relation to each hub.

7 Whitworth University, "Office of Church Engagement," accessed September 28, 2018, https://www.whitworth.edu/cms/administration/church-engagement/.

8 See Sittser's work *Resilient Faith: How the Early Christian "Third Way" Changed the World* (Grand Rapids: Brazos, 2019) for an example of the latter.

9 Wimmer served in this capacity until his death in 2020.

10 Whitworth University, "Whitworth Awarded $1 Million from Lilly Endowment to Fund Ekklesia Project, New Office of Church Engagement," *Whitworth University News*, December 4, 2013, https://news.whitworth.edu/2013/12/whitworth-awarded-1-million-from-lilly.html.

11 Bill Robinson, "Academics," *Of Mind and Heart*, December 2001, https://digitalcommons.whitworth.edu/cgi/viewcontent.cgi?article=1010&context=mind-and-heart.

12 *Foundation Directory Online Professional*, s.v. "Lilly Endowment, Inc." (Organization Name) and "Spokane, WA" (Geographic Focus), accessed September 20, 2018, https://fdo.foundationcenter.org/.

13 Robinson, "Academics."

14 Robinson, "Academics."

15 *Foundation Directory Online Professional*, s.v. "Lilly Endowment, Inc." (Organization Name) and "Spokane, WA" (Geographic Focus); Whitworth University, "Whitworth Receives $1 Million Grant from Lilly Endowment Inc. to Create New Christian Churches," *Whitworth University News*, October 29, 2018, https://news.whitworth.edu/2018/10/whitworth-receives-1-million-grant-from.html.

16 See Martin Ruef, *The Entrepreneurial Group: Social Identities, Relations, and Collective Action* (Princeton, N.J.: Princeton University Press, 2010) for an incisive study of the role of collaboration in entrepreneurship.

17 Steve Taylor similarly observes how organizational structures support conditions for ecclesial adaptation. As Taylor notes: "[E]cclesial innovation requires ordering" (Steve Taylor, *First Expressions: Innovation and the Mission of God* [London: SCM Press, 2019], 207).

18 According to 2012 data from the National Congregations Study, only 12.6 percent of congregations have an average worship attendance of more than 250 people. A growing percentage of congregations report that 100 or fewer people regularly participate in the religious life of their congregation (Association of Religion Data Archives, National Congregations Study, Cumulative Dataset, 2012, accessed September 22, 2018, https://www.thearda.com/).

19 For the 2019 Summit, Ministry Partners receive a $100 scholarship to attend the annual conference, which makes the base rate (before food and lodging) $200.

20 When asked about their engagement with the OCE, Ministry Partners regularly identify their friendship with the organizers as the primary occasion for their partnership.

21 Hugh Heclo's account of "institutional distrust" characterizes congregations' distrust of educational institutions (Hugh Heclo, *On Thinking Institutionally* [Boulder, Colo.: Paradigm, 2008], 26).
22 These include: Called to Faithful Preaching, Called to Youth Ministry, Called to Refugees and Immigrants, Called to Creation Care, Called to Reconciliation, Called to the City, Called to Formational Worship, and Called to Church Planting.
23 Whitworth University, "Whitworth Institute for Ministry Conference Set for July 23–27," *Whitworth University News*, July 20, 2018, https://news.whitworth.edu/2018/06/whitworth-institute-of-ministry.html.
24 Whitworth University, "Whitworth Ministry Summit Promo," YouTube video, March 5, 2019, 1:02, https://www.youtube.com/watch?time_continue=4&v=qwteIqw44JQ.
25 The text reads: ". . . but those who hope in the LORD will renew their strength. They will soar on wings like eagles; they will run and not grow weary, they will walk and not be faint" (NIV).
26 Whitworth University, "Academy of Christian Discipleship," accessed September 28, 2018, https://www.whitworth.edu/cms/administration/church-engagement/academy-of-christian-discipleship/.
27 Although participation varies by congregation, First Presbyterian Church of Missoula had forty-one participants in their latest offering of the Academy of Christian Discipleship.
28 With the recent addition of this position to the annual university budget, the Fellows Program is nearly financially sustainable.
29 OCE staff report that fellows raised approximately $50,000 to support the 2018 fellowship period.
30 This participant asked to remain unnamed.
31 Originally called "Learning Communities," these were renamed to reflect the vocational orientation of these collaborative learning environments. As noted in the description of the PC's work and mission that follows, they have also recently launched a Learning Communities initiative.
32 Sittser explains this relationship: "So we're moving more and more towards institutionalization, but not in a kind of formalistic, programmatic way. There's relationship underneath it."
33 Specifically, they used Sittser's emerging work at the time about the "third way" as the paradigm to organize their reflection and conversation.
34 For example, the Youth Worker Learning Community also gathers monthly with United, which is a network of youth workers in Spokane (United Youth Ministry Network, accessed October 1, 2018, https://unitedspokane.org/), and the Church Planting Learning Community is part of the Pacific Northwest Church Planting Movement, which has a vision to identify, develop, and deploy four hundred missional leaders across the Pacific Northwest in ten years (Pacific Northwest Church Planting Movement, "Home," accessed October 1, 2018, https://www.pnwmovement.com/), and the Refugee and Immigrant Learning Community is connected to World Relief Spokane, which connects local churches and immigrant communities (World Relief Spokane, "About Us," accessed October 1, 2018, https://worldreliefspokane.org/mission).
35 See Jerry Sittser, *A Grace Disguised: How the Soul Grows through Loss*, expanded ed. (Grand Rapids: Zondervan, 2004).

36 With only one exception, all of the individuals who use this language identify as white/Caucasian and male. Although this current research does not provide adequate data to explore the nature of this correlation, future research may consider the possible correlation between this particular social location and how the language of "post-Christian" or "post-Christendom" is deployed to describe the marginal position of Christian thought, practice, and organizations. Further, the use of "Christendom," as used here to describe the shifting landscape of organized religious life, assumes that Christianity once held a favored place in society. However, as Christopher James observes, this assessment could be questioned. For example, James introduces his study of church-plants in Seattle by noting: "While religion has been on the decline in the Northwest as elsewhere, this has not been a fall from cultural dominance as in other parts of the country; Christendom never really took hold in Cascadia" (James, *Church Planting in Post-Christian Soil*, 26). Although Cascadia has pronounced cultural and geographical differences that distinguish it from the Inland Northwest, his assessment demonstrates the need to consider whether Christendom ever took hold in the region served by the OCE.

37 The Third Way is a program facilitated by Sittser, McGonigal, and guest faculty as part of the Academy of Christian Discipleship. The course provides an introduction to Christian thought and practice, with particular attention to the history of Christian engagement with culture. The course also provided a platform for Sittser to refine the content for his book *Resilient Faith*.

38 Killen, "Introduction," 10.

39 James Wellman notes how the Pacific Northwest's distinct cultural context provides an amenable environment for "entrepreneurial evangelicals" in *Evangelical vs. Liberal: The Clash of Christian Cultures in the Pacific Northwest* (New York: Oxford University Press, 2008), 39–44.

40 United States Census Bureau, s.v. "Spokane city, Washington," accessed October 3, 2018, QuickFacts, https://www.census.gov/quickfacts/fact/table/spokanecitywashington/PST045217#PST045217.

41 United States Census Bureau, s.v. "Spokane Valley city, Washington," accessed October 3, 2018, QuickFacts, https://www.census.gov/quickfacts/spokanevalleycitywashington.

42 United States Census Bureau, s.v. "Spokane Valley city, Washington"; United States Census Bureau, s.v. "Spokane city, Washington."

43 See Dale E. Soden, *Outsiders in a Promised Land: Religious Activists in Pacific Northwest History* (Corvallis: Oregon State University Press, 2015); Dwayne A. Mack, *Black Spokane: The Civil Rights Struggle in the Inland Northwest* (Norman: University of Oklahoma Press, 2014).

44 Downtown Spokane Heritage Walk, "Spokane History," accessed October 5, 2018, https://www.historicspokane.org/HeritageTours/downtown/history.html.

45 For example, a visitor's guide to Washington describes Spokane as "one of the state's newest culinary hot spots" (Washington Hospitality Association, *Washington State Visitors' Guide* [2018], 119).

46 For example, Spokane's population increased 3.7 percent from 2010 to 2017, while Portland's grew by 11 percent and Seattle's grew by 19.1 percent over the same period (United States Census Bureau, s.v. "Portland city, Oregon," accessed October 3, 2018, QuickFacts, https://www.census.gov/quickfacts/fact/table/

portlandcityoregon,US/PST045221; United States Census Bureau, s.v. "Seattle city, Washington," accessed October 3, 2018, QuickFacts, https://www.census.gov/quickfacts/fact/table/seattlecitywashington,portlandcityoregon,US/PST045221).

47 Moody Bible Institute also had a campus in Spokane. It closed in 2018 (Chad Sokol, "Moody Bible Institute to Close Spokane Campus," *Spokesman-Review*, November 10, 2017, https://www.spokesman.com/stories/2017/nov/10/moody-bible-institute-to-close-spokane-campus/).

48 United States Census Bureau, s.v. "Spokane city, Washington." Spokane Valley is only slightly higher at $48,015 (United States Census Bureau, s.v. "Spokane Valley city, Washington").

49 The median household income in 2017 for Boise was $54,547 and $43,602 for Missoula, Montana (United States Census Bureau, s.v. "Boise city, Idaho," "Missoula city, Montana," "Spokane city, Washington," QuickFacts, accessed October 5, 2018, https://www.census.gov/quickfacts/fact/table/boisecitycityidaho,missoulacitymontana,spokanecitywashington/INC110217).

50 For example, see the interactive maps from the 2012 and 2016 presidential elections from the *New York Times* (Matthew Bloch et al., "An Extremely Detailed Map of the 2016 Election," *New York Times*, July 25, 2018, https://www.nytimes.com/interactive/2018/upshot/election-2016-voting-precinct-maps.html#4.45/44.27/-108.58; Nate Cohn and Toni Monkovic, "What This 2012 Map Tells Us about America, and the Election," *New York Times*, October 18, 2016, https://www.nytimes.com/2016/10/19/upshot/what-this-2012-map-can-tell-us-about-the-2016-election.html).

51 McKay notes that this feedback was well received and OCE staff express a similar sentiment, but it nonetheless reflects a constant challenge for the OCE's ongoing work.

52 Like many other institutions of Christian higher education, Whitworth has undergone an ongoing discernment process about the nature of its relationship with its founding denomination. This is reflected in their Statement on Denominational Relationships (Whitworth University, "Statement of Denominational Relationship," accessed October 10, 2018, https://www.whitworth.edu/cms/about/statement-on-denominational-relationships/).

53 In 2018, James Leman estimated that First Church saw attendance of around 130–35.

54 For example, Patricia Killen describes the region as an "open religious environment" where religious expression vacillates between "expansiveness" and "self-absorption" (Killen, "Introduction," 10, 14).

2 "HOPE AND CARE IN THE NEIGHBORHOOD"

1 Mike Seely, "For a Seattle Enclave, Isolation May Be Its Salvation," *New York Times*, April 12, 2019, https://www.nytimes.com/2019/04/12/travel/seattle-south-park.html.

2 Parish Collective, "Learn How It Works," accessed June 1, 2019 (a website update in 2021 no longer includes this exact language; for the latest description of their work, see https://www.parishcollective.org/). This summary of the PC mission reflects a composite of different ways their work is framed for different contexts.

3   Paul Sparks, Tim Soerens, and Dwight Friesen, *The New Parish: How the Neighborhood Is Transforming Mission, Discipleship and Community* (Downers Grove, Ill.: InterVarsity Press, 2014), 23.
4   Sparks, Soerens, and Friesen, *New Parish*, 23.
5   Sparks, Soerens, and Friesen, *New Parish*, 68.
6   As a video introducing the Parish Collective's work explains: "Living local; it's a global movement taking place right in your own neighborhood and it's catching on like wildfire" (Parish Collective, "About," accessed June 1, 2019, https://parishcollective.org/about/).
7   See John McKnight and Peter Block, *The Abundant Community: Awakening the Power of Families and Neighborhoods* (San Francisco: Berrett-Koehler, 2010). According to one pastor and parish leader, John McKnight, Peter Block, and Walter Brueggemann are the "unofficial elders of the Parish Collective."
8   Sparks, Soerens, and Friesen, *New Parish*, 99.
9   The community Golladay describes here is located in Chattanooga, Tenn. As noted below and expanded in chapter 4, a distinctive component of the PC's work is the network of partnerships and parish-based expressions that extend beyond the Pacific Northwest.
10 Sparks, Soerens, and Friesen, *New Parish*, 74. The identification of the neighborhood as the ecclesial center neither denigrates nor denies the importance of congregations and related forms of Christian organization. As the three observed: "This is not to downplay church gatherings or religious structures. It is to call attention to just how far they have become disconnected from the particulars of ordinary life" (68).
11 Peter Block, *Community: The Structure of Belonging* (San Francisco: Berrett-Koehler, 2008), 79.
12 "Harvest" here refers to Jesus' words in Matthew 9:37–38: "The harvest is plentiful, but the laborers are few; therefore ask the Lord of the harvest to send out laborers into his harvest" (NRSV). According to this participant, the "subversion" offered here reflects an understanding that the harvest doesn't need saving, but "the harvest feeds us."
13 Tim Soerens and Christiana Rice, "Five Hopeful Signs That Dare Us to Be the Church," *Parish Collective*, March 29, 2016, https://medium.com/parish-collective/five-hopeful-signs-that-dare-us-to-be-the-church-641b75239e2c.
14 Although this observation came from only one of the founders, it is attributed to both because Sparks and Soerens were both present in this interview.
15 Although this represents a minor semantic distinction, if unaddressed, this slight fissure has the potential to become a divisive point.
16 The existing and ongoing "movement" of neighborhood-based ecclesial life has recently garnered some attention. For example, Christopher James' study of church plants in Seattle includes several communities that reflect the PC's commitments. Typologically categorized under his "Neighborhood Incarnation" model, James identifies this model as the "the most robustly missional practical ecclesiology in the field" (James, *Church Planting in Post-Christian Soil*, 177). James concludes that "this model deserves increased theological and practical consideration by practitioners and theologians alike" (177). As Lee Hardy similarly notes, the place-based forms of practice that organize the PC's work have also garnered attention from scholars who are interested in ecclesial renewal beyond

the Pacific Northwest (Lee Hardy, *The Embrace of Buildings: A Second Look at Walkable City Neighborhoods* [Grand Rapids: Calvin College Press, 2017], 129).

17. It is difficult to date the formation of the PC due to its organic character and some ambiguity among organizers about when it started. In the absence of a single date, I have dated the formation of the PC to the first Inhabit Conference, which occurred in 2010.

18. Sparks, Soerens, and Friesen, *New Parish*, 8.

19. In particular, organizers identify Michael Frost and Alan Hirsch's *The Shaping of Things to Come: Innovation and Mission for the 21st-Century Church* (Peabody, Mass.: Hendrickson, 2003) as a key moment for the conversation around an alternative vision for ecclesial life.

20. There is not a single narrative for the PC's early stages. Katt's narration has been used here because it illustrates the range of challenges and the collaborative process that gave rise to the Parish Collective.

21. Sparks, Soerens, and Friesen provide a summary of the network of relationships that gave rise to the Parish Collective in *New Parish*, 8–14.

22. Launched in 1997 as branch of Western Seminary, The Seattle School of Theology & Psychology is now independently accredited. Prior to 2011, the institution was known as Mars Hill Graduate School.

23. Craig Detweiler. Detweiler was serving as president of The Seattle School of Theology & Psychology at the time of this interview, but he resigned in February 2019 (Seattle School of Theology & Psychology, "Dr. Craig Detweiler Resigns as President," February 27, 2019, https://theseattleschool.edu/blog/craig-detweiler-resigns-president/).

24. *Foundation Directory Online Professional*, s.v. "M. J. Murdock Charitable Trust" (Organization Name) and "Seattle School of Theology & Psychology" (Recipient), accessed November 1, 2018, https://fdo.foundationcenter.org/.

25. The authors express their appreciation for the funding from the M. J. Murdock Charitable Trust (Sparks, Soerens, and Friesen, *New Parish*, 197).

26. This interviewee follows this by noting that this has to shift in a way that "preserves some of these core, connected, relational values and stay nimble and decentralized, while also organizing ourselves with a bit more systematic strategy."

27. Sparks, Soerens, and Friesen, *New Parish*, 14. At the time of this writing, the PC is in a critical phase in its ongoing growth and development. Soerens received a 2018 Reflective Leadership grant from Leadership Education at Duke Divinity School, which is funded by Lilly Endowment, Inc. (Leadership Education at Duke Divinity School, "Reflective Leadership Grants," accessed November 10, 2018, https://leadership.divinity.duke.edu/what-we-offer/grants/reflective-leadership-grants/).

28. Parish Collective, "6-Series Document" (2019).

29. Parish Collective, "6-Series Document."

30. Parish Collective, "Connect," accessed December 5, 2018, https://parishcollective.org/join-in/.

31. Of these, more than 45 percent (1,178) are located in the Pacific Northwest and 88 percent (2,283) are located in North America. Of the remaining 12 percent, there are high concentrations in the United Kingdom, Australia, and New Zealand.

32. See Sparks, Soerens, and Friesen, *New Parish*, 99. See also McKnight and Block, *Abundant Community*.

33 Parish Collective, "6-Series Document."
34 Parish Collective, "New Parish Learning Communities" handout (2019).
35 Parish Collective, "6-Series Document."
36 Parish Collective, "6-Series Document."
37 Called "Parish Portraits," these are delivered in a Pecha Kucha format that combines twenty images with a seven-minute description of a particular neighborhood.
38 Parish Collective, "New Parish Learning Communities."
39 For example, the two-day Inhabit Conference lists more than seventy individuals as plenary speakers, musicians, or workshop facilitators.
40 Lauren Goldbloom, who serves as an area connector in Spokane, Washington, offers a corroborating perspective, when she describes her work as "not in any sense a 'church' space," placing "church" in scare quotes as she speaks.
41 Tim Soerens, *Everywhere You Look: Discovering the Church Right Where You Are* (Downers Grove, Ill.: InterVarsity Press, 2020), 69.
42 Hardy, *Embrace of Buildings*, 29.
43 Much like "Pacific Northwest," "Cascadia" describes a variety of geographic regions and cultural practices. In its widest sense, it is a synonym for the Pacific Northwest. As used here, it has a much narrower scope that is limited to the region west of the Cascade Mountains. See Mark Wexler, "Conjectures on Workplace Spirituality in Cascadia," in Todd, *Cascadia*, 217–19.
44 Douglas Todd, introduction to Todd, *Cascadia*, 2, 5.
45 Killen, "Memory," 66.
46 Derek Erwin, "Report: Seattle Leads the Nation as Fastest Growing Tech Hub," *Startup Finance Blog*, October 30, 2018, https://www.lightercapital.com/blog/report-seattle-leads-nation-as-fastest-growing-tech-hub/.
47 Nick Wingfield, "Next Big Tech Corridor? Between Seattle and Vancouver, Planners Hope," *New York Times*, October 2, 2016, https://www.nytimes.com/2016/10/03/technology/next-big-tech-corridor-between-seattle-and-vancouver-planners-hope.html.
48 MOHAI, "Bezos Center for Innovation," accessed December 6, 2018, https://mohai.org/exhibit/bezos-center-for-innovation/. Although unnamed, this "climate" includes an economic context.
49 Wellman, *Evangelical vs. Liberal*, 271.
50 Todd, introduction to Todd, *Cascadia*, 11.
51 James, *Church Planting in Post-Christian Soil*, 31.
52 James, *Church Planting in Post-Christian Soil*, 125.
53 University of Washington, "Climate in the Pacific Northwest," accessed February 18, 2020, https://cig.uw.edu/learn/.
54 Todd, introduction to Todd, *Cascadia*, 4.
55 For example, Soerens was a cofounding advisor for Impact Hub-Seattle (Seattle Impact Hall, "About Us," accessed December 1, 2018, https://impacthubseattle.com/ [the site rebranded and now goes by Seattle Impact Hall]).
56 For Jung, his engagement with the PC provided a theology that affirmed what he was already doing.
57 This quotation is a composite of several different sections of my interview with Carlson.

58 Although the internal logic of emergent/ing church resists the concept of a fixed "tradition," Phyllis Tickle notes how emergence Christians have "shared sensibilities, values, and positions" (Phyllis Tickle, *Emergence Christianity* [Grand Rapids: Baker, 2012], 115).

59 As Rice observes, the mission of the PC is "connection oriented."

60 This description combines insights from Gerardo Marti and Gladys Ganiel, *The Deconstructed Church: Understanding Emerging Christianity* (Oxford: Oxford University Press, 2014); Scot McKnight et al., *Church in the Present Tense: A Candid Look at What's Emerging* (Grand Rapids: Brazos, 2011); Josh Packard, *The Emerging Church: Religion on the Margins* (Boulder, Colo.: Lynne Rienner/FirstForumPress, 2012); and Michael Clawson and April Stace, eds., *Crossing Boundaries, Redefining Faith: Interdisciplinary Perspectives on the Emerging Church Movement* (Eugene, Ore.: Wipf & Stock, 2016).

61 Michael Clawson, "A Brief History of the Emerging Church Movement in the United States," in Clawson and Stace, *Crossing Boundaries, Redefining Faith*, 22–23.

62 Michael Clawson and April Stace, introduction to Clawson and Stace, *Crossing Boundaries, Redefining Faith*, 7.

63 See Marti and Ganiel, *Deconstructed Church*.

64 Clawson, "Brief History," 27.

65 Marti and Ganiel, *Deconstructed Church*, 25.

66 Gerardo Marti, "Emerging Christianity through a Social Scientific Lens: The ECM as a Case of Religious Institutional Entrepreneurship," in Clawson and Stace, *Crossing Boundaries, Redefining Faith*, 62.

67 Marti and Ganiel, *Deconstructed Church*, 5.

68 See Elaine A. Heath, "A New Day Rising in the Church," in *The Hyphenateds: How Emergence Christianity Is Re-traditioning Mainline Practice*, ed. Phil Snider (Danvers, Mass.: Chalice Press, 2011), 26–35.

69 Dwight J. Friesen, *Thy Kingdom Connected: What the Church Can Learn from Facebook, the Internet, and Other Networks* (Grand Rapids: Baker, 2009), 72. Lloyd Chia identifies Friesen as an "emergent thinker and author" (Lloyd Chia, "From Boundaries to Borderlands: The Emerging Church's Imaginative Work of Fostering Relationships across Difference," in Clawson and Stace, *Crossing Boundaries, Redefining Faith*, 155).

70 Soerens, *Everywhere You Look*, 9.

71 Tickle, *Emergence Christianity*, 115.

72 Marking a point of decisive departure from Emerging Christianity, the PC identifies the need to "dance well with institutions" and clearly states that they are not "anti-institutional." While some participants still identify a tension between institutionalized and grassroots, neighborhood-based religious expressions, at the organizational level, the PC partners with established institutions (e.g., seminaries, denominations, and parachurch organizations) to equip students, ministers, and local leaders.

73 Chia attributes this to Tony Jones (Chia, "From Boundaries to Borderlands," 147), but the referenced blog post does not include this phrase.

74 A "critical case" is an instance that has "strategic importance in relation to the general problem" (Flyvbjerg, *Making Social Science Matter*, 78).

75 Dale E. Soden, "Contesting the Soul of an Unlikely Land: Mainline Protestants, Catholics, and Reform and Conservative Jews in the Pacific Northwest," in Killen

and Silk, *Religion & Public Life in the Pacific Northwest*, 75; James Wellman, "The Churching of the Pacific Northwest: The Rise of Sectarian Entrepreneurs," in Killen and Silk, *Religion & Public Life in the Pacific Northwest*, 81.

76 For an early account that notes the adaptive spirit that permeates organized religious life within the Pacific Northwest, see Patrick J. Harris, "William Keil and the Aurora Colony: A Communal Society Crosses the Oregon Trail," in *Religion and Society in the American West: Historical Essays*, ed. Carl Guarneri and David Alvarez (Lanham, Md.: University Press of America, 1987), 425.

77 Killen, "Introduction," 10, 14.

78 This analysis stops short, however, of considering how the adaptive ethos that distinguishes religion in the Pacific Northwest reflects and impacts the individual and collective forms of religious thought and practice.

79 Nicholas Wolterstorff, *In This World of Wonders: Memoir of a Life in Learning* (Grand Rapids: Eerdmans, 2019), 210.

3 THE STRUCTURE OF ADAPTIVE CHANGE

1 See Benac and Weber-Johnson, *Crisis and Care* for a discussion of the relationship between crisis, care, and imagination in the wake of the 2020 crises.

2 Walter Brueggemann, *Virus as a Summons to Faith: Biblical Reflections in a Time of Loss, Grief, and Uncertainty* (Eugene, Ore.: Cascade, 2021), 1.

3 See Abraham Kuyper, *Rooted & Grounded: The Church as Organism and Institution*, trans. Nelson Kloosterman (Grand Rapids: Christian's Library Press, 2013), in which Kuyper describes the church as an "organism and institution" (15).

4 Sharon Parks, "A Convocation of Ecclesial Entrepreneurs," March 30–31, 2021.

5 Anticipating the structure of part II, Bonhoeffer similarly observes how his work attends to the "[s]tructure of the *sanctorum communio*" (Dietrich Bonhoeffer, *DBWE* 1:223).

6 Of these three terms, the glossary prepared by Heifetz and his colleagues provide definitions for holding environment, social system, but not community. They do provide a short definition for "community" in their discussion of the need to identify one's own loyalties in order to lead adaptive work. "Community," as used here, refers to "[c]urrent family members, friends, and groups with whom you identify outside of work in your current social, political, and religious affiliations" (Ronald Heifetz, Alexander Grashow, and Marty Linsky, *The Practice of Adaptive Leadership: Tools and Tactics for Changing Your Organization and the World* [Cambridge, Mass.: Harvard University Press, 2009], 187). Although this definition identifies a set of intimate, personal relationships with "community," their use elsewhere presents a more fluid understanding.

7 Heifetz, Grashow, and Linsky, *Practice of Adaptive Leadership*, 305. The definition of holding environment is the longest definition offered in their glossary.

8 Heifetz, *Leadership without Easy Answers*, 105.

9 Heifetz, Grashow, and Linsky, *Practice of Adaptive Leadership*, 155.

10 Patrick Reyes, *The Purpose Gap: Empowering Communities of Color to Find Meaning and Thrive* (Louisville: Westminster John Knox, 2021), 78.

11 Willie James Jennings, *After Whiteness: An Education in Belonging* (Grand Rapids: Eerdmans, 2020), 104.

12 Heifetz, *Leadership without Easy Answers*, 22. Since its publication in 1994, Heifetz's *Leadership without Easy Answers* and various companion pieces have found

an audience both within and beyond the church and Christian organizations. For example, Heifetz's work and theory influences Gil Rendle's *Quietly Courageous: Leading the Church in a Changing World* (Lanham, Md.: Rowman & Littlefield, 2019); Kevin Ford's *Transforming Church: Bringing Out the Good to Get to Great* (Colorado Springs, Colo.: David C. Cook, 2008); and Lovette Weems' *Church Leadership: Vision, Team, Culture, and Integrity*, rev. ed. (Nashville: Abingdon, 2010).

13   The chief aim of Heifetz's work is to develop a "conceptual framework" that provides "practitioners with a practical philosophy of leadership" in order to "launch more focused empirical research" (8–9). For Heifetz, theory development has the principal aim of enriching leadership practice as well as the study of leaders and their communities. In contrast, the dominant approach to theory-building in the sociology of organizations seeks to describe the social world and the organizational agents and actors within a given system (cf. Howard Aldrich and Martin Ruef, *Organizations Evolving*, 2nd ed. [London: Sage, 2006]).

14   For example, Sparks, Soerens, and Friesen engage Heifetz to develop their account of "adaptive presence" (Sparks, Soerens, and Friesen, *New Parish*, 117–21) and Rice and Frost consider Heifetz's account of adaptive leadership to develop an account of "adaptive missional leadership" (Michael Frost and Christiana Rice, *To Alter Your World: Partnering with God to Rebirth Our Communities* [Downers Grove, Ill.: InterVarsity Press, 2017], 106).

15   Attending to the values that animate adaptive change provides a site for interdisciplinary engagement between organizational theory, leadership studies, and theology. Despite the relative absence of religion from organization studies, recent articles identifying a "theological turn" (Bruno Dyck, "God on Management: The World's Largest Religions, the 'Theological Turn,' and Organization and Management Theory and Practice," in *Religion and Organization Theory*, ed. Paul Tracey, Nelson Phillips, and Michael Lounsbury, Research in the Sociology of Organizations 41 [Bingley, UK: Emerald Group, 2014], 23) in organization studies and calls for greater attention to values in organization studies (Philip Selznick, "On Sustaining Research Agendas: Their Moral and Scientific Basis," in *Institutions and Ideals: Philip Selznick's Legacy for Organizational Studies*, ed. Matthew Kraatz, Research in the Sociology of Organizations 44 [Bingley, UK: Emerald Group, 2015]; Matthew Kraatz and Ricardo Flores. "Reinfusing Values," in Kraatz, *Institutions and Ideals*; Mayer Zald, "Organization Studies as a Scientific and Humanistic Enterprise: Toward a Reconceptualization of the Foundations of the Field," *Organization Science* 4, no. 2 [1993]) suggest the timeliness of renewed reflection about the relevance of organizational theory to the study of religion, and vice versa. Following Philip Selznick, one of the founders of organizational studies, Heifetz identifies values as the fulcrum for adaptive change (*Leadership without Easy Answers*, 23; 289, n. 40). As Bass et al. observe, Christian practical wisdom expresses communities' engagement with the shared values that animate their common life (Bass et al., *Christian Practical Wisdom*). For an insightful discussion of Selznick's contribution to organizational studies, see Kraatz, *Institutions and Ideals*.

16   Heifetz, Grashow, and Linsky, *Practice of Adaptive Leadership*, 3.
17   Heifetz, *Leadership without Easy Answers*, 31.
18   See Frost and Rice, *To Alter Your World* and Leroy Barber, *Embrace: God's Radical Shalom for a Divided World* (Downers Grove, Ill.: InterVarsity Press, 2016).

19 It is beyond the scope of this project to consider different points of emphasis in their respective understandings of shalom; what is important to note is that they engage in a common form of theological interpretation, giving vision and purpose to their work according to this biblical-theological motif. Specifically, the concept provides a rationale for how their shared pursuit of interconnected, collaborative work necessarily involves attending to the particular challenges that confront individuals in their communities and working to promote justice. As Leroy Barber—who is a partner for the PC's Learning Communities initiative—writes: "We were created out of relationship and for relationship; we're relational at our core. We cannot help but function in community, and when we're not in community, we suffer consequences. . . . Human flourishing requires that we establish, mend, and maintain relationships with other people" (Barber, *Embrace*, 51). McGonigal has similarly explored the biblical theme of shalom through his research and writing.

20 Sittser, too, seeks to demonstrate how the early Christian movement offers a pattern for contemporary thought and practice. He writes: "The early church thus launched a different kind of movement in the ancient world. . . . It proved highly adaptable, resourceful, and successful in functioning within the empire. Not that it was entirely successful. No renewal movement ever is, as history shows, even in the case of the movements we most admire and wish to emulate" (Sittser, *Resilient Faith*, 114).

21 Frost and Rice, *To Alter Your World*, 97.

22 Notably, Sparks uses this language to make a minor distinction from Heifetz's paradigm.

23 Sparks, Soerens, and Friesen, *New Parish*, 59.

24 When interviewed just over two years later, this individual no longer serves in a local context. Rather, she now serves alongside individuals across the community as a "community chaplain," enriching the ecclesial ecology through convening and boundary crossing work.

25 James K. A. Smith, *Desiring the Kingdom: Worship, Worldview, and Cultural Formation* (Grand Rapids: Baker Academic, 2009).

26 Heifetz, *Leadership without Easy Answers*, 254.

27 Heifetz, *Leadership without Easy Answers*, 75.

28 Rendle, *Quietly Courageous*, 16.

29 Heifetz, Grashow, and Linsky, *Practice of Adaptive Leadership*, 74.

30 Ironically, concerns about financial stability are more pronounced within the OCE, despite their considerable grant assets.

31 As Trey Wince observes from his work with innovators beyond the Pacific Northwest: "I see this moment in our church's history as one of significant hope. Like it or not, desperation prompts innovation, and the table is well set for both" (Trey Wince, "Trump, Vegan Soup, and Automobiles," in Benac and Weber-Johnson, *Crisis and Care*, 36).

32 The bakery closed in 2019 (Don Chareunsy, "Petit Chat Village Bakery in North Spokane Closes Its Doors," *Spokesman-Review*, August 20, 2019, https://www.spokesman.com/stories/2019/aug/20/petit-chat-village-bakery-in-north-spokane-closes-/).

33 Debbie Wong, "A Prayer in Search of Holy Connection," *The Work of the People*, accessed December 20, 2020, https://www.theworkofthepeople.com/prayer-in-search-of-holy-connection.

34 In a widely discussed piece published on March 20, Andy Crouch, Kurt Keilhacker, and Dave Blanchard distinguish between a blizzard, winter, and a little ice age to describe this cultural-ecclesial moment. A "blizzard" blows in quickly and then passes; the chill of "winter" subsides after several months. A "little ice age," however, brings a "years-long disruption." Citing Gideon Lichfield, they conclude: "We're not going back to normal" (Andy Crouch, Kurt Keilhacker, and Dave Blanchard, "Leading beyond the Blizzard: Why Every Organization Is Now a Startup," *Praxis Journal*, March 20, 2020, https://journal.praxislabs.org/leading-beyond-the-blizzard-why-every-organization-is-now-a-startup-b7f32fb278ff).

35 Osmer, *Practical Theology*, 21. Osmer is describing the experiences that catalyze the interpretive activity for individuals and communities. Much as Osmer notes, events that "puncture our taken-for-granted world" invite reflection that leads to "new interpretive patterns" (21–22).

36 Vivek Murthy, *Together: The Healing Power of Connections in a Sometimes Lonely World* (New York: HarperCollins, 2020).

37 William Bridges, *Managing Transitions: Making the Most of Change*, 4th ed. (Boston: Da Capo Press, 2016).

38 Bridges, *Managing Transitions*, 9. Robert Dale describes a similar pattern of congregational change in *To Dream Again: How to Help Your Church Come Alive* (Eugene, Ore.: Wipf & Stock, 2004).

39 Charles Taylor, *A Secular Age* (Cambridge, Mass.: Harvard University Press, 2007), 2–3. Taylor distinguishes two additional senses in which the term "secularity" can be understood: (1) the emptying of public space of reference to God or "to any reference to ultimate reality" and (2) the diminishment of religious belief and practice. While his work largely explores the third option, as defined above, the other two apply equally to the Pacific Northwest.

40 Heifetz, Grashow, and Linsky, *Practice of Adaptive Leadership*, 74.

41 Gary Gunderson, *Boundary Leaders: Leadership Skills for People of Faith* (Minneapolis: Fortress, 2004).

42 Gunderson, *Boundary Leaders*, 10.

43 Gunderson, *Boundary Leaders*, 27–28.

44 Gunderson, *Boundary Leaders*, 109–10.

45 For an insightful discussion of liminality, see Timothy Carson et al., *Crossing Thresholds: A Practical Theology of Liminality* (Cambridge: Lutterworth, 2021).

46 Gunderson uses the phrase "social architecture" (Gunderson, *Boundary Leaders*, 109).

47 Gunderson describes this ecology as "webs of transformation" (Gunderson, *Boundary Leaders*, 110).

48 Sharon Parks, "Convocation of Ecclesial Entrepreneurs." Parks continues: "I sometimes just deeply grieve that much of the church is being held hostage to the last reformation, when we are in reformation time. . . . [T]hey are so good at paying attention to what is happening in the present when others are looking through the spectacles of yesterday. And I think that what this conversation is wanting to do is pay exquisite attention to what is happening in the present rather than seeing the present through the spectacles of yesterday. It's not that yesterday

doesn't matter, bringing history to this is part of paying exquisite attention." Many other participants in this focus group also used the language of "hinge point" to describe their cultural-ecclesial moment.

49 Sparks, Soerens, and Friesen, *New Parish*, 144–45.
50 E. E. Cummings, *Complete Poems: 1913–1962* (New York: Harcourt Brace Javonovich, 1972), 462.
51 Heifetz, *Leadership without Easy Answers*, 253.
52 Heifetz, *Leadership without Easy Answers*, 87.
53 Heifetz, *Leadership without Easy Answers*, 76.
54 Block, *Community*, 105.
55 Block, *Community*, 106.
56 Elliot Eisner, *The Educational Imagination: On the Design and Evaluation of School Programs* (New York: Macmillan, 1979).
57 Heifetz, Grashow, and Linsky, *Practice of Adaptive Leadership*, 172.
58 Although Heifetz observes how the questions that invite adaptive work "produce owners," across these communities, the OCE's and PC's guiding questions evoke an imagination that stretches beyond ownership.
59 Heifetz, Grashow, and Linsky, *Practice of Adaptive Leadership*, 63.
60 Heifetz, Grashow, and Linsky, *Practice of Adaptive Leadership*, 49.
61 Farley, *Theologia*, 87–88.
62 Bonnie J. Miller-McLemore, "The Clerical and Academic Paradigm," in *Christian Theology in Practice: Discovering a Discipline* (Grand Rapids: Eerdmans, 2012), 160–84.
63 Callid Keefe-Perry directed my attention to the relevance of critiques of the clerical paradigm and academic paradigm.
64 Martin Ruef, "The Emergence of Organizational Forms: A Community Ecology Approach," *AJS* 106, no. 3 (2000): 670.
65 For Heifetz, community represents both the situation where adaptive challenges emerge and the requisite condition for adaptive work to begin. Even as Heifetz describes the relational space where adaptive challenges are identified and where adaptive work takes place as "community," he neglects to specify either the social entity he envisions, or the conditions that nurture the form of community required for adaptive work. Rather, his use of community suggests a range of possible definitions without identifying a clear social referent. Despite the ambiguity on this point, what is clear is that the forms of connection and partnership that organize the OCE and PC serve a similar function: they provide a holding environment for their adaptive work.
66 Heifetz, Grashow, and Linsky, *Practice of Adaptive Leadership*, 305. The definition of holding environment is the longest definition offered in their glossary.
67 For example, speaking about the need for more leaders within her community, one parish leader observes how some individuals are unwilling to leave the comfort of the "institutional church."
68 Heifetz, *Leadership without Easy Answers*, 105.
69 Heifetz, Grashow, and Linsky, *Practice of Adaptive Leadership*, 155.
70 Heifetz, Grashow, and Linsky, *Practice of Adaptive Leadership*, 156.
71 For example, Whitworth president Beck Taylor notes how funding from Murdock has enabled him to gather regularly with other leaders in Christian higher education from within and beyond the region.

72 Institute for Advanced Studies of Culture, "Thriving Cities," accessed May 15, 2019, https://vimeo.com/135908974.
73 Sparks and Soerens note the impact of innovative design, which emphasizes experimentation and iteration, for their work.
74 The three stories in the Gospels (Matthew 9:16–17; Mark 2:21–22; Luke 5:36–39) note how new wine goes into new wineskins, but this individual inverts the order in this comment. Although the new wine is important, the structure—the new wineskin—directs the collective imagination their work demands.
75 Gunderson, *Boundary Leaders*, 110.
76 Gunderson, *Boundary Leaders*, 26.
77 As noted above, the premise of Heifetz's account of adaptive challenge is that existing solutions are no longer adequate for the challenges besetting a community. As a result, he describes the need for "new ways that build from the best of the past" (Heifetz, Grashow, and Linsky, *Practice of Adaptive Leadership*, 69), a new vantage point to "clarify a complex situation" (Heifetz, *Leadership without Easy Answers*, 22) and the creation of a new social architecture around an adaptive challenge. But the ends that organize and animate each step of this process remain obliquely defined.
78 Tod Bolsinger, *Canoeing the Mountains: Christian Leadership in Uncharted Territory* (Downers Grove, Ill.: InterVarsity Press, 2015).
79 Sparks, Soerens, and Friesen, *New Parish*, subtitle.
80 Soerens and Rice, "Five Hopeful Signs That Dare Us to Be the Church."
81 Louis Menand, "An Introduction to Pragmatism," in *Pragmatism: A Reader*, ed. Louis Menand (New York: Vintage Books, 1997), xiv.
82 The balcony metaphor serves two purposes. First, following Heifetz's description of "balcony spaces" (Heifetz, *Leadership without Easy Answers*, 252–54), these are individuals who have a particular perspective above the day-to-day challenges that can enrich our reflection and practice. Second, much like the balcony in the United States congressional chambers, these individuals were invited to listen in on the conversation on the main floor. I intentionally centered conversation among the participants from these organizations, while also inviting feedback from balcony guests at key moments in the conversation. For a description of convening as a form of practical theological inquiry, see Dustin Benac, "The Craft of Theology and Qualitative Research," in *The Wiley-Blackwell Companion to Theology and Qualitative Research*, ed. Pete Ward and Knut Tveitereid (Malden, Mass.: Wiley-Blackwell, forthcoming).
83 Gibbs, "Everything Is an Experiment," 127–31.

4 ANCHORS AND WEBS

1 Mike Carr, "Geography, Spirituality and Social Change in Cascadia: A Bioregional Perspective," in Todd, *Cascadia*, 127–42.
2 Dustin Benac, "Research Memo," February 8, 2019.
3 Institute for Advanced Studies of Culture, "Thriving Cities."
4 Paul DiMaggio predicted in 1998 that students of organizations and religion were entering an auspicious time for cross-pollinating forms of inquiry. "Insofar as students of religion concern themselves with such formal organizations as congregations, denominations, and religiously affiliated schools and service organizations," writes DiMaggio, "[I]t seems plausible that they may also benefit from

applying insights and methods from the study of organizations in their research" (Paul DiMaggio, "The Relevance of Organizational Theory to the Study of Religion," in *Sacred Companies: Organizational Aspects of Religion and Religious Aspects of Organizations*, ed. N. J. Demerath et al. [New York: Oxford University Press, 1998], 19). Nevertheless, as Paul Tracey et al. observed in 2014: "Despite its central importance in nearly all societies, religion has been largely neglected in the study of organizations and management" (Paul Tracey, Nelson Phillips, and Michael Lounsbury, "Taking Religion Seriously in the Study of Organizations," in Tracey, Phillips, and Lounsbury, *Religion and Organization Theory*, 3). For students of religion who hope to employ organizational theory in their field, however, DiMaggio cautions that they "will have to adapt" organizational theory's conceptual and methodological categories (DiMaggio, "Relevance of Organizational Theory to the Study of Religion," 20). And, following Tracey, this adaptation departs from the dominant approach to organizational research.

5   Paul DiMaggio and Walter Powell, "The Iron Cage Revisited: Institutional Isomorphism and Collective Rationality in Organizational Fields," *American Sociological Review* 48, no. 2 (1983): 148.

6   W. Richard Scott, *Institutions and Organizations: Ideas, Interests, and Identities*, 4th ed. (London: Sage, 2014), 106.

7   DiMaggio and Powell, "Iron Cage Revisited," 148.

8   DiMaggio and Powell, "Iron Cage Revisited," 148.

9   DiMaggio and Powell, "Iron Cage Revisited," 148.

10 W. Richard Scott and Gerald F. Davis, *Organizations and Organizing: Rational, Natural, and Open Systems Perspectives* (Upper Saddle River, N.J.: Pearson, 2007), 118.

11 When applied to the study of religion, the study of organizational fields enabled researchers to consider the broader field that informed Bishops' votes at the Second Vatican Council (Melissa J. Wilde et al., "Religious Economy or Organizational Field? Predicting Bishops' Votes at the Second Vatican Council," *American Sociological Review* 75, no. 4 [2010]: 586–606), identify the network of partners that support congregational life in America (Nancy Ammerman, *Pillars of Faith: American Congregations and Their Partners* [Berkeley: University of California Press, 2005]), and examine the shifting values that contributed to the move to ordain women in American denominations (Mark Chaves, *Ordaining Women: Culture and Conflict in Religious Organizations* [Cambridge, Mass.: Harvard University Press, 1997]).

12 Smith, Schneider, and Dickson, "Meso Organizational Behavior," 161.

13 Henry Louis Taylor Jr. and Gavin Luter, *Anchor Institutions: An Interpretive Review Essay* (Buffalo, N.Y.: Anchor Institutions Task Force, 2013).

14 Steven Johnson notes how the "adjacent possible" contributes to the formation of new ideas and innovations (Steven Johnson, *Where Good Ideas Come From: The Natural History of Innovation* [New York: Riverhead Books, 2010], 25–42).

15 Walter Powell, "Expanding the Scope of Institutional Analysis," in *The New Institutionalism in Organizational Analysis*, ed. Walter Powell and Paul DiMaggio (Chicago: University of Chicago Press, 1991), 200. Powell's description of "institutional change" in this sentence applies equally to the study of these two sites and the organizations that support them within the neo-institutional understanding of organizations as institutions.

16 Scott and Davis, *Organizations and Organizing*, 280.
17 Scott and Davis, *Organizations and Organizing*, 278.
18 Published during the early phase of the PC's organization, Dwight Friesen's *Thy Kingdom Connected* draws insight from network theory to develop a "networked paradigm" that reflects a "richly interconnective vision of interpersonal relations [that] requires a deep understanding of the self-in-relationship, which makes possible the offering of our individuated self to the other" (Friesen, *Thy Kingdom Connected*, 26). Although it is not clear to what extent Friesen's early engagement with network theory informed the structure of the PC, his work does suggest that organizers of the PC have been working to adapt network theory to ecclesial thought and practice from the early stages of their work.
19 Walter Powell, "Neither Market nor Hierarchy: Network Forms of Organization," *Research in Organizational Behavior* 12 (1990): 323.
20 Powell, "Neither Market nor Hierarchy," 322.
21 Powell, "Neither Market nor Hierarchy," 324.
22 Although unacknowledged in his study, vocations of religious leadership and service in higher education—as a teacher and administrator—also require and cultivate know-how.
23 Powell, "Neither Market nor Hierarchy," 324.
24 Powell, "Neither Market nor Hierarchy," 324. Powell's observation about the priority of "know-how" within social networks also represents a form of practical wisdom.
25 Powell, "Neither Market nor Hierarchy," 324.
26 As Powell notes, the transmission of resources and information in networked forms of organization (as opposed to hierarchies) introduces the risk that new meaning may evolve (Powell, "Neither Market nor Hierarchy," 325).
27 Powell, "Neither Market nor Hierarchy," 325.
28 Powell, "Neither Market nor Hierarchy," 325–26.
29 Powell, "Neither Market nor Hierarchy," 324.
30 Ronald Burt, *Structural Holes: The Social Structure of Competition* (Cambridge, Mass.: Harvard University Press, 1992), 28.
31 Aldrich and Ruef, *Organizations Evolving*, 71.
32 See Mark Granovetter, "The Strength of Weak Ties: A Network Theory Revisited," *Sociological Theory* 1 (1983): 201; Aldrich and Ruef, *Organizations Evolving*, 71.
33 Ferguson, *Square and the Tower*, 30.
34 Burt, *Structural Holes*, 13.
35 Ida Momennejad, Ajua Duker, and Alin Coman, "Bridge Ties Bind Collective Memories," *Nature Communications* 10 (2019): 1–8.
36 Aldrich and Ruef, *Organizations Evolving*, 71.
37 If, as I argued in chapter 3, these hubs share a common value for relational presence, the work that organizes them departs from the economic logic that organizes Burt's account. Rather than trying to leverage weak ties in order to gain a strategic advantage, as Burt suggests, they connect disconnected individuals and communities.
38 Stephen Bourgatti and Pacey Foster, "The Network in Organizational Research: A Review and Typology," *Journal of Management* 29, no. 6 (2003): 1000–1001.
39 Aldrich and Ruef, *Organizations Evolving*, 88.
40 Ruef, "Emergence of Organizational Forms," 670.

41　Ferguson, *Square and the Tower*, 42.
42　As Lee Ranie and Berry Wellman observe, individuals and organizations "exist now in information and communication ecologies that are strikingly different from the ones that existed just a generation ago" (Lee Ranie and Berry Wellman, *Networked: The New Social Operating System* [Cambridge, Mass.: MIT Press, 2012], 255). Powell similarly identifies the need for attention to "the ecology of network forms" (Powell, "Neither Market nor Hierarchy," 372).
43　My use of "ecological" here differs in two significant ways from its use in organizational ecology. First, my description of this approach draws heavily from Michael Hannan and John Freeman's work in organizational ecology, but I use this term in relation to the specific sites that I consider here. It is not necessary, in my opinion, to restrict the use of an ecological lens to longitudinal studies of population-level data. Rather, this analytical approach can be combined with insights from particular organizations in order to understand both the ecological conditions that contribute to the founding and disbanding of organizations at gestational or palliative stages. At the same time, the study of transitional periods at specific organizations can promote a better understanding of the social processes that introduce change within a broader organizational ecology.

　　Second, I combine insights from organizational ecology with an evolutionary approach to organizational change. Although proponents of the evolutionary approach have presented it as a meta-theory to organizational change, the two approaches—ecological and evolutionary—bear sufficient conceptual similarity (not to mention both drawing upon organic metaphors) to permit this pairing. Moreover, the evolutionary approach provides resources to explain organizational change within specific organizations in a way that complements insights from organizational ecology.
44　Michael Hannan and John Freeman, *Organizational Ecology* (Cambridge, Mass.: Harvard University Press, 1989), 6.
45　Aldrich and Ruef, *Organizations Evolving*, 37.
46　Hannan and Freeman, *Organizational Ecology*, 41.
47　Hannan and Freeman, *Organizational Ecology*, 13.
48　Scott and Davis aptly summarize: "Rather than being planned or internally induced, the sources of change are often located in the wider environment—in the dynamics of the population-level demographic processes or in political demands and normative pressures stemming from, for example, the nation-state or the professions" (*Organizations and Organizing*, 246).
49　Scott and Davis, *Organizations and Organizing*, 64.
50　James, *Church Planting in Post-Christian Soil*, 136. In a similar manner, my own writing and engagement with these two hubs has the capacity to convey legitimacy to their work.
51　Bass et al., *Christian Practical Wisdom*, 5.
52　Bass et al., *Christian Practical Wisdom*, 5.
53　Beyond the Pacific Northwest, religious organizations have "long served as foundries of organizational forms and issues," and, as N. J. Demerath and Terry Schmitt conclude: "There is immense potential for research payoff in attending to them" (N. J. Demerath and Terry Schmitt, "Transcending Sacred and Secular: Mutual Benefits in Analyzing Religious and Nonreligious Organizations," in Demerath et al., *Sacred Companies*, 396).

54 This includes the master's program at Seattle Pacific University's School of Theology and Claremont School of Theology's planned relocation to Willamette University in Salem, Oregon.
55 Hannan and Freeman speak of "managers," but I refer to "leaders" in my account. Although there is some distinction in the leadership and management literature, the revision here provides conceptual clarity across my broader account.
56 Hannan and Freeman, *Organizational Ecology*, 41.
57 Hannan and Freeman, *Organizational Ecology*, 41.
58 Hannan and Freeman, *Organizational Ecology*, 41.
59 Herbert Simons, *Administrative Behavior: A Study of Decision-Making Processes in Administrative Organization*, 2nd ed. (New York: Macmillan, 1957), 240.
60 Hannan and Freeman, *Organizational Ecology*, 41.
61 Chapter 5 provides a thoroughgoing discussion and definition of "ecclesial ecology." For my earliest use of this term, see my essay "Theological Education for a New Age." As noted: "This [ecclesial] ecology includes the various identifiable forms of organized, ecclesial life such as congregations, theological schools, Christian colleges and universities, philanthropic centers and nonprofits—but it also includes the various experiments and expressions of creative deviance that take place in the boundary spaces between existing and emerging orders."

5 REIMAGINING CHURCH

1 This participant reviewed and approved my descriptions in this scene prior to publication.
2 This rhetorical move reflects Dykstra's own approach in *Growing in the Life of Faith*. After introducing the formative function of Christian practices, Dykstra observes: "Certainly, this claim is not the kind that I think can be proven. It is more the kind of claim for which one can provide witness or testimony, and I hope to provide enough of that to see whether it stimulates testimony of a similar kind in you" (53). In a similar manner, my description and constructive assessment of these hubs seeks to provide a form of testimony that stimulates a similar form of adaptive work within other communities of faith.
3 See Bass et al., *Christian Practical Wisdom*, which develops an account of Christian practical wisdom through interpenetrating movements of showing and telling "how it operates" (16).
4 Sharon Parks, *Leadership Can Be Taught: A Bold Approach for a Complex World* (Boston: Harvard Business School Publishing, 2005), 210.
5 See Parks, *Leadership Can Be Taught* for a full description of leadership as artistry.
6 Craig Dykstra, "Pastoral and Ecclesial Imagination," in Bass and Dykstra, *For Life Abundant*, 48.
7 Craig Dykstra, "Reconceiving Practice," in *Shifting Boundaries: Contextual Approaches to the Structure of Theological Education*, ed. Barbara G. Wheeler and Edward Farley (Louisville: Westminster John Knox, 1991), 35–66.
8 Dykstra, "Pastoral and Ecclesial Imagination," 51.
9 Willie James Jennings, *The Christian Imagination: Theology and the Origins of Race* (New Haven, Conn.: Yale University Press, 2010) demonstrates the complex interplay between embodiment, theology, collective memory, social structures, and the practices that have historically guided communities of faith. As Bass observes in her contribution to *Christian Practical Wisdom*, Jennings' work "cuts

like a two-edged sword" (240), simultaneously leveling a pointed critique at the death-dealing capacity of Christian thought and opening up new imaginative vistas beyond a deformed Christian imagination. While chapter 6 will briefly explore the complex interplay between race and the adaptive work that organizes these sites, this relationship represents a growing edge for these hubs and a potential avenue for future research.

10 Dykstra, "Pastoral and Ecclesial Imagination," 43.
11 Dykstra, "Pastoral and Ecclesial Imagination," 43.
12 Dykstra, "Pastoral and Ecclesial Imagination," 59.
13 Dykstra, "Pastoral and Ecclesial Imagination," 48.
14 Dykstra, "Pastoral and Ecclesial Imagination," 48.
15 William Sullivan, introduction to *Educating Clergy: Teaching Practices and Pastoral Imagination*, by Charles R. Foster et al. (San Francisco: Jossey-Bass, 2006), 9.
16 Christian Scharen and Eileen Campbell-Reed similarly note how the adaptive challenges that confront seminarians, theological education, and communities require pastoral imagination (Christian Scharen and Eileen Campbell-Reed, "Learning Pastoral Imagination: A Five-Year Report on How New Ministers Learn in Practice," *Auburn Studies* 21 [2016]: 4–46). Their study extends Dykstra's concept by drawing upon an understanding of *phronesis* in order to argue that "pastoral imagination emerges as an integrative, embodied, relational capacity" (5).
17 Dykstra, "Pastoral and Ecclesial Imagination," 52.
18 Dykstra, *Growing in the Life of Faith*, 44.
19 Dykstra, "Pastoral and Ecclesial Imagination," 54. Dykstra's writing and history of institutional service demonstrates a commitment to listening. For example, as he notes in his essay, he refined these concepts by engaging in several years of formal and informal conversations with pastors and seminarians.
20 The formation of an imagination for adaptive leadership requires learning to pause, and the slow, disciplined, reflective creativity that emerges through this process (Parks, *Leadership Can Be Taught*, 227).
21 Dykstra, "Pastoral and Ecclesial Imagination," 57.
22 See Dorothy C. Bass and Craig Dykstra, "Times of Yearning, Practices of Faith" and "A Way of Thinking about a Way of Life," in Bass, *Practicing Our Faith*, 1–12, 203–17.
23 Bass and Dykstra, "Times of Yearning, Practices of Faith," 1–2.
24 Dorothy C. Bass, new preface to Bass, *Practicing Our Faith*, xiii.
25 See Foster et al., *Educating Clergy*; Scharen and Campbell-Reed, "Learning Pastoral Imagination"; Kathleen A. Cahalan, *Introducing the Practice of Ministry* (Collegeville, Minn.: Liturgical Press, 2010).
26 Dykstra, "Pastoral and Ecclesial Imagination," 43.
27 Scharen and Campbell-Reed approach this concept when they observe how "new ministers cultivate pastoral imagination when they apprentice themselves to the particular world where their ministry is situated" ("Learning Pastoral Imagination," 33), but their account neglects Dykstra's symbiotic conception of pastoral and ecclesial imagination.
28 See R. Stephen Warner, "The Place of the Congregation in the Contemporary American Religious Configuration," in *American Congregations*, vol. 2, *New*

Perspectives in the Study of Congregations, ed. James Wind and James Lewis (Chicago: University of Chicago Press, 1994), 54.

29 Kathryn Tanner, *Christianity and the New Spirit of Capitalism* (New Haven, Conn.: Yale University Press, 2019), 214.

30 The priority of this concept in the PC's collective lexicon reflects the influence of Walter Brueggemann's work and friendship. Specifically, Brueggemann, in *The Prophetic Imagination*, 2nd ed. (Minneapolis: Fortress, 2001), describes the linguistic and epistemological work that contributes to the formation of an alternative community. Although the first edition was published thirty years before Dykstra's essay, they demonstrate similar attention to the relationships between practice, imagination, and Christian ministry.

31 Sparks, Soerens, and Friesen, *New Parish*, 85.

32 Sparks, Soerens, and Friesen, *New Parish*, 185–86. The authors provide various other forms of shorthand for this idea (e.g., "counter-imagination" [41], "communal imagination" [127], "parish imagination" [141]), but "new imagination" provides the fullest description of what they envision.

33 It is beyond the scope of the present inquiry, but future research may fruitfully explore how charisma represents the antithesis of the practical wisdom that reflects and emerges from pastoral imagination.

34 Ketola acknowledges how this exposure proved "disruptive" in her life and context, but she also notes how Soerens and Sparks provided timely support, presence, and encouragement.

35 Sparks, Soerens, and Friesen, *New Parish*, 141.

36 Here McGonigal is describing a conversation he had with John Wimmer, who served as a program director in the religion division at Lilly Endowment, Inc. and started the Indianapolis Center for Congregations in Indianapolis, Indiana.

37 Dykstra, "Pastoral and Ecclesial Imagination," 43.

38 The priority of the neighborhood at First Church Spokane, where Leman serves as pastor, provides a striking point of resonance with the PC's organizing mission. However, when asked if he was aware of the PC or *The New Parish*, Leman said he was not familiar with their work.

39 Dykstra, "Pastoral and Ecclesial Imagination," 48.

40 Dykstra, "Pastoral and Ecclesial Imagination," 57.

41 My description here constructively extends research that locate congregations within "religious ecologies" by considering the broader ecclesial context in which change occurs. See Nancy Ammerman, *Congregations and Community* (New Brunswick, N.J.: Rutgers University Press, 1997); Nancy Eiesland and Stephen Warner, "Ecology: Seeing the Congregation in Context," in *Studying Congregations: A New Handbook*, ed. Nancy Ammerman et al. (Nashville: Abingdon, 1998), 40–77.

42 Joel Podolny's discussion of networks as "pipes" and "prisms" informs my use of "prism" here. Although Podolny uses the metaphor to suggest that networks enable "the qualities of actors [to be] inferred by potential exchange partners," my use serves a different purpose (Joel Podolny, "Networks as Pipes and Prisms of the Market," *AJS* 107, no. 1 [2001]: 58). Rather than providing an indication or status, the prismatic character of the ecclesial ecology refracts the pastoral and ecclesial imagination that emerges in relation to these places. When combined with the densely relational and pneumatic properties of this ecology, the imaginative work

43 Heifetz uses the phrase "creative deviance" to describe the kind of leadership that catalyzes and sustains adaptive change (Heifetz, *Leadership without Easy Answers*, 183). I have adapted Heifetz's language here to describe how adaptive organizations can catalyze change within an ecclesial ecology.
44 Another interviewee similarly notes how her family created a context for her to understand and experience belonging and "gave [her] a taste of God's love."
45 Dykstra, *Growing in the Life of Faith*, 39.
46 Dykstra, *Growing in the Life of Faith*, xx, 38.
47 Although the final topic, religious language, does not identify a specific social locale, it nevertheless remains important. Specifically, religious language provides both the means and the medium to encounter, apprehend, and grow in the life of faith.
48 Recent work by Edward Farley, Mary McClintock Fulkerson, John Swinton, and Harriet Mowat identifies the "situation" as a primary site for practical theological reflection, providing a close analogue for Dykstra's concept of "place." However, there is not a direct correspondence between the two concepts. For example, a situation is comprised of the "way various items, powers, and events in the environment gather to evoke responses from participants" (Mary McClintock Fulkerson, *Places of Redemption: Theology for a Worldly Church* [Oxford: Oxford University Press, 2007], 36). While this concept helpfully directs attention to the situated nature of religious practice and communities of faith—and to their complexity—Dykstra's use of "place" offers a narrower theological and social referent. Specifically, Dykstra's account demonstrates the priority of particular kinds of places in a way that considers their interrelationship and their quotidian features in light of the reality and promises of God.
49 Dykstra, *Growing in the Life of Faith*, 133.
50 Miller-McLemore, *Christian Theology in Practice*, 36.
51 Dykstra, *Growing in the Life of Faith*, 73.
52 Dykstra's work reflects some engagement with the concept of "ecology" as early as 1999. For example, he identifies Urie Bronfenbrenner's *The Ecology of Human Development* (Cambridge, Mass.: Harvard University Press, 1981) as a source that informs his description of the conditions that contribute to formation in and through practice (Dykstra, *Growing in the Life of Faith*, 79, n. 7).
53 Craig Dykstra, "Cultivating Thriving Communities of Faith: The Promise of Strategic Religious Philanthropy," Thomas H. Lake Lecture at the Lilly Family School of Philanthropy (Bloomington, Ind.: IUPUI, March 27, 2014), 3.
54 José Humphreys, *Seeing Jesus in East Harlem: What Happens When Churches Show Up and Stay Put* (Downers Grove, Ill.: InterVarsity Press, 2018), 20.
55 To constructively extend Jennifer Ayres' eco-theological vision, the adaptive work that organizes these sites invites "an ecologically grounded Christian practical theology [that] concerns itself with the cultivation and nurture of people of faith who inhabit God's world well" (Jennifer Ayres, "Cultivating the 'Unquiet Heart': Ecology, Education, and Christian Faith," *Theology Today* 74, no. 1 [2017]: 58).

56 For example, support for spiritual direction and discipleship or expertise in growing a community garden.
57 Dykstra describes faith as "qualitatively different"; Christ's "true and efficacious presence" in the Holy Spirit is active in the inner heart and pervades the mind, and this is the ultimate condition of our knowing (Dykstra, *Growing in the Life of Faith*, 21).
58 See Jürgen Moltmann, *The Church in the Power of the Spirit* (Minneapolis: Fortress, 1993), 291.
59 Edward Farley's *Theologia* includes a similar interest in institutions, but his account lacks critical, theological reflection about the institutional conditions that are needed to actualize his vision. For example, he contends that there exists a need for a "new institutionality" (Farley, *Theologia*, 16), but he neglects to develop a constructive appraisal for the form of institutional life that could attend to the importance of the embodied and habituated forms of knowing outlined in his account.
60 Dykstra, "Pastoral and Ecclesial Imagination," 57.
61 As Scott and Davis noted in chapter 4, the study of organizational fields "calls attention to organizations that are not linked by direct connections but, because they are operating under similar conditions, exhibit similar structural characteristics and types of relationships" (Scott and Davis, *Organizations and Organizing*, 118).
62 Bass and Dykstra, introduction to *For Life Abundant*, 13. Bass and Dykstra are speaking here about practical theology, but their insight applies equally to the imagination required for this adaptive work, which is itself an expression of practical theology.
63 Craig Dykstra and James Hudnut-Beumler, "The National Organizational Structures of Protestant Denominations: An Invitation to a Conversation," in *The Organizational Revolution: Presbyterians and American Denominationalism*, ed. Milton Coalter, John Mulder, and Louis Weeks (Louisville: Westminster John Knox, 1992), 330.

6 ADAPTIVE CHURCH

1 Bonhoeffer, *DBWE* 8:389.
2 Bonhoeffer, *DBWE* 5:25.
3 The use of Bonhoeffer and Luke-Acts in this way introduces a critical interpretive question: Given the historical and cultural difference between Bonhoeffer, early Christian communities, and these hubs, does his work present an appropriate source to consider the adaptive work that organizes them? While there has been a recent resurgence in academic and popular reflection about Bonhoeffer's contemporary relevance (see "Why Is Dietrich Bonhoeffer Relevant Today?" *Faith & Leadership*, November 26, 2019, https://faithandleadership.com/why-dietrich-bonhoeffer-relevant-today; Lori Brandt Hale and Reggie L. Williams, "Is This a Bonhoeffer Moment?" *Sojourners*, February 2018, https://sojo.net/magazine/february-2018/bonhoeffer-moment), Bonhoeffer is used here primarily as a catalyst for theological reflection. As Wayne Whitson Floyd observes: "Bonhoeffer's thought is perhaps most fertile when it is allowed to act as a catalyst for the theological work of others" (Wayne Whitson Floyd, "Bonhoeffer," in *The Modern Theologians: An Introduction to Christian Theology since 1918*, 3rd ed., ed. David

Ford [Malden, Mass.: Blackwell, 2005], 57). Similarly, the turn to Luke-Acts constructively extends the priority of Scripture and early Christian communities for organizers across each hub (see Sittser, *Resilient Faith*; Soerens, *Everywhere You Look*).

4 C. Kavin Rowe, *World Upside Down: Reading Acts in the Graeco-Roman Age* (Oxford: Oxford University Press, 2009). As Rowe astutely notes, Luke-Acts presents a particular "way of knowing," carried by a constellation of narrative, practice, and assembly, that "from the outside can ally appear to be upside down" (136).

5 See Samuel Wells, *Improvisation: The Drama of Christian Ethics* (Grand Rapids: Brazos, 2004); L. Gregory Jones and Andy Hogue, *Navigating the Future: Traditioned Innovation for Wilder Seas* (Nashville: Abingdon, 2021).

6 Rather, practitioners often note how their work is proceeding without "templates."

7 John Swinton, *Dementia: Living in the Memories of God* (Grand Rapids: Eerdmans, 2012), 21.

8 This line intentionally mirror's Bonhoeffer's claim at the rhetorical hinge of *Sanctorum Communio*: "The whole theological reflection thus far not only leads to the discussion of the *sanctorum communio*, but is possible and meaningful from the perspective of the *sanctorum communio*" (Bonhoeffer, *DBWE* 1:122–23).

9 Reed follows by noting how she is now trying to be a good neighbor and a homemaker, even though she would have dismissed the latter term at an earlier stage in her life.

10 Soerens and Rice, "Five Hopeful Signs That Dare Us to Be the Church."

11 Sittser, *Resilient Faith*, 110–11.

12 For an illuminating study of early Christianity and its relevance to contemporary Christian thought and practice, see C. Kavin Rowe, *One True Life: The Stoics and Early Christians as Rival Traditions* (New Haven, Conn.: Yale University Press, 2016).

13 Sittser, *Resilient Faith*, 13.

14 The material that appears here has been revised and adapted from an earlier version in *The Bonhoeffer Legacy: An International Journal*. See Dustin Benac, "A Bonhoefferian Approach to Social Analysis: Life Together as *Communio*, Relation, and Possibility," *The Bonhoeffer Legacy: An International Journal* 5, no. 2 (2018): 63–81.

15 Bonhoeffer, *DBWE* 1:78.

16 Bonhoeffer, *DBWE* 1:212.

17 Bonhoeffer, *DBWE* 1:49.

18 Bonhoeffer, *DBWE* 1:208–12.

19 Bonhoeffer, *DBWE* 1:250.

20 Bonhoeffer writes: "To understand the church as a community is not enough; it is indeed a community, but one that is concretely defined as a community of spirit. And as such it is not merely a modified or special version of the general category of 'community'; rather it constitutes an antinomic new basic-relation that we must now examine" (Bonhoeffer, *DBWE* 1:261).

21 Bonhoeffer, *DBWE* 1:157.

22 Bonhoeffer, *DBWE* 1:191.

23. For a brilliant reading of Paul that arrives at a similar conclusion, see Susan Eastman, *Paul and the Person: Reframing Paul's Anthropology* (Grand Rapids: Eerdmans, 2017), 146–49.
24. Bonhoeffer, *DBWE* 1:213.
25. Bonhoeffer, *DBWE* 1:121.
26. Charles Marsh, *Reclaiming Dietrich Bonhoeffer: The Promise of His Theology* (Oxford: Oxford University Press, 1994), 141.
27. For Bonhoeffer, "[t]he community of saints as the community of penitent sinners is held together by the unity of the body of Christ" (Bonhoeffer, *DBWE* 1:214).
28. Bonhoeffer, *DBWE* 1:213–14.
29. The basic insight Bonhoeffer develops here anticipates his later understanding of a two-fold priority of these basic social relations in *Creation and Fall*: (1) humankind exists and finds freedom in relation to the other, because (2) this primal form of existence represents an *analogia relationis* to the Creator God.
30. Bonhoeffer, *DBWE* 1:223. Bonhoeffer writes: "We have been speaking of 'the' empirical church. But does this phenomenon exist at all? . . . The answer to this question will tell us more about the structure of the sanctorum communion" (223).
31. Departing from other translators, I have chosen to translate *Gesellschaft* as "organization" rather than "society." Although Bonhoeffer uses Tönnies' categories to organize his thought, his understanding of the Christological genesis for social relations presents Christ, rather than economics, as the grounding principle for *Gesellschaft*. Further, Bonhoeffer's attention to the particularity and connectedness that emerges in Christ directly contradicts Tönnies' description of *Gesellschaft* as "a group of people who . . . live peacefully alongside each other . . . without being essentially united—indeed, on the contrary, they are here essentially detached" (Ferdinand Tönnies, *Community and Civil Society*, ed. Jose Harris, trans. Jose Harris and Margaret Hollis [Cambridge: Cambridge University Press, 2001], 52). Bonhoeffer's use of *Gesellschaft* to describe the objective reality of the church is better translated as "organization." Although, in select places, Bonhoeffer also uses *Organisation* and its derivatives to characterize the structure of the empirical church (Bonhoeffer, *DBWE* 1:208), I translate *Gesellschaft* as "organization" in order to capture Bonhoeffer's attention to the organized, concrete, historical, and relational forms of social existence that emerge in and around Christ.
32. Bonhoeffer signals his reliance on Tönnies when he observes in a footnote: "Tönnies's insight, that 'community is the lasting and genuine form of living together, society only transitory and superficial' is verified phenomenologically" (Bonhoeffer, *DBWE* 1:101, n. 30).
33. Bonhoeffer, *DBWE* 1:182.
34. Bonhoeffer, *DBWE* 1:191.
35. Bonhoeffer writes: "The church-community exists through Christ's action. It is elected in Christ from eternity. It is the new humanity in the new Adam" (Bonhoeffer, *DBWE* 1:137–38).
36. Bonhoeffer, *DBWE* 1:139.
37. Bonhoeffer, *DBWE* 1:223.
38. Bonhoeffer, *DBWE* 1:252–53. As noted previously, I have departed from the translators of the DBW in my translation of *Gesellschaft*.
39. Bonhoeffer, *DBWE* 1:264.

40 Bonhoeffer, *DBWE* 1:266.
41 Marsh summarizes it in this way: "[T]he being of God in revelation is not being-in-potentiality [*Sein als Seinskönnen*] but being in Christ as the concreteness of community" (Marsh, *Reclaiming Dietrich Bonhoeffer*, 128).
42 Bonhoeffer, *DBWE* 1:78.
43 Bonhoeffer, *DBWE* 1:80.
44 Bonhoeffer's writings attend to the shifting social structures and forms of practice that support collective action amid a period of profound social change. As demonstrated here, Tönnies' categories provide a framework for Bonhoeffer's reflection, even as Bonhoeffer's use of *Gemeinschaft* and *Gesellschaft* deploys these concepts within an original conceptual frame. Bonhoeffer, however, is not alone in trying to understand and describe the shifting social structures that organize a common life. For example, Gilles Deleuze and Félix Guattarri distinguish between "taproot" and "rhizome" patterns of thought and social order (Gilles Deleuze and Félix Guattarri, *A Thousand Plateaus: Capitalism and Schizophrenia*, trans. Brian Massumi [Minneapolis: University of Minnesota Press, 1987]).
45 Readers who take particular interest in Bonhoeffer's analysis at this point may enjoy two later works that employ a similar line of analysis: Claude Welch, *The Reality of the Church* (New York: Charles Scribner's Sons, 1958) and James Gustafson, *Treasure in Earthen Vessels: The Church as a Human Community* (New York: Harper & Brothers, 1961).
46 The language of "transforming relationship" is drawn from Friesen's description of The Seattle School of Theology & Psychology's mission, but it aptly describes the work of the PC as well.
47 Clifford Green, *Bonhoeffer: A Theology of Sociality*, rev. ed. (Grand Rapids: Eerdmans, 1999), 271.
48 This theme is present throughout the arc of Bonhoeffer's work and secondary literature. For example, Bonhoeffer talks about the church as the "qualified world" according to "God's own entry into it and for it" (*DBWE* 12:263). *Sanctorum Communio* describes how the basic social structures are reformed and transcended in Christ, and *Discipleship* shows how the image of Christ transforms "those who have heard the call to be disciples" (*DBWE* 4:281). Secondary literature demonstrates a similar emphasis. For example, Green describes Bonhoeffer's interdisciplinary engagement as an attempt "to qualify and transform these borrowed concepts" (Green, *Bonhoeffer*, 26); Marsh identifies the "ontological transformation of people in Christ" (Marsh, *Reclaiming Dietrich Bonhoeffer*, 133); and Reggie Williams directs attention to the "transformation that Bonhoeffer experienced in Harlem" (Reggie Williams, *Bonhoeffer's Black Jesus: Harlem's Renaissance Theology and an Ethic of Resistance* [Waco, Tex.: Baylor University Press, 2014], 135).

Transformation also represents a site of conceptual resonance with organizational theory. As Aldrich and Ruef note in *Organizations Evolving*, the process and possibility of transformation represents a perennial and polarizing debate in organizational studies. For the present account, their work helpfully defines transformation and identifies three axes of organizational transformation: goals, boundaries, and activities. Reflecting the basic insight of their approach, this present study seeks to consider "the conditions under which change occurs" (132). For a full description of organizational transformation, see Aldrich and Ruef, *Organizations Evolving*, 132–58.

49 Bonhoeffer, *DBWE* 2:112.
50 Bonhoeffer, *DBWE* 2:116.
51 For a similar conclusion, see Dykstra's description of the symbiotic relationship between pastoral and ecclesial imagination in the previous chapter. See especially Dykstra, "Pastoral and Ecclesial Imagination," 43.
52 Bonhoeffer writes: "Faith invariably discovers itself already in the church; it is there already when it becomes aware of its presupposition" (Bonhoeffer, *DBWE* 2:117).
53 Bonhoeffer, *DBWE* 2:113.
54 Bonhoeffer, *DBWE* 2:126.
55 Bonhoeffer, *DBWE* 2:131.
56 Bonhoeffer, *DBWE* 2:89.
57 Bonhoeffer, *DBWE* 1:3, 127.
58 Following Bonnie Miller-McLemore, attending to the way represents one of the domains of inquiry for practical theology (Miller-McLemore, "Introduction," 9).
59 James Davison Hunter, *To Change the World: The Irony, Tragedy, and Possibility of Christianity in the Late Modern World* (Oxford: Oxford University Press, 2010), 44. Hunter similarly considers how networks provide a site to consider how religion contributes to social change.
60 Joel Green, *The Gospel of Luke* (Grand Rapids: Eerdmans, 1997), 9–10.
61 All biblical references come from the New Revised Standard Version.
62 Rowe, *World Upside Down*.
63 Luke's use of the perfect ἐκκέχυται (10:45) to express the surprise of those who came with Peter suggests the ongoing impact of the gift of the Spirit for those on whom it came.
64 A common reading of Acts divides Luke's account into two roughly equal parts or phases: chapters 1 through 12 recount events related to the early church in Jerusalem, while chapters 13 through 28 focus more narrowly on Paul's missionary journeys. For representative readings, see Bruce Malina and John Pilch, *Social-Science Commentary on the Book of Acts* (Minneapolis: Fortress, 2008); Charles Talbert, *Reading Acts: A Literary and Theological Commentary* (Macon, Ga.: Smyth & Helwys, 2005). While such readings note important differences related to the emphasis and actors in the narrative, these readings risk obscuring the continuity across these sections
65 Rowe, *World Upside Down*, 134.
66 Flavius Josephus, *Jewish War* 3.4.2.
67 Richard Pervo, *Acts: A Commentary* (Minneapolis: Fortress, 2009), 291.
68 Notably, not by the displaced representatives of the Jerusalem Church.
69 Dieter Zeller, *Exegetical Dictionary of the New Testament*, vol. 1, ed. Horst Balz and Gerhard Schneider (Grand Rapids: Eerdmans, 1999), 152.
70 The extent to which Luke is aware of this material is debated, but the echo remains pronounced.
71 C. Kavin Rowe, *Early Narrative Christology: The Lord in the Gospel of Luke* (Berlin: de Gruyter, 2006).
72 A similar construction is used in Luke 2:40 to characterize Jesus' growth as a child. Despite minor differences in the use of articles (Luke 2:40 does not include definite articles), the commonality suggests a correlation between the grace of God in the growth of Jesus and that same grace in the growth of the church. Bruce Metzger observes the uncommon inclusion of the definite article τήν after χάριν in 11:23

conveys particular force and may suggest Barnabas' noteworthy excitement about the evident expression of God's grace (Bruce Metzger, *A Textual Commentary on the Greek New Testament* [New York: United Bible Society, 1994], 343).

73 The infinitive διδάξαι leaves ambiguity.
74 On the limits of technocratic approaches to teaching, see Jacques Ellul, *The Technological Society*, trans. John Wilkinson (New York: Vintage Books, 1964) and Ivan Illich, *Deschooling Society* (London: Marion Boyars, 1970).
75 Edward Farley, *Ecclesial Man: A Social Phenomenology of Faith and Reality* (Philadelphia: Fortress, 1975).
76 Rowe, *One True Life*, 129.
77 H. Richard Niebuhr expresses the relationship between history, story, and community: "In our history association means community, the participation of each living self in a common memory and common hope no less than in a common world of nature" (H. Richard Niebuhr, *The Meaning of Revelation* [New York: Macmillan, 1946], 71).
78 While F. F. Bruce characterizes Antioch as a Christian "base" (F. F. Bruce, *The Book of Acts* [Grand Rapids: Eerdmans, 1988], 223), this understates the complexity of the social logic presented by Luke's narration. The term "network" provides a more appropriate designation. Although critics may characterize the use of this term as anachronistic, Holland Hendrix's use of networks to study benefactor/patron relations in Thessalonica demonstrates the relevance of this category to studies of early Christian communities (Holland Hendrix, "Benefactor/Patron Networks in the Urban Environment: Evidence from Thessalonica," in *Social Networks in Early Christian Environments: Issues and Methods for Social History*, ed. L. Michael White [Atlanta: Society of Biblical Literature, 1992], 39–58).
79 Malina and Pilch, *Social-Science Commentary on the Book of Acts*, 88.
80 Attention to the Pauline tradition highlights the absence of conflict at Antioch in Luke's narration. As Galatians 2 outlines, even though Antioch came to comprise a networked community of faith, it may have also served as a site of the decisive confrontation between Peter and Paul. The inclusion of these diverse traditions within the canonical material does not invalidate either account, but expresses an "internal coherence" that expresses unity even amid a history of conflict (Markus Bockmuehl, *Seeing the Word: Refocusing New Testament Study* [Grand Rapids: Baker, 2006], 121–30).
81 Adam M. Klienbaum, "Organizational Misfits and the Origins of Brokerage in Intrafirm Networks," *Administrative Science Quarterly* 57, no. 3 (2012): 407–52.
82 Καταγγέλλω occurs 10 times in Acts—more than anywhere else in the New Testament. All but one of these uses occurs in or after Acts 13:5. For a description of the importance of proclamation, see Karl Barth, *CD* 1.2/§20.
83 Rowe writes: "Of the things we should learn from Acts' ecclesiological vision, none is quite as important as the very basic sense that thinking theologically about the church requires us to discern the interconnections that make up a total way of life.... [I]f we wish to talk about ecclesiology according to Acts, we must talk primarily about a theologically explicated habit of being that is noticeably different from the larger practices and assumptions that shape daily life in the Greco-Roman world" (C. Kavin Rowe, "Ecclesiology in Acts," *Interpretation: A Journal of Bible and Theology* 66, no. 3 [2012]: 269).

84 This conclusion must be held in tension with Luke's measured evaluation of the state. For Luke, rulers exalting themselves over the Lord represent the primary subject of critique, not the state (cf. Talbert, *Reading Acts*, 113).

85 Alasdair MacIntyre, *Whose Justice? Which Rationality?* (Notre Dame, Ind.: University of Notre Dame Press, 1988).

86 See Rowe, *One True Life*; Pierre Hadot, *Philosophy as a Way of Life: Spiritual Exercises from Socrates to Foucault*, trans. Michael Chase (Oxford: Blackwell, 1995).

87 Bonhoeffer writes, "The word of scripture, the hymns of the church, and the prayer of the community should form part of every daily worship that they share together" (Bonhoeffer, *DBWE* 5:52–53).

88 Rodney Stark's description of Christians' responses to early epidemics demonstrate the power of care amid times of crisis (Rodney Stark, *The Rise of Christianity: How the Obscure, Marginal Jesus Movement Became the Dominant Religious Force in the Western World in a Few Centuries* [San Francisco: Harper, 1997], 82).

89 Richard Hays, *The Moral Vision of the New Testament: Community Cross, New Creation—A Contemporary Introduction to New Testament Ethics* (New York: HarperOne, 1996), 302.

90 Mark Knight, "Sin and Salvation," in *The Oxford Handbook of Dietrich Bonhoeffer*, ed. Michael Mawson and Philip Ziegler (New York: Oxford University Press, 2019), 210–24.

91 Knight, "Sin and Salvation," 218.

92 Sin leads to "broken community and isolation" (Bonhoeffer, *DBWE* 1:107).

93 Bonhoeffer, *DBWE* 5:31.

94 Bonhoeffer, *DBWE* 5:32–33.

95 Nevertheless, this theme appears indirectly through the shared interest in shalom and the possibility to understand sin as the fracture of shalom.

96 Bonhoeffer, *DBWE* 10:546.

97 Bonhoeffer, *DBWE* 10:542.

98 Bonhoeffer, *DBWE* 8:188, emphasis in original.

99 Three individuals did not identify their gender. In select cases, individuals identified as white, but then provided some caveat (e.g., grew up in Japan, descendant of Native Americans). Notably, these homogeneous markers of race and gender also reflect my own embodiment. For a further discussion of the self-reflexivity that informs this research, see appendix A.

100 For example, my field notes from these events read: "[The PC's Inhabit is] mostly white with a mix of young and greying"; "[The OCE's Summit] skews toward grey—seems like the balance in the room is flipped [from Inhabit]. Approximately ninety percent white."

101 Ruef, *Entrepreneurial Group*, 60.

102 Ruef, *Entrepreneurial Group*, 81.

103 Michael Mawson, *Christ Existing as Community: Bonhoeffer's Ecclesiology* (Oxford: Oxford University Press, 2018), 66.

104 Bonhoeffer, *DBWE* 5:93.

105 Willie James Jennings, *Acts: A Theological Commentary* (Louisville: Westminster John Knox, 2017), 149.

106 See Patrick Reyes, "Grandma's Table: Memories of Survival and Adaptation," in Benac and Weber-Johnson, *Crisis and Care*, 49–54.

107 Williams, *Bonhoeffer's Black Jesus*, 140.

108 Alan Roxburgh, *Joining God in the Great Unraveling: Where We Are & What I've Learned* (Eugene, Ore.: Cascade, 2021).

109 Bonhoeffer identifies the need for "a new language [*eine neue Sprache*]" (Bonhoeffer, *DBWE* 8:389) in the aforementioned letter addressed to a friend's son on the occasion of his baptism, but he did not develop this theme. Similarly, even though his early engagement with transcendental philosophy in his academic work introduced him to the language of "practical reason" (Bonhoeffer, *DBWE* 2:40, 45), he did not explore this concept.

The narrative in Luke-Acts similarly identifies the importance of wisdom: Jesus is "filled with wisdom" as a child and "increased in wisdom" as he grew (Luke 2:40, 52); the Scriptures that guide a community are called the "Wisdom of God" (Luke 11:49); wisdom is a feature for those tasked to care for widows (Acts 6:3). Nevertheless, the narrative stops short of detailing the practical wisdom that animates early Christian networks.

7 "WE'RE BETTER TOGETHER"

1 Beyond my description of each hub's team, I have chosen not to identify individuals with a particular mode of leadership. I obscure identities at this point to avoid placing individuals within a particular mode, potentially compromising their local leadership.

2 Lest my description of Reformation Day be read solely as an appeal for change, it is helpful to note how Seattle Pacific University describes this event: "Remembering Luther's intent to reform (not split from) the Roman Catholic Church, we view today not as a time of triumph, but one of renewal, repentance, and revival, as we ponder the meaning of Semper Reformanda 'always being reformed.'" (Seattle Pacific University, "Five Hundred Years Ago Today," Facebook, October 31, 2017, https://m.facebook.com/story/graphql_permalink/?graphql_id=UzpfSTEyNDU5ODQ3MDk2NTk2MDoxNTM4OTQzNzk2MTk4MDgw).

3 Dustin Benac, "Seattle Pacific University School of Theology Post-interview Memo," October 31, 2017.

4 Bass et al., *Christian Practical Wisdom*, 5.

5 See Patrick Reyes, *Nobody Cries When We Die: God, Community, and Surviving to Adulthood* (Atlanta: Chalice Press, 2016) for a model of contextual, collective discernment.

6 See L. Gregory Jones, *Christian Social Innovation: Renewing Wesleyan Witness* (Nashville: Abingdon, 2016) for a resonant description.

7 Charles Marsh, introduction to *Lived Theology: New Perspectives on Method, Style, and Pedagogy* (New York: Oxford University Press, 2017), 10.

8 Beyond this discussion of Christian practical wisdom, scholars in other fields have similarly identified the need for renewed attention to practical wisdom (*phronesis*) in research and public life. For example, see MacIntyre, *Ethics in the Conflict of Modernity*; Barry Schwartz and Kenneth Sharpe, *Practical Wisdom: The Right Way to Do the Right Thing* (New York: Riverhead Books, 2010); Flyvbjerg, *Making Social Science Matter*; John Uhr, *Prudential Public Leadership: Promoting Ethics in Public Policy and Administration* (New York: Palgrave Macmillan, 2015); and Peter Eckel and Cathy Trower, *Practical Wisdom: Thinking Differently about College and University Governance* (Sterling, Va.: Stylus, 2019). The authors of these volumes do not understand and develop the concept of practical wisdom in

9   Sparks, Soerens, and Friesen, *New Parish*, 167.
10   See Frost and Rice, *To Alter Your World*, 97–113. Both *The New Parish* and *To Alter Your World* engage Heifetz to identify the need for leadership, but they do so at a later point in their work.
11   Sittser, *Resilient Faith*, 88. Sittser's work includes a chapter that discusses authority, noting how authority was "derivative" for early Christians (95), but his work stops short of offering a clear description of the form of leadership that is required then and now. Ostensibly, the work of the OCE takes up the task Sittser identifies in his conclusion.
12   The description of leadership as "being with" combines insights from an array of scholars and practitioners. It principally reflects Sam Wells' development of this motif (see *A Nazareth Manifesto: Being with God* [Malden, Mass.: John Wiley & Sons, 2015], *Incarnational Ministry: Being with the Church* [Grand Rapids: Eerdmans, 2017], and *Incarnational Mission: Being with the World* [Grand Rapids: Eerdmans, 2018]). It also draws inspiration from David Kelsey's *Eccentric Existence*, where Kelsey similarly contends that the Christian tradition presents "a picture of human existence as eccentric, centered outside itself in the triune God in regard to its being, value, destiny, identity, and proper existential orientations to its ultimate and proximate contexts" (David Kelsey, *Eccentric Existence: A Theological Anthropology*, 2 vols. [Louisville: Westminster John Knox, 2009], 2:893). Finally, this motif reflects Bonhoeffer's Christological understanding of the inseparability "being-with-each-other (*Miteinander*)" and "being-for-each-other (*Füreinander*)" (Bonhoeffer *DBWE* 1:182).
13   Wells, *Incarnational Mission*, 15.
14   This insight reflects calls for more collaborative approaches to religious leadership. "Many customary styles of leadership in local communities are proving insufficient," William Clark and Daniel Gast note, and then conclude: "The health of our church communities calls for collaborative approaches" (William Clark and Daniel Gast, "Introduction: Collaborative Leadership for Local Church Communities," in *Collaborative Parish Leadership: Contexts, Models, Theology*, ed. William Clark and Daniel Gast [London: Lexington, 2017], 1).
15   Benac and Weber-Johnson, "Ecclesial Imagination for Organizational Transformation," 168. This description of organizational midwifery resembles Rice and Frost's formulation, but it more clearly indicates how midwifery contributes to the transformation of organizations and communities.
16   Catalysts in both hubs described their leadership as an "apostolic" orientation. This language references Alan Hirsch's APEST (Apostle, Prophet, Evangelist, Shepherds, Teachers) typology. For a description of "Apostle," see Alan Hirsch, *5Q: Reactivating the Original Intelligence and Capacity of the Body of Christ* (Columbia: 100 Movements, 2017), xxxiii, 99–102, 113.
17   Michael Moynagh, *Church in Life: Innovation, Mission, and Ecclesiology* (Eugene, Ore.: Cascade, 2018), 60.
18   Sparks, Soerens, and Friesen, *New Parish*, 179.
19   Block, *Community*, 203.
20   Sparks, Soerens, and Friesen, *New Parish*, 175.

Notes to Pages 195–209   293

21. The Surveyor's mode of "being with" should not be confused with the premodern understanding of *curiositas*. As characterized here, the Surveyor's mode of being pursues a form of hospitality to individuals and ideas, seeking to support the conditions that enable each to form and flourish. See Paul Griffiths, *Intellectual Appetite: A Theological Grammar* (Washington, D.C.: Catholic University of America Press, 2009) for a lucid introduction to this term.
22. Biola University, "A Foot in Each World: Vocation between Academia and the Church—Gerald Sittser," last modified May 17, 2017, https://cct.biola.edu/foot-world-vocation-academia-church-gerald-sittser/.
23. Kate Bowler, *The Preacher's Wife: The Precarious Power of Evangelical Women Celebrities* (Princeton, N.J.: Princeton University Press, 2019), xxi.
24. Sparks, Soerens, and Friesen, *New Parish*, 14. Organizers of both hubs similarly identify individuals who functioned as Guides at critical stages in their adaptive process.
25. Dante Alighieri, *The Purgatorio*, trans. Henry Wadsworth Longfellow (New York: Barnes & Noble, 2005), VI.71. Nevertheless, Dante also refers to Virgil by a host of other names, e.g., "escort," "conductor," "comforter," "master," "lord," and "leader." The plurality of names Dante attributes to his guide bespeaks the diverse vocations that reflect this posture. Summarizing Virgil's role within *The Divine Comedy*, Vittorio Montemaggi aptly notes: "[H]e leads others to the light" (Vittorio Montemaggi, *Reading Dante's* Commedia *as Theology: Divinity Realized in Human Encounter* [Oxford: Oxford University Press, 2016], 235).
26. Dante, *The Purgatorio* XXX.50–51.
27. When organizers gathered to discuss this paradigm, they often self-identified with the form of leadership that occupied the opposite position in this model. I explore this relationship as a "polarity" organized around three axes of innovation: connection, care, and change.
28. The absence of a clearly identifiable Champion for the PC's work is one of the striking features of this research.
29. See Marlon Hall's description of an "ecotone" ("Experience Is the Path to Discovering Your 'Why' with Anthropologist Marlon Hall," interview by Sean Waldron, *Tension Theory* (podcast), October 22, 2019, 44:11, https://www.tensiontheory.com/podcast/25).
30. See Gunderson, *Boundary Leaders*.
31. M. J. Murdock Charitable Trust, "About the Trust," accessed January 17, 2020, https://murdocktrust.org/about-the-trust/.
32. Frequently speaking in terms of "we," the practical wisdom that informs the Connector-Convener's work links the Connector-Convener's language to the collective.
33. Kevin Doyle Jones, "Neighborhood Economics: Local Funding for Entrepreneurs without a Rich Uncle," *Impact Alpha*, August 4, 2017, https://impactalpha.com/neighborhood-economics-emerging-ecosystem-approach-is-gaining-momentum-97ad2c143768/.
34. Soerens follows by describing the potential reach of this catalytic change in terms that reflect the ecclesial ecology. Specifically, he notes how change affects "systems, potentially of seminaries, of parachurch organizations."
35. The priority of friendship across these hubs and in this broader account is consistent with Chloe Lynch's thesis about how friendship provides the basis for

36 Wells, *Incarnational Mission*.
37 Parks approaches this concept, but she stops short of fully exploring the implications of practical wisdom for the forms of knowledge and formation that adaptive work requires. For example, she identifies the need to attend to the "habitual ways of responding" (Parks, *Leadership Can Be Taught*, 6).
38 Heifetz, *Leadership without Easy Answers*, 13; Parks, *Leadership Can Be Taught*, 2.
39 Nevertheless, these hubs similarly serve as centers that generate new language, literature, and resources to support leaders and communities of faith.
40 Swinton and Mowat, *Practical Theology and Qualitative Research*, 24.
41 Osmer, *Practical Theology*, 4.
42 Osmer, *Practical Theology*, 192.
43 For accounts that emphasize the contributions of servant leadership, see Bernice Ledbetter, Robert Banks, and David Greenhalgh, *Reviewing Leadership: A Christian Evaluation of Current Approaches*, 2nd ed. (Grand Rapids: Baker Academic, 2016); Justin Irving and Mark Strauss, *Leadership in Christian Perspective: Biblical Foundations and Contemporary Practices for Servant Leaders* (Grand Rapids: Baker Academic, 2019).

The beginning of this note (item 35) continues from the previous page: ecclesial leadership (see Chloe Lynch, *Ecclesial Leadership as Friendship: Explorations in Practical, Pastoral and Empirical Theology* [New York: Routledge, 2019]). Jack Barentsen kindly notified me of this resonance with Lynch's account.

44 This language is particularly clustered around the OCE's network.
45 Larry Rasmussen, "Shaping Communities," in Bass, *Practicing Our Faith*, 118.

8 A MOMENT OF RENOVATING VIRTUE

1 William Wordsworth, *The Prelude*, ed. J. C. Maxwell (New Haven, Conn.: Yale University Press, 1971), bk. XII, ll. 208–18. The theme for bk. XII, "Imagination and Taste: How Impaired and Restored," harmonizes with the role of imagination in my argument.
2 Genesis 1:2 (NRSV).
3 Dustin Benac, "December 4, 2019 Research Memo."
4 Wordsworth, *The Prelude*, bk. XII, ll. 208–18.
5 Derived from the Latin root *renovare*, "renovating" describes an act of renewing, restoring, or reviving. Far from a solitary endeavor, virtue requires a connection to a broader community, finding its proper end in relation to others. Renovating virtue, as described here, also requires wisdom to discern the appropriate form of response at this particular site of rupture.
6 The phrase "brought up short" comes from Richard Osmer (Osmer, *Practical Theology*, 21). Robert Creech directed my attention to Osmer's language.
7 To borrow language lines from Linda Buckmaster: "This is all we have / in this life, all we own: / a flowering / an opening / a gap between stones / for tiny tender roots" (Linda Buckmaster, "Flowering," in *Poetry of Presence: An Anthology of Mindfulness Poems*, ed. Phyllis Cole-Dai and Ruby Wilson [West Hartford, Conn.: Grayson Books, 2017], 133).
8 For a description of the wisdom that guides other communities as they cross over, see Dustin Benac and Erin Weber-Johnson, "What Do These Stones Mean?" in Benac and Weber-Johnson, *Crisis and Care*, 139–46.
9 Richard Osmer concludes *Practical Theology* by describing the "pragmatic task" of practical theology as responding to the question "How might we respond?"

10 Peter Block similarly observes how restorative community "value[s] possibility and relatedness over problems, self-interest, and the rest of the stuck community's agendas." The guiding question is "What can we create together?" (47).

11 The material in this section is primarily based on responses to the question "What else is needed for you, your organization, or those you serve or will serve to either continue to fulfill or more faithfully fulfill your/their particular organizational mission?"

12 As McGonigal notes, there is a "realization" that the OCE "will always be in the grants business."

13 Sittser is seventy and McGonigal is sixty-nine at the time of this writing. Since Sittser and McGonigal started the OCE in the final stages of their careers, age is neither a new nor an unexpected challenge.

14 Sparks is fifty-one, Soerens is forty-one, and Rice is forty-one at the time of this writing.

15 The Parish Collective Board, for which Jonathan Brooks serves as the current chair, signals one intentional effort to build around leadership that reflects the diversity of the communities they serve.

16 Shannon Hopkins and Mark Sampson, "Seeing Our Rooted Good: Trees, Pandemics, and Economic Imagination," in Benac and Weber-Johnson, *Crisis and Care*, 90, 88. As Hopkins and Sampson note, the new language of interconnection emerges by simply "look[ing] at trees" (88). Accordingly, my qualitative work throughout this project has centered individuals in relation to the broader the ecclesial and arboreal ecology that surrounds them. The trees that surround religious life in the Pacific Northwest ground my qualitative research in material reality and root my theological redescription in an imagination of interconnectedness.

17 The phrase "adjacent possibilities" comes from Johnson, *Where Good Ideas Come From*, 23. Patricia Killen kindly directed me to Johnson's language.

18 Bookended by reflections on the adaptive possibilities for pastors and ecclesial entrepreneurs, the remaining topics are organized alphabetically.

19 Elizabeth Conde-Frazier similarly describes the need for "a collaborative educational ecology" (80). For an insightful account of the history of theological education and recent innovations that support a more collaborative mode of education, see Elizabeth Conde-Frazier, "*Las Estructuras Crean Hábitos*: A Collaborative Educational Ecology," in *Atando Cabos: Latinx Contributions to Theological Education* (Grand Rapids: Eerdmans, 2021), 80–102.

20 Jeff Astley and Colin Crowder provide a resonant description of the scope and aims of Christian education in their introduction to *Theological Perspectives on Christian Formation: A Reader on Theology and Christian Education*, ed. Jeff Astley, Leslie Francis, and Colin Crowder (Grand Rapids: Eerdmans, 1996), x–xix.

21 Charles Foster, *From Generation to Generation: The Adaptive Challenge of Mainline Protestant Education in Forming Faith* (Eugene, Ore.: Wipf & Stock, 2012), 96–119. Consistent with my broader argument, Foster introduces his account as a

response to the adaptive challenges that engage congregations and their denominations (Foster, *From Generation to Generation*, 1–21).

22 This statement identifies an ongoing need for educational institutions; it does not suggest that it is necessary to maintain all existing institutions that contribute to Christian education. Indeed, as David Dockery suggests, the host of challenges that confront Christian higher education "will keep the issue of collaboration near the top of the list of important matters for many campus" (David Dockery, "Change, Challenge, and Confession: Looking toward the Future of Christian Higher Education," *Christian Education Journal* 16, no. 2 [2019]: 298). Dockery identifies the need to reconnect with local congregations for educational institutions (302). Dockery's analysis focuses on the challenges that confront Christian higher education, but theological educational institutions similarly need to expand their roster of collaborators and partners.

23 This interviewee first identifies "old people" and then follows these comments by identifying the need for "money." The material quoted here provides an interpretive bridge between these two concepts.

24 It is possible to provide a finer distinction between nonprofit organizations and parachurch ministries. However, I have combined these into a single category, "nonprofit ministries." Without diminishing the defining features of either category, this designation reflects the similar vocation that individuals across these organizations pursue.

25 More than half (51 percent) of participants in Scharen and Campbell-Reed's study have positions of ministerial service outside full-time congregational ministry. Of those, 35 percent are in chaplaincy, nonprofit ministry, or part-time congregational ministry positions (Scharen and Campbell-Reed, "Learning Pastoral Imagination," 10–13).

26 Brooks is quoting Leroy Barber, the Director of Innovation for an Engaged Church in the Pacific Northwest Conference of the United Methodist Church. Barber has partnered with the PC to launch a series of learning communities throughout the region.

27 Heifetz, *Leadership without Easy Answers*, 235–76.

28 Heifetz identifies: pacing the work; managing oneself; distinguishing between the role and the self; externalizing conflict; finding suitable and complementary partners; listening to oneself; finding a sanctuary; preserving a sense of purpose; and learning perpetually. For an extended discussion of staying alive, see Ronald Heifetz and Marty Linsky, *Leadership on the Line: Staying Alive through the Dangers of Change* (Boston: Harvard Business School Publishing, 2002).

29 My description of anti-institutionalism is not synonymous with institutional distrust. While institutions have the capacity to support the conditions for innovation, they also have the capacity to perpetuate patterns of injustice, inequality, and harm.

30 The life of the church and the principal task of the practical theologian both emerge from the ordinary character of Christian existence. See Ward, *Introducing Practical Theology*, 3. Jennifer Herdt astutely describes the importance of formation for discipleship, which occurs in diverse educational contexts. See Jennifer Herdt, "Forming Humanity: Practices of Education Christianly Considered," in *Everyday Ethics: Moral Theology and the Practices of Ordinary Life*, ed. Michael Lamb and Brian A. Williams (Washington, D.C.: Georgetown University Press, 2019), 65–80.

31 To return to Nicholas Wolterstorff's reflections in the introduction, other experiments may be "something like" these hubs, "yet infinitely beyond" in contextually specific ways (Wolterstorff, *In This World of Wonders*, 210).

APPENDIX A

1 The nomenclature in this appendix draws on the title of appendix B in Kate Bowler's *Blessed* (Kate Bowler, *Blessed: A History of the American Prosperity Gospel* [New York: Oxford University Press, 2013], 249–62).
2 Natalie Wigg-Stevenson, *Ethnographic Theology: An Inquiry into the Production of Theological Knowledge* (New York: Palgrave Macmillan, 2014), 2 (emphasis in original).
3 Wigg-Stevenson, *Ethnographic Theology*, 170.
4 Bonhoeffer, *DBWE* 2:32.
5 Bonhoeffer, *DBWE* 1:3, 127.
6 Dustin Benac, "November 25, 2019, Research Memo (Postdated)."
7 For a full description of how I approached my empirical research as a practical theologian, see Benac, "Craft of Theology and Qualitative Research."
8 Swinton and Mowat, *Practical Theology and Qualitative Research*, 235.
9 Swinton and Mowat, *Practical Theology and Qualitative Research*, 261.
10 See appendix B for a full list of participants.
11 For an example of convening in organizational studies, see Mauro Magatti, introduction to *Social Generativity: A Relational Paradigm for Social Change*, ed. Mauro Magatti (London: Routledge, 2018), 1–7; Generativita.it, "Generativity," last modified 2019, http://generativita.it/it/generativita/.
12 As this individual also noted: "This very conversation, I feel like this is the thing that's needed so profoundly. We have to do our work obviously, but the collaborative potential and the openness that feels like it's there right now, it feels quite special, honestly."

APPENDIX C

1 Primary partners are those institutions that are integral to your particular institutional mission.

Bibliography

Adler, Paul. Introduction to *The Oxford Handbook of Sociology and Organizational Studies: Classical Foundations*, edited by Paul Adler, 3–19. Oxford: Oxford University Press, 2009.

Aldrich, Howard E., and Martin Ruef. *Organizations Evolving*. 2nd ed. London: Sage, 2006.

Alighieri, Dante. *The Purgatorio*. Translated by Henry Wadsworth Longfellow. New York: Barnes & Noble, 2005.

Ammerman, Nancy. *Congregations and Community*. New Brunswick, N.J.: Rutgers University Press, 1997.

———. *Pillars of Faith: American Congregations and Their Partners*. Berkeley: University of California Press, 2005.

Association of Religion Data Archives. National Congregations Study, Cumulative Dataset, 2012. Accessed September 22, 2018. https://www.thearda.com/.

Astley, Jeff, and Colin Crowder. "Theological Perspectives on Christian Education: An Overview." In *Theological Perspectives on Christian Formation: A Reader on Theology and Christian Education*, edited by Jeff Astley, Leslie Francis, and Colin Crowder, x–xix. Grand Rapids: Eerdmans, 1996.

Austin, Thad. "Collaborative Partnerships: Christian Ministry in a Post-pandemic World." In *Crisis and Care: Meditations on Faith and Philanthropy*, edited by Dustin Benac and Erin Weber-Johnson, 55–60. Eugene, Ore.: Cascade, 2021.

Ayres, Jennifer. "Cultivating the 'Unquiet Heart': Ecology, Education, and Christian Faith." *Theology Today* 74, no. 1 (2017): 57–65. doi: 10.1177/0040573616689836.

Barber, Leroy. *Embrace: God's Radical Shalom for a Divided World*. Downers Grove, Ill.: InterVarsity Press, 2016.

Barth, Karl. *Church Dogmatics*. 4 vols. New York: T&T Clark, 2009.

Bass, Dorothy C., ed. *Practicing Our Faith: A Way of Life for a Searching People*. 2nd ed. San Francisco: Jossey-Bass, 2010.

———. Preface to *Practicing Our Faith: A Way of Life for a Searching People*, 2nd ed., edited by Dorothy C. Bass. San Francisco: Jossey-Bass, 2010.

Bass, Dorothy C., and Craig Dykstra. Introduction to *For Life Abundant: Practical Theology, Theological Education, and Christian Ministry*, edited by Dorothy C. Bass and Craig Dykstra, 1–17. Grand Rapids: Eerdmans, 2008.

———. "Times of Yearning, Practices of Faith." In *Practicing Our Faith: A Way of Life for a Searching People*, 2nd ed., edited by Dorothy C. Bass, 1–12. San Francisco: Jossey-Bass, 2010.

———. "A Way of Thinking about a Way of Life." In *Practicing Our Faith: A Way of Life for a Searching People*, 2nd ed., edited by Dorothy C. Bass, 203–17. San Francisco: Jossey-Bass, 2010.

Bass, Dorothy C., Kathleen A. Cahalan, Bonnie J. Miller-McLemore, James R. Nieman, and Christian B. Scharen. *Christian Practical Wisdom: What It Is, Why It Matters*. Grand Rapids: Eerdmans, 2016.

Benac, Dustin. "A Bonhoefferian Approach to Social Analysis: Life Together as *Communio*, Relation, and Possibility." *The Bonhoeffer Legacy: An International Journal* 5, no. 2 (2018): 63–81.

———. "The Craft of Theology and Qualitative Research." In *The Wiley-Blackwell Companion to Theology and Qualitative Research*, edited by Pete Ward and Knut Tveitereid. Malden, Mass.: Wiley-Blackwell, forthcoming.

———. "Theological Education for a New Age." *Presbyterian Outlook*, September 25, 2018, https://pres-outlook.org/2018/09/theological-education-for-a-new-age/.

Benac, Dustin, and Erin Weber-Johnson, eds. *Crisis and Care: Meditations on Faith and Philanthropy*. Eugene, Ore.: Cascade, 2021.

———. "Ecclesial Imagination for Organizational Transformation: Hospice Care, Midwifery, and the Ordering of a Common Life." *Practical Theology* 12, no. 2 (2019): 158–74. doi: 10.1080/1756073X.2019.1595316.

———. "What Do These Stones Mean?" In *Crisis and Care: Meditations on Faith and Philanthropy*, edited by Dustin Benac and Erin Weber-Johnson, 139–46. Eugene, Ore.: Cascade, 2021.

Biola University. "A Foot in Each World: Vocation between Academia and the Church—Gerald Sittser." Last modified May 17, 2017. https://cct.biola.edu/foot-world-vocation-academia-church-gerald-sittser/.

Bloch, Matthew, Larry Buchanan, Josh Katz, and Kevin Quealy. "An Extremely Detailed Map of the 2016 Election." *New York Times*, July 25, 2018, https://www.nytimes.com/interactive/2018/upshot/election-2016-voting-precinct-maps.html#4.45/44.27/-108.58.

Block, Peter. *Community: The Structure of Belonging*. San Francisco: Berrett-Koehler, 2008.

Bockmuehl, Markus. *Seeing the Word: Refocusing New Testament Study*. Grand Rapids: Baker, 2006.

Bolsinger, Tod. *Canoeing the Mountains: Christian Leadership in Uncharted Territory*. Downers Grove, Ill.: InterVarsity Press, 2015.

Bonhoeffer, Dietrich. *Act and Being*. Translated by Martin Rumscheidt. Vol. 2 of *Dietrich Bonhoeffer Works*. Edited by Wayne Whitson Floyd and Hans-Richard Reuter. Minneapolis: Fortress, 2009.

———. *Barcelona, Berlin, New York: 1928–1931*. Translated by Douglas Stott. Vol. 10 of *Dietrich Bonhoeffer Works*. Edited by Clifford Green. Minneapolis: Fortress, 2008.

———. *Berlin: 1932–1933*. Translated by Isabel Best, David Higgins, and Douglas Stott. Vol. 12 of *Dietrich Bonhoeffer Works*. Edited by Larry Rasmussen. Minneapolis: Fortress, 2009.

———. *Discipleship*. Translated by Barbara Green and Reinhard Krauss. Vol. 4 of *Dietrich Bonhoeffer Works*. Edited by John D. Godsey and Geffrey B. Kelly. Minneapolis: Fortress, 2003.

———. *Letters and Papers from Prison*. Translated by Isabel Best, Lisa Dahill, Reinhard Krauss, and Nancy Lukens. Vol. 8 of *Dietrich Bonhoeffer Works*. Edited by John de Gruchy. Minneapolis: Fortress, 2010.

———. *Life Together and Prayerbook of the Bible*. Translated by Daniel Bloesch and James Burtness. Vol. 5 of *Dietrich Bonhoeffer Works*. Edited by Geffrey B. Kelly. Minneapolis: Fortress, 2005.

———. *Sanctorum Communio: A Theological Study of the Sociology of the Church*. Translated by Reinhard Krauss and Nancy Lukens. Vol. 1 of *Dietrich Bonhoeffer Works*. Edited by Clifford B. Green. Minneapolis: Fortress, 1998.

Bourgatti, Stephen, and Pacey Foster. "The Network in Organizational Research: A Review and Typology." *Journal of Management* 29, no. 6 (2003): 991–1013.

Bowler, Kate. *Blessed: A History of the American Prosperity Gospel*. New York: Oxford University Press, 2013.

———. *The Preacher's Wife: The Precarious Power of Evangelical Women Celebrities*. Princeton, N.J.: Princeton University Press, 2019.

Bridges, William. *Managing Transitions: Making the Most of Change*. 4th ed. Boston: Da Capo Press, 2016.

Bronfenbrenner, Urie. *The Ecology of Human Development*. Cambridge, Mass.: Harvard University Press, 1981.

Bruce, F. F. *The Book of Acts*. Grand Rapids: Eerdmans, 1988.

Brueggemann, Walter. *The Prophetic Imagination*. 2nd ed. Minneapolis: Fortress, 2001.

———. *Virus as a Summons to Faith: Biblical Reflections in a Time of Loss, Grief, and Uncertainty*. Eugene, Ore.: Cascade, 2021.

Buckmaster, Linda. "Flowering." In *Poetry of Presence: An Anthology of Mindfulness Poems*, edited by Phyllis Cole-Dai and Ruby Wilson, 133. West Hartford, Conn.: Grayson Books, 2017.

Burt, Ronald. *Structural Holes: The Social Structure of Competition*. Cambridge, Mass.: Harvard University Press, 1992.

Byassee, Jason. Foreword to *Christian Witness in Cascadian Soil: Coworkers with God in the Land of Hiking, Hipsters, and Hand-Crafted Lattes*, by Ross Lockhart, ix–xi. Eugene, Ore.: Cascade, 2021.

Byassee, Jason, and Ross Lockhart. *Better than Brunch: Missional Churches in Cascadia*. Eugene, Ore.: Cascade, 2020.

Cahalan, Kathleen A. *Introducing the Practice of Ministry*. Collegeville, Minn.: Liturgical Press, 2010.

———. "Unknowing: Spiritual Practices and the Search for a Wisdom Epistemology." In *Christian Practical Wisdom: What It Is, Why It Matters*, by Dorothy C. Bass, Kathleen A. Cahalan, Bonnie J. Miller-McLemore, James R. Nieman, and Christian B. Scharen, 275–321. Grand Rapids: Eerdmans, 2016.

Carr, Mike. "Geography, Spirituality and Social Change in Cascadia: A Bioregional Perspective." In *Cascadia: The Elusive Utopia: Exploring the Spirit of the Pacific Northwest*, edited by Douglas Todd, 127–42. Vancouver, B.C.: Ronsdale Press, 2008.

Carson, Timothy, Rosy Fairhurst, Nigel Rooms, and Lisa Withrow. *Crossing Thresholds: A Practical Theology of Liminality*. Cambridge: Lutterworth, 2021.

Centre for the Study of Christianity and Culture. "Churches, COVID-19 and Communities: Experiences, Needs, and Supporting Recovery." University of York, March 2021.

Chareunsy, Don. "Petit Chat Village Bakery in North Spokane Closes Its Doors." *Spokesman-Review*, August 20, 2019. https://www.spokesman.com/stories/2019/aug/20/petit-chat-village-bakery-in-north-spokane-closes-/.

Chaves, Mark. *American Religion: Contemporary Trends*. 2nd ed. Princeton, N.J.: Princeton University Press, 2017.

———. *Ordaining Women: Culture and Conflict in Religious Organizations*. Cambridge, Mass.: Harvard University Press, 1997.

———. "Religious Organizations: Data Resources and Research Opportunities." *American Behavioral Scientist* 45 (2002): 1523–49.

Chia, Lloyd. "From Boundaries to Borderlands: The Emerging Church's Imaginative Work of Fostering Relationships across Difference." In *Crossing Boundaries, Redefining Faith: Interdisciplinary Perspectives on the Emerging Church Movement*, edited by Michael Clawson and April Stace, 139–63. Eugene, Ore.: Wipf & Stock, 2016.

Christerson, Brad, and Richard Flory. *The Rise of Network Christianity: How Independent Leaders Are Changing the Religious Landscape*. New York: Oxford University Press, 2017.

Clark, William, and Daniel Gast. "Introduction: Collaborative Leadership for Local Church Communities." In *Collaborative Parish Leadership: Contexts, Models, Theology*, edited by William Clark and Daniel Gast, 1–8. London: Lexington, 2017.

Clawson, Michael. "A Brief History of the Emerging Church Movement in the United States." In *Crossing Boundaries, Redefining Faith: Interdisciplinary Perspectives on the Emerging Church Movement*, edited by Michael Clawson and April Stace, 17–44. Eugene, Ore.: Wipf & Stock, 2016.

Clawson, Michael, and April Stace, eds. *Crossing Boundaries, Redefining Faith: Interdisciplinary Perspectives on the Emerging Church Movement*. Eugene, Ore.: Wipf & Stock, 2016.

———. Introduction to *Crossing Boundaries, Redefining Faith: Interdisciplinary Perspectives on the Emerging Church Movement*, edited by Michael Clawson and April Stace, 1–16. Eugene, Ore.: Wipf & Stock, 2016.

Cohn, Nate, and Toni Monkovic. "What This 2012 Map Tells Us about America, and the Election." *New York Times*, October 18, 2016. https://www.nytimes.com/2016/10/19/upshot/what-this-2012-map-can-tell-us-about-the-2016-election.html.

Conde-Frazier, Elizabeth. *Atando Cabos: Latinx Contributions to Theological Education*. Grand Rapids: Eerdmans, 2021.

Crouch, Andy, Kurt Keilhacker, and Dave Blanchard. "Leading beyond the Blizzard: Why Every Organization Is Now a Startup." *Praxis Journal*, March 20, 2020. https://journal.praxislabs.org/leading-beyond-the-blizzard-why-every-organization-is-now-a-startup-b7f32fb278ff.

Cummings, E. E. *Complete Poems: 1913–1962*. New York: Harcourt Brace Javonovich, 1972.

Dale, Robert. *To Dream Again: How to Help Your Church Come Alive*. Eugene, Ore.: Wipf & Stock, 2004.

Deleuze, Gilles, and Félix Guattarri. *A Thousand Plateaus: Capitalism and Schizophrenia*. Translated by Brian Massumi. Minneapolis: University of Minnesota Press, 1987.

Demerath, N. J., and Terry Schmitt. "Transcending Sacred and Secular: Mutual Benefits in Analyzing Religious and Nonreligious Organizations." In *Sacred Companies: Organizational Aspects of Religion and Religious Aspects of Organizations*, edited by N. J. Demerath, Peter Hall, Terry Schmitt, and Rhys Williams, 381–400. New York: Oxford University Press, 1998.

DiMaggio, Paul. "The Relevance of Organizational Theory to the Study of Religion." In *Sacred Companies: Organizational Aspects of Religion and Religious Aspects of Organizations*, edited by N. J. Demerath, Peter Hall, Terry Schmitt, and Rhys Williams, 7–23. New York: Oxford University Press, 1998.

DiMaggio, Paul, and Walter Powell. "The Iron Cage Revisited: Institutional Isomorphism and Collective Rationality in Organizational Fields." *American Sociological Review* 48, no. 2 (1983): 147–60.

Dockery, David. "Change, Challenge, and Confession: Looking toward the Future of Christian Higher Education." *Christian Education Journal* 16, no. 2 (2019): 296–308. doi: 10.1177/0739891319846716.

Downtown Spokane Heritage Walk. "Spokane History." Accessed October 5, 2018. https://www.historicspokane.org/HeritageTours/downtown/history.html.

Dyck, Bruno. "God on Management: The World's Largest Religions, the 'Theological Turn,' and Organization and Management Theory and Practice." In *Religion and Organization Theory*, edited by Paul Tracey, Nelson Phillips, and Michael Lounsbury, 23–62. Research in the Sociology of Organizations 41. Bingley, UK: Emerald Group, 2014.

Dykstra, Craig. "Cultivating Thriving Communities of Faith: The Promise of Strategic Religious Philanthropy." Thomas H. Lake Lecture at the Lilly Family School of Philanthropy. Bloomington, Ind.: IUPUI, March 27, 2014.

———. *Growing in the Life of Faith: Education and Christian Practices*. 2nd ed. Louisville: Westminster John Knox, 2005.

———. "Pastoral and Ecclesial Imagination." In *For Life Abundant: Practical Theology, Theological Education, and Christian Ministry*, edited by Dorothy C. Bass and Craig Dykstra, 41–61. Grand Rapids: Eerdmans, 2008.

———. "Reconceiving Practice." In *Shifting Boundaries: Contextual Approaches to the Structure of Theological Education*, edited by Barbara G. Wheeler and Edward Farley, 35–66. Louisville: Westminster John Knox, 1991.

Dykstra, Craig, and James Hudnut-Beumler. "The National Organizational Structures of Protestant Denominations: An Invitation to a Conversation." In *The Organizational Revolution: Presbyterians and American Denominationalism*, edited by Milton Coalter, John Mulder, and Louis Weeks, 306–30. Louisville: Westminster John Knox, 1992.

Eastman, Susan. *Paul and the Person: Reframing Paul's Anthropology*. Grand Rapids: Eerdmans, 2017.

Eckel, Peter, and Cathy Trower. *Practical Wisdom: Thinking Differently about College and University Governance*. Sterling, Va.: Stylus, 2019.

Egan, Timothy. *The Good Rain: Across Time and Terrain in the Pacific Northwest*. New York: Alfred Knopf, 1990.

Eiesland, Nancy, and Stephen Warner. "Ecology: Seeing the Congregation in Context." In *Studying Congregations: A New Handbook*, edited by Nancy Ammerman, Jackson Carrol, Carl Dudley, and William McKinney, 40–77. Nashville: Abingdon, 1998.

Eisner, Elliot. *The Educational Imagination: On the Design and Evaluation of School Programs*. New York: Macmillan, 1979.

Ellul, Jacques. *The Technological Society*. Translated by John Wilkinson. New York: Vintage Books, 1964.

Erwin, Derek. "Report: Seattle Leads the Nation as Fastest Growing Tech Hub." *Startup Finance Blog*, October 30, 2018. https://www.lightercapital.com/blog/report-seattle-leads-nation-as-fastest-growing-tech-hub/.

Farley, Edward. *Ecclesial Man: A Social Phenomenology of Faith and Reality*. Philadelphia: Fortress, 1975.

———. *Theologia: The Fragmentation and Unity of Theological Education*. Philadelphia: Fortress, 1983.

Ferguson, Niall. *The Square and the Tower: Networks, Hierarchies and the Struggle for Global Power*. New York: Penguin, 2017.

Flick, Uwe. *Managing Quality in Qualitative Research*. 2nd ed. Thousand Oaks, Calif.: Sage, 2018.

Floyd, Wayne Whitson. "Bonhoeffer." In *The Modern Theologians: An Introduction to Christian Theology since 1918*, 3rd ed., edited by David Ford, 43–61. Malden, Mass.: Blackwell, 2005.

Flyvbjerg, Bent. *Making Social Science Matter: Why Social Inquiry Fails and How It Can Succeed Again*. Cambridge: Cambridge University Press, 2001.

Ford, Kevin. *Transforming Church: Bringing Out the Good to Get to Great*. Colorado Springs, Colo.: David C. Cook, 2008.

Foster, Charles. *From Generation to Generation: The Adaptive Challenge of Mainline Protestant Education in Forming Faith*. Eugene, Ore.: Wipf & Stock, 2012.

Foster, Charles R., Lisa E. Dahill, Lawrence A. Goleman, and Barbara Wang Tolentino. *Educating Clergy: Teaching Practices and Pastoral Imagination*. San Francisco: Jossey-Bass, 2006.

Foundation Directory Online Professional. s.vv. "Lilly Endowment, Inc." (Organization Name) and "Spokane, WA" (Geographic Focus). https://fdo.foundationcenter.org/.

Frey, Sylvia, and Betty Wood. *Come Shouting to Zion: African American Protestantism in the American South and British Caribbean to 1830*. Chapel Hill: University of North Carolina Press, 1998.

Friesen, Dwight J. *Thy Kingdom Connected: What the Church Can Learn from Facebook, the Internet, and Other Networks*. Grand Rapids: Baker, 2009.

Frost, Michael, and Alan Hirsch. *The Shaping of Things to Come: Innovation and Mission for the 21st-Century Church*. Peabody, Mass.: Hendrickson, 2003.

Frost, Michael, and Christiana Rice. *To Alter Your World: Partnering with God to Rebirth Our Communities*. Downers Grove, Ill.: InterVarsity Press, 2017.

Fulkerson, Mary McClintock. *Places of Redemption: Theology for a Worldly Church*. Oxford: Oxford University Press, 2007.

Generativita.it. "Generativity." Last modified 2019. http://generativita.it/it/generativita/.

Gibbs, Sunia. "Everything Is an Experiment." In *Crisis and Care: Meditations on Faith and Philanthropy*, edited by Dustin Benac and Erin Weber-Johnson. Eugene, Ore.: Cascade, 2021.

Goodrich, Charles, Kathleen Moore, and Frederick Swanson. Introduction to *In the Blast Zone: Catastrophe and Renewal on Mount St. Helens*, edited by Charles Goodrich, Kathleen Moore, and Frederick Swanson, ix–xvii. Corvallis: Oregon State University Press, 2008.

Granovetter, Mark. "The Strength of Weak Ties: A Network Theory Revisited." *Sociological Theory* 1 (1983): 201–33.

Green, Clifford. *Bonhoeffer: A Theology of Sociality*. Rev. ed. Grand Rapids: Eerdmans, 1999.

Green, Joel. *The Gospel of Luke.* Grand Rapids: Eerdmans, 1997.

Griffiths, Paul. *Intellectual Appetite: A Theological Grammar.* Washington, D.C.: Catholic University of America Press, 2009.

Gunderson, Gary. *Boundary Leaders: Leadership Skills for People of Faith.* Minneapolis: Fortress, 2004.

Gustafson, James. *Treasure in Earthen Vessels: The Church as a Human Community.* New York: Harper & Brothers, 1961.

Hadot, Pierre. *Philosophy as a Way of Life: Spiritual Exercises from Socrates to Foucault.* Translated by Michael Chase. Oxford: Blackwell, 1995.

Hale, Lori Brandt, and Reggie L. Williams. "Is This a Bonhoeffer Moment?" *Sojourners*, February 2018. https://sojo.net/magazine/february-2018/bonhoeffer-moment.

Hall, Marlon. "Experience Is the Path to Discovering Your 'Why' with Anthropologist Marlon Hall." Interview by Sean Waldron, *Tension Theory* (podcast), October 22, 2019, 44:11. https://www.tensiontheory.com/podcast/25.

Hannan, Michael, and John Freeman. *Organizational Ecology.* Cambridge, Mass.: Harvard University Press, 1989.

Hardy, Lee. *The Embrace of Buildings: A Second Look at Walkable City Neighborhoods.* Grand Rapids: Calvin College Press, 2017.

Harris, Patrick J. "William Keil and the Aurora Colony: A Communal Society Crosses the Oregon Trail." In *Religion and Society in the American West: Historical Essays*, edited by Carl Guarneri and David Alvarez, 425–47. Lanham, Md.: University Press of America, 1987.

Hatch, Mary Jo. *Organizations: A Very Short Introduction.* Oxford: Oxford University Press, 2011.

Hays, Richard. *The Moral Vision of the New Testament: Community Cross, New Creation—A Contemporary Introduction to New Testament Ethics.* New York: HarperOne, 1996.

Heath, Elaine A. "A New Day Rising in the Church." In *The Hyphenateds: How Emergence Christianity Is Re-traditioning Mainline Practice*, edited by Phil Snider, 26–35. Danvers, Mass.: Chalice Press, 2011.

Heclo, Hugh. *On Thinking Institutionally.* Boulder, Colo.: Paradigm, 2008.

Heifetz, Ronald. *Leadership without Easy Answers.* Cambridge, Mass.: Harvard University Press, 1994.

Heifetz, Ronald, Alexander Grashow, and Marty Linsky. *The Practice of Adaptive Leadership: Tools and Tactics for Changing Your Organization and the World.* Cambridge, Mass.: Harvard University Press, 2009.

Heifetz, Ronald, and Marty Linsky. *Leadership on the Line: Staying Alive through the Dangers of Change.* Boston: Harvard Business School Publishing, 2002.

Hendrix, Holland. "Benefactor/Patron Networks in the Urban Environment: Evidence from Thessalonica." In *Social Networks in Early Christian Environments: Issues and Methods for Social History*, edited by L. Michael White, 39–58. Atlanta: Society of Biblical Literature, 1992.

Herdt, Jennifer. "Forming Humanity: Practices of Education Christianly Considered." In *Everyday Ethics: Moral Theology and the Practices of Ordinary Life*, edited by Michael Lamb and Brian A. Williams, 65–80. Washington, D.C.: Georgetown University Press, 2019.

Hirsch, Alan. *5Q: Reactivating the Original Intelligence and Capacity of the Body of Christ*. Columbia: 100 Movements, 2017.

Hopkins, Shannon, and Mark Sampson. "Seeing Our Rooted Good: Trees, Pandemics, and Economic Imagination." In *Crisis and Care: Meditations on Faith and Philanthropy*, edited by Dustin Benac and Erin Weber-Johnson, 85–91. Eugene, Ore.: Cascade, 2021.

Humphreys, José. *Seeing Jesus in East Harlem: What Happens When Churches Show Up and Stay Put*. Downers Grove, Ill.: InterVarsity Press, 2018.

Hunter, James Davison. *To Change the World: The Irony, Tragedy, and Possibility of Christianity in the Late Modern World*. Oxford: Oxford University Press, 2010.

Illich, Ivan. *Deschooling Society*. London: Marion Boyars, 1970.

Institute for Advanced Studies of Culture. "Thriving Cities." Accessed May 15, 2019. https://vimeo.com/135908974.

Irving, Justin, and Mark Strauss. *Leadership in Christian Perspective: Biblical Foundations and Contemporary Practices for Servant Leaders*. Grand Rapids: Baker Academic, 2019.

James, Christopher. *Church Planting in Post-Christian Soil: Theology and Practice*. New York: Oxford University Press, 2018.

Jennings, Willie James. *Acts: A Theological Commentary*. Louisville: Westminster John Knox, 2017.

———. *After Whiteness: An Education in Belonging*. Grand Rapids: Eerdmans, 2020.

———. *The Christian Imagination: Theology and the Origins of Race*. New Haven, Conn.: Yale University Press, 2010.

Johnson, Steven. *Where Good Ideas Come From: The Natural History of Innovation*. New York: Riverhead Books, 2010.

Jones, Kevin Doyle. "Neighborhood Economics: Local Funding for Entrepreneurs without a Rich Uncle." *Impact Alpha*, August 4, 2017. https://impactalpha.com/neighborhood-economics-emerging-ecosystem-approach-is-gaining-momentum-97ad2c143768/.

Jones, L. Gregory. *Christian Social Innovation: Renewing Wesleyan Witness*. Nashville: Abingdon, 2016.

Jones, L. Gregory, and Andy Hogue. *Navigating the Future: Traditioned Innovation for Wilder Seas*. Nashville: Abingdon, 2021.

Kelsey, David. *Eccentric Existence: A Theological Anthropology*. 2 vols. Louisville: Westminster John Knox, 2009.

Killen, Patricia O'Connell. "Introduction—Patterns of the Past, Prospects for the Future: Religion in the None Zone." In *Religion & Public Life in the Pacific Northwest:*

The None Zone, edited by Patricia O'Connell Killen and Mark Silk, 9–20. Walnut Creek, Calif.: AltaMira Press, 2004.

———. "Memory, Novelty and Possibility in This Place." In *Cascadia: The Elusive Utopia: Exploring the Spirit of the Pacific Northwest*, edited by Douglas Todd, 65–85. Vancouver, B.C.: Ronsdale Press, 2008.

Killen, Patricia O'Connell, and Mark Shibley, "Surveying the Religious Landscape: Historical Trends and Current Patterns in Oregon, Washington, and Alaska." In *Religion & Public Life in the Pacific Northwest: The None Zone*, edited by Patricia O'Connell Killen and Mark Silk, 25–49. Walnut Creek, Calif.: AltaMira Press, 2004.

Killen, Patricia O'Connell, and Mark Silk, eds. *Religion & Public Life in the Pacific Northwest: The None Zone*. Walnut Creek, Calif.: AltaMira Press, 2004.

King, David. "The Surprising Financial Strength of American Congregations." *Insights Newsletter*, January 28, 2020. https://philanthropy.iupui.edu/news-events/insights-newsletter/2020-issues/january-2020-issue-2.html.

Klemme, E. J., and B. F. Kumler in *The Pacific Northwest Pulpit*. Compiled by Paul Little. New York: United Methodist Book Concern, 1915.

Klienbaum, Adam M. "Organizational Misfits and the Origins of Brokerage in Intrafirm Networks." *Administrative Science Quarterly* 57, no. 3 (2012): 407–52.

Knight, Mark. "Sin and Salvation." In *The Oxford Handbook of Dietrich Bonhoeffer*, edited by Michael Mawson and Philip Ziegler, 210–24. New York: Oxford University Press, 2019.

Kraatz, Matthew, ed. *Institutions and Ideals: Philip Selznick's Legacy for Organizational Studies*. Research in the Sociology of Organizations 44. Bingley, UK: Emerald Group, 2015.

Kraatz, Matthew, and Ricardo Flores. "Reinfusing Values." In *Institutions and Ideals: Philip Selznick's Legacy for Organizational Studies*, edited by Matthew Kraatz, 353–81. Research in the Sociology of Organizations 44. Bingley, UK: Emerald Group, 2015.

Kuyper, Abraham. *Rooted & Grounded: The Church as Organism and Institution*. Translated by Nelson Kloosterman. Grand Rapids: Christian's Library Press, 2013.

Lamott, Anne. *Traveling Mercies: Some Thoughts on Faith*. New York: Pantheon Books, 1999.

Leadership Education at Duke Divinity School. "Reflective Leadership Grants." Accessed November 10, 2008. https://leadership.divinity.duke.edu/what-we-offer/grants/reflective-leadership-grants/.

Ledbetter, Bernice, Robert Banks, and David Greenhalgh. *Reviewing Leadership: A Christian Evaluation of Current Approaches*. 2nd ed. Grand Rapids: Baker Academic, 2016.

Lynch, Chloe. *Ecclesial Leadership as Friendship: Explorations in Practical, Pastoral and Empirical Theology*. New York: Routledge, 2019.

MacIntyre, Alasdair. *Ethics in the Conflict of Modernity: An Essay on Desire, Practical Reason, and Narrative*. Cambridge: Cambridge University Press, 2016.

———. *Whose Justice? Which Rationality?* Notre Dame, Ind.: University of Notre Dame Press, 1988.

Mack, Dwayne A. *Black Spokane: The Civil Rights Struggle in the Inland Northwest*. Norman: University of Oklahoma Press, 2014.

Maddox, Randy. "Practical Theology: A Discipline in Search of a Definition." *Perspectives in Religious Studies* 18 (1991): 159–69.

Magatti, Mauro. Introduction to *Social Generativity: A Relational Paradigm for Social Change*, edited by Mauro Magatti. London: Routledge, 2018.

Malina, Bruce, and John Pilch. *Social-Science Commentary on the Book of Acts*. Minneapolis: Fortress, 2008.

Marsh, Charles. Introduction to *Lived Theology: New Perspectives on Method, Style, and Pedagogy*. New York: Oxford University Press, 2017.

———. *Reclaiming Dietrich Bonhoeffer: The Promise of His Theology*. Oxford: Oxford University Press, 1994.

Marti, Gerardo. "Emerging Christianity through a Social Scientific Lens: The ECM as a Case of Religious Institutional Entrepreneurship." In *Crossing Boundaries, Redefining Faith: Interdisciplinary Perspectives on the Emerging Church Movement*, edited by Michael Clawson and April Stace, 45–70. Eugene, Ore.: Wipf & Stock, 2016.

Marti, Gerardo, and Gladys Ganiel. *The Deconstructed Church: Understanding Emerging Christianity*. Oxford: Oxford University Press, 2014.

Mawson, Michael. *Christ Existing as Community: Bonhoeffer's Ecclesiology*. Oxford: Oxford University Press, 2018.

McKnight, John, and Peter Block. *The Abundant Community: Awakening the Power of Families and Neighborhoods*. San Francisco: Berrett-Koehler, 2010.

McKnight, Scot, Kevin Corcoran, Peter Rollins, and Jason Clark. *Church in the Present Tense: A Candid Look at What's Emerging*. Grand Rapids: Brazos, 2011.

Menand, Louis. "An Introduction to Pragmatism." In *Pragmatism: A Reader*, edited by Louis Menand, xi–xxiv. New York: Vintage Books, 1997.

Metzger, Bruce. *A Textual Commentary on the Greek New Testament*. New York: United Bible Society, 1994.

Miller-McLemore, Bonnie J. *Christian Theology in Practice: Discovering a Discipline*. Grand Rapids: Eerdmans, 2012.

———. "Disciplining: Academic Theology and Practical Knowledge." In *Christian Practical Wisdom: What It Is, Why It Matters*, by Dorothy C. Bass, Kathleen A. Cahalan, Bonnie J. Miller-McLemore, James R. Nieman, and Christian B. Scharen, 175–231. Grand Rapids: Eerdmans, 2016.

———. "Introduction: The Contributions of Practical Theology." In *The Wiley-Blackwell Companion to Practical Theology*, edited by Bonnie J. Miller-McLemore, 1–20. Malden, Mass.: Wiley-Blackwell, 2012.

M. J. Murdock Charitable Trust. "About the Trust." Accessed January 17, 2020. https://murdocktrust.org/about-the-trust/.

MOHAI. "Bezos Center for Innovation." Accessed December 6, 2018. https://mohai.org/exhibit/bezos-center-for-innovation/.

Moltmann, Jürgen. *The Church in the Power of the Spirit*. Minneapolis: Fortress, 1993.

Momennejad, Ida, Ajua Duker, and Alin Coman, "Bridge Ties Bind Collective Memories." *Nature Communications* 10 (2019). doi: 10.1038/s41467-019-09452-y.

Montemaggi, Vittorio. *Reading Dante's* Commedia *as Theology: Divinity Realized in Human Encounter*. Oxford: Oxford University Press, 2016.

Moynagh, Michael. *Church in Life: Innovation, Mission, and Ecclesiology*. Eugene, Ore.: Cascade, 2018.

Murthy, Vivek. *Together: The Healing Power of Connections in a Sometimes Lonely World*. New York: HarperCollins, 2020.

News Tribune Editorial Board. "Yes, Tacoma's Historic Churches Can Be Rescued. Let's Celebrate This Success Story." *News Tribune*, April 6, 2021. https://www.thenewstribune.com/opinion/editorials/article250450861.html?fbclid=IwAR3GVlAK-zF4LDAmzVnHFiH7XKT87K7c1lRVM02-rrT-KMdG4r2JpVE1cT0.

Niebuhr, H. Richard. *The Meaning of Revelation*. New York: Macmillan, 1946.

O'Donovan, Oliver. *Self, World and Time*. Vol. 1 of *Ethics as Theology*. Grand Rapids: Eerdmans, 2013.

Oliver, Mary. "When I Am among the Trees." In *Poetry of Presence: An Anthology of Mindfulness Poems*, edited by Phyllis Cole-Dai and Ruby R. Wilson, 44. West Hartford, Conn.: Grayson Books, 2017.

Osmer, Richard. *Practical Theology: An Introduction*. Grand Rapids: Eerdmans, 2008.

Pacific Northwest Church Planting Movement. "Home." Accessed October 1, 2018. https://www.pnwmovement.com/.

Packard, Josh. *The Emerging Church: Religion on the Margins*. Boulder, Colo.: Lynne Rienner/FirstForumPress, 2012.

Parish Collective. "6-Series Document." 2019.

———. "About." Accessed June 1, 2019. https://parishcollective.org/about/.

———. "Connect." Accessed December 5, 2018. https://parishcollective.org/join-in/.

———. "Learn How It Works." Accessed June 1, 2019. (A website update in 2021 no longer includes this exact language. For the latest description of their work, see https://www.parishcollective.org/.)

———. "New Parish Learning Communities." Handout. 2019.

Parks, Sharon. "A Convocation of Ecclesial Entrepreneurs." March 30–31, 2021.

———. *Leadership Can Be Taught: A Bold Approach for a Complex World*. Boston: Harvard Business School Publishing, 2005.

Pervo, Richard. *Acts: A Commentary*. Minneapolis: Fortress, 2009.

Pew Research Center. "In U.S., Decline of Christianity Continues at Rapid Pace: An Update on America's Changing Religious Landscape." October 17, 2019. https://

www.pewforum.org/2019/10/17/in-u-s-decline-of-christianity-continues-at-rapid-pace/.

Pfeffer, Jeffrey. *New Directions for Organizational Theory: Problems and Prospects*. New York: Oxford University Press, 1997.

Podolny, Joel. "Networks as Pipes and Prisms of the Market." *American Journal of Sociology* 107, no. 1 (2001): 33–60.

Powell, Walter. "Expanding the Scope of Institutional Analysis." In *The New Institutionalism in Organizational Analysis*, edited by Walter Powell and Paul DiMaggio, 183–203. Chicago: University of Chicago Press, 1991.

———. "Neither Market nor Hierarchy: Network Forms of Organization." *Research in Organizational Behavior* 12 (1990): 295–336.

Ranie, Lee, and Berry Wellman. *Networked: The New Social Operating System*. Cambridge, Mass.: MIT Press, 2012.

Rasmussen, Larry. "Shaping Communities." In *Practicing Our Faith: A Way of Life for a Searching People*, 2nd ed., edited by Dorothy C. Bass, 117–30. San Francisco: Jossey-Bass, 2010.

Rendle, Gil. *Quietly Courageous: Leading the Church in a Changing World*. Lanham, Md.: Rowman & Littlefield, 2019.

Reyes, Patrick. "Grandma's Table: Memories of Survival and Adaptation." In *Crisis and Care: Meditations on Faith and Philanthropy*, edited by Dustin Benac and Erin Weber-Johnson, 49–54. Eugene, Ore.: Cascade, 2021.

———. *Nobody Cries When We Die: God, Community, and Surviving to Adulthood*. Atlanta: Chalice Press, 2016.

———. *The Purpose Gap: Empowering Communities of Color to Find Meaning and Thrive*. Louisville: Westminster John Knox, 2021.

Robinson, Bill. "Academics." *Of Mind and Heart*, December 2001. https://digitalcommons.whitworth.edu/cgi/viewcontent.cgi?article=1010&context=mind-and-heart.

Roozen, David, and James Nieman, eds. *Church, Identity, and Change: Theology and Denominational Structure in Unsettled Times*. Grand Rapids: Eerdmans, 2005.

Rowe, C. Kavin. *Early Narrative Christology: The Lord in the Gospel of Luke*. Berlin: de Gruyter, 2006.

———. "Ecclesiology in Acts." *Interpretation: A Journal of Bible and Theology* 66, no. 3 (2012): 259–69.

———. *One True Life: The Stoics and Early Christians as Rival Traditions*. New Haven, Conn.: Yale University Press, 2016.

———. *World Upside Down: Reading Acts in the Graeco-Roman Age*. Oxford: Oxford University Press, 2009.

Roxburgh, Alan. *Joining God in the Great Unraveling: Where We Are & What I've Learned*. Eugene, Ore.: Cascade, 2021.

Ruef, Martin. "The Emergence of Organizational Forms: A Community Ecology Approach." *American Journal of Sociology* 106, no. 3 (2000): 658–714.

———. *The Entrepreneurial Group: Social Identities, Relations, and Collective Action.* Princeton, N.J.: Princeton University Press, 2010.

Scharen, Christian, and Aana Marie Vigen, eds. *Ethnography as Christian Theology and Ethics.* New York: Continuum, 2011.

Scharen, Christian, and Eileen Campbell-Reed. "Learning Pastoral Imagination: A Five-Year Report on How New Ministers Learn in Practice." *Auburn Studies* 21 (2016): 1–61.

Scheitle, Christopher. *Beyond the Congregation: The World of Christian Nonprofits.* New York: Oxford University Press, 2010.

Schwartz, Barry, and Kenneth Sharpe. *Practical Wisdom: The Right Way to Do the Right Thing.* New York: Riverhead Books, 2010.

Scott, W. Richard. *Institutions and Organizations: Ideas, Interests, and Identities.* 4th ed. London: Sage, 2014.

Scott, W. Richard, and Gerald F. Davis. *Organizations and Organizing: Rational, Natural, and Open Systems Perspectives.* Upper Saddle River, N.J.: Pearson, 2007.

Seattle Impact Hall. "About Us." Accessed December 1, 2018. https://impacthubseattle.com/.

Seattle Pacific University. "Five Hundred Years Ago Today." Facebook, October 31, 2017. https://m.facebook.com/story/graphql_permalink/?graphql_id=UzpfSTEyNDU5ODQ3MDk2NTk2MDoxNTM4OTQzNzk2MTk4MDgw.

Seattle School of Theology & Psychology. "Dr. Craig Detweiler Resigns as President." February 27, 2019. https://theseattleschool.edu/blog/craig-detweiler-resigns-president/.

Seattle Times Staff. "The Unchurched Northwest." *Seattle Times*, October 11, 2005. https://www.seattletimes.com/opinion/the-unchurched-northwest/.

Seely, Mike. "For a Seattle Enclave, Isolation May Be Its Salvation." *New York Times*, April 12, 2019. https://www.nytimes.com/2019/04/12/travel/seattle-south-park.html.

Selznick, Philip. "On Sustaining Research Agendas: Their Moral and Scientific Basis." In *Institutions and Ideals: Philip Selznick's Legacy for Organizational Studies*, edited by Matthew Kraatz, 9–20. Research in the Sociology of Organizations 44. Bingley, UK: Emerald Group, 2015.

Shakespeare, Lyndon. *Being the Body of Christ in the Age of Management.* Eugene, Ore.: Cascade, 2016.

Sharman, Linda. "The Seeley Mudd Chapel—Making a House a Home." *Whitworth Alumni Magazine* 48, no. 1 (1979): 1.

Silk, Mark. "The Pacific Northwest Is the American Religious Future." *Religion News Service*, June 4, 2019. https://religionnews.com/2019/05/31/the-pacific-northwest-is-the-american-religious-future/.

Simons, Herbert. *Administrative Behavior: A Study of Decision-Making Processes in Administrative Organization.* 2nd ed. New York: Macmillan, 1957.

Singleton, Royce, and Bruce Straights. *Approaches to Social Research*. 5th ed. New York: Oxford University Press, 2005.

Sittser, Gerald. *Resilient Faith: How the Early Christian "Third Way" Changed the World*. Grand Rapids: Brazos, 2019.

Sittser, Jerry. *A Grace Disguised: How the Soul Grows through Loss*. Expanded ed. Grand Rapids: Zondervan, 2004.

Smith, D. Brent, Benjamin Schneider, and Marcus Dickson. "Meso Organizational Behavior: Comments on the Third Paradigm." In *The Sage Handbook of Organization Studies*, 2nd ed., edited by Steward Clegg, Cynthia Hardy, Thomas Lawrence, and Walter Nord, 149–64. London: Sage, 2006.

Smith, James K. A. *Desiring the Kingdom: Worship, Worldview, and Cultural Formation*. Grand Rapids: Baker Academic, 2009.

Soden, Dale E. "Contesting the Soul of an Unlikely Land: Mainline Protestants, Catholics, and Reform and Conservative Jews in the Pacific Northwest." In *Religion & Public Life in the Pacific Northwest: The None Zone*, edited by Patricia O'Connell Killen and Mark Silk, 51–77. Walnut Creek, Calif.: AltaMira Press, 2004.

———. *Outsiders in a Promised Land: Religious Activists in Pacific Northwest History*. Corvallis: Oregon State University Press, 2015.

Sokol, Chad. "Moody Bible Institute to Close Spokane Campus." *Spokesman-Review*, November 10, 2017. www.spokesman.com/stories/2017/nov/10/moody-bible-institute-to-close-spokane-campus/.

Soerens, Tim. *Everywhere You Look: Discovering the Church Right Where You Are*. Downers Grove, Ill.: InterVarsity Press, 2020.

Soerens, Tim, and Christiana Rice. "Five Hopeful Signs That Dare Us to Be the Church." *Parish Collective*, March 29, 2016. https://medium.com/parish-collective/five-hopeful-signs-that-dare-us-to-be-the-church-641b75239e2c.

Sparks, Paul, Tim Soerens, and Dwight Friesen. *The New Parish: How the Neighborhood Is Transforming Mission, Discipleship and Community*. Downers Grove, Ill.: InterVarsity Press, 2014.

Stark, Rodney. *The Rise of Christianity: How the Obscure, Marginal Jesus Movement Became the Dominant Religious Force in the Western World in a Few Centuries*. San Francisco: Harper, 1997.

Sullivan, William. Introduction to *Educating Clergy: Teaching Practices and Pastoral Imagination*, by Charles R. Foster, Lisa E. Dahill, Lawrence A. Goleman, and Barbara Wang Tolentino. San Francisco: Jossey-Bass, 2006.

Swinton, John. *Dementia: Living in the Memories of God*. Grand Rapids: Eerdmans, 2012.

Swinton, John, and Harriet Mowat. *Practical Theology and Qualitative Research*. 2nd ed. London: SCM Press, 2016.

Talbert, Charles. *Reading Acts: A Literary and Theological Commentary*. Macon, Ga.: Smyth & Helwys, 2005.

Tanner, Kathryn. *Christianity and the New Spirit of Capitalism*. New Haven, Conn.: Yale University Press, 2019.

Taylor, Charles. *A Secular Age*. Cambridge, Mass.: Harvard University Press, 2007.

Taylor, Henry Louis, Jr., and Gavin Luter. *Anchor Institutions: An Interpretive Review Essay*. Buffalo, N.Y.: Anchor Institutions Task Force, 2013.

Taylor, Steve. *First Expressions: Innovation and the Mission of God*. London: SCM Press, 2019.

Tickle, Phyllis. *Emergence Christianity*. Grand Rapids: Baker, 2012.

Todd, Douglas. Introduction to *Cascadia: The Elusive Utopia: Exploring the Spirit of the Pacific Northwest*, edited by Douglas Todd, 1–29. Vancouver, B.C.: Ronsdale Press, 2008.

Tönnies, Ferdinand. *Community and Civil Society*. Edited by Jose Harris. Translated by Jose Harris and Margaret Hollis. Cambridge: Cambridge University Press, 2001.

Tracey, Paul, Nelson Phillips, and Michael Lounsbury. "Taking Religion Seriously in the Study of Organizations." In *Religion and Organization Theory*, edited by Paul Tracey, Nelson Phillips, and Michael Lounsbury, 3–21. Research in the Sociology of Organizations 41. Bingley, UK: Emerald Group, 2014.

Uhr, John. *Prudential Public Leadership: Promoting Ethics in Public Policy and Administration*. New York: Palgrave Macmillan, 2015.

United States Census Bureau. QuickFacts. Accessed October 3, 2018. https://www.census.gov/quickfacts/fact/table/US/PST045219.

United Youth Ministry Network. "Top." https://unitedspokane.org/.

University of Washington. "Climate in the Pacific Northwest." Accessed February 18, 2020. https://cig.uw.edu/learn/.

Ward, Pete. *Introducing Practical Theology: Mission, Ministry, and the Life of the Church*. Grand Rapids: Baker Academic, 2017.

Warner, R. Stephen. "The Place of the Congregation in the Contemporary American Religious Configuration." In *New Perspectives in the Study of Congregations*, edited by James Wind and James Lewis, 54–99. Vol. 2 of *American Congregations*. Chicago: University of Chicago Press, 1994.

Washington Hospitality Association. *Washington State Visitors' Guide*, 2018.

Watkins, Clare. "Organizing the People of God: Social-Science Theories of Organization in Ecclesiology." *Theological Studies* 52 (1991): 689–711.

Weems, Lovette. *Church Leadership: Vision, Team, Culture, and Integrity*. Rev. ed. Nashville: Abingdon, 2010.

Welch, Claude. *The Reality of the Church*. New York: Charles Scribner's Sons, 1958.

Wellman, James. "The Churching of the Pacific Northwest: The Rise of Sectarian Entrepreneurs." In *Religion & Public Life in the Pacific Northwest: The None Zone*, edited by Patricia O'Connell Killen and Mark Silk, 79–105. Walnut Creek, Calif.: AltaMira Press, 2004.

———. *Evangelical vs. Liberal: The Clash of Christian Cultures in the Pacific Northwest*. New York: Oxford University Press, 2008.

Wells, Samuel. *Improvisation: The Drama of Christian Ethics*. Grand Rapids: Brazos, 2004.
———. *Incarnational Ministry: Being with the Church*. Grand Rapids: Eerdmans, 2017.
———. *Incarnational Mission: Being with the World*. Grand Rapids: Eerdmans, 2018.
———. *A Nazareth Manifesto: Being with God*. Malden, Mass.: John Wiley & Sons, 2015.
Wexler, Mark. "Conjectures on Workplace Spirituality in Cascadia." In *Cascadia: The Elusive Utopia: Exploring the Spirit of the Pacific Northwest*, edited by Douglas Todd, 215–39. Vancouver, B.C.: Ronsdale Press, 2008.
Whitworth University. "Academy of Christian Discipleship." Accessed September 28, 2018. https://www.whitworth.edu/cms/administration/church-engagement/academy-of-christian-discipleship/.
———. "The Campaign for Whitworth." *Whitworth Today* 87, no. 2 (2018): 5.
———. "Office of Church Engagement." Accessed September 28, 2018. https://www.whitworth.edu/cms/administration/church-engagement/.
———. "Statement of Denominational Relationship." Accessed October 10, 2018. https://www.whitworth.edu/cms/about/statement-on-denominational-relationships/.
———. "Whitworth Awarded $1 Million from Lilly Endowment to Fund Ekklesia Project, New Office of Church Engagement." *Whitworth University News*, December 4, 2013. https://news.whitworth.edu/2013/12/whitworth-awarded-1-million-from-lilly.html.
———. "Whitworth Institute for Ministry Conference Set for July 23–27." *Whitworth University News*, July 20, 2018. https://news.whitworth.edu/2018/06/whitworth-institute-of-ministry.html.
———. "Whitworth Ministry Summit Promo." YouTube video, March 5, 2019, 1:02. https://www.youtube.com/watch?time_continue=4&v=qwteIqw44JQ.
———. "Whitworth Receives $1 Million Grant from Lilly Endowment Inc. to Create New Christian Churches." *Whitworth University News*, October 29, 2018. https://news.whitworth.edu/2018/10/whitworth-receives-1-million-grant-from.html.
"Why Is Dietrich Bonhoeffer Relevant Today?" *Faith & Leadership*, November 26, 2019. https://faithandleadership.com/why-dietrich-bonhoeffer-relevant-today.
Wigg-Stevenson, Natalie. *Ethnographic Theology: An Inquiry into the Production of Theological Knowledge*. New York: Palgrave Macmillan, 2014.
Wilde, Melissa J., Kristin Geraty, Shelley L. Nelson, and Emily A. Bowman. "Religious Economy or Organizational Field? Predicting Bishops' Votes at the Second Vatican Council." *American Sociological Review* 75, no. 4 (2010): 586–606.
Williams, Reggie L. *Bonhoeffer's Black Jesus: Harlem's Renaissance Theology and an Ethic of Resistance*. Waco, Tex.: Baylor University Press, 2014.
Wince, Trey. "Trump, Vegan Soup, and Automobiles." In *Crisis and Care: Meditations on Faith and Philanthropy*, edited by Dustin Benac and Erin Weber-Johnson, 33–38. Eugene, Ore.: Cascade, 2021.
Wingfield, Nick. "Next Big Tech Corridor? Between Seattle and Vancouver, Planners Hope." *New York Times*, October 2, 2016. https://www.nytimes.com/2016/10/03/technology/next-big-tech-corridor-between-seattle-and-vancouver-planners-hope.html.

Winner, Lauren. *The Dangers of Christian Practice: On Wayward Gifts, Characteristic Damage, and Sin.* New Haven, Conn.: Yale University Press, 2018.

Wolterstorff, Nicholas. *In This World of Wonders: Memoir of a Life in Learning.* Grand Rapids: Eerdmans, 2019.

Wong, Debbie. "A Prayer in Search of Holy Connection." *The Work of the People.* Accessed December 20, 2020. https://www.theworkofthepeople.com/prayer-in-search-of-holy-connection.

Wordsworth, William. *The Prelude.* Edited by J. C. Maxwell. New Haven, Conn.: Yale University Press, 1971.

World Relief Spokane. "About Us." Accessed October 1, 2018. https://worldreliefspokane.org/mission.

Yin, Robert. *Case Study Research and Applications: Design and Methods.* 6th ed. London: Sage, 2018.

Yong, Amos. *Renewing the Church by the Spirit: Theological Education after Pentecost.* Grand Rapids: Eerdmans, 2020.

Zald, Mayer. "Organization Studies as a Scientific and Humanistic Enterprise: Toward a Reconceptualization of the Foundations of the Field." *Organization Science* 4, no. 2 (1993): 513–28.

Zeller, Dieter. *Exegetical Dictionary of the New Testament.* Vol. 1. Edited by Horst Balz and Gerhard Schneider. Grand Rapids: Eerdmans, 1999.

Index of Subjects

adaptive: adaptive challenges, 86, 276n77; adaptive change, 60, 67–71, 81, 92–93, 95–96, 104, 126, 132–40, 148, 184, 199, 212, 230–33; adaptive leadership, 89, 212; adaptive wisdom, 70, 89, 100; adaptive work, 11, 13, 33, 43, 69, 71–77, 86–88, 92–100, 105–26, 140–42, 170–78, 184–85, 199–203, 212–13
Alki Beach, 218
anthropology, 259n25, 259n29
Aurora Commons, 56
authority, 4, 86, 88–93, 95, 222; academic and clerical paradigms, 90–91; axes of innovation, 191, 194; for early Christians, 176, 187, 292n11; leadership, 191, 194, 206; reimagined, 165

being with, xvii, 184–99, 203–13, 226, 292n12, 293n21
belonging, ix, 32, 48, 53, 69–71, 75, 79, 84, 96, 99, 101, 154, 157–67, 171–75, 178–79, 186–87, 193, 218–19, 223, 225–26, 230, 232, 283n44
Birmingham, Ala., 51
Boise, Ida., 33, 147, 235, 266n49

boundary zone, 83–85, 87, 174; challenge of, 2, 13, 77, 79–80, 96; possibility, 90, 220, 226; uncertainty, 87, 168, 174

Cascade Mountains, 55, 269n43
Cascadia, 5, 53, 54, 57; *see also* Pacific Northwest
Catholic, 1, 257n8, 270n75, 291n2
Chicago, Ill., 22, 100, 145
Christian education, 3, 20, 71, 91, 226, 295n20, 296n22
Christian practical wisdom, 6, 9–14, 71, 110, 124–26, 237, 261n42; conditions for, 151; defined, 9, 185–86; in an adaptive church, 180, 184, 186, 211, 214, 232
Christian Practical Wisdom: What It Is, Why It Matters, 9, 261n45, 261n46, 262n48, 262n49, 272n15, 279n51, 279n52, 280n3, 280n9, 291n4
Christian practice, 21, 36, 134, 171, 231, 233, 260n34, 280n2
church planting, 30, 264n22; church planting networks, 40, 118; examples of, 36–37, 264n34
Cincinnati, Ohio, 46, 51

Cliff/Cannon, South Hill, 52
collective learning, 10, 87–88; *see also* questions
Columbia Plateau, 33
Columbia River, 33, 103
Community: The Structure of Belonging, 267n11
connection, 4–5, 10–13, 18–27, 55–74, 85–87, 98, 99, 104–19, 141–43, 154–55, 166, 169–72, 218, 220–28, 253, 270n59, 294n5; belonging, 53, 178, 187; disconnection, 44, local, 34, 48, 124, 149, 199; leadership, 189–95, 199, 208–14, 293n27; *see also* collaboration
convening, 20, 30, 45, 49, 51, 74, 103, 149, 156, 193, 203–5, 253, 273n24, 297n11; practical theology, 236
COVID-19: challenges of, 81, 82, 252–53; pandemic, 4, 76, 81, 82, 83, 219; post-pandemic, 4, 82; pre-pandemic, 81, 82; response to, 82, 171, 253; *see also* crisis
crisis, 57, 67–68, 83, 89, 91, 209, 252, 290n88; possibility, 219; response to, 96, 122, 209; *see also* precarity

denominations, 41, 144, 270n72, 276n4, 277n11; Christian Reformed Church, 45; Methodist, 51, 81, 296n26; Presbyterian, 28, 35, 36, 37
Discipleship, 172, 287n48

ecclesial ecology, 3, 10–13, 20, 103–4, 152, 164, 186, 219–21, 232, 293n34; adaptive possibility, 224–31; as place, 140–42; as prism, 143–48, 282n42; defined, 8, 139; leadership, 191–215; level of analysis, 234–35, 260n40; shifting, 67, 125–26, 133, 150, 179, 187, 283n43; vitality, 9, 151, 170, 176
ecclesiology, 183, 228, 233, 234, 260n38, 267m16, 290n83
economics, 33, 286n31
ecumenism, 74

Elliott Bay, 218
Emergent Church, 58, 270n58
Emerging Church: Emergent Village network, 58; Emerging-Missional traditions, 12, 57–60; tradition, 57–59
entrepreneurship: ecclesial, 191, 199, 201, 206, 211; in the Pacific Northwest, 3, 23; religious, 3, 53, 120; research on, 92, 176, 263n16, 270n66
ethnography: *see* qualitative research

Faith & Leadership, 284n3
finances, 79; funding, 22–23, 30, 45–48, 94, 116, 174, 221, 229–30, 275n71; stability, 2, 13, 79, 221–22, 273n30; *see also* economics
formation, 7, 10, 11, 32, 52, 58, 70, 71, 88, 92, 94, 109, 110, 111, 115, 121, 134, 135, 140–41, 147, 150, 152, 162–65, 168, 277n14
friendship, 21, 22, 25, 43, 44, 69, 93, 106, 107, 111, 112, 140, 175, 176, 187, 209, 222, 226 230, 263n20, 294n35
Fuller Theological Seminary, 115, 124, 258n8

Gemeinschaft, 160, 161, 163, 287n44
Gen X, 45
Gesellschaft, 160, 161, 286n31, 286n38, 287n44
Growing in the Life of Faith, 259n34, 280n2, 281n18, 283n45, 283n46, 283n49, 283n51, 283n52, 284n57

Hamilton, Ontario, 51
holding environments: *see* organizational environments
hope, 2, 19, 27, 39, 80–81, 84, 100–101, 179, 206, 210, 216, 220, 224, 252, 264n25, 273n31, 289n77

imagination, 6, 10, 17 32, 53, 60, 70–74, 90–91, 100, 110, 132, 144, 149, 156, 179, 193, 196, 210, 213–15, 218, 222, 224, 226, 229, 230, 282n32, 282n33, 294n1; Christian imagination, 281n9; collective imagination, 9, 51–52,

133, 157, 219, 276n74; conjunctive imagination, 220, 231; ecclesial imagination, 8, 10, 12, 14, 131, 133–43, 145–48, 150–55, 164, 169–70, 176–78, 214, 225–27; pastoral imagination, 131, 133–43, 145, 148, 150–55, 214
improvisation, 153
Inland Northwest, 17, 26, 32, 33, 35, 265n36
innovation, 3, 5–6, 32, 34, 53, 60, 6–68, 75, 80, 91–92, 120, 132–33, 152, 154, 165, 173, 185, 190–91, 201, 205, 210, 212, 223, 226–30, 273n31
institutions: changing, 2, 3, 19, 60, 124; connection to, 4–5, 48, 136, 141, 223; distrust, 26, 264n21; educational, 2, 13, 20, 26, 33, 90, 105, 123, 142, 145, 147, 183, 226; hubs, 13, 104, 121, 219; leading within, 190, 205–6, 223; new, 3, 135, 151, 230
isolation, 2, 13, 40–44, 55, 79–80, 83, 85–86, 89, 95, 143, 150, 158, 173, 175, 187; *see also* loneliness

landscapes: cultural, 5, 20; geographic, 5, 17, 33, 53; religious, 36, 81–83, 150–51; shifting, 2, 13, 30, 61, 108, 184; social, 4, 5, 53, 195, 207–9
leadership: Caretaker, 187, 189, 190, 198, 199–200, 203–5, 208; Catalyst, 187, 190–91, 198–201, 203, 205–6, 208–9; Champion, 187, 190–92, 198–200, 203, 206–10, 230, 293n28; Connector-Convener, 187, 192–95, 198, 201, 203, 205, 208–10, 229, 293n32; Guide, 187, 197–202, 206, 208; Surveyor, 187, 195–96, 198–201, 203, 205, 207–9, 230, 293n21
Leadership Can Be Taught, 280n4, 280n5, 281n20, 294n37, 294n38
leadership teams, 199, 202–3
Leadership Without Easy Answers, 262n55, 271n8, 271n12, 272n15, 272n17, 273n26, 273n27, 275n51, 275n52, 275n53, 276n68, 276n77, 276n82, 283n43, 294n38, 296n27
Life Together, 171, 172
life together, 40, 48, 54, 84, 98, 146, 154–56, 168, 218; belonging, 159–62; possibility, 162–65; relation, 157–59; *see also* community
Lilly Endowment, 22, 45, 48, 208, 263n10, 263n12, 263n15, 269n27, 282n36
local church, 20–21, 25–26, 28, 30, 36, 40, 74, 136, 170
loneliness, 2, 13, 41, 44, 51, 79–80, 83, 95
loss, 83

M. J. Murdock Charitable Trust, xi, 22, 28, 94, 193, 205, 235, 268n24, 268n25
mainline, 1, 12, 28, 35–37, 58, 100, 126, 136, 201
methods: *see* qualitative research
Ministry Partner Network, 24, 29, 114, 116
missional church, 12, 57–60, 126
Missoula, Mont., 24, 28, 31, 33, 34, 262n47, 266n49

The Navigators, 47
neighborhood, 1–2, 12, 34, 36, 39–59, 67–68, 72–73, 79, 81–82, 85–88, 92, 95, 97–98, 106–7, 116, 124, 131, 136–38, 146–50, 155–56, 164, 189, 194, 199–201, 209, 219, 225, 267n6, 267n16, 270n72, 282n38; *see also* parish
network: Christian thought and practice, 10, 58, 69, 168–70, 187, 222, 289n78; disequilibrium, 69, 93; Ministry Partner Network, 24–29, 35–36; neighborhood, 39–40, 48, 51, 124, 268n2; network theory, 11, 104–5, 108–20, 258n15, 278n18; rebuilding, 19–23, 31, 41, 43, 49, 60, 85, 95, 138, 142–43; reflexive ecclesiology network, 234

The Northwest Church Planting Networks, 118
Office of Church Engagement: adaptive possibilities, 221–24; challenges, 75–78; collaborators, 20–23; mission, 18–20; place, 32–35; programmatic structure, 24–32; tradition, 35–37; values, 71–75
On Thinking Institutionally, 264n21
Opportunity Presbyterian Church, 154
Organizational Ecology, 279n44, 279n46, 279n47, 280n56, 280n57, 280n58, 280n60
organizational environments, 3, 104; ambiguous set, 12, 92, 95, 200, 221; fixed set, 12, 92, 94, 200–201, 221, 225
organizational fields, 105, 108, 120, 260n40, 277n11, 284n61
organizational theory, 7–8, 104–5, 139, 272n15
Overlake Christian Church, 143

Pacific Northwest: American religious future, 3–6, 215; defined, 262n47; entrepreneurship, 13, 70, 265n39; ministry, 20, 22, 31, 71, 96, 98, 100; religious life, 12, 26, 32–35, 37, 53–58, 60, 74, 108, 166, 258n14; way of life, 154–57; *see also* Cascadia
Pacific Northwest Church Planting Movement, 30, 36, 264n34
Pacific Northwest Presbytery, 22
parish, 39–42, 45–46, 48–49, 52, 59, 79, 98, 116, 122, 133, 137, 143, 146–47, 156, 186, 197; *see also* neighborhood
Parish Collective: adaptive possibilities, 221–24; challenges, 70–80; collaborators, 43–48; mission, 40–42; place, 53–57; programmatic structure, 48–53; tradition, 57–60; values, 71–75
The Parish Project, 45
philanthropy, 4, 71, 197, 230, 259

phronesis, 155, 194, 261n42, 281n16, 291n8; *see also* Christian practical wisdom
Pike Place Market, 45, 131
polarities, 188, 207, 208–11
Portland, Oreg., 1, 2, 3, 5, 8, 10, 39, 44, 46, 53, 54, 93, 100, 106, 112, 146, 235, 265n46
possibility, 5, 10, 42, 44–45, 53, 60, 69, 83–87, 93, 107–8, 124, 132, 134, 140, 142, 147, 150–52, 154, 157, 160, 162–65, 168, 172–73, 175, 179, 217–31
post-Christendom, 2, 3, 13, 19, 27, 31, 77, 79–80, 265n36
post-Christian, 31, 265n36
power, 27, 30, 60, 86–87, 156, 164–66, 168, 173, 178–79, 189, 219, 229, 236
practical theology, 6–9, 113, 148, 186, 212–14, 220, 236, 260n38, 261n43
Practical Theology and Qualitative Research, 260n38, 261n41, 261n43, 294n40, 297n8, 297n9
The Practice of Adaptive Leadership, 271n6
precarity, 68, 81, 83, 100, 166–67, 170, 175, 230; *see also* uncertainty

qualitative research, 233, 262n52, 295n16; ethnography, 260n36, 297n2, 297n3; methods, 8, 261n42
questions: for an adaptive church, 150–52; leadership, 191, 193–94, 198, 206–7; the power of questions, 86–89, 95, 275n58

race, 176, 178, 246, 249, 281n9, 290n99
Redmond, Wash., 143
Religion and Organization Theory, 273n15, 277n4
Resistencia Coffee, 39

Sacred Companies, 277n4, 279n53
Sanctorum Communio, 157–59, 172, 271n5, 285n8
San Diego, Calif., 46, 51

Seattle, Wash., 4, 5, 32, 34, 39, 44, 45, 46, 47, 48, 51, 53, 55, 56, 57, 59, 112, 123, 131, 146, 171, 183, 218, 219, 227, 235, 265n36, 265n46, 267n16

Seattle School of Theology & Psychology, 43, 46, 48, 51, 123, 268n22, 268n23, 268n24, 287n46

South Park neighborhood, 39

Spokane, Wash., 4, 17, 24, 29, 30, 32, 33, 34, 35, 36, 52, 55, 68, 73, 81, 98, 100, 112, 115, 122, 145, 146, 154, 208, 217, 235, 257n8, 264n12, 264n15, 264n34, 265n40, 265n44, 265n46, 266n47, 266n49, 269n40, 273n32

Spokane River, 32, 33, 34, 81

Spokane Valley, Wash., 32, 68, 154, 265n41, 265n42, 266n48

structure, 10, 41, 43, 69–71, 79, 86, 106, 139, 223, 276n74; belong, ix, 155, 162, 187, 230; Bonhoeffer, 160, 162–63; conditions for change, 95–100, 104, 109, 177; organizational studies, 112, 117, 120, 123–25

Tacoma, Wash., 39, 43, 44, 46, 112, 236, 259n31

theological education: academic paradigm, 90; clerical paradigm, 90–91; new models, 184, 226, 280n61

theological redescription, 154, 164–65, 173, 295n16

Thresholds, 47, 118

transformation: barriers, 33, 193; collective, 9, 69, 75, 87, 90, 96, 97–98, 100, 155–57, 162, 164–65, 186, 191, 194, 210; conditions, 121, 160–61, 163, 178, 186, 189, 213; imagination, 52, 136; individual, 97, 154–55; neighborhood, 39, 42, 53 79, 97; organizational, 13, 72, 84, 97, 157, 163, 187, 292n15

uncertainty, 3, 12, 67, 69, 77, 80–87, 92–93, 95, 100, 104, 121, 125–26, 140, 162, 166–75, 196, 202–3, 219–20, 224, 226, 230–32; *see also* precarity

United Kingdom, 51, 117, 268n31

V3, 118

values: in adaptive change, 11–13, 84, 92–93, 97, 213; in organizational studies, 105, 109; priority, 71–75, 208; structure, 69–70

Vancouver, B.C., 5, 53–55, 100, 112, 155

Vancouver, Wash., 103, 235

way of life, 6, 8, 72, 90, 153–56, 165, 179, 187, 224; early Christian, 166–67, 169–75, 289n83; neighborhood, 41; practical theology, 6–7, 134–35, 141, 212, 259n34

Whitworth University, 17, 20, 103, 118, 123, 263n5, 263n7, 263n10, 263n15, 264n23, 264n24, 264n26, 267n52; religious, 72, 90, 134, 143, 156, 166–67, 170, 171, 173, 175, 179, 224, 260n34, 289n83

Wiley-Blackwell Companion to Practical Theology, 259n33

World Relief, 29, 112, 118, 264n34

Young Life, 118

Index of Names

Adler, Paul, 260n28
Aldrich, Howard, 119, 272n13, 278n31, 278n32, 278n36, 278n39, 279n45, 287n48
Alighieri, Dante, 293n25
Ammerman, Nancy, 277n11, 283n41
Arntzen, Courtney, 24, 33, 138, 240–41, 262n47
Austin, Thad, 4, 241, 259n17
Ayres, Jennifer, x, 283n55, 296n30

Barber, Leroy, 272n18, 273n19, 296n26
Barth, Karl, 289n82
Bass, Dorothy C., 9, 260n34, 261n43, 261n45, 261n46, 281n22, 281n23, 281n24, 281n33
Beatrice, 198
Bell, Rob, 58
Benac, Dustin, 257n5, 259n17, 259n28, 261n42, 276n1, 276n82, 285n14, 291n3, 294n3, 294n8, 297n6, 297n7
Blanchard, Dave, 274n34
Block, Peter, 42, 159, 200, 267n7, 267n11, 295n10
Bockmuehl, Markus, 289n80
Bolsinger, Tod, 97, 276n78
Bonhoeffer, Dietrich, 13, 153, 271n5, 284n1, 284n2, 284n3, 286n24, 286n25, 286n26, 286n27, 286n28, 286n29, 286n30, 286n31, 286n32, 286n33, 286n34, 286n35, 286n36, 286n37, 286n38, 286n39, 287n40, 287n41, 287n42, 287n43, 287n44, 287n45, 287n47, 287n48, 288n49, 288n50, 290n87, 290n90, 290n92, 290n93, 290n94, 290n96, 290n97, 290n98, 290n103, 290n104, 290n107
Bowler, Kate, xii, 293n23, 297n1
Bridges, William, 274n37, 274n38
Brooks, Jonathan, xix, 62, 145, 176, 240, 241, 295n15
Brueggemann, Walter, 68, 200, 271n2, 282n30
Burt, Ronald, 278n30, 278n34, 278n37
Byassee, Jason, 5, 241, 259n27, 259n32

Campbell-Reed, Eileen, 281n16, 281n25, 281n27
Carlson, Andy, 56
Chaves, Mark, x, 256, 257n4, 258n9, 258n16, 277n11
Conde-Frazier, Elizabeth, 295n19
Crouch, Andy, 274n34
Cummings, E. E., 86, 275n50

Dante, 197, 198, 293n25, 293n26
Davis, Gerald F., 277n10
Deleuze, Gilles, 287n44
Demerath, N. J., 277n4, 279n53
DiMaggio, Paul, 276n4, 277n5, 277n7, 277n8, 277n9, 277n15
Driscoll, Mark, 59
Dykstra, Craig, ix, xi, 13, 132, 259n34, 261n43, 280n2, 280n6, 280n7, 280n8, 281n10, 281n11, 281n12, 281n13, 281n14, 281n16, 281n17, 281n18, 281n19, 281n20, 281n22, 281n23, 281n26, 281n27, 283n45, 283n46, 283n48, 283n49, 283n51, 283n52, 283n53, 284n57, 284n60, 284n62, 284n63

Eisner, Elliot, 275n56
Ellul, Jacques, 289n74

Fairbanks, Rob, 20, 30, 240
Farley, Edward, 258n11, 280n7, 283n48, 284n59, 289n75
Ferguson, Niall, 120, 258n15
Flyvbjerg, Bent, 8, 261n42
Foster, Charles, 225, 281n15, 281n25, 295n21
Freeman, John, 121, 279n43, 279n44, 279n46, 279n47, 280n55, 280n56, 280n57, 280n58, 280n60
Friesen, Dwight, 40, 43, 239, 267n3, 267n4, 267n5, 267n8, 267n10, 270n69, 278n18
Frost, Michael, 59, 268n19, 272n14, 272n18, 292n10, 292n15
Fulkerson, Mary McClintock, 283n48

Gibbs, Sunia, 5, 100, 259n29
Goldbloom, Laura, 68
Golladay, Anna, 41, 240
Goodwin, Andrew, 29, 31, 240
Green, Clifford, 162, 287n47, 287n48
Griffiths, Paul, 293n21
Guattarri, Félix, 287n44
Gunderson, Gary, 84, 274n41, 274n42, 274n43, 274n44, 274n46, 274n47
Gustafson, James, 287n45

Hadot, Pierre, 290n86
Hall, Marlon, 293n29
Hannan, Michael, 121, 279n43, 279n44, 279n46, 279n47
Harder, Dave, 85, 124, 131, 240
Hatch, Mary Jo, 260n38
Hays, Richard, 290n89
Heath, Elaine A., 270n68
Heclo, Hugh, 264n21
Heifetz, Ronald, 13, 69, 70, 75, 262n55, 271n6, 271n7, 271n8, 271n9, 271n12, 296n27, 296n28
Helms, James, 93, 106, 241
Herdt, Jennifer, 296n30
Hirsch, Alan, 59, 268n19, 292n16
Hopkins, Shannon, 224, 295n16
Hudnut-Beumler, James, 284n63
Humphreys, José, 142, 283n54
Hunter, James Davidson, 288n59

Illich, Ivan, 289n74

James, Christopher, 53, 259n23, 259n30, 265n36, 267n16
Jennings, William James, 271n11, 290n105
Johnson, Steven, 277n14
Jones, L. Gregory, x, 262n50, 285n5, 291n6
Jones, Rich, 50, 240
Jung, Barry, 55, 240

Katt, Ben, 43, 140, 184, 240
Kelsey, David, 292n12
Ketola, Jessica, 137, 219, 241
Killen, Patricia O'Connell, x, 4, 53, 257n7, 258n14, 259n19, 259n20, 259n21, 259n25, 259n29, 266n54, 295n17
King, David, 258n10
Kuyper, Abraham, 271n3

Lamott, Anne, 2, 257n3
Lauckner, Kirk, 47, 240
Leman, Abby, 24, 140, 149
Leman, James, 73, 81, 88, 138, 145, 240–41, 266n53, 282n38

Lind, Kevin, 67, 68, 74, 154, 240–41
Linsky, Marty, 271n6, 271n7, 271n9, 272n16, 273n29, 274n40, 275n57, 275n59, 275n60, 275n66, 275n69, 275n70, 276n77, 296n28
Lounsbury, Michael, 272n15, 277n4

MacIntyre, Alasdair, 261n42, 290n85
Marsh, Charles, 286n26, 287n41, 287n48, 291n7
Marti, Gerardo, 58, 270n60, 270n63, 270n65, 270n66, 270n67
Martin, Erin, 1–2, 257n2
McGonigal, Terry, 18, 20–21, 208, 240–41
McInturff, Kathryn, 19, 28, 240
McKay, Mike, 31, 34, 138, 240–41, 266n51
McKnight, John, 50, 267n7
McKnight, Scot, 270n60
McQueen, Josh, 143, 240–41
Miller-McLemore, Bonnie J., 259n33, 262n48, 275n62, 288n58
Moltmann, Jürgen, 284n58
Moore, Steve, xi, 94, 103, 193, 205, 240–41
Mowat, Harriet, 8, 213, 260n38, 261n41, 261n43, 283n48
Murthy, Vivek, 83, 274n36

Niebuhr, H. Richard, 289n77
Nieman, James, 260n36

O'Donovan, Oliver, 261n42
Oliver, Mary, 17, 262n2
Osmer, Richard, 83, 213, 260n38, 261n43, 294n6, 294n9, 294n41, 294n42

Parks, Sharon, 86, 212, 242, 271n4, 275n48, 280n4, 280n5
Powell, Walter, 109, 277n5, 277n7, 277n8, 277n9, 277n15, 278n19, 278n20, 278n21, 278n23, 278n24, 278n25, 278n26, 278n27, 278n28, 278n29

Rasmussen, Larry, 294n45
Reed, Karen, 148, 155, 240

Reyes, Patrick, xi, 178, 272n10, 290n106, 292n5
Rice, Christiana, xix, 43, 47, 61, 200, 240, 267n13, 272n14, 272n18
Robinson, Bill, 22, 263n11, 263n13, 263n14
Rowe, C. Kavin, x, 166, 285n4, 285n12, 288n62, 288n65, 288n71, 289n76, 289n83
Roxburgh, Alan, 59, 291n108
Ruef, Martin, 92, 263n16, 272n13, 275n64

Sampson, Mark, 234, 295n16
Scharen, Christian B., 9, 260n36, 281n16, 281n25, 281n27, 296n25
Scott, W. Richard, 277n6, 277n10
Selznick, Philip, 272n15
Shakespeare, Lyndon, 258n9
Silk, Mark, 3, 12, 257n7, 258n12, 258n14
Sittser, Gerald (Jerry), xix, 18, 20, 22, 63, 187, 240–41, 264n32, 264n33, 264n35, 293n22
Smith, James K. A., 273n25
Smith, Mindy, 18, 19, 25, 144, 222, 240–41
Soerens, Coté, 39
Soerens, Tim, xix, 39, 44, 61, 110, 131, 240–41, 267n3, 267n4, 267n5, 267n8, 267n10, 267n13, 267n14, 268n18, 268n21, 268n25, 268n27, 268n32, 269n41
Sparks, Paul, 39, 44, 131, 240–41, 267n3, 267n4, 267n5, 267n8, 267n10, 267n14, 272n14, 276n73, 276n79, 293n24
Stark, Rodney, 290n88
Strong, Doug, 183, 239
Swinton, John, 8, 213, 260n38, 261n41, 261n43, 283n48, 285n7, 294n40

Tanner, Kathryn, 135, 282n29
Taylor, Beck, 21, 23, 111, 239–40, 275n71
Taylor, Charles, 83, 274n39
Taylor, Steve, 263n17

Thornbury, Kimberly, xi, 229, 241
Tickle, Phyllis, 270n58, 270n71
Todd, Douglas, 53, 55, 259n18, 259n19, 269n43, 269n44, 269n50, 269n54
Tönnies, Ferdinand, 160, 286n31, 286n32
Tracey, Paul, 272n15, 277n4, 277n5

Uhr, John, 291n8

Vigen, Aana Marie, 260n36
Virgil, 197–98, 293n25

Ward, Pete, 260n36, 260n38, 262n43, 276n82

Welch, Claude, 287n45
Wellman, James, 53, 265n39, 269n49, 271n75
Wells, Samuel, 285n5
Wigg-Stevenson, Natalie, 233, 287n2, 297n3
Wimmer, John, 22, 208, 282n36
Wolterstorff, Nicholas, 61, 271n79, 297n31
Wordsworth, William, 217–18, 294n1, 294n4

Index of Scripture

Genesis		3:15	167
1:2	294n2	3:26	167
Isaiah		4:10	167
40:31	27	6:3	291n109
Matthew		7:54–8:1	166
9:37–38	267n12	9:26–27	177
9:16–17	276n74	10:1–48	166
Mark		11:2	177
2:21–22	96, 276n74	11:19	166
Luke		11:19–13:4	165, 166
1:26	167	11:20	166
2:40	288n72, 291n109	11:21	166, 167
2:52	291n109	11:23	167, 288n72
5:36–39	96, 276n74	11:24	167
10:25–42	167	11:26	167, 168
10:45	288n63	11:27	171
11:4	173	11:30	169
11:23	167, 288n72	12:5	171
11:49	291n109	12:6–11	175
12:28	167	12:12–17	171
14:47	166	12:23	171
24:47	173	12:24	171
John		12:25–13:3	169
1:46	33	13:4	167
Acts		13:4–28:31	169
2:24	167	13:5	170, 289n82
2:38	173	13:38	173

14:26	169	Galatians	
15:1	177	2	289n80
15:22–23	169	Colossians	
15:30	169	1:24	167
15:35	169	1 Thessalonians	
15:36–41	177	1:6–7	167
18:22	169		
2 Corinthians			
1:4	167		
1:6	167		